Distributed Computing

ACADEMIC PRESS RAPID MANUSCRIPT REPRODUCTION

This is volume 20 in A.P.I.C. Studies in Data Processing
General Editors: Fraser Duncan *and* M. J. R. Shave
A complete list of titles in this series appears at the end of this volume

Distributed Computing

Edited by

FRED B. CHAMBERS

Logica Ltd.
London, England

DAVID A. DUCE
GILLIAN P. JONES

Computing Division
Rutherford Appleton Laboratory
Didcot, England

1984

ACADEMIC PRESS
(Harcourt Brace Jovanovich, Publishers)
London Orlando San Diego New York
Toronto Montreal Sydney Tokyo

UNIX™ is a Trademark of AT&T Bell Laboratories

Ada® is a registered Trade Mark of the U.S. Government (Ada Joint Program Office)

Chapter 21 is reproduced from *Workshop on the Analysis of Concurrent Systems—Proceedings,* Lecture Notes in Computer Science (to appear), by kind permission of Springer-Verlag

ACADEMIC PRESS, INC. (LONDON) LTD.
24-28 Oval Road,
London NW1 7DX

United States Edition published by
ACADEMIC PRESS, INC.
Orlando, Florida 32887

LIBRARY OF CONGRESS CATALOG CARD NUMBER: 84-48446
ISBN 0-12-167350-2

Preface

This book helps to mark the completion of the Distributed Computing Systems research programme (DCS) sponsored by the U.K. Science and Engineering Research Council. The DCS programme, from 1977-1984, culminated in a conference at the University of Sussex, Brighton, U.K. in September 1984. The conference included a series of tutorials on major topics in distributed computing, based on the contents of this volume. When the programme first started, there was relatively little research in distributed computing underway in the U.K., and it was to promote research in what was seen as a key area for the future, that the programme was conceived. During the lifetime of the programme the field grew enormously both in the breadth of activity and the depth of understanding. Within the programme itself, a number of research themes emerged, and these have been reflected in the organization of the book.

The book aims to give a basic grounding in each of the areas covered. A general familiarity with the relevant aspects of computing is assumed, but specialist knowledge is not required. The book should be of interest to researchers and practitioners in the field, academic and industrial, and will also serve as an introductory text for new researchers. It is appropriate as an undergraduate or postgraduate text for a single-term introductory course on distributed systems.

The book is divided into five parts corresponding to the five themes covered.

● **Part I** describes the **dataflow** approach to parallel computation, one of the bases on which parallel super computer of the future will be constructed. This part is contributed by John Glauert, John Gurd, Chris Kirkham and Ian Watson, all members of the Manchester dataflow project, a DCS funded investigation which has established a world lead in this approach. Topics covered include the basic principles of dataflow computing, the evolution of dataflow computer architectures and the high level languages used to program them. Details of the Manchester prototype dataflow computer structure, instruction set and performance are presented. The single-assignment programming language SISAL is introduced.

● **Part II** is concerned with **declarative languages,** and with computer architectures to support their evaluation. The essence of the declarative approach to programming is to shift the burden of determining in detail *how* something must be done, from the programmer to the architecture. The first chapter in this part, by John Darlington, introduces the reader to *functional languages* and their conventional implementation. The next chapter, by Bill Clocksin, introduces *logic languages* and their conventional implementations. The remaining chapters, by Richard Kennaway and Ronan Sleep, describe the origins and rise of novel architectures to support such languages, and the parallel approach to implementation.

- **Part III** addresses **loosely-coupled distributed systems.** Such systems are multi-computer configurations that do not share immediate memory and can be dispersed over wide geographical areas. They form much the greater part of the distributed systems that have investigated and are in use today. The chapters in this part, by Keith Bennet, Ian Wand and Andy Wellings, describe the general architecture of such systems and examine the detailed requirements of their various components, operating systems appropriate to this environment and related programming languages.

- **Part IV** deals with **closely-coupled distributed systems,** typically systems which *do* share a common memory. The alternative architectures that may be adopted for the design of such systems; the structure and features of typical programming languages; the nature of run-time support software; and software development tools for debugging and testing applications, are considered in turn. This part concludes with two case studies describing the overall design of hardware and software for experimental multi-microprocessor systems (Cyba-M, developed at Swansea and UMIST; and POLYPROC, University of Sussex).

- **Part V** by Robin Milner and Samson Abramsky faces the essential questions of **modelling and verifying** concurrent systems. What is a good mathematical model of concurrency? Can there be a common model for both hardware and software? A concurrent program may be thought of alternatively as software to be compiled or as description of the behaviour of a piece of hardware. The development of fundamental notations for such programs' description is explored and some approaches to verifying them mathematically are illustrated using simple examples.

The editors of this book were the Industrial Coordinator, Academic Coordinator and Technical Secretary of the DCS Programme when it terminated. We, and the contributors, wish to acknowledge the many researchers whose work has contributed to this book.

We are particularly grateful to Paul, Arthur, Frits and many others at CWI for their assistance, patience and understanding during the preparation of the book. Finally, we would like to thank Alan Kinroy, Duncan Gibson and Elizabeth Fielding for their sterling work in producing the many diagrams in the book.

Easter 3, 1984   Fred B Chambers
                                                                    David A Duce
                                                                    Gillian P Jones

Contributors

S. Abramsky   Department of Computing, Imperial College, 180 Queen's Gate, London SW7 2BZ

D. Aspinall   Department of Computation, University of Manchester Institute of Science and Technology, P. O. Box 88, Manchester, M60 1QD

K. H. Bennett   Department of Computer Science, University of Keele, Keele, Staffs ST5 5BG

W. F. Clocksin   Computer Laboratory, University of Cambridge, Corn Exchange Street, Cambridge CB2 3QG

J. Darlington   Department of Computing, Imperial College, 180 Queen's Gate, London SW7 2BZ

J. R. W. Glauert   School of Computing Studies, University of East Anglia, University Village, Norwich NO4 8BC

R. L. Grimsdale   School of Engineering and Applied Sciences, University of Sussex, Falmer, Brighton BN1 9QT

J. R. Gurd   Department of Computer Science, University of Manchester, Oxford Road, Manchester M13 9PL

F. Halsall   School of Engineering and Applied Sciences, University of Sussex, Falmer, Brighton BN1 9QT

J. R. Kennaway   School of Computing Studies, University of East Anglia, University Village, Norwich NO4 8BC

C. C. Kirkham   Department of Computer Science, University of Manchester, Oxford Road, Manchester M13 9PL

A. J. R. G. Milner   Department of Computer Science, James Clerk Maxwell Building, The King's Buildings, Mayfield Road, Edinburgh EH9 3JZ

M. R. Sleep   School of Computing Studies, University of East Anglia, University Village, Norwich NO4 8BC

I. C. Wand   Department of Computer Science, University of York, Heslington, York YO1 5DD

I. Watson   Department of Computer Science, University of Manchester, Oxford Road, Manchester M13 9PL

A. J. Wellings   Department of Computer Science, University of York, Heslington, York YO1 5DD

Contents

Part I

The Dataflow Approach

J. R. W. Glauert
J. R. Gurd
C. C. Kirkham
I. Watson

1 Fundamentals of Dataflow

J. R. Gurd

1.1 INTRODUCTION

It is becoming apparent that future requirements for computing speed, system reliability, software manageability and cost-effectiveness will entail the development of alternative computer architectures to replace the traditional 'von Neumann' organization on which our present computing practices are based. Dataflow architecture is one possible alternative which aims for high-speed computing via efficient exploitation of software parallelism in a highly parallel system of processing hardware. The name 'dataflow' is derived from the graphical model of computation which is used to describe how programs are executed. In this model data is active and flows asynchronously through the two-dimensional program, activating each instruction when all the required input data has arrived. This is in direct contrast to the 'von Neumann' model in which data passively resides in store whilst instructions are executed one-at-a-time according to a defined sequence controlled by a 'program counter'.

Dataflow architectures, as described in this part of the book, are only one alternative to traditional computers. Several other models with similar characteristics are emerging, and these are sometimes confused with dataflow systems, usually because they too are driven by their data. In particular, string reduction and graph reduction systems fall into this category. In the following we will concentrate on 'pure' dataflow architectures.

This part of the book is divided into four chapters, covering fundamentals, hardware techniques, machine-level programming and high-level software. This first chapter opens with a discussion of the nature of software parallelism, the possible ways of representing it, and some implications for parallel machine-code design. This provides an introduction to dataflow notation and also demonstrates the important distinction between static and dynamic dataflow systems. The chapter concludes with a discussion of techniques for compiling from various high-level programming languages into dataflow object-code.

In Chapter 2 on hardware we consider the requirements for executing dataflow code and exploiting the exposed software parallelism. We then study three different system designs which have been, or are being, constructed as experimental research vehicles for further work applying and refining dataflow techniques. The chapter closes with a discussion of dataflow system performance.

Chapter 3, on machine-level programming, studies the languages which are used to specify graph programs for the Manchester Dataflow Machine. The lowest-level interface is via a compact textual representation of the binary messages which are sent to load the program store. This is difficult for humans to use as a programming vehicle, and it is more normal to use the Template Assembler (TASS) which is also described.

Chapter 4 describes a specific high-level language for dataflow programming, SISAL, illustrated by a number of examples of language constructs and some complete programs. SISAL is a single-assignment language with Pascal-like syntax. It is currently being used for evaluation of a variety of multiprocessing strategies.

1.2 PARALLELISM IN SOFTWARE

Two kinds of parallelism can be found in software. The first kind occurs when a common operation (or set of operations) is to be applied to many separate sets of data. An example is the element-wise addition of several arrays, as in the Fortran program:

```
        DO 10 I = 1,100
        F(I) = A(I) + B(I) + C(I) + D(I)
    10  CONTINUE
```

The second kind is found when different operations (or sets of operations) are to be applied to separate (or even common) sets of data. This may be found in many blocks of assignment statements, for example, the following Fortran code:

```
        A = E - G
        B = H * Z
        C = E * H + F
        D = E + G
```

These forms of parallelism have been known for a long time and their importance in influencing parallel hardware design has been recognized. Flynn [1] classified hardware systems as SIMD (single-instruction-stream, multiple-data-stream) if they exploit the first kind of software parallelism, and MIMD (multiple-instruction-stream, multiple-data-stream) if they exploit the second kind.

Nowadays this classification is considered overly simple, but no generally accepted alternative taxonomy is emerging. The difficulty seems to be that parallel hardware may be deployed at a different level of 'granularity' to the obvious software parallelism. For example, in an instruction pipeline, small parts of the execution of successive instructions are processed concurrently by overlapping, regardless of any program parallelism at the instruction level, or above. In the absence of a level-independent taxonomy of parallel systems comparison of different architectures is by *ad hoc* methods. We have found it useful to distinguish between 'regular' and 'irregular' parallelism when comparing the abilities of dataflow systems with those of more conventional parallel systems.

Regular parallelism exists wherever the same task is to be performed many times over, usually on disjoint data. With connected data it may be necessary to exploit regular parallelism via a pipeline, as in the instruction pipeline cited above. With unconnected data, as in the case of the first (SIMD) kind of software parallelism, a lock-step parallel array of hardware can be used, as in the DAP [2] or ILLIAC IV [3]. In either case, the actions to be performed concurrently are highly regular, and the performance of the systems depends critically on whether or not the program can provide sufficient work with the required amount of the required form of regularity.

Most of the parallel computers so far constructed exploit regular parallelism of one form or another. In practice it has proved surprisingly difficult to arrange for programs to provide, continuously, sufficient parallelism of the desired nature. Consequently applications run at variable speed, the regular parts executing rapidly, whilst other sections are necessarily slower. In many cases the slow segments dominate overall performance and reduce the total speedup of programs to a small fraction of that intended.

Irregular parallelism exists wherever different tasks are potentially concurrently executable, sometimes on common data. This corresponds to the second (MIMD) form of software parallelism. An independent array of parallel hardware, such as in the CDC 6600 [4] (on a small scale) or the C.mmp [5] and Cm* [6] multiprocessors (on a large scale), is needed for implementation. Where common data is involved complex interlocking mechanisms are necessary to prevent unintentional accesses being made (e.g. reading data before it has been defined, or writing before all prior reads have been completed). Note that hardware mechanisms which exploit irregular parallelism will also be able to handle regular parallelism. The reverse is not usually the case.

Few systems have been constructed to exploit irregular parallelism on a large scale, and it is in this area that many interesting experiments in computer architecture are now being conducted. The best known examples use parallelism at the 'process' level, derived from programming languages such as Concurrent Pascal [7], Modula [8], Distributed Processes [9], and Communicating Sequential Processes [10] and implemented on shared-memory or message-passing multiprocessors. Dataflow systems exploit irregular parallelism at a lower level, approximating to the conventional machine-code instruction-level.

Whether parallelism is regular or not, the key issue in developing a system to exploit it is to provide an effective notation for expressing potential parallelism in programs. In the following section we develop a notation for instruction-level irregular parallelism by examining the nature of inherent parallelism in a small segment of conventional Fortran code.

1.3 PROGRAMS AS GRAPHS

Consider the following set of Fortran assignments which multiply together the 'variables' I1, I2, I3, I4, I5 and I6 and put the result in 'variable' K:

$$
\begin{aligned}
L &= I1 * I2 \\
M &= I3 * I4 \\
N &= I5 * I6 \\
K &= L * M * N
\end{aligned}
$$

To discover the potential software parallelism we must discard the traditional view of a program as a list of instructions which manipulate data in fixed storage locations in a defined sequence. Instead we need to concentrate on the role the individual storage locations play as they temporarily hold data values whilst the latter pass between operations in the program. The pattern of store accesses brought about by the sequence of activation of instructions is normally contrived by the programmer to achieve the combinations of data with operators dictated by the particular problem being solved. The fact that this is specified as a one-at-a-time process owes more to the history of the development of computers than to inherent constraints in the problems that computers are used to solve.

1.3.1 Data Dependence Graphs

An alternative view of the combination of data with operators is obtained by constructing a data dependence graph for the program [11, 12]. Algorithms for this task are in common use for conventional machines in optimizing compilers. In the example above, we simply draw a number of arcs over the program, one arc for each variable. The tail of an arc shows where the variable is assigned, and the head shows where the variable is consumed (by appearing on the right-hand side of an assignment statement). In more complex examples more than one arc may be required for a variable when it appears on the right-hand side of more than one assignment statement. Multiple assignments, where a variable is assigned a value at more than one point in the program, can be dealt with by systematically renaming the variables so that a version is created without multiple assignments, but with the same meaning as the original. Where variables appear only on the right-hand side they are assumed to be input data to the program segment. The resultant graph for our example is shown in **Figure 1-1**.

This diagram is more visually attractive if it is rearranged to show enforced sequence down the page, with potential concurrency across the page, as shown in **Figure 1-2**.

In this graphical form it is possible to omit all the variable names as they are now superfluous, being constrained to be the same at head and tail of each arc. If names are required (as an aid to understanding, or for writing a textual version of the graph), they can be written just once, alongside the appropriate arc. Each assignment statement can be simplified to a description of the expression to be computed. In many cases this will be a simple arithmetic operation, as in the case of the multiplication in our example, shown in **Figure 1-3**.

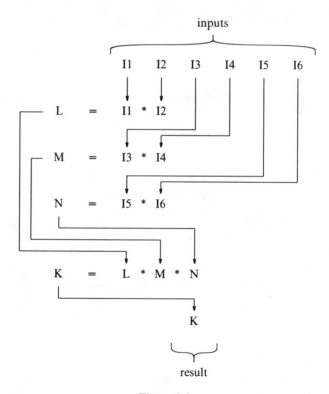

Figure 1-1

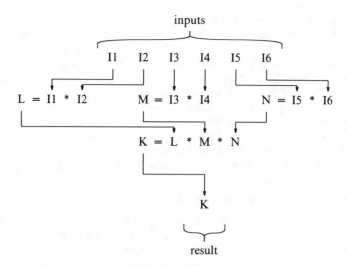

Figure 1-2

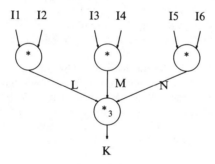

Figure 1-3

1.3.2 Machine-Level Graph Programs

We have now constructed a simple statement-level data dependence graph. Note that it retains the meaning of the original program, but it also shows potential parallelism and enforced sequence in a two-dimensional format. In order to illustrate all the program parallelism available for exploitation by instruction-level parallel hardware it is necessary to decompose the program even further. Of course the level to which we descend is completely arbitrary. We could build a system capable of multiplying three values together in one instruction (in which case the above graph would not need further reduction), or we could go to the extreme of implementing only boolean operators (AND, OR, NOT, etc.) in hardware, and building up more complex operators using standard techniques (in which case our example graph would require considerable further decomposition). Most of the dataflow computers currently under construction use an instruction-level comparable to that of a 16-bit minicomputer with extended arithmetic capabilities. We shall assume this level in the remainder of this part of the book. This implies the availability of straightforward monadic and dyadic arithmetic operators on integer and floating-point numbers, and we will also assume the existence of operators which generate and manipulate boolean values.

In our example program it will be noted that the lowest expression evaluation in the graph is not a machine instruction at this level. Consequently it must be implemented by a subgraph of instructions such as either of those shown in **Figure 1-4**.

In this particular example it is immaterial which of these alternatives is used, and a compiler could choose between them arbitrarily. In other cases there will be efficient and inefficient options and compilers will need to be sensitive to the assessment criteria if they are to produce optimal code under a wide range of conditions. To develop such assessment criteria we need to know how programs will actually execute on a specific parallel hardware configuration. This is too difficult to discuss in detail here, but we shall finish this chapter with a brief description of an abstract dataflow implementation model from which the basic principles of execution may be derived.

1.3.3 Execution of Machine-Level Graphs

Consider a complete machine-level program graph for our example in which each multiply instruction is given an identification number, as shown in **Figure 1-5**. Remember that the purpose of this notation is to allow all potentially concurrent instructions to execute simultaneously. In the original sequential program we would expect the multiplications to be performed in the order {1}, {2}, {3}, {4}, {5}, producing the answer in five multiplication times. On the graph above we can see that either of the parallel execution orderings {1, 2, 3}, {4}, {5} or {1, 2}, {3, 4}, {5} will produce the answer in three multiplication times (given at least three and two multipliers, respectively). The problem for the parallel execution model is to cause one of these parallel execution orderings to be followed.

It is difficult to arrange activation of instructions by some parallel equivalent of a program counter. In the first place such program counters would have to be associated with processors, and the variable amounts of parallelism that could occur might require large numbers of these processors, many of which could frequently become idle. Secondly, the idea of a program counter is closely linked to the concept of a linear data store with fixed locations for each program variable. Large numbers of active instructions would

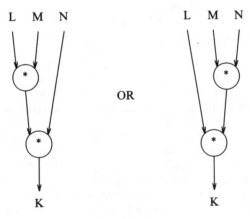

Figure 1-4

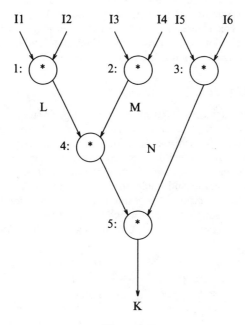

Figure 1-5

imply large numbers of active store locations with attendant problems of multiplexing the required accesses. In addition to this each horizontal 'band' of instructions would have to be synchronized so that the next lower band could not start processing until all current instructions had terminated. This implies that a program would proceed at the speed of the slowest operation in each band. Apart from these problems, the task of allocating instructions to processors would be extremely difficult.

These arguments constitute a compelling reason for abandoning program counters in instruction-level parallel computers. The key to making this transition is to notice that a data dependence graph shows how *instructions are dependent on data.* It is not sensible to execute an instruction before all the data it requires is available. Conversely, once an instruction has finished executing, all other instructions that are waiting for its output data can be activated safely. The simplest way to execute a graph program so as to obey these rules is to send data directly from instruction to instruction according to the data dependence arcs, and to allow each instruction to execute when and only when it has all its required input data available. In this way the graph program execution will be *data-driven.*

We can illustrate data-driven execution of graph programs by introducing data-carriers, known as 'tokens' after Petri-net notation [13], onto the data dependence graph. Each token carries one data value. A token is constrained to move (at any speed it can) from the tail to the head of one data dependence arc. Tokens wait at the heads of their dependence arcs until all other arcs (if there are others) pointing to the same instruction also have tokens at their heads. At this time this instruction can be executed, taking an arbitrary amount of time to complete, after which its result token(s) is(are) placed on its output arc(s). The tokens causing the execution are no longer needed, and so they will be removed from their (input) arcs.

The sequence of 'snapshots' in **Figure 1-6** shows how our example program could be used to evaluate 6! by sending tokens with integer values 1 to 6 to the program inputs I1 to I6, respectively. Tokens are shown on the dependence arcs as black discs with the associated values written alongside. The way in which the data appears to flow through the program graph during execution is the reason for the name 'dataflow'.

1.4 GENERALIZED DATAFLOW GRAPHS

The multiplication program considered above is not a general example of conventional computing practice. The only arithmetic operation used is multiplication and there are no control structures, such as conditionals or loops. In this section we consider enhancements to the dataflow notation which help to accommodate more general programs.

The first point to be made is that *any* form of machine instruction can be represented by a node in a dataflow graph and could therefore be executed in parallel with other instructions. This property makes the graph notation useful for exploiting irregular software parallelism. The simplest case in which this is advantageous is in the evaluation of general arithmetic expressions in which any arithmetic machine instructions could be

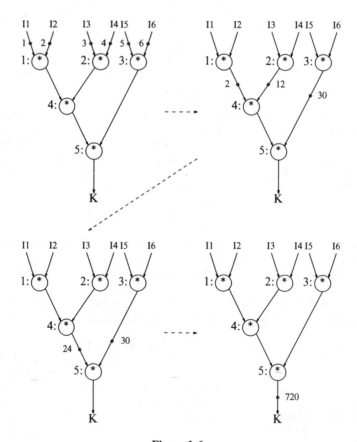

Figure 1-6

used. Such expressions can be converted easily into graphs. In fact most conventional compilers already generate 'expression evaluation trees', when parsing high level programs, before they generate the required linear object code. The dataflow execution model demonstrates how such trees may be evaluated directly, in time proportional to their height, using parallel instruction execution. At a higher level, the model also allows whole expressions to be evaluated concurrently. Additional parallelism can be found when control structures are invoked.

1.4.1 Conditionals

The simplest control structure is the conditional (**if** ... **then** ... **else** ... **fi**). We can construct a data dependence graph for a conditional statement using *conditional dependence arcs* which are controlled by the runtime evaluation of a boolean predicate. These arcs are implemented using the two 'switching' machine instructions, known as *branch* and *merge*, shown in **Figure 1-7** and **Figure 1-8**.

These may be visualized as two-way switches inserted into the arcs of a standard dependence graph. Each switch selects one of two possible routes for an incoming data token, the other route being left inactive. The route is selected according to the value of

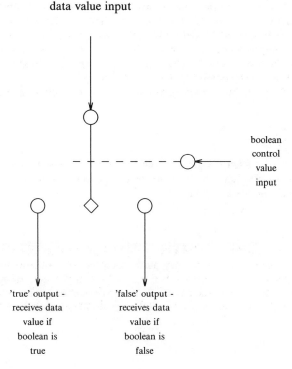

Figure 1-7

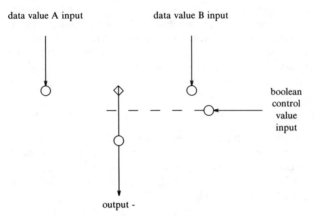

data value A input   data value B input

boolean
control
value
input

output -

receives data value A if boolean is true

or data value B if boolean is false

Figure 1-8

a boolean control token. The data and control tokens wait for each other at the inputs to the switch exactly as they would at a dyadic or triadic arithmetic instruction. Where it is certain that only one of the data inputs to a *merge* instruction will be generated, and in proper correspondence to the associated boolean (e.g. from a previous *branch* instruction using the same control value), the *merge* may be omitted from the machine code and the two data arcs conjoined, as shown in **Figure 1-9**.

Using the extended instruction set we can implement a conditional Fortran statement such as:

C = A
IF (I .EQ. J) C = F

by the graph shown in **Figure 1-10** in which '⊥' indicates that tokens travelling down this arc will be destroyed, and the '=?' instruction generates a boolean value indicating whether its two data inputs are equal.

1.4.2 Loops

Switch instructions are most powerful when used to implement graphical loops and functions. These are important because they allow complex computations to be defined by relatively small programs, in the same way as conventional loops, subroutines or procedures. However, these reentrant constructs pose substantial implementation problems in a parallel computer because of the possibility of simultaneous activation of the reentrant code.

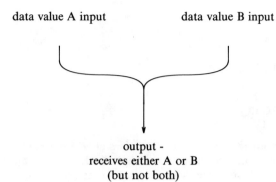

output -
receives either A or B
(but not both)

Figure 1-9

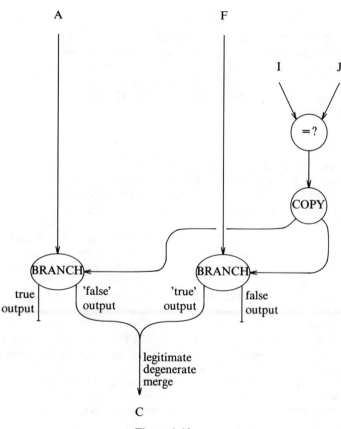

Figure 1-10

As an example, consider the Fortran program segment below:

```
        I = N
        J = 1
10      IF (I .LE. 0) GOTO 99
        J = I * J
        I = I - 1
        GOTO 10
99      M = J
```

This is an iterative program which computes values of N! for variable N (i.e. not just 6!). It translates into the machine-level graph of **Figure 1-11**. Detailed analysis of this graph reveals that it is possible for more than one token to occupy the arcs labelled '?' and '??'. Consequently, it is essential that the arcs of the graph behave as first-in-first-out queues (otherwise the loop could terminate early because of overtaking on the arc labelled '?'). Unfortunately implementation of unbounded queues proves to be difficult, so it is usual in practical dataflow systems to restrict the normal 'firing rule' so that instructions can only be executed when their output arc is empty.

This is the simplest way of implementing reentrant graph programs, but it is not completely general because it prohibits concurrent reentrancy. It only permits loops which are reactivated in strict sequence. Although a limited amount of parallelism can be obtained by pipelining within the cycles of a loop, there is often further parallelism which can only be extracted by a more general scheme (as described in the next two sections). Systems which implement this first scheme, allowing only sequential, cyclic reentrancy, are known as *static* dataflow systems [14].

1.4.3 Functions

A typical case in which concurrent reentrancy is required is when the programmer defines a *function* (i.e. a user-defined subgraph) which is to be called from several places within the program. This is somewhat similar to a Fortran subroutine. It is, of course, possible to create many copies of the machine code representing the function and to plant them 'in-line' at the appropriate places. However, this is wasteful of instruction storage for large functions and those which are called frequently. It also prohibits the use of recursion since this implies provision of infinitely expanded program graphs. Consequently, two alternative implementation schemes for reentrant programs have been proposed.

The first such scheme permits concurrent reentrancy via an *apply* instruction, planted at the start of a user-defined subgraph, which creates a new copy of the subgraph each time it is activated [15]. All input tokens to a subgraph activation are gathered together at the *apply* instruction and are then transferred to the unique new copy of the reentrant code. An *exit* instruction, placed at the end of the copy of the subgraph, gathers together all the output tokens for the activation and transfers them back to the output arcs of the appropriate *apply* instruction. The copy of the reentrant code is then destroyed. The operation of this scheme is analogous to conventional macro-expansion in that extra code and data space is allocated whenever it is called for. This avoids data having to share code concurrently.

An alternative scheme allows data to share code by 'tagging' tokens as they enter into and exit from the reentrant areas [16, 17]. This system is similar to the use of a stack for implementing procedures and functions on conventional machines, except that the concurrent activation of shared graph code requires that each token be *individually* tagged with the appropriate 'name-base' instead of using global stack registers to identify the

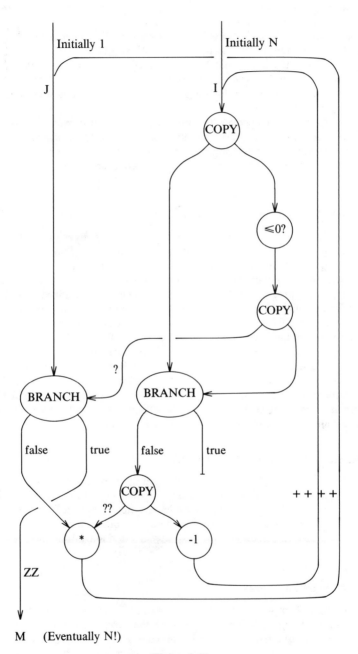

Figure 1-11

currently active data space. In visual terms tagging can be thought of as the process of *colouring* the data tokens [18]. The graph execution rules need to be modified so that only tokens of the same colour (i.e. those carrying identical tags) can group together to cause execution of an instruction. Special instructions are needed to create new tags at entry to, and to restore old tags at exit from, the reentrant code. Of course, tokens must carry extra bits to denote the tag.

Note that token-tagging can be used to distinguish data belonging to different cycles around a loop. For example, in the program shown in **Figure 1-11**, assuming all input tags have value zero, the tags could be incremented each time round the loop at the points labelled ' + + ', and zeroed on exit from the loop at the point labelled 'ZZ'. In this case it is no longer necessary for the arcs to act as first-in-first-out queues, and the 'firing rule' can be derestricted.

Systems using the above schemes to implement concurrently reentrant functions are known as *dynamic* dataflow systems. The first scheme is called the *dynamic code-copying* scheme. The second scheme is known as the *dynamic tagged*, or *dynamic code-sharing* scheme. Hybrid dynamic systems use both code-sharing and code-copying in order to limit the size of the tag.

1.4.4 Structured Data

Compact programs can also be written using data structuring, by which a single variable name is used to refer to a large collection of simple data items. Two schemes have been developed to implement data structures in dataflow graph programs.

The first scheme uses separate storage to hold the structures and represents each structure travelling in the program graph by a *pointer* token. A specialized *structure store* is responsible for executing read and write operations on structures, and also for issuing the appropriate pointers [19]. All other instructions are as described above, and operate on scalar data, or control the flow of pointer tokens through the program graph.

An alternative scheme uses the tagging system described in the previous section [20]. Each element of a data structure is a normal token which carries a unique tag defining the position of the element in the structure. Tag-sensitive instructions are used to manipulate the structure in the required way. This scheme is particularly useful for implementing regular structures, such as arrays, whose elements are all subject to continuous processing (as, for example, in signal processing applications).

1.5 COMPILATION OF GRAPH CODE

The examples introduced earlier demonstrate that it is possible to generate dataflow graphs from a conventional high-level programming language such as Fortran. However, the analysis algorithm that forms data dependence graphs from such languages is highly complex and takes a long time to execute. There exist other languages which are easier to translate and these are receiving the majority of attention in dataflow research projects.

1.5.1 Conventional Languages

The principal difficulties with conventional languages reside in possible side-effects due to *explicit* use of storage locations (accessed by the programmer as 'variables'). Data dependence analysis is often hampered by obscure array index expressions which are impossible to analyse at compile-time and thus requires some assistance from the programmer to indicate how the arrays will be accessed. However, the worst problem is that of aliasing via the use of unbounded arrays or arithmetic operations on pointers. No amount of compile-time analysis can help unravel devious or undisciplined use of such language 'features'. The only method of control is to ban the facilities from the language [21].

1.5.2 Single-Assignment Languages

Single-assignment languages (SALs) have no concept of sequential execution and no direct control statements such as the GOTO. To combat the ambiguities that might arise from reassigning values to variables, the languages allow each variable to be assigned just once in a program. Constructs which permit controlled reassignment in special cases, such as loops, are provided. SALs tend to use data structures, such as arrays and streams, that can be readily implemented in dataflow graphs. There are often strict type and scope rules. In particular, it is common to prohibit all forms of side-effect in reentrant constructs. The net results are languages that provide ideal textual syntax for the description of dataflow graphs [22, 23, 16, 24, 25].

Many SALs were developed without reference to dataflow execution, and they are similar to the *functional* or *applicative* languages which have been developed without reference to any particular means of execution.

1.5.3 Functional Languages

Functional languages are based on the mathematics of functional algebra and have no concepts of storage state and assignment [26]. They are sometimes referred to as *zero-assignment* languages. In fact, if assignment is restricted to occur only once for each variable in a program, the effect is the same as if there were no assignment at all and 'assignment' statements were treated as *definitions* of the variables. In this sense SALs and functional languages are identical and it should come as no surprise to find that absence of GOTOs and side-effects are common to them both. However, functional algebra allows more powerful programming constructs than are used in SALs because it permits construction of higher order functions and abstract data structures. Consequently the two groups are not directly equivalent. Nevertheless they have enough in common to make it attractive to implement functional languages on dataflow systems.

Several attempts have been made to compile dataflow code from higher order functional languages [27]. These indicate that it is possible to implement such languages fully, but there are many doubts as to the efficiency of programs produced in this way. Recent research has concentrated on developing mixed data-driven/demand-driven architectures for such languages [28].

1.6 SUMMARY OF DATAFLOW GRAPHS

Dataflow graphs are a convenient notation for representing parallel computations. They permit conditional constructs, loops, functions (including recursion), and data structuring. Translation to dataflow graphs is feasible from a wide range of high-level programming languages.

There is a natural classification for dataflow systems according to the way they handle reentrant code. The three classes of system are known as *static, dynamic code-copying,* and *dynamic tagged* schemes.

1.7 REFERENCES

1. M. J. Flynn, "Some Computer Organisations and Their Effectiveness," *IEEE Transactions on Computers* **C-21**(9), p.948 (September 1972).

2. S. F. Reddaway, "DAP - A Distributed Array Processor," *Proceedings of 1st ACM Symposium on Computer Architecture* (December 1973).

3. G. H. Barnes et. al., "The ILLIAC IV Computer," *IEEE Transactions on Computers* **C-17**(8), p.746 (August 1968).

4. J. E. Thornton, *Design of a Computer: The CDC6600,* Scott Foresman & Co (1970).

5. W. A. Wulf and C. G. Bell, "C.mmp - A multi-mini-processor," *Proceedings of AFIPS FJCC* **41**, p.765 (September 1972).

6. R. J. Swan, S. H. Fuller, and D. P. Siewiorek, "Cm* - A Modular Multimicroprocessor," *Proceedings of AFIPS NCC* **46**, p.637 (June 1977).

7. P. Brinch Hansen, "The Programming Language Concurrent Pascal," *IEEE Transactions on Software Engineering* **SE-1**(2) (June 1975).

8. N. Wirth, "Modula: A Language for Modular Multiprogramming," *Software - Practice & Experience* **7**(1), p.3 (January 1977).

9. P. Brinch Hansen, "Distributed Processes : A Concurrent Programming Concept," *Communications of the ACM* **21**(11), p.934 (November 1978).

10. C. A. R. Hoare, "Communicating Sequential Processes," *Communications of the ACM* **21**(8), p.666 (August 1978).

11. F. E. Allen and J. Cocke, "A Program Data Flow Analysis Procedure," *Communications of the ACM* **19**(3), p.137 (March 1976).

12. D. J. Kuck et. al., "Dependence Graphs and Compiler Optimisations," *Proceedings of 8th ACM Symposium on Principles of Programming Languages*, p.207 (January 1981).

13. J. L. Peterson, "Petri Nets," *ACM Computing Surveys* **9**(3), p.223 (September 1977).

14. J. B. Dennis and D. P. Misunas, "A Preliminary Architecture for a Basic Data Flow Processor," *Proceedings of 2nd IEEE Symposium on Computer Architecture*, p.126 (January 1975).

15. G. S. Miranker, "Implementation of Procedures on a Class of Dataflow Processors," *Proceedings of International Conference on Parallel Processing*, p.77 (August 1977).

16. Arvind, K. P. Gostelow, and W. Plouffe, "An Asynchronous Programming Language and Computing Machine," Technical Report TR114a, Department of Information and Computer Science, University of California at Irvine (December 1978).

17. I. Watson and J. R. Gurd, "A Prototype Data Flow Computer with Token Labelling," *Proceedings of AFIPS NCC* **48**, p.623 (June 1979).

A 'multiple instruction stream, multiple data stream' capability is necessary in order that different processing resources can be executing different operations at the same time. A large number of machines of this type have been proposed and a significant number built, for example C.mmp [2] and Cm* [3]. They usually consist of a number of conventional processors, each with their own program and data stores connected together via either a common store or a communication network (crossbar switch, common bus, slotted ring etc.). They are intended to be programmed in a relatively conventional language such as Modula [4] which has facilities for expressing communication between parallel processes. The user is required explicitly to divide a program into suitable parallel sections which can be mapped on to the physical machine structure.

This view of computation not only places a severe burden on the user but also constrains the architecture. The communication between processes is bidirectional and is unpredictable both in peak and average bandwidth. In order to produce satisfactory performance, an architecture is required which allows very high speed communication between random processors in the network. In practice the machine designers have compromised assuming that the data rates could be controlled and hence the machines have failed to realize their potential. This is not surprising as such random high speed communication is very difficult to achieve.

If a viable architecture of this type were developed then the dataflow approach with its software advantages would certainly be applicable to such a structure. However, the constraints imposed by the communicating process view of parallel computation are relaxed in a dataflow environment and it is possible to consider more realistic physical implementations of MIMD computers.

2.1.2 Fine Grain Versus Coarse Grain Parallelism

It is clearly possible to apply dataflow principles over a wide range of problem structures from individual machine operations to processes at the level discussed above. If the correct process divisions are chosen then it is probable that the communication bandwidth for a given rate of computation will be minimized.

Conversely, if a low level is chosen then the number of inputs required before an operation can be executed will be smaller and hence the mechanism required to detect this condition in a physical machine will be simplified.

It is also necessary to consider how the machine is to be programmed. With a small number of notable exceptions (e.g APL), programming languages express computations at a relatively fine grain level of operation. Although there are many worthwhile attempts to produce 'very high level' programming languages they still retain the capability of performing scalar addition etc. If these operations are required for general purpose computation then this is the level at which the programmer will compose at least some portion of his code. If a number of such operations must then be 'bundled' for execution by the machine then this would need to be automated if the programming philosophy is to be maintained. Of course, the natural function/procedure divisions may be appropriate to minimize communication, but they may not. The automation of the task then becomes complex.

A further factor in the decision is the choice of static or dynamic task allocation. This is particularly important if coarse grain parallelism is considered. If high level operations are allocated to processing resources statically at the start of the problem execution, then each processor need only have access to the code which it will execute. In a dynamic scheme there is a requirement for access to the whole program from each individual processor. If each contains all the code, this could be a large overhead in storage, but if large portions of code are passed around dynamically this increases the bandwidth

18.   J. B. Dennis, "First Version of a Dataflow Procedure Language," *Lecture Notes in Computer Science* 5, p.187 (1974).

19.   D. P. Misunas, "Structure Processing in a Dataflow Computer," *Proceedings of Sagamore Conference on Parallel Computation* (August 1975).

20.   Bowen D.L, "Implementation of Data Structures in a Dataflow Computer," Ph.D. Thesis, Department of Computer Science, University of Manchester (May 1981).

21.   Arvind and R. A. Ianucci, "A Critique of Multiprocessing von Neumann Style," Technical Memo 226, MIT Laboratory for Computer Science (1983).

22.   W. B. Ackerman and J. B. Dennis, "VAL - A Value-Oriented Algorithmic Language Preliminary Reference Manual," Technical Report 218, MIT Laboratory for Computer Science (June 1979).

23.   W. B. Ackerman, "Dataflow Languages," *IEEE Computer* 15(2), p.15 (February 1982).

24.   J. R. W. Glauert, "High Level Languages for Dataflow Computers," *Pergamon-Infotech State of the Art Report on Programming Technology*, p.173 (March 1982).

25.   J. McGraw, S. Skedzielewski, S. Allan, D. Grit, R. Oldehoeft, J. R. W. Glauert, I. Dobes, and P. Hohensee, "SISAL - Streams and Iteration in a Single-Assignment Language," Language Reference Manual Version 1.0, Lawrence Livermore National Laboratory (July 1983).

26.   J. Backus, "Can Programming be Liberated from the von Neumann Style? A Functional Style and its Algebra of Programs," *Communications of the ACM* 21(8), p.613 (August 1978).

27.   G. Richmond, "A Dataflow Implementation of SASL," M.Sc. Thesis, Department of Computer Science, University of Manchester (October 1982).

28.   J. Darlington and M. Reeve, "ALICE: A Multiprocessor Reduction Machine for the Parallel Evaluation of Applicative Languages," *Languages and Computer Architecture* (October 1981).

2 Architecture and Performance

I. Watson

2.1 INTRODUCTION

The dataflow model represents a parallel computation as a directed graph removing any requirement for unnecessary sequencing. If the model can be mapped on to a physical machine structure it should be possible to overcome many of the problems which have been encountered in the design of parallel machines based on more conventional computational models in which sequencing is fundamental. We will consider a variety of approaches to machine design in an attempt to explain how the architecture of current dataflow machines has arisen.

An equally important feature of the dataflow approach is the development of a parallel programming style which retains the power of current programming languages but removes any necessity to express parallelism explicitly and requires no knowledge of the machine structure. Although conventional high level programming languages reflect the basic sequential nature of the machines which execute the compiled code, the details of more complex architectural features (instruction pipelines, virtual memory etc.) are usually completely hidden. There is much evidence that, if the programmer is required to take account of machine level features (vectorization, overlays etc.), then the programming task becomes significantly more complex and error prone. This situation can only be compounded by the introduction of parallelism. It will be seen that this attempt to hide the physical structure from the programmer has a significant influence when considering practical implementation.

2.1.1 Existing Parallel Machines

A great deal of work has been done on parallel computer structures. Before considering a completely new architectural approach we should first consider the two major types of 'conventional' parallel computer architecture to see if the dataflow model is relevant.

Array processors (e.g. DAP [1]) have been designed to exploit the parallelism which exists in problems where similar operations can be performed on every element of an array concurrently with each processor executing the same sequence of instructions. This 'single instruction stream, multiple data stream' parallelism is only a small subset of that which can be expressed in dataflow form and a machine structure of this type is unsuited to the general case.

requirements and the overheads of process allocation. In order that efficient use is made of parallel resources, it is important that they do not become idle, the chances of idleness are significantly increased in a scheme which allocates processes statically using coarse grain parallelism.

The choice is not straightforward, and this is reflected in the machine structures that have been proposed and constructed. On balance, it appears that the fine grain parallelism approach is winning but this may only be a temporary lead.

2.2 MACHINE TOPOLOGIES

An obvious physical realization of a dataflow machine could consist of a processor for each computational node on the graph together with a reconfigurable communication network to provide the interconnections. There are two objections to this. Such a system would be grossly inefficient because inactive nodes would result in inactive processors. This might be overcome if several nodes were allocated to each processor. However, the complexities of the required communication are such that no physical machine based on these principles has been attempted.

An abstraction from the 'physical' interconnection of the dataflow graph can lead to more realistic structures for physical machines. If each node is allocated a unique identifier, the interconnections can be held in a node description as the identifier of the next node (together with an input number) to which data will be sent when computed. It is then possible to replace the explicit interconnection paths by a generalized communication network. A data value, when computed, uses the next node information as a routing director to find the processor which contains the required operation. It should now be clear how such a technique would allow a dataflow program to be mapped on to a conventional multi-processor where a number of nodes are statically allocated to each of the processors.

At this point it is worthwhile noting that the communication required is essentially uni-directional. A result value is computed and the computational resources used can be released to another task immediately. No reply is needed and, as long as the processor which contains the destination node has other work to do, the transit time to the destination is not critical. It should also be noted that there is no requirement to maintain ordering through the communication network. It is these aspects of the dataflow model which relax the architectural constraints on the physical structure and render the crossbar-switch approach to multi-processor design unnecessary.

2.2.1 Tree Structures

A large number of computational problems have the property that they start slowly, build up to a crescendo of activity, and then collapse to produce a relatively small result. This has led to an interest in tree structured machines, an example of which, using a binary tree, is shown in **Figure 2-1**.

A major reason for the interest in this physical structure is the ease with which it could be mapped on to VLSI using 'Recursive H' techniques. **Figure 2-2** shows the basic principles of this method.

Although other computational models are also applicable, it is possible to see how a dataflow computation might map on to such a structure. The initial nodes are placed at the root of the tree and, as they produce their results, they are passed down, eventually reaching the leaves where maximum activity takes place. As the computation collapses the results can be passed back to the root. Unfortunately, as one might imagine, it is almost impossible to devise a general strategy whereby a computation can be mapped

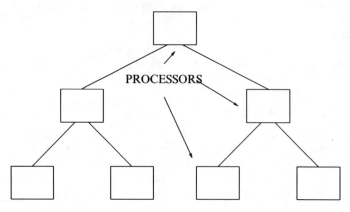

Figure 2-1

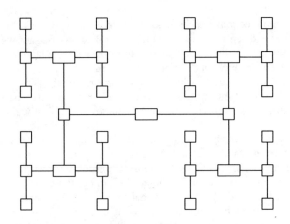

Figure 2-2

statically on to such a structure so as to produce sensible use of the resources.

A dynamic allocation scheme is necessary. If the root processor holds a complete description of the dataflow graph, it can decide from the results which it produces which areas of the graph are to be activated next; and pass these together with the data to its sub-processors. If the distribution strategy is carefully chosen, then the computation could spread itself nicely over the structure.

A machine which operates in this way was conceived and partially constructed by Al Davis at the University of Utah. One processing node became operational in 1978 [5] and using information about the characteristics of this a complete structure was evaluated by simulation. The results of this work indicate that many problems still exist in this approach. Not only does the distribution occupy significant resources, but also the strategy is still complex. Computations which appear to become very active may cease due to run-time conditions which cannot be predicted and large sections of the physical tree which have been allocated may suddenly become idle. The limited communication available then makes re-distribution of the computation a very inefficient task. A further problem arises when the leaves of the tree are reached and processors discover that they are in possession of a rapidly expanding section of the code.

Recognizing these difficulties there have been several proposals for machine topologies which can be classified as 'virtually tree structured' [6]. The physical machine structures can be viewed as 'folded trees' so that the communication is more general. Most of these ideas have not aimed at dataflow, but the more recent related area of Reduction Machines for the implementation of functional languages. It remains to be seen whether practical implementations of these ideas will work. There are still overheads of task distribution and unfortunately many of the physical interconnection schemes are not obviously suited to VLSI implementation.

2.2.2 Ring Structures·

The tree structured approach to machine design has been driven by the possibilities of highly parallel computers which exploit the potential of VLSI technology; the dataflow computational model is then viewed as a possible method of using these machines.

An alternative approach is to take the dataflow model as the driving force and design machines which make maximum use of its capabilities. The particular technological constraints of VLSI, although important, should only be addressed when the feasibility of these parallel structures is fully understood. This has resulted in a variety of ring-structured dataflow machine designs.

The most serious problem in any multi-processor structure is the provision of a flexible interconnection scheme with high bandwidth. The uni-directional communication property and the lack of a requirement for very rapid transit time between processors are exploited in ring-structured dataflow machines to overcome this problem. **Figure 2-3** shows the basic outline of such a machine.

A processor is assumed to contain:

(1)   A description of the dataflow graph.

(2)   A mechanism for assembling incoming data into complete packets for execution.

The switching mechanism is composed of individual 2×2 switches, each of which contains buffers at its input to hold incoming data. Routing information within the data packet indicates which of the switch outputs it is directed towards. The overall structure is therefore effectively a set of parallel pipelines. An N input, N output switch requires $N/2(\log N)$ individual elements and any route through the switch is a $\log N$ stage pipeline. It can be shown that, assuming random contention for switching resources, such a structure achieves a throughput bandwidth which approaches its theoretical maximum. However its complexity is manageable in a practical implementation. As the communication is uni-directional, the only price paid is the pipeline delay between processors. As long as the processors are kept active and the pipeline is kept full by parallelism in the program, then no degradation of performance should result.

This structure has been presented without any mention of the exact dataflow computational model used or the level of granularity employed. The basic structure is largely independent of these factors and as such has formed the basis of most of the major dataflow machines which have been, or are in the process of being, constructed. The differences between these machines are reflected in the detailed structure of the processors.

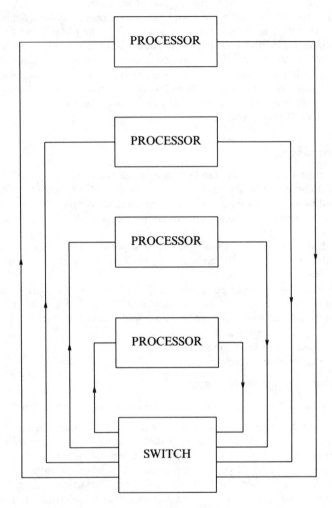

Figure 2-3

2.3 PRACTICAL MACHINES

Although it has been mentioned that the dataflow principle is applicable to any level of granularity and the choice is not immediately obvious, all the major projects have chosen to implement the model at the level of simple machine instructions. The prevailing view amongst those closely involved is that programming languages require this. Others believe that the major impact of dataflow ideas will be at a higher level. Whatever the final outcome, the projects which are currently in progress are providing a great deal of useful information in the area of parallel machine design. It is worthwhile therefore to examine some of the architectures in more detail.

2.3.1 The MIT Static Dataflow Machine

A machine which uses the static dataflow model of computation is being implemented currently by a team led by Jack Dennis at MIT. It uses bit-sliced microengines connected via a general purpose unidirectional routing network [7]. In this system the three major dataflow tasks of:

> accessing the program description;
> gathering tokens to produce executable packets;
> executing instructions;

are implemented in software in the processor modules.

A key factor in the design of the MIT system is the ability to expand its power by adding extra processors via an extended communications switch.

The desire to expand power by adding hardware is common to all dataflow system designs. There is keen debate about the maximum size of switch that can be constructed (or that will be feasible in the forseeable future). There is an obvious relationship between the power of individual processors, the total power, and the size of the switch. Because the MIT system uses conventional microprocessor software to emulate the dataflow model, it runs relatively slowly and large switches will be needed for substantial applications (e.g. weather forecasting). It is envisaged in the MIT design that switches of size 500×500 and more can be implemented using byte-wide 2×2 routers.

Other researchers are less confident that switches of this size will be practicable. Consequently they have concentrated on improving the execution rates of individual processors by designing their internal structure to be dataflow oriented.

2.3.2 The MIT Dynamic Dataflow Machine

Another research group at MIT, under the leadership of Arvind, is constructing a VLSI-based dataflow processor with many of the characteristics of the ring-structured system. The main features of this system are that (1) data structure accesses are handled separately from ordinary token activities, and (2) there is a two-tiered communication system [8]. The processor design is outlined in **Figure 2-4**.

The three major dataflow activities are handled by separate hardware, in particular the token gathering operation is performed by a small associative store. Data structure operations are treated separately so that (1) they can be performed quickly, and (2) the potentially large numbers of tokens involved do not occupy space in the expensive unmatched-token store. The two-tiered communication structure relieves the general communications switch of excess traffic as long as programs exhibit strong 'locality' (i.e. processing activity is localized in subgraphs and processors rather than communicating randomly with other subgraphs/processors). Locality also benefits the size of the unmatched-token store, and current plans at MIT are to implement a small 64-word store.

Reduced traffic in the communications switch allows bit-wide data paths to be used. The proposed building block for this MIT system is an 8×8 bit-wide module. Using program locality still further, large-size switches can be made rather less complex than the networks proposed for other systems.

This design relies heavily on strong program locality. The language Id [9] also developed by Arvind's team, has appropriate properties, and the system is being designed around this language.

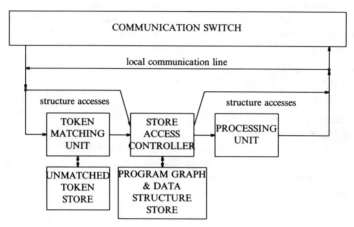

Figure 2-4

2.3.3 The Manchester Dynamic Dataflow Machine

A research group at Manchester University under the leadership of John Gurd and Ian Watson has constructed a specialized 'ring-structured' dataflow processor with funding from the Distributed Computing Systems Programme of the Science and Engineering Research Council of Great Britain [10, 11]. In this ring-structure the three dataflow tasks (i.e. matching tokens together; finding the next instruction; and processing of instructions) are implemented in three separate hardware modules. The individual actions in these modules are dependent solely on the module input data so that successive actions may be overlapped by connecting the modules in a pipeline. One extra pipeline module is provided to queue excess tasks when highly parallel programs are running. The overall ring-structure is therefore a four-stage pipeline as shown in **Figure 2-5**.

The fundamental unit of data in the switch is a token-package representing a tagged token on an arc of the program graph. The token has a data type and value, and a tag. The arc is represented by the address (in the program graph store) of the instruction at its head (known as the 'destination'). The token is the smallest data package in the system, and so the queue module is positioned adjacent to the switch, at the input to the ring.

Queued tokens are presented one-at-a-time to the matching unit, which is responsible for grouping together tokens with the same tag heading for the same destination instruction. In the Manchester system tokens may be grouped together in ones or twos, so that triadic instructions and above cannot be supported. Tokens which expect to find a partner, but which arrive at the matching unit before the partner does, are kept in the unmatched-token store until the partner arrives. At this time (or, in the case of a single-input instruction, when the first and only token arrives) all the required input data and the common tag and destination fields are sent to the instruction fetch unit as a token-pair package.

The program graph is stored as an array of instructions each representing one operator and its associated output arc(s). The destination field of an incoming token-pair is used as an address to fetch the next instruction which contains an opcode and up to two destination fields. This produces a complete executable package which is sent to the processing unit. Here the specified opcode is executed using the collected data and tag as operands, and the result token(s) is(are) finally returned to the communications switch

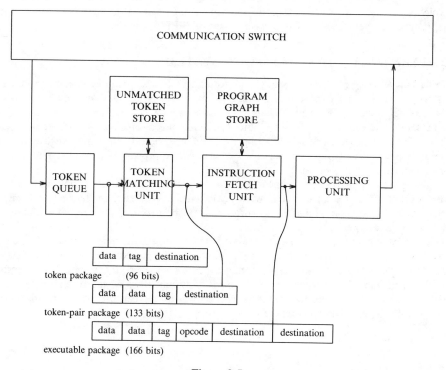

Figure 2-5

input.

The critical part of this system is the matching unit. The task of pairing tokens together is an act of association and so the unmatched-token store is (pseudo-)associative in nature; it is implemented using a hardware-hashing mechanism. In the technology chosen for the prototype version the average match time is 450 nanoseconds [12]. This limits the instruction execution rate of the ring-structured processor to just over 2 million instructions per second (MIPS). The prototype instruction processing element is some fifteen times slower than this and so a serially-activated parallel array of up to 15 such elements is required as a processing unit. At the time of writing the prototype system is running at just less than 2MIPS with 12 elements in the array.

The prototype implementation is tailored to stable, MSI, medium-speed, TTL technology. Higher speed could be obtained using faster logic and storage components, for example ECL. Comparable speed might be obtained if design were tailored to VLSI technology.

2.3.4 Other Projects

Several other projects are worthy of mention. A research system built in 1978 by a team led by Don Oxley at Texas Instruments used four microprocessors and a 990/10 host, connected together via a time-multiplexed communication ring [13]. This was a very low performance system but served to demonstrate some basic dataflow principles. A dataflow machine is being developed at NTT in Japan by Makoto Amamiya and his group [14]. Their hardware has been operational for about one year. The LAU project led by Jean-Claude Syre at CERT Toulouse in France [15] produced a working machine which was closely related to dataflow. Additional information on dataflow systems and languages has been published in a special issue of IEEE Computer [16].

2.4 PERFORMANCE OF DATAFLOW SYSTEMS

Little has yet been published about the performance of these dataflow systems in practical applications. The most comprehensive results obtained so far have come from the Manchester project [17]. These relate to the performance of the parallel processing elements within a single ring structure but nevertheless are impressive. A number of small but realistic programs of widely differing structure, with both regular and irregular parallelism, were run on a ring with between one and twelve processing elements. The results are summarized in **Figure 2-6**.

The speedup remains almost linear until the bandwidth limitations of the ring pipeline are approached. Since those results were published the store sizes in the ring have been expanded so that more realistic sized problems can be executed. The initial evidence is that the previous performance is maintained.

The next stage of the Manchester project is to investigate the performance of a multi-ring structure. This is being done using a microprocessor based system with two 68000 machines providing the function of a ring processor. A four ring system has recently become operational and will soon be extended to twenty rings. If the results of this are equally satisfactory, then the dataflow approach will be capable of producing very efficient high speed parallel computers.

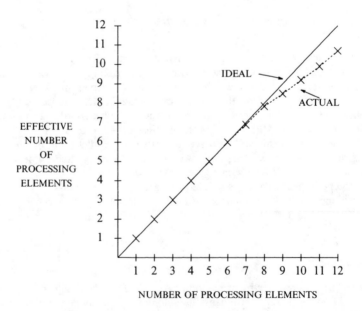

NUMBER OF PROCESSING ELEMENTS

Figure 2-6

2.5 REFERENCES

1. S. F. Reddaway, "DAP - A Distributed Array Processor," *Proceedings of 1st ACM Symposium on Computer Architecture* (December 1973).

2. W. A. Wulf and C. G. Bell, "C.mmp - A multi-mini-processor," *Proceedings of AFIPS FJCC* **41**, p.765 (September 1972).

3. R. J. Swan, S. H. Fuller, and D. P. Siewiorek, "Cm* - A Modular Multimicroprocessor," *Proceedings of AFIPS NCC* **46**, p.637 (June 1977).

4. N. Wirth, "Modula: A Language for Modular Multiprogramming," *Software - Practice & Experience* **7**(1), p.3 (January 1977).

5. A. L. Davis, "The Architecture and System Methodology of DDM1: A Recursively Structured Data Driven Machine," *Proceedings of 5th ACM Symposium on Computer Architecture*, p.210 (April 1978).

6. F. W. Burton and M. R. Sleep, "Executing Functional Programs on a Virtual Tree of Processors," *Languages and Computer Architecture* (October 1981).

7. J. B. Dennis and D. P. Misunas, "A Preliminary Architecture for a Basic Data Flow Processor," *Proceedings of 2nd IEEE Symposium on Computer Architecture*, p.126 (January 1975).

8. Arvind and V. Kathail, "A Multiple Processor Dataflow Machine that Supports Generalised Procedures," *Proceedings of 8th ACM Symposium on Computer Architecture*, p.291 (May 1981).

9. Arvind, K. P. Gostelow, and W. Plouffe, "An Asynchronous Programming Language and Computing Machine," Technical Report TR114a, Department of Information and Computer Science University of California at Irvine (December 1978).

10. J. R. Gurd and I. Watson, "Data Driven System for High Speed Parallel Computing," *Computer Design* **9**(6), p.91 (June 1980).

11. J. R. Gurd and I. Watson, "Data Driven System for High Speed Parallel Computing," *Computer Design* **9**(7), p.97 (July 1980).

12. J. G. D. da Silva and I. Watson, "A Pseudo-Associative Matching Store with Hardware Hashing," *Proceedings of the IEE* **130E**(1), p.19 (January 1983).

13. D. Johnson, "Automatic Partitioning of Programs in Multiprocessor Systems," *Proceedings of IEEE COMPCON* (April 1980).

14. M. Amamiya et. al., "A Dataflow Processor Array System for Solving Partial Differential Equations," *Proceedings of International Symposium on Applied Mathematics and Information Science*, Kyoto University (March 1982).

15. J-C. Syre et. al., "LAU System - A Parallel Data-Driven Software/Hardware System Based on Single-Assignment," *Parallel Computers - Parallel Mathematics*, p.347 (1977).

16. "Special Issue on Dataflow Systems," *IEEE Computer* **15**(2) (February 1982).

17. J. R. Gurd and I. Watson, "Preliminary Evaluation of a Prototype Dataflow Computer," *Proceedings of 9th World Computer Congress IFIP'83 September 1983*, p.545.

3 Assembler Level Programming

C. C. Kirkham

3.1 MANCHESTER DATAFLOW MACHINE FEATURES

As described previously, the Manchester Data Flow Machine at present consists of a single ring. The *node* store, one of the units in the ring, holds an encoding of the program graph, and the purpose of this chapter is to explain this encoding and to describe the features which graphs on the Manchester Machine may contain.

3.1.1 Instruction Format

For easily understood reasons, nodes on dataflow graphs for the Manchester machine are restricted in the following ways:

> There may be 1 or 2 input arcs.
> There may be 0, 1 or 2 output arcs.

The restriction on the number of inputs enables matching in the *matching unit* to be implemented in a straightforward manner, while that on the number of output arcs is determined by the size of an instruction. There are few occasions when no outputs are required, so the instruction encoding does not cater for this option and all nodes must have 1 or 2 destinations. If a node has a single destination it can also have a literal as one of the inputs, but then it may only have a single incoming arc. A *destination* in an instruction identifies the node to which the arc is connected, which of the two possible input points at which it is attached, and also the *matching function*. The latter indicates to the matching unit what it should do with a token on this arc, namely whether to attempt to match it with another token or not. The matching function was introduced as a result of an early change in the ring design to put the matching unit before rather than after the node store. However it has since been significantly generalized to provide other facilities as will be described below.

3.1.2 Matching Functions

The usual purpose of the matching function is given above, namely to allow the matching store to decide whether an operand will need to be matched with another going to the same node. In common use, therefore, only two matching functions are useful, namely BY (bypass), for operands going to monadic operators or dyadic operators with a literal, and EW (extract-wait), for operands which need to be paired. The remaining 6 matching functions are provided for special purposes which will only be hinted at here. For a more complete explanation of the use of some of the more unusual matching functions see Catto et. al. [1]. The naming of the matching functions, other than BY, follows a pattern which will now be explained. When an operand arrives at the matching store a search is made, pseudo-associatively, for a matching operand. Either this succeeds or it does not, and for each of these circumstances there is an action required of the matching store. Matching functions are named by giving the first letter of the action on successful match followed by the first letter of the action otherwise. The possible actions are:

Successful match actions

Extract   remove the matched operand from the matching store.

Preserve   leave a copy of the matched operand in the matching store.

Increment   leave an incremented copy of the matched operand.

Decrement   leave a decremented copy of the matched operand.

In all cases the incoming operand and the operand with which it matched are sent on to the node store as a pair of operands for a dyadic operator.

Unsuccessful match actions

Wait   insert the operand in the store for subsequent matching.

Defer   give up for now and try again later.

Abort   invent a matched operand of type Empty to form a pair.

Generate   as Abort, but also store the incoming operand in the matching store as if it were going to the opposite input point to this node.

Not all combinations are found to be useful, and below is a list of the seven implemented with a brief indication as to where they are used.

EW The normal matching function for dyadic operators.

ED Used in non-deterministic situations such as entry to critical sections - a form of busy waiting.

PD Used to store values such as array elements at a node in the graph.

ID Used at the entry to monitors to generate a stream of requests.

DD Used in reference counting so that stored objects can be disposed of when no longer required.

EA Used in guarded commands - i.e. in non-deterministic situations.

PG Used in 'lazy evaluation'.

3.2 THE INSTRUCTION SET

The instruction set has been divided into two distinct partitions. One class contains orders which only ever generate *one* 'logical' result and are known as *single result* orders. The other orders have *two* 'logical' results and are known as *double result* orders. The significance of 'logical' above is that the two possible result arcs are used for different purposes and values - it does not refer to how many copies of the result are produced. Thus there is a duplicate order provided to produce two copies of its input, but this is a single result instruction. The classic example of a double result instruction is the order to perform integer division which produces the quotient on one output arc, and the remainder on the other. With a single result instruction the node can produce one or two copies of the single result, depending on the number of destinations in the node. With a double result instruction the situation is more complicated. If only one of the logical results is required this is indicated by the prefix to the instruction, and then the available destinations can be used to provide one or two copies of this result. Otherwise the prefix indicates that both results are required, in which case the left result is sent to the first destination, and the right result to the second. Thus the possible prefix values are:

N   for a single result order.

D   for a double result order using both logical results.

L   for a double result order using the left result only.

R   for a double result order using the right result only.

3.2.1 Example Orders

The DUP (duplicate) order is very easy to describe. It takes a single operand of any type, and copies it to its single logical result. Of course, to be useful, this order usually uses both destinations to obtain two copies of that result. Notice that the type of the operand is mentioned here. This is because all values in the machine have a type, and most orders are sensitive to this type. Thus the SBI (subtract integers) order is also a single result order, this time with two operands. If both operands are of type integer the result is produced by subtracting the second operand from the first, and is also of type integer. The error behaviour of SBI when the operands are not of type integer, or when the resultant value overflows the range of integer values, will be described below.

As mentioned above DRM (divide integers with remainder) is a double result order. It requires two input operands, both of type integer. The left result is then the integer quotient, and the right result is the remainder. The BRR order is an implementation of branch, mentioned in **Figure 1-7**. It is also a double result order, with two operands. However in this case the types of the operands may differ. The right operand must be of type boolean, and is used to decide which logical result should receive a copy of the left operand, which can be of any type. If the right operand is *true* the right-hand result is produced, otherwise the left. The error behaviour of each of these orders will be described in the next section.

3.2.2 Error Behaviour

The above description has entirely omitted any mention of the behaviour of the orders in error situations. This is by no means a trivial detail as will be seen from the varying forms of error behaviour which will be discussed in this section. As a general rule the host computer is informed whenever an error is detected. This allows the user to abort the program by some crude external mechanism, such as resetting the machine! This is necessary because a program with a large amount of parallelism can perform a large amount of computation in parallel with, and completely independent of, its fault generating fragment. It will not in general be desirable for programs to check repeatedly whether any error has occurred to cause termination and this is left to the host.

However, there are also situations where errors need not indicate that the program should be halted. For example a program may not need to worry about the correct value of an expression which overflowed if it is determining the smaller of two expressions; it need only give up if both expressions overflow. All that is required is that no program should produce wrong answers as a result of detected errors. The Manchester Machine has a data type 'Error' which is usually produced as the result by a node which detected an error. The value part contains information about the position of the error and the nature of the error. The above discussion means that in general error values should not change into non-error values as a result of the operation of a node.

There is only one way to produce an error at a DUP node, and that is by providing it with a right-hand input. This will cause a 'type error' to occur, and the result produced will be of type 'error' to indicate this. However the DUP node is quite important in considering error handling, as it is specified to pass on its operand regardless of type. Thus error values are propagated just like any others.

SBI however can produce an error token as a result in a variety of ways. Firstly, if the operands are of correct type but the result of the subtraction is out of range an integer overflow error will occur. If either of the operands are of type error, however, this error will be passed on unchanged. If both operands are of type error, the left will be passed on - and the information in the right operand will be lost. Finally, a type error will occur if either (or both) operands are of neither integer nor error types. This error behaviour is designed to fit the principles enunciated above, and is general for arithmetic operations. DRM shows how this has to be complicated in the case of double result orders. When DRM produces an error result, which it can do for any of the reasons given for SBI, it does so to *both* results.

BRR is more interesting, however, in that only one result is used for error tokens. This is because branch orders are used to implement loops, and it is possible by correct use to cause a loop to terminate if an error occurs in evaluating its termination condition. Of course the result of the loop is still an error, but it is desirable to terminate the loop cleanly when this happens. Thus, because BRR is meant to implement **repeat** loops, where a true condition terminates, an error type for the right-hand operand causes it to be sent to the right result only. The right result is also used for the type error token if the right hand operand is of a type which is neither boolean nor error. There is a BRW order, to implement **while** loops, which differs from BRR only in the fact that it sends error tokens to the left result instead.

3.2.3 Dynamic Arcs

Most arcs in a dataflow graph are static. That is they are fixed and join one node to another in a permanent way. However there are situations when the destination to which a node should send its result needs to be different for separate activations of that node. The classic example of this is when a function returns a result to the part of the graph that called it. In a manner analogous to that of conventional computers, we wish to have the choice whether to duplicate the code of the function body everywhere it is called or whether to have just a single copy to which arguments are passed and from which results are returned to the calling graph. Passing arguments into a function body presents no difficulty, but a dynamic arc is required to obtain the result. The destination for this arc is the right operand to the SDS instruction which creates the arc, the left operand being the value to be sent. Thus the return information when a function is called consists of the destination to which the resulting value should be returned.

3.2.4 Labelling

As mentioned earlier, the Manchester Machine uses 'labelling' to allow graphs to be multiply used. Thus there are three label fields associated with each operand and these are known as the *activation name*, the *iteration level* and the *index*. For much of the time, the use of labels is not apparent as the matching store only matches operands with identical labels and most orders produce results with the same labels as their inputs. However there are orders whose purpose is to manipulate the label fields in various ways, and some of these will now be described.

The YIL order yields the iteration label of its single operand as the single result. The type of this result is *ordinal*, a restricted range of non-negative integers. SIL normally produces a left result which is the same as the left operand but with its iteration level equal to the value of the right operand. The right logical result is used in cases where the type of the right operand is not ordinal, or where the label produced by this operation could not be represented in the space available for it. The ADL order is similar, except that the right operand in this case must be of type integer, and its value is added to the iteration level rather than replacing it. In this case a negative iteration level, which would be illegal, also produces an error on the right output. There are orders which correspond to these for manipulating the index and activation name fields of the label, and other orders have also been introduced.

3.2.5 Other Orders

There are many other orders in the Manchester Machine. Among the more complex are special purpose orders proposed by Bowen [2] to implement and manipulate data structures. For details of the full instruction set of the machine, see the Basic Programming Manual [3].

3.3 THE MACHINE-LEVEL USER INTERFACE

The interface between the ring and the outside world is provided by the host, now a VAX-11/780, via the switch. All input to the ring and output from it is in the form of 'messages'. Indeed all information passing round the ring is in this same form. Labelled operands passing from the processing unit to the matching store via the switch and the token queue form 'normal' messages. This is the expected traffic when a program is executing. However programs are loaded, and various monitoring actions also need to take place, and these are implemented by means of 'special' messages. These are destined for particular units on the ring, and are passed on unchanged by all other units. At the indicated unit the special message is removed from the ring, and causes the requested action to occur. For example, there is a special message to load an entry in the node store, and this is how programs are loaded. Another important use of special messages is in providing output from the ring to the host by means of special messages to the host which the switch diverts from the token queue. Indeed all forms of monitoring provided by the machine generate special messages to the host, including the monitoring of errors mentioned above.

Figure 3-1 gives a listing of a program in the most low-level form, namely as the textual representation of the special messages required to load it into the node store. SPNLN indicates a 'special message to the node store to load a node', and therefore prefixes each order of the program. The data is in the form of normal messages to be inserted into the token queue when the program is to be executed. This program is shown as a dataflow graph in **Figure 3-2**.

```
;
; Simple iterative factorial program
;
SPNLS0    0            11
SPNLN0    0NDUP0       1LBY0        2LEW
SPNLN0    1NSBI0       6LBY         I1
SPNLN0    2DBRR0       4REW0        10LBY
SPNLN0    3NCEI0       7LBY         I0
SPNLN0    4NMLI0       5LBY
SPNLN0    5LADL0       2LEW         I1
SPNLN0    6NDUP0       8LEW0        3LBY
SPNLN0    7NDUP0       2REW0        8REW
SPNLN0    8LBRR0       4LEW0        9LBY
SPNLN0    9LADL0       1LBY         I1
SPNLN0    10ROPT0      11LBY        G0
SPNLN0    11NKIL0      0LBY
;
; and the data is
;
NI5 0 0 0 0 0LBY
```

Figure 3-1

3.4 THE TEMPLATE ASSEMBLER (TASS)

As you can see, the SPNLN form is rather tedious to read or write. In addition it lacks many of the facilities commonly found in conventional assemblers, such as labels and macros. Anyone writing the SPNLN code has to explicitly generate all the DUP nodes to produce multiple copies of a value, and must also be careful about using only one output from any node with a literal input. TASS, for 'Template Assembler', rectifies these deficiencies and provides its user with a cleaner view of the machine. This cleaner view is also useful to compilers, and in fact TASS was mainly intended as an intermediate code to be generated by high-level language compilers. Although it is instructive about the way in which the machine works, it has never been our intention to make users write assembly language programs, and therefore even TASS is not too attractive. Probably some kind of graphical program generation tool would provide the best user interface at this level [4].

In TASS nodes are named. If the node has only a single logical result this name represents the result and can be used as an operand in other nodes. It can be used as many times as required, with TASS supplying any DUPs necessary. If the node has two logical results, then the node name represents both of them, and must be qualified before it can be used as an operand. This qualification takes the form of the a selection of the left or right output, following the name with .L or .R respectively. Indeed if a double result operation is used but only one of the results is required, the node itself may be qualified and then the name represents the single specified result as with a single result operation. Hence:

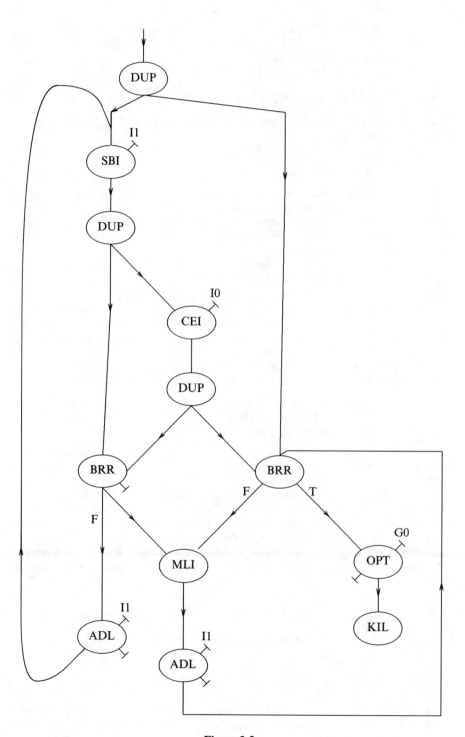

Figure 3-2

```
aplusb = (ADI a b);              ! adds a and b - both results
                                 ! of earlier operations
resdivc = (DRM aplusb c);
quotient = (DRM aplusb c).L;     ! Does the division a 2nd time,
                                 ! but only keeps the left result
zero = (SBI resdivc.L quotient); ! This will be zero
```

Literals are represented by strings, and are very similar to their SPNLN form. They can however be named, e.g.

```
pi = "R3.14159";
halfrem = (DRM resdivc.R "I2").L;
```

TASS carefully removes the restriction that only one result may be used of a double result operator if a literal is present. It does so by planting two copies of the operator if both logical results are required, and supplying the same inputs to them both. However, notice that it is still an error to write an operation with two literals, and the use of names for literals can make this less obvious!

It is one of the characteristic features of the Manchester Dataflow Machine that there is no 'merge' operation. That is to say, no node is required at the point in a dataflow graph where two arcs join to provide the input to a single input point. Obviously such situations should only occur after careful thought by the programmer to check that only one of the arcs should deliver a result with any particular label, and this will be the case when the value is the result of a conditional computation, for example. The simple notation used above does not deal with this situation however - for an operand is a name (or a literal). TASS therefore uses a Merge operator to maintain this simplicity, and this does not inconvenience the user who must anyway be aware of this situation. Thus

```
thenres = (BRR thenval bool).R;
elseres = (BRR elseval bool).L;
res = (Merge thenres elseres);
```

leaves res as the name to be used where the result of the conditional expression is required. Of course no code is planted for a Merge! Merge can have any number of arguments.

There are situations where Merge is not quite enough. An example is where the values of arguments are sent into the body of a function by each call. To use Merge would require a knowledge of how many calls there are in the program, and although this information can be obtained it could be a significant amount of work for such a trivial reason. To deal with this, TASS provides a way of naming the input points of a node and then linking operands to them. The input point is filled in with a dummy value, '_'. Thus

```
inarg = (DUP _);
argpoint = L'inarg;              ! naming the input point.
```

When a value, say x, is to be linked to this position, it is done as follows

```
(Link argpoint x);
```

This mechanism could, of course, be used instead of Merge - but each mechanism has a sensible use and both are provided.

One complication introduced by using names in TASS is that the addresses of nodes are no longer known, and a mechanism must be provided for literals of type destination.

These can be derived from the identifications of input points given above in the following way

inargdest = D'argpoint;

This makes inargdest a literal of type destination with a value of the input to the DUP node given earlier. Thus, to give a more complicated example, a program to add the integer results of calls to two different functions, f and g, would contain

fplusg = (ADI _ _);
thisfret = (SYN D'L'fplusg trig).L;
thisgret = (SYN D'R'fplusg trig).L;
(Link fretpt thisfret);
(Link gretpt thisgret);

where fretpt and gretpt are the positions in the bodies of f and g respectively to which return addresses are sent, i.e. the right hand input points of their SDS nodes.

TASS is quite a general system, and the description above was designed to illustrate its simple use as a dataflow assembly language. It also quite naturally provides macro facilities and is used in rather different styles by the two compilers which code generate into TASS.

As a simple illustration, **Figure 3-3** contains a TASS version of the program given earlier in graphical and SPNLN forms.

```
(I "TASS" "TSM") ;
! Iterative factorial calculation
in      = (Data "I 5") ;
n       = (DUP in) ;
mer_n   = (Merge n newn) ;
ndec    = (SBI mer_n "I 1") ;
endtest = (CEI ndec "I 0") ;
muln    = (BRR ndec endtest).L ;
newn    = (ADL muln "I 1").L ;
mer_fac = (Merge n newfac) ;
endbr   = (BRR mer_fac endtest) ;
cand    = (MLI muln endbr.L) ;
newfac  = (ADL cand "I 1").L ;

(OPT endbr.R "G 0") ;

(Finish) ;
```

Figure 3-3

3.5 REFERENCES

1.   A. J. Catto, J. R. Gurd, and C. C. Kirkham, "Nondeterministic Dataflow Programming," *Proceedings of 6th ACM European Regional Conference*, p.435 (April 1981).

2.   Bowen D.L, "Implementation of Data Structures in a Dataflow Computer," Ph.D. Thesis Department of Computer Science, University of Manchester (May 1981).

3.   C. C. Kirkham, "The Manchester Prototype Dataflow System: Basic Programming Manual (4th Edition)," Internal Report, Department of Computer Science University of Manchester (November 1983).

4.   A. L. Davis and R. M. Keller, "Dataflow Program Graphs," *IEEE Computer* **15**(2), p.26 (February 1982).

4 High Level Dataflow Programming

J. R. W. Glauert

4.1 INTRODUCTION

In Chapter 1 it was explained that the most attractive way to program dataflow systems is to use a language based on a functional style. This chapter gives a tutorial introduction to the language SISAL, developed as a result of collaboration between the Manchester Dataflow Group and a number of other researchers at Lawrence Livermore National Laboratory, Digital Equipment Corporation, and Colorado State University.

It will be assumed that the reader has some knowledge of conventional languages such as Pascal [1] and Algol68 [2]. SISAL will be described by comparison with such languages and many features of the syntax will appear familiar. The underlying semantics of SISAL are very different from those of conventional languages, however. A program places few constraints on the order of evaluation, allowing much implicit parallelism which can be exploited by a dataflow system.

No attempt will be made to describe the complete SISAL language, nor to give a formal syntax or semantics. The reader should consult the SISAL Language Reference Manual [3] for further details. The language is introduced through a series of examples illustrating many of its notable features, and then some complete programs are discussed.

4.2 PROGRAM STRUCTURE

4.2.1 Functions

SISAL does not allow *procedures*, but heavy use is made of *functions*, which are always free from side-effects. A SISAL program contains a *main function* which is evaluated to yield the result of the program. SISAL functions consist of a header and an expression. Expressions may yield multiple results as illustrated by the following complete program:

```
% Return the value of the argument, its square, and square root
function Test ( Arg: real returns real, real, real )
    Arg, Arg*Arg, sqrt( Arg )
end function
```

Wherever the syntax for computing a tuple of values occurs, indicated by separating a list of expressions by commas, the individual expressions may be computed in parallel by a dataflow system. Since there are no side effects it is also possible to compute sub-expressions independently.

SISAL functions may be recursive and may take and return arguments of any type. The syntax for calling functions is conventional.

All values are strictly typed but it is usually unnecessary to give types since they can be derived from the form of an expression. No implicit type coercions are performed. The types of function arguments and results must be given, however, as illustrated above.

4.2.2 Compound Expressions

In common with other Functional languages, SISAL has no concept of variables to which repeated assignments can be made. There is no control structure to specify the order of evaluation of statements. Instead there are facilities for declaring *named values*. There is a rich syntax for the expressions used to define such values. This provides the full expressive power found in conventional languages while allowing the implicit parallelism in an algorithm to be exploited.

The *compound expression* allows a number of local definitions to be made and used in the final result expression:

```
% Find Real solutions ax² + bx + c = 0

Root1, Root2 : =
    let
        d := sqrt( b*b - 4*a*c );
        t := 2*a
    in
        (-b + d) / t,  (-b - d) / t
    end let
```

4.2.3 Conditional Expressions

There are no conditional statements in the form found in Pascal, but instead there are conditional expressions similar to those available in Algol68. The following SISAL expression could be used to compute the absolute value of a variable, although a built-in function, **abs**, is also available for the purpose:

```
% Compute the absolute value of Arg

AbsArg : = if Arg > 0.0 then Arg else -Arg end if
```

There can be only one statement defining *AbsArg* so a value must be provided by both **then** and **else** arms of the expression. It is often required to define the values of several names on the basis of a single condition. This facility is provided by the syntax for handling tuples of values already used in the examples above:

```
% Sort two values into order

Lesser, Greater : = if A < B then A, B else B, A end if
```

4.2.4 Iterative Expressions

Repetitive computation is essential for most programming tasks. Since SISAL provides recursive functions it is possible to express repetitive computation in recursive form. It can be argued, however, that an iterative style is more natural for many algorithms. SISAL has a form of expression which allows a sequence of values to be computed, the final result being chosen when some condition is met. Each name concerned is given an initial value and there is a rule for computing a new value in terms of the old. Hence it is possible to repeat some computation, evaluating successive approximations to a solution, until an acceptable result is obtained:

```
% Calculate the Square Root of X using Newton's method

Root : =
    for initial
        R := X / 2.0
    repeat
        R := (old R + X / old R) / 2.0
    until abs( R - old R ) < Epsilon
    returns value of R
    end for
```

The keyword **old** preceding an identifier references the value bound to the name before the body of the loop was invoked, while the unadorned name refers to the new value. Hence the initial value is referred to as **old** during the first invocation of the body.

The keyword **until** may be replaced by **while**, in which case the sense of the test is reversed. It must be stressed that SISAL does not follow Pascal in using **while** and **repeat** to distinguish loop bodies which may be skipped entirely from those which are always executed at least once.

SISAL does provide the equivalent of both types of iteration, however, for in addition to the form:

for initial <decls> **repeat** <body> <test> **returns** <expr> **end for**

which always invokes the body at least once, there is also:

for initial <decls> <test> **repeat** <body> **returns** <expr> **end for**

The iterative construct also allows the use of recurrence equations. The next example computes the factorial of a number N using **while** and the form which tests before invoking the loop body:

```
% Iterative computation of N Factorial

FacN : =
    for initial
        C, P := 1, 1;
    while C < N
    repeat
        C := old C + 1;
        P := old P * C
    returns value of P
    end for
```

It will be seen that the effect is to multiply together all the values in the sequence represented by C. The order of multiplication is not significant and a suitable parallel implementation could improve on the essentially sequential algorithm given. SISAL allows reduction operators to be applied to the sequences of values returned from the iterative construct:

    % Use of a Reduction Operator to compute N Factorial

    FacN : =
        for initial
            C := 1
        while C < N
        repeat
            C := **old** C + 1
        returns value of product C
        end for

This example introduces a new form of the **returns** clause. As well as returning the last value bound to a name, it is also possible to combine all the values associated with the name in the **init** clause and successive loop cycles.

4.2.5 Forall Expressions

It is often required to perform the same computation on each of a set of values. In conventional languages it is necessary to use an iterative construct even if the computation for each value in the set is independent and evaluation could have proceeded in parallel. The factorial example used above could have generated the sequence of numbers to be multiplied together without using a recurrence equation.

SISAL has another style of **for** expression for computing a set of results for each value produced by a generator. The simplest generator yields all the integers in a range. The example below computes the factorial and also provides the sum of the squares of the numbers from one to N:

    % Compute Factorial N and the Sum of Squares to N

    FacN, SumSq : =
        for C **in** 1, N
            Sq := C * C
        returns value of product C, **value of sum** Sq
        end for

The **returns** clause has the same syntax for both varieties of **for** expression. The results computed for each binding created by the generator are available in the **returns** clause. The set of bindings may be empty, as in the case where N is less than one. If the **returns** clause employs a reduction operator, the appropriate unit value will be returned, so the example above would yield one for FacN and zero for SumSq.

4.3 DATA STRUCTURE

4.3.1 Arrays

So far only simple data values have been illustrated, although practical programs will require more sophisticated data structures. SISAL permits arrays of any type of value. The following type declarations introduce one and two dimensional arrays of **real** numbers:

```
type Vector  =  array [ real ];
type Matrix  =  array [ array [ real ] ];
```

Arrays are similar to those in Algol68, values having bounds determined at run-time by their defining statements. The statements below show forms for building array values, including an array with no elements and an array whose elements are all the same. In the case of an empty array it is not possible to determine the type from context, so the type **Vector** is given explicitly.

Array access uses conventional syntax and there are functions for enquiring the bounds and number of elements in an array. Array catenation appends the elements of the second array to the first, continuing the bounds from the upper bound of the first array:

```
Arr1 : = array [ 1: 1.0; 2: 4.0 ];
Arr2 : = array Vector [ ];
Arr3 : = array_fill( 1, 10, 0.0 );

El2 : = Arr1[ 2 ];
Size3 : = array_size( Arr3 );
Up2 : = array_limh( Arr2 );

Arr4 : = Arr1 || Arr3;
```

The repetitive constructs can be combined with array data structures in a flexible fashion. Previous examples have shown how the series of values computed in an iterative loop may be added or multiplied together. It is also possible to form the series of values into an array:

```
% Double Each Element of Array ArrA

ArrB : =
    for I in 1, 10
        Double : = ArrA[I] * 2.0
    returns array of Double
    end for
```

The **for in** repetitive form can be used to operate on all elements of an array simultaneously. A generator for use with arrays makes the elements of the array available directly without explicit subscripting as in the version below:

```
% Double Each Element of Array ArrA

ArrB : =
    for El in ArrA
        Double : = El * 2.0
    returns array of Double
    end for
```

The number of values generated depends on the size of the array. The corresponding indices are available via the extended generator:

```
for El in ArrA at_index Ix
```

For each invocation of the **for in** expression body there will be corresponding bindings to El and Ix.

The SISAL **dot** construction allows corresponding elements of more than one array to be processed. The example below computes the inner product of two arrays and forms an array containing the sum of the corresponding elements of the original arrays:

% Compute Inner Product of ArrA and ArrB and Pointwise Sum

```
InnerProd, ArrC : =
    for ElA in ArrA dot ElB in ArrB
        P : = ElA * ElB;
        S : = ElA + ElB
    returns value of sum P, array of S
    end for
```

There is also a **cross** product syntax, useful for handling matrices, equivalent to nesting of **for in** expressions.

4.3.2 Streams

It is intended that SISAL arrays should be thought of as single objects to be manipulated as a whole. Hence an implementation will generally require that all elements of an array have been given values before any part of the array may be used. As a consequence there may be synchronization after a repetitive construct which generates an array.

SISAL *streams*, on the other hand, may be viewed as sequences of values, produced in order, individual elements being available as soon as they are computed. Functions operating on streams may act as filters, passing on only some of the input values, or computing a function of the values as they arrive.

The operations available on streams are more limited than those on arrays. Streams may be built in much the same way as arrays, although no index values are required. The size of a stream may be enquired and the first element may be extracted. A function is available which strips off the first element, leaving the rest of the stream:

```
type IntStream = stream [ integer ];

Str1 : = stream [ 1, 4, 9, 25 ];
Str2 : = stream_rest( Str1 );

El2 : = stream_first( Str2 );
Size : = stream_size( Str2 );
```

The repetitive constructs may yield streams as well as arrays, and values of the result will be made available as soon as possible. The transforming and filtering applications of streams are illustrated by the following two examples. The first squares every element of a stream while the second rejects negative elements:

% Transform a Stream by Squaring each element

```
ResStr : =
    for El in ArgStr
        Sq : = El * El
    returns stream of Sq
    end for
```

% Remove Negative elements from a Stream

ResStr : =
    for El **in** ArgStr
       Neg : = (El < 0.0)
    returns stream of El **unless** Neg
    end for

In the second example the resulting stream is formed by appending each element in the stream to the result, unless the corresponding value of Neg is true. There is a keyword **when** which complements **unless**.

Streams of any data type are permitted, although the intended application of streams makes a type which is a **stream** of a **stream**, of little interest.

4.3.3 Records

Record types may be used. Creation of records is similar to that for arrays, but uses field names rather than index values. Field selection is as in Pascal:

    type Complex = **record** [Re, Im: **real**];

    X : = **record** [Re: 10.0; Im: 3.1];
    Y : = **record** [Re: X.Re; Im: -X.Im];
    Z : = X **replace** [Im: -X.Im];

The expression for Z yields the same value as Y; the **replace** form is useful for manipulating records with many fields and yields the record given as its first argument, but with some fields taking new values.

4.4 OTHER LANGUAGE FEATURES

A number of aspects of SISAL have been omitted from this introductory tutorial. There are a number of additional operations available on arrays and streams, and further reduction operations are provided. Simple **boolean** and **character** types are available, along with the familiar operations on those types.

The only form of expression omitted, **tagcase**, is used to access a type which acts as the disjoint union of existing types. A tag value indicates the component type present in a particular instance of the union type and is used to select the appropriate clause of the **tagcase** expression. **Union** types may be defined recursively, allowing data structures such as trees and linked lists to be constructed without the use of a pointer type.

A major area not mentioned in this introduction is the handling of errors by SISAL. Every operation and every form of expression in a SISAL program has a well-defined behaviour in the presense of errors. Each data type contains special error values which are returned as the result of any expression of the given type generating an error, or receiving an argument which is an error value. Errors will therefore propagate through expressions and be returned as the result of the program. A program may take special action in the presence of recoverable errors by using the special boolean function **is_error** which can be applied safely to any value.

4.5 SOME COMPLETE SISAL PROGRAMS

The programs given below are adapted from Appendix D of the SISAL Language Reference Manual [3].

4.5.1 Sorting

The first example uses a parallel algorithm based on QuickSort. The parallel **for** expression yields three arrays, containing all values less than, equal to, or greater than the pivot:

```
% QUICKSORT
%
% Split the argument array on the basis of the first element,
% applying the algorithm recursively to the two unsorted arrays

type Vector = array [ real ]

function QuickSort ( Info: Vector returns Vector )

if array_size( Info ) < 2
then
      Info
else
    let
        Piv = Info[1];
        L, M, R :=
            for Data in Info
            returns
                array of Data when (Data < Piv),
                array of Data when (Data = Piv),
                array of Data when (Data > Piv)
            end for
    in
        QuickSort( L ) || M || QuickSort( R )
    end let
end if

end function
```

4.5.2 Prime Numbers

The second example uses stream filters to compute a sequence of Prime numbers using the Sieve of Eratosthenes:

```
% SIEVE
%
% Create a Stream of all Prime Numbers less than N²
% by the Sieve Method

type IntStream = stream [ integer ]

function Sieve ( N: integer returns IntStream )

    function Filter ( S: IntStream; N: integer returns IntStream )

        let
            P := stream_first( S );
            R := stream_rest( S );
            F: =
                if P > N
                then R
                else
                    let
                        G : =
                            for V in R
                            NotPrime : = (mod( V, P ) = 0)
                            returns stream of V unless NotPrime
                            end for
                    in Filter( G, N )
                    end let
                end if
        in stream [P] || F
        end let

    end function

    let
        StartList : =
            for I in 2, N*N
            returns stream of I
            end for
    in Filter( StartList, N )
    end let

end function
```

4.5.3 Quadrature

The final example is a recursive Adaptive Quadrature program for integrating a given function over a specified range. The original example is more complete, handling error situations.

```
% QUADRATURE
%
% Integrate the function F over the given range

function Integrate ( Low, High: real returns real )

    % The Function to Integrate
    function F ( X: real returns real )
    X * X
    end function

    % Compute Approximation using Trapezoidal Rule
    function Area ( Low, FLow, High, FHigh: real returns real )
    (High - Low) * (FHigh + FLow) / 2.0
    end function

    % Recursively sub-divide are until approximation is acceptable
    % Provided with functions at end points and crude area of Trapezium
    function Quad( Low, FLow, High, FHigh, Trap: real returns real )
        let
            Mid := (Low + High) / 2.0;
            FMid := F( Mid );
            LTrap := Area( Low, FLow, Mid, FMid );
            HTrap := Area( Mid, FMid, High, FHigh );
        in
            if Abs( LTrap + HTrap - Trap ) < Epsilon
            then LTrap + HTrap
            else
                Quad(Low,FLow,Mid,FMid,LTrap) +
                Quad(Mid,FMid,High,FHigh,HTrap)
            end if
        end let
    end function

let
    FLow := F( Low );
    FHigh := F( High );
in
    Quad( Low, FLow, High, FHigh, Area( Low, FLow, High, FHigh ) )
end let

end function
```

4.6 REFERENCES

1.   K. Jensen and N. Wirth, *PASCAL User Manual and Report,* Springer-Verlag, New York (1975).

2.   A. van Wijngaarden et. al., *Revised Report on the Algorithmic Language Algol68,* Springer-Verlag, Berlin (1976).

3.   J. McGraw, S. Skedzielewski, S. Allan, D. Grit, R. Oldehoeft, J. R. W. Glauert, I. Dobes, and P. Hohensee, "SISAL - Streams and Iteration in a Single-Assignment Language," Language Reference Manual Version 1.0, Lawrence Livermore National Laboratory (July 1983).

Part II

Declarative Systems

W. F. Clocksin
J. Darlington
J. R. Kennaway
M. R. Sleep

5 Functional Programming

J. Darlington

5.1 INTRODUCTION

Functional languages have had a small band of very enthusiastic advocates for many years now. Their origins as practical languages can perhaps be traced to the development of LISP by John McCarthy in the early 60's but their ancestry goes directly back to the lambda calculus and recursion equation notations developed by workers in mathematical logic in the 1930's. For the last ten years functional languages and related technologies have been developed by, amongst others, Backus, Burge, Burstall, Henderson, Landin, MacQueen, Turner and the author. With notable exceptions this has been, until lately, largely a British phenomenon. However, functional languages are now beginning to attract a much wider interest and several developments, not least the advent of highly parallel VLSI architectures, are promising to translate the theoretical advantages of these languages into practical reality.

This article attempts to introduce the reader to the functional languages, briefly describing most aspects concerned with their development, implementation and use.

5.1.1 Foundations of Functional Languages

Functional languages trace their origins to the *lambda calculus* developed by Alonzo Church in the 1930's [1]. This calculus arose from work on basic computability theory and in particular the attempt to define precisely the intuitive notion of which functions, of the positive integers, could be computed in a mechanical or algorithmic way. Church's proposal, which became known as *Church's Thesis*, was that these effectively calculable functions should be identified with those functions that are expressible in a simple calculus, the lambda calculus. Although not amenable to formal proof Church's Thesis is now universally regarded as true, which makes the lambda calculus not a bad base on which to design a programming language.

In Church's lambda calculus expressions, called *lambda expressions*, are used to denote functions. Thus the expression

$$\lambda x . x^2 + 2$$

denotes the function which when applied to a number squares it and adds 2 to it. A lambda expression has two parts. The part up to the dot is called the bound variable and the part after the dot is called the body. The process of putting the two halves together is termed abstraction, as the function denoted by the lambda expression is abstracted from its body.

Functions denoted by lambda expressions are applied in the normal way by juxtaposing them with their argument, thus

$$(\lambda x.\ x^2 + 2)\ (5)$$

denotes the application of the denoted function to the value 5 and evaluates to 27.

A lambda expression can also appear in an argument position as in

$$(\lambda f.\ f(5))\ \lambda x.x^2 + 2$$

which evaluates again to 27. Note that the bound variable f in this case is 'function valued'.

These lambda expressions form the well formed formulas of the *lambda calculus*. The calculus is completed by a set of rules of lambda conversion i.e. rules that convert one lambda expression to another without changing its meaning. These rules are purely syntactic and can be applied without knowing the meaning of the expression.

There are three such rules. The first (the *alpha-rule*) says that we can change the name of the bound variables as long as we do it consistently. The second (the *beta-rule*) is the most important, and corresponds to function application. It says that lambda expressions of the form $(\lambda x.M)\ N$ can be converted to the form $M[N/x]$ i.e. M with N substituted for x, again as long as we do it consistently. The third rule is the opposite of the beta-rule and says that any expression can be converted to an abstracted function re-applied to appropriate arguments.

The basic idea behind the lambda calculus is that application of these rules corresponds to evaluating a program (or effectively computing a function) as they can be applied mechanically. An application of the beta-rule is termed a *reduction*. If A can be converted to B using only alpha and beta rules A is said to be reducible to B. An expression that cannot be reduced any further is said to be in *normal form*. Normal form lambda expressions correspond to the result of evaluating a program. Normal forms are unique (up to applications of the alpha-rule).

In reducing a lambda expression there may be several choices of what to do next. The main theorem of the lambda calculus, the *Church-Rosser theorem*, states that it does not matter in what order things are done, all paths lead to the same result. Furthermore if B is a normal form of A, A is convertible to B using only reduction steps. These results make the lambda calculus a very tractable discipline on which to base a computational formalism.

Another formalism that also has had an influence on the design of several functional languages, *Kleene recursion equations* [2], has the same origins as Church's lambda calculus, namely the search for a formal notation to try and capture the notion of effectively computable functions. Kleene recursion equations again are a method of denoting functions, in this case by sets of mutually recursive equations.

For example the equations

$$
\begin{aligned}
Ack(n, 0) &= n + 1 \\
Ack(0, m + 1) &= Ack(1, m) \\
Ack(n + 1, m + 1) &= Ack(Ack(n, m + 1), m)
\end{aligned}
$$

define the famous *Ackermann function*. The general form of these recursion equations is a set of, possibly mutually recursive, equalities concerning the functions being defined. The form of expression allowed on the left hand side of these equations is restricted and they are meant to be used in a left to right manner as production rules. There may be several equations mentioning the same function on the left hand side and these equations are distinguished by the terms occurring in the argument position, e.g. the first equation above is meant to be used for evaluating the Ackermann function when its second argument is zero, the second equation when the first argument is zero and the second non zero and the third when both arguments are non zero.

The functions definable using Kleene style recursion equations are exactly those definable using lambda expressions which gives even greater credence to the claim that they both correspond to the set of all effectively calculable functions.

5.2 FUNCTIONAL PROGRAMMING

The object of writing a functional program is, not surprisingly, to define a set of functions. Thus functional programming can be carried out in any conventional language, such as Pascal, which has a function definition capability. As we shall see, however, there are fundamental differences between functions as defined in Pascal and those defined in functional languages.

5.2.1 Introduction

In a functional language, such as HOPE or KRC, a program is a set of equations defining functions in terms of other simpler or primitive functions.

For example

max(x, y) = **if** x > y **then** x *else* y

defines the well known maximum function in terms of the primitives **if then else** and >.

The program

maxof3(x, y, z) = max(max(x, y), z)
max(x, y) = **if** x > y **then** x **else** y

shows the use of a defined function in the definition of a more complex function. Notice that in the above program there is no ordering implied on the equations. The execution of a functional language program involves evaluating an expression using the equations of the program as directed, left to right, rewrite rules. Thus, for example, to find the maximum of the three numbers 3, 5, 7 one evaluates the expression maxof3(3, 5, 7) which goes through the following rewrites before being reduced to the number 7

maxof3(3, 5, 7)
⟹ max(max(3, 5), 7)
⟹ max(**if** 3 > 5 **then** 3 **else** 5, 7)
⟹ max(5, 7)
⟹ **if** 5 > 7 **then** 5 **else** 7
⟹ 7

Functional programming systems are usually interactive. A user, characteristically, is allowed to develop his program incrementally by adding or deleting equations and at any time he can ask the system to evaluate a typed in expression. The system responds by printing back the reduced answer.

Functions can, of course, be defined in terms of themselves, using recursion.

factorial(n) = **if** n = 0 **then** 1 **else** n * factorial(n-1)

Many functional languages rather than having one equation for each function being defined allow the programmer to write several equations, each one dealing with a particular case in the manner of Kleene recursion equations.

Thus

```
factorial(0) = 1
factorial(n + 1) = (n + 1) * factorial(n)
```

defines exactly the same factorial function as above. The first equation deals with the case where the number input is zero and the second with all numbers that are greater than zero. Note that in order to preserve the property that the order of the equations is not important we require that for any value at most one equation should apply. This is most easily achieved by requiring that the cases covered by each equation are disjoint.

5.2.2 Data Structures

Structures are handled in functional languages by introducing a special class of functions, called *constructor functions*. No equations are written to define constructor functions, they simply act to build data structures. More accurately terms built out of constructor functions and constants (i.e. unary constructor functions) name data structures.

For example lists can be defined by introducing two constructor functions. One, *nil*, names the empty list. Traditionally the other, two argument, constructor is written as an infix operator ".". Thus the term 1.(2.nil) names the list with two elements 1 and 2 conventionally written as [1, 2].

Equations can be written to define functions over structures just as they can over scalars.

For example

```
length(nil) = 0
length(x.l) = 1 + length(l)
```

defines the function that calculates the length of a list. Note how the ability to write patterns in the left hand side of the equation not only gives one the ability to decide what case to select but also the ability to decompose the structure and name the component parts. Thus the "l" on the right hand of the second equation names the tail of the list input i.e. the list minus its first element. This process of *pattern matching* is a feature of the advanced functional languages shared with the logic languages and adds great power, often removing the need to define explicit conditionals or selector functions.

Evaluating a program manipulating structures involves exactly the same process as evaluating one involving only scalars. Thus to calculate the length of the list that we would informally write as [1, 2] we reduce the expression length(1.(2.nil)). The reduction process continues, as before, until no further reductions are possible and the expression consists solely of constructor functions or constants. This is illustrated in **Figure 5-1**, which assumes + as a built in primitive.

Note that we can formally treat scalars as terms built from the constructor functions 0 and successor (written as + 1). Thus it makes sense to write n + 1 in the left hand side pattern or even n + 2 but not n + m. The two former expressions being syntactic sugar for successor(n) and successor(successor(n)) respectively but the later implies a non deterministic split of the input value which is not allowed.

This view of structures as terms in constructor functions allows functional languages to deal directly with structures that would be termed 'abstract' in more conventional languages. For example binary trees shaped as shown in **Figure 5-2** can be introduced by defining two new constructor functions, *atom* to build the leaf objects and *tree* to build interior nodes. Thus the tree in **Figure 5-2** is named by the term

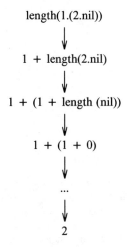

Figure 5-1

Figure 5-2

    tree(tree(atom(1), atom(2)), atom(3))

and a function to rotate such tree structures can be written as

    rotate(atom(n)) = atom(n)
    rotate(tree(t1, t2)) = tree(rotate(t2), rotate(t1))

Thus rotate(tree(tree(atom(1),atom(2)),atom(3))) reduces to:

    tree(atom(3),tree(atom(2),atom(1)))

which names the tree shown in **Figure 5-3**.

5.2.3 Higher Order Functions

All realistic functional languages are what is termed *higher order*. This means that functions themselves can be passed around as data objects just as scalars or lists. This is in keeping with the doctrine that in a soundly based programming language all objects

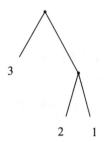

Figure 5-3

should have full 'rights' and that there should not be first and second class citizens.

Thus in functional languages there are expressions that evaluate to objects that are function valued. We have actually already seen such objects. Having defined a program (equations) for the function factorial, the identifier factorial has as value the factorial function. Functions are applied to their arguments by juxtaposition in the normal way, with or without bracketing according to the style of parsing used e.g.

> factorial 3 or factorial(3)

It is often convenient to be able to define a function without having to give it a name that is globally available as is the case with factorial. Several functional languages utilize lambda expressions for this purpose. For example a lambda expression of the form **lambda** n $\Rightarrow$ 2 * n evaluates to a function which multiplies the number to which it is applied by 2. Thus **(lambda** n $\Rightarrow$ 2 * n) 4 evaluates to 8.

The following program computes the list of all the factorials from 1 to n by first constructing the list of integers from 1 to n and then using the map function to apply the factorial function to each element. Note that the second argument of map is function valued.

listoffact(n)	= map(listo(n), fact)
map(nil, f)	= nil
map(n.l, f)	= f(n).map(l,f)
listo(n)	= listfromto(1, n)
listfromto(i, j)	= **if** i $>$ j **then** nil
	else i.listfromto(i + 1, j)
fact(0)	= 1
fact(n + 1)	= (n + 1) * fact(n)

Similarly

> listofsquares(n) = map(listo(n), **lambda** n $\Rightarrow$ n^2)

produces the list of squares of numbers up to n. Note that it is of course impossible to use a lambda expression to denote a function that needs to use recursion in its definition as there is no function name available to apply to achieve the recursive call!

An alternative mechanism employed in some functional languages is the use of partial parameterization. Here a function of several arguments is applied to fewer arguments than required to produce a function 'expecting' the missing arguments.

For example given the max function which expects two arguments max(x, y) = **if** x > y **then** x **else** y

we can apply it to only one argument as in max(3) to produce a function of one argument that when applied to a number returns that number if it is greater than 3 and 3 otherwise. i.e.

max(3) 4 is equivalent to max(3, 4).

The existence of higher order functions provides the basis for a powerful programming style in functional languages. For any data structure one can define a set of general purpose '*iterators*' that walk over the data structures applying functions passed as parameters in various ways. Given a rich enough set of these higher order functions most programs can be implemented as specific instantiations of these functions, removing the need to write explicit recursions in the main program.

Functions can also be written that return functions as values. The classic example is function composition

compose(f, g) = **lambda** x $\Rightarrow$ f(g(x))

so compose(**lambda** n $\Rightarrow$ n^2, **lambda** n $\Rightarrow$ 2 * n)4 evaluates to 64.

This use of function forming functions (sometimes known as functionals) leads to a style of functional programming popularized by Burge and Backus and embodied in the language FP (see below). Here programs are constructed at a higher level of functional abstraction and the main building blocks are function forming functions such as compose. In effect a program that would normally be expressed as a sequence of transformations on objects is replaced by a sequence of transformations on functions the result of which is then applied to the object.

5.2.4 Set Expressions

One powerful idea that has been adopted in several functional languages is the use of *set abstraction*. *Relative set abstraction* was first introduced in Zermelo-Frankel set theory as a mechanism for defining sets in terms of qualified selections from other sets. It has been adopted into functional languages to provide a convenient syntax for a particular higher order iterator over sets.

For example, consider the problem of calculating all the right angled triangles that can be constructed, whose sides are integer valued and less than a given size. If we represent a triangle as a triple of integers representing the sizes of the three sides this function can be written directly thus,

triangles(n) = $\{(n1, n2, n3) \mid 0 \leqslant n1, n2, n3 \leqslant n \ \& \ n1^2 + n2^2 = n3^2\}$

A set iteration consists of two parts: a *generator*, in this case 0 < n1, n2, n3 $\leqslant$ n, producing candidates for possible inclusion in the answer set; and a predicate, in this case $n1^2 + n2^2 = n3^2$, selecting which of these are to be included.

Set abstraction was first employed as a specification language in [3], its incorporation into a functional programming language as an executable feature was first suggested in [4] and implemented in [5]. SETL [6], used sets as a basic control primitive. HOPE, KRC and Miranda all use set expressions. For an elegant exposition of the power of set expressions see [7].

5.2.5 Qualified Expressions

Often the right hand side of an equation will contain more than one occurrence of the same subexpression as in

$$g(x) = \textbf{if } x = 0 \textbf{ then } 0$$
$$\textbf{else } x + (g(x/2) * g(x/2))$$

This repetition of the same expression will do no harm to the meaning of the program because, as we shall see below, it is an important property of functional languages that the same expression in the same context always evaluates to the same result. However, the repeated re-evaluation of the same expression can have disastrous consequences for the efficiency of the execution, especially if, as in our example, the redundancy occurs in a recursive call that will exponentially amplify it.

This potential inefficiency is simply overcome in functional languages by the use of *qualified expressions* which allow the programmer to name the repeated expression and then refer to it by that name.

Thus many languages employ a construct such as

B **where** y = A

where the variable named y can be used to refer to the expression A throughout B. So our example above could be written

$$g(x) = x + (y * y) \textbf{ where } y = g(x/2)$$

It is important to realize that this is not assignment as the value of y does not change throughout its use. The meaning of any expression involving **where** is always equivalent to that of the expression where the qualified variable has been resubstituted with the expression it denotes.

Many languages allow the use of pattern matching in **where** expressions just as they allow it on the left hand side of equations. Thus

$$\text{quotrem}(x, y) \quad = \textbf{if } x < y \textbf{ then } (0, x)$$
$$\textbf{else } (1 + m, n)$$
$$\textbf{where } (m, n) = \text{quotrem}(x - y, y)$$

is a function to calculate the quotient and remainder of a pair of numbers. Note that quotrem as well as taking a pair of numbers as arguments returns a pair of numbers and that pattern matching (of a simple form) is used in the **where** construct.

5.2.6 Typing

The concept of *typing* is orthogonal to whether a language is functional or not; however functional languages have several advantages when it comes to developing powerful typing systems, and many functional languages have typing systems in advance of any available elsewhere. Three of the most developed functional languages ML, HOPE and Miranda (see below) all employ the *polymorphic typing* system developed by Robin Milner [8]. This supports a strong typing discipline but allows variables to appear in type statements thus avoiding many of the rigidities found in strong typing as employed in, say, Pascal.

Using the Milner algorithm one can either ask the user to give the types of his functions prior to their definition, and then check that the expressions he types in are consistent with the information he has given; or infer the types of the functions as he inputs them, and signal an error if it is impossible to do this consistently.

HOPE adopts the former strategy, ML and Miranda the latter. For example in HOPE before defining the factorial function one would have to give its type

dec fact : num → num
fact(0) = 1
fact(n + 1) = (n + 1) * fact(n)

In ML and Miranda the type would be inferred (from knowledge of the types of the basic functions) and presented to the user.

Polymorphism appears trivially in the definition of the identity function (a function one would actually never need to write in a functional language). In HOPE this would be

typevar alpha *(introducing a type variable)*
dec id : alpha → alpha
id(x) = x

Thus id is restricted only in that the type of its output must be the same as the type of its input. It can be applied to objects of any type, numbers, characters, trees etc.

Polymorphism is much more useful when it is applied to data structures. Thus, for example, the same list building and manipulating functions can be used for lists of numbers or lists of lists or lists of trees in contrast to the situation in Pascal where these all would be different types requiring separate function definitions.

Functions are, of course, a type and the full definition of our compose function in HOPE would be

typevar alpha, beta, gamma
dec compose: (beta → gamma) × (alpha → beta) → (alpha → gamma)
compose(f, g) = **lambda** n ⇒ f(g(n))

(If E1 and E2 are type expressions E1 → E2 is the type expression denoting functions from E1 to E2).

The Milner algorithm is not generally applicable to non-functional languages. It is our experience that the combination of strong typing and polymorphism provides a very powerful aid to correct program development and is essential for any realistic programming language.

One crucial point to note is that functional languages are *deterministic*. For any given input they will always give the same answer. Furthermore all pure functional languages have the Church-Rosser property: alternative sequences of evaluation, if they terminate, always lead to the same answer.

The above describes the main features of most modern functional languages. There are matters we have not considered such as syntactic extensions and modular structures but we have covered the main building blocks. Functional languages are characterized by the small number of basic concepts employed and the consistent way these are combined to form powerful notations. Most functional languages are very simple to learn once the basic concepts have been grasped.

5.3 FUNCTIONAL PROGRAMMING METHODOLOGIES

5.3.1 The Importance of Functional Languages

The reasons why functional languages are considered important and a significant advance on conventional languages are threefold. First, it is held they are intrinsically more powerful languages than conventional ones, so program construction is a simpler and less error prone task. Second, formal manipulation of functional programs is possible, enabling the process of program transformation, the systematic derivation of efficient programs from specifications, to be supported. Third, parallel evaluation of functional programs is easy to organize, allowing the design of very fast, extensible, multi-processor machines. We will return to these points in more detail below but it is worth taking some time to consider the theoretical reason behind all these claimed benefits.

Pure functional languages are *referentially transparent*. This means that programs written in functional languages can be considered static objects and that the meaning of an expression in a functional language depends on the meaning of its component subexpressions and not on the history of any computation performed prior to the evaluation of that expression. There is thus a clean notion of equivalence between expressions and equivalent expressions can be freely substituted for each other in any context without changing the meaning of the whole expression. Clearly mathematics is referentially transparent and 3 + 2 is equivalent to 5, so 3 + 2 can be substituted for 5 in the expression 8 * 5 yielding 8 * (3 + 2) without changing the meaning of the whole (40).

It would be very difficult to consider doing mathematics with a language that was not referentially transparent; it is one of the ground rules for any notation to be comprehensible and manipulable and this applies to notations for writing programs as much as notations for writing mathematics.

Languages with variables that can be assigned to are not usually referentially transparent. The meaning of an expression involving such variables can vary according to the history of the computation performed prior to the evaluation of that expression.

Thus a programmer writing a functional language program is free to concentrate on the declarative reading of his program, *what* will be computed not *how* it will be computed, as the meaning of the program will be independent of the order of its evaluation. A programmer in a conventional, sequential, language must take care that all his operations are performed in the right order to achieve the correct result, an extra intellectual responsibility, and one that mitigates against comprehensibility, modularity or modifiability.

5.3.2 Specification

Programming in functional languages lends itself very nicely to a process of specification or prototyping prior to the development of efficient programs. It is very natural, when using a functional language, to develop a model of the system one is attempting to build. If one disregards the need for efficiency it is very natural to write programs in a functional language that very directly specify what is to be computed. The point is that specification and program are written in the same notation and specifications can be run or interrogated to test out one's ideas on an emerging system or demonstrate the intended capability to a customer.

The power of functional languages for specification purposes can be extended by removing some of the restrictions placed on the notation to permit efficient interpretation. As we saw earlier functional languages are a subset of a general equational language, a subset chosen to allow the equations to be used as directed rewrite rules. If one is not concerned initially with evaluation one can remove these restrictions and allow a user to define functions using general equations.

For example given a definition of multiplication by repeated addition

$$\text{mult(a, 0)} = 0$$
$$\text{mult(a, b+1)} = a + \text{mult(a, b)}$$

It is natural to specify a function to perform (exact) division by the general equation

$$\text{mult(div(n, m), m)} = n$$

Such an equation serves perfectly well to define div, it is just not, at first glance, a program that would enable us to compute divisions.

Other ways a functional language can be extended for specification purposes include allowing equations over infinite sets or lists that are not constructable but perfectly well defined. For example the following 'program' specifies the ordered list of numbers that are composites of 2, 3 and 5, the well known Hamming problem,

$$\text{hamming} = \text{order(composites)}$$
$$\text{composites} = \{2^i \star 3^j \star 5^k \mid i, j, k \geqslant 0\}$$
$$\text{order(S)} = \text{min(S). order(remove(min(S), S))}$$
$$\text{min(S)} = \{s \mid s \in S \textbf{ forall } s' \in S : s' \geqslant s\}$$
$$\text{remove (x, S)} = \{s \mid s \in S \& s \neq x\}$$

The point is that composites is an infinite set so min(composites) is not executable. However the above serves as a perfectly adequate specification of hamming which can be at least symbolically evaluated and interrogated using theorem provers rather than efficient program executors and can be systematically transformed to an efficient program.

5.3.3 Transformation

Having established a satisfactory specification the next step is to develop an efficient program to accomplish the task. The idea underlying *transformation* is that the specification should be systematically manipulated in order to produce this program. The critical requirement is therefore for a set of manipulation rules that allow programs to be transformed improving their efficiency while leaving their meaning unaltered. It is a great advantage of the functional languages that such a set of manipulation rules can be simply provided. Because functional languages are referentially transparent they can be manipulated just as familiar mathematical forms are manipulated. The '=' sign in a functional program really is equality and equivalent expressions can, by and large, be interchanged freely without the need for elaborate checking. This is the basis for the *unfold/fold* system of program transformation first developed in [9]. This is a set of six simple rules for transforming functional programs. These rules have been proved correct once and for all so there is no way their application can change the meaning of a program, thus doing away with the need for a separate proof of the correctness of each transformation attempted. Such a simple set of rules would be impossible to obtain for a conventional language such as Pascal.

The example below shows a very simple transformation of a program to compute the average of a list of numbers to a more efficient version.

Specification/Initial Program

$$
\begin{aligned}
\text{average(l)} &= \text{div(sum(l), count(l))} \\
\text{sum(nil)} &= 0 \\
\text{sum(n.l)} &= n + \text{sum(l)} \\
\text{count(nil)} &= 0 \\
\text{count(n.l)} &= 1 + \text{count(l)}
\end{aligned}
$$

Transformation

Introduce a new function (guaranteed to preserve the meaning of the program as it does not overlap with any case previously defined).

$$\text{av(l)} = (\text{sum(l), count(l)}) \qquad\qquad \text{(A)}$$

Instantiate this equation

$$\text{av(nil)} = (\text{sum(nil), count(nil)})$$

Symbolically evaluate this equation

$$\text{av(nil)} = (0, 0) \qquad\qquad \text{(B)}$$

Again instantiate (A)

$$\text{av(n.l)} = (\text{sum(n.l), count(n.l)})$$

Symbolically evaluate

$$\text{av(n.l)} = (n + \text{sum(l)}, 1 + \text{count(l)})$$

Re-arrange

$$\text{av(n.l)} = (n + u, 1 + v)$$
$$\qquad \textbf{where } (u, v) = (\text{sum(l), count(l)})$$

Use (A) 'backwards'

$$\text{av(n.l)} = (n + u, 1 + v)$$
$$\qquad \textbf{where } (u, v) = \text{av(l)} \qquad\qquad \text{(C)}$$

Rewrite the original equation for average

$$\text{average(l)} = \text{div(u, v)}$$
$$\qquad \textbf{where } (u, v) = (\text{sum(l), count(l)})$$

Again use (A) backwards

$$\text{average(l)} = \text{div(u, v)}$$
$$\qquad \textbf{where } (u, v) = \text{av(l)} \qquad\qquad \text{(D)}$$

Final Program

The net result of the above manipulations is three new equations (B, C, D) that have been systematically derived from the initial program and taken together constitute a more efficient program for average

average(l) = div(u, v) **where** (u, v) = av(l)

av(nil) = (0, 0)
av(n.l) = (n + u, 1 + v) **where** (u, v) = av(l)

As well as being correct the unfold/fold system has been shown to be powerful in that it is capable of expressing a wide variety of substantial transformations, e.g [10, 11].

The simple formal nature of transformations in a functional language presents the possibility of at least partially mechanizing the process. The system described in [12] enables a user to design his program, by writing a structured transformation plan utilizing high level transformation operators, that is executed by the system that implements the transformation as a sequence of the lowest level, correctness preserving, operators. Such a system, we consider, combines the precision and accuracy of formally based program development with the practicality and intelligibility of structured program design. The fact that the program design is itself a formal object, the transformation plan, has very important advantages when it comes to program modification and maintenance. It is ironic that of all the professions, programming itself is still relatively unautomated. It seems necessary that computers contribute materially to the programming process if software development is ever to reach the standards of accuracy, reliability and replicability that are required. The combination of functional languages, specification, transformation and semi-automatic program development systems seems to offer a feasible route.

5.3.4 Parallel Evaluation

The design of computer architectures to take advantage of the opportunities for parallelism inherent in functional and related languages is dealt with in depth elsewhere in this volume. It is worth pointing out here, however, that the reason why it is much simpler to organize parallel evaluation for functional programs than for programs in a sequential language is exactly the same reason as conveys all the other advantages alluded to above, namely possession of referential transparency.

For example consider our original program for the average example give above

average(l) = div(sum(l), count(l))

If we attempt to evaluate average(1.(2.(3.nil))) application of this equation leaves us with

div(sum(1.(2.(3.nil))), count(1.(2.(3.nil))))

to compute.

It is clear that the computation of sum(1.(2.(3.nil))) can proceed independently of the computation of count(1.(2.(3.nil))) because of the absence of any time dependent behaviour. They can therefore be computed in parallel with consequent gain in efficiency. Note that the transformation performed above only affects an improvement if the target machine is a sequential one. It is often the case that a parallel implementation allows the efficient execution of what would otherwise be viewed as preliminary specifications or inefficient initial programs. We are not claiming that the advent of parallel architectures will do away with the need for the careful design of good algorithms, either by program transformation or by informal manual methods; they will, however, lift the level in doing away with the final, awkward, step of fitting the functional program to the sequential nature of the machines currently in use.

5.4 SEQUENTIAL IMPLEMENTATION OF FUNCTIONAL LANGUAGES

Anyone implementing a functional language on a conventional, sequential, machine faces several problems. The very nature of the languages makes them somewhat unsuited to the machines in existence today and in order to preserve their pure nature, which is really their raison d'etre, one has either to put up with a certain degree of inefficiency or expect the compiler to do more work than would be necessary for a sequential language, such as Pascal. It has been the case traditionally that functional languages are happiest when implemented on machines with large unsegmented virtual address spaces and significant amounts of real memory. However certain very impressive implementations have been developed lately and functional languages are beginning to be fitted onto machines at the micro end of the range.

It is very gratifying to be able to report that implementations of functional languages on parallel machines seem easier than on sequential machines. It is our experience on the ALICE project [13], that in a parallel context many of the problems previously associated with implementing functional languages either disappear or have much more efficient solutions. A HOPE compiler for ALICE, written in HOPE itself, described in [14], illustrates this point well.

5.4.1 Implementation via Transformation to a Sequential Language

Instead of attempting to implement a functional language on a sequential machine by direct interpretation or compilation one can transform the functional language program to a program in a conventional sequential language which can then be evaluated in the traditional way. Early work on program transformation tended to regard functional languages as purely specification languages and envisaged a final phase of translation to a sequential language. With the growing interest in functional languages as programming languages in their own right this route has been neglected; it could still offer some advantages. The main point is that almost all the transformations necessary to produce an efficient sequential program can be carried out as source to source transformations at the functional level, where programs are more amenable to manipulation, and the final translation to a conventional language can be automatic. Even features such as storage overwriting, which do not have a meaning in a functional language, can still be treated at the functional level as described in [11]. Working at this level it is possible to achieve much more significant transformations than if the equivalent program were expressed in a sequential language and one may actually end up with a more efficient program starting with an inefficient functional language specification, rather than attempting to directly write an efficient sequential language program.

5.4.2 Interpretation and Source Reduction

The simplest way to implement a functional language is to develop a *source interpreter* that mimics the operational semantics for functional languages we described earlier, i.e. expression rewriting. Here the program and expression to be evaluated are parsed to give tree structures and the interpretive loop consists of detecting a rewritable subexpression within the expression being evaluated and performing the appropriate substitution. Such interpreters are, of course, rather slow in execution but can be instrumented to provide a great deal of intelligible information about program execution and therefore make excellent program development tools.

5.4.3 S.E.C.D. Machine Implementations

Many implementations of functional languages that use compilation are based on the S.E.C.D. machine. This is an abstract machine developed by Landin [15] to support the evaluation of lambda calculus expressions. It is a register transfer machine and its name derives from the designation of the four principal registers used.

As with all machines the S.E.C.D. machine has its own machine code. Thus a functional language program is compiled to a program in this machine code which when executed, according to the semantics of the S.E.C.D. machine, terminates with a value equivalent to that which would have been obtained by direct reduction of the functional language program.

The main problem to be overcome in the design of such an abstract machine is to fully support functions. Functions can be created dynamically and applied at points remote from their definition. To be implemented correctly functional languages must obey static binding rules, that is any free variables in a function body must take on the values they had when the function was defined, not the values they have when the function is applied. This is handled in S.E.C.D. style implementations by representing dynamically created functions by an object called a *closure* which can be viewed as a pair consisting of the function body and the *environment* pertaining at the time of that function's definition. Thus when such a function is applied the current environment is suspended and replaced by the environment part of the closure.

The four registers in an S.E.C.D. machine are

S the stack, which is used to hold intermediate values generated during the evaluation of an expression.

E the environment, which holds the values bound to variables during evaluation.

C the control list, the machine language program being executed.

D the dump, a stack used to hold the suspended computation when a new function is applied.

An excellent description of the S.E.C.D. machine and the way it can be used to support a functional language can be found in [16].

5.4.4 Graph Reduction Implementations

All languages, functional or otherwise, in current use today employ variables as a convenient way of referring to entities created during computation. So even if one does not allow variables to be assigned to, one is still faced with the task of deciding what is the current value of a particular variable symbol. The S.E.C.D. machine uses the classic technique of employing an environment, some association of variable symbols with their current values, to tackle this problem. This is not the only solution though and several functional language implementations have pursued the alternative solution of actually replacing the occurrence of the variable symbol by its value, that is copying the function body with the appropriate substitutions made, rather than creating a new environment and leaving the function body unaltered.

The technique of evaluating a functional language program by rewriting an expression where the expression is represented in (directed, acyclic) graph form is, not unnaturally, known as *graph reduction*. An impressive implementation of a functional language that uses a compilation approach to graph reduction is described in [17]. Here a compiler for a functional language FC, a subset of ML, operates by compiling each function, viewed as a rewrite rule, to a sequence of instructions for an abstract graph reduction machine, called the *G-machine*. The G-machine code for a function manipulates the graph to reduce a function application to its value. The G-code is then translated into sequences of native code for a VAX-11 that directly perform the required rewrites. The resulting implementation is very fast indeed.

The furthest one can go in avoiding the use of variables, and therefore the need for closures, is to compile the program to a form that does not involve variables at all. Turner [18] presents an approach following this route where the program is compiled to a machine code consisting entirely of *combinators* from combinatory logic [19]. The compiled program then consists entirely of an expression built from applications of a fixed set of combinators. There is a set of rewrite rules for certain combinator configurations that is fixed across all programs so evaluation consists simply of reducing the combinator expression using these rules. The simplicity of this idea has prompted a hardware realization in the form of a sequential combinator reduction machine [20].

The appeal of the combinator approach is that it reduces the problem of evaluating a functional program to a small number of primitives. The disadvantage is that the combinators define rather small transformations and combinator expressions for non-trivial user functions may become quite large and thus require a correspondingly greater number of steps to interpret. Hughes [21] refines the combinator idea and uses an infinite (program dependent) set of 'super-combinators'. A program is translated into an expression containing super-combinators and a set of super-combinator definitions.

5.5 FUNCTIONAL LANGUAGES

5.5.1 LISP

LISP started life as a pure functional language [22]. It was quickly 'improved' by adding features, such as assignment, designed to increase performance on sequential machines. There has been widespread use of LISP particularly in the US Artificial Intelligence community for many diverse applications, powerful user support environments have been developed (e.g. INTERLISP) and powerful single user workstations have been designed for LISP. Recently there has been a resurgence of interest in pure LISP, and LISPKIT [16] represents an interesting return to pure LISP.

5.5.2 ML

ML is a functional language developed at Edinburgh University as part of the LCF theorem proving project [23]. Although initially conceived as a meta-language (hence ML) to direct proof systems it is a powerful general purpose higher order functional language employing the Milner polymorphic typing algorithm. There are several implementations of ML, primarily in LISP.

5.5.3 HOPE

HOPE is a polymorphically typed higher order recursion equation based functional language. It is a successor to an earlier first order recursion equation based language, NPL [5], that itself grew from work on program transformation. The first implementation of HOPE was at Edinburgh University [24]. There are now implementations at Bell Labs and at Imperial College, London, where it was the initial language behind the design of the parallel graph reduction machine, ALICE [13].

5.5.4 SASL, KRC, Miranda

Turner has been responsible for a series of higher order functional languages [25], culminating in Miranda which is a polymorphically typed, higher order, recursion equation based functional language. Several implementations of these languages exist in C and BCPL.

5.5.5 FP

FP is a functional language developed by John Backus and popularized by his Turing Lecture [26]. FP has a style that can best be described as APL'ish as it shuns the use of variables and concentrates on the use of operators. FP has many enthusiastic followers, particularly in the U.S; several implementations have been developed and several novel architectures designed around FP.

5.6 APPLICATIONS OF FUNCTIONAL LANGUAGES

Functional languages have potentially universal applicability. They are general purpose programming languages and could ultimately replace sequential languages completely. However, we have a long way to go before this happens. With the outstanding exception of LISP it is probably fair to characterize functional languages as emerging from adolescence into full maturity. They have much theoretical potential but they are only just beginning to become widely appreciated. Many significant applications have been carried out, some of which are mentioned below. Experience with these projects seems to bear out the advantages claimed for functional languages.

By far the widest experience has been with LISP. Since its development in the 1960's it has become **the** language of the U.S. Artificial Intelligence community and has spread widely into other fields. LISP's sparsity of syntax and the fact that programs and data share the same representation makes it very attractive as a systems programming language and almost all advanced AI language implementation work is carried out in LISP.

A feature of LISP's development is the large amount of effort that has gone into the development of programming environments. INTERLISP is the best known of these and has grown over the years as the result of many people's efforts and now provides a very powerful collection of editing, debugging and general programming support tools.

A multiplicity of applications have been written in LISP including algebraic manipulation systems, planning and learning systems, robot controllers and automatic programming systems. One must record that all these systems have been written in 'dirty' LISP but recently interest has revived in the pure subset and some large systems are being recoded. Interest in LISP has extended to the development of high powered work stations optimized for LISP which have now been in commercial production for many years and are proving very popular, especially in the U.S.

Around the universities there has been much interest in, and use of, pure functional languages. HOPE has been used at Edinburgh to write sophisticated mathematical and program specification packages [27]. Also at Edinburgh, Feather used NPL to fully specify the text formatter from Kernighan and Plauger [28], and transformed this, completely mechanically, to an efficient implementation [29].

At Imperial much of the system and application software for the ALICE graph reduction machine [13] is written in HOPE. In particular Ian Moor has developed a HOPE compiler for ALICE that is completely written in HOPE. This covers the whole language and certainly qualifies as a significant sized application at around 5,000 lines of

HOPE [14]. Other system software written in HOPE includes the meta-language program transformation system [12], and a variety of text and structure editors. Several of the interesting application programs have been written as student projects. It is worth recording our local experience that undergraduate students, by and large, take to functional languages very enthusiastically, and their productivity and accuracy is markedly higher using functional rather than conventional languages. Applications that have been developed include a picture description package in HOPE [30], that allows complicated scenes to be described purely declaratively or statically; a tax guidance program; and an intelligent structure editor that allows a user to input a language syntax definition in B.N.F., and produces for him a structure editor/program input system for that language.

An interesting experiment is reported in [31]. Here an experiment was performed implementing the Unix parser generator Yacc in SASL and comparing it to the sequential implementation. The conclusions can be summarized as supporting the claims made for functional languages as regards programmer productivity and code compactness (although the latter was not improved by as much as had been hoped); confirming that strong typing and data encapsulation are even more essential in a functional language than an imperative one; and indicating that debugging of functional language programs is a difficult activity needing more research attention.

Henderson has used LISPKIT extensively to develop an operating system and suite of program development tools [32].

In the U.S. Buneman and his colleagues at the University of Pennsylvania have developed a functional language with a data base query facility. This language FQL [33], is actually in commercial use and being used by, amongst others, travelling salesmen who use it to interrogate their companies' data bases over phone lines.

5.7 FUTURE DEVELOPMENT OF FUNCTIONAL LANGUAGES

Research in functional languages is continuing apace in all areas of application, programming methodology and support, language design, implementation techniques and machine design. We consider that the future prospects are very promising as all the developments in supporting technologies are moving in directions that will enable the theoretical advantages of functional languages to be fully exploited. The prospect of a complete functional language programming environment, allowing program specification and formal transformation, all running on a highly parallel VLSI machine, is very attractive and should be easily obtainable before the end of the decade. Such developments will enable functional languages to offer significant cost performance advantages both in software production and execution speed.

It is invidious to highlight any particular development in what is a very exciting field but two aspects that are particularly exciting are the adoption of functional languages by commercial concerns and the growing convergence between the logic and functional languages.

As we saw earlier there have been sufficient applications of functional languages to demonstrate their practical utility, but real progress will only be made when organizations, separate from sites developing functional languages, use them on problems of commercial interest to them. This is starting to happen to a significant degree and provides valuable feedback to the designers of these languages.

The logic and functional languages are basically similar. Both are based on mathematical notations providing the opportunity for formally based program development and parallel evaluation. The differences are that functional languages are deterministic, they are often typed, to our eyes they have a richer and more readable syntax and make powerful use of higher order facilities. What they lack in comparison to logic languages is the sort of control structure that allows a relation, once defined, to be used in several modes. Analysis of the reason for this difference points to the fact that the logic languages employ unification, a generalization of the pattern matching employed in functional languages. However it has been shown [34] and [35], that unification can be smoothly incorporated into functional languages.

The resulting languages possess all the control structure flexibility of the logic languages while retaining all existing advantages of the functional languages. Parallel developments on the logic side open up the very real possibility of a unified logic and functional language being developed in the near future.

5.8 REFERENCES

1. A. Church, "An Unsolvable Problem in Elementary Number Theory," *American Journal of Mathematics* **58**, pp.345-363 (1936).

2. S. C. Kleene, "General Recursive Functions of Natural Numbers," *Mathematical Annals* **112**, pp.727-742 (1936).

3. Z. Manna and R. A. Waldinger, "Knowledge and Reasoning in Program Synthesis," Technical Note 98, A.I. Center SRI (1974).

4. J. Darlington, "Applications of Program Transformation to Program Synthesis," *Proc. Colloquium on Proving and Improving Programs*, pp.133-144, Arc et Senans, France (1975).

5. R. M. Burstall, "Design Considerations for a Functional Programming Language," *Proc. Infotech State of the Art Conference*, Copenhagen (1977).

6. J. Schwartz, *On Programming. An Interim Report on the SETL Project,* Courant Institute of Mathematical Sciences, New York University (1973).

7. D. A. Turner, "The Semantic Elegance of Functional Languages," *Invited Paper ACM/MIT Conference on Functional Languages and Computer Architecture*, Portsmouth, Massachussetts (1981).

8. A. J. R. G. Milner, "A Theory of Type Polymorphism in Programming," CSR-9-77, Dept of Computer Science, University of Edinburgh (1977).

9. R. M. Burstall and J. Darlington, "Some Transformations for Developing Recursive Programs," *JACM* **24**(1), pp.44-67 (1977).

10. H. Partsch, "A Transformational Approach to Parsing," Internal Report Project CIP, Technical University of Munich (1983).

11. I. W. Moor, "A Study of Algorithm Derivations," Internal Report, Dept. of Computing, Imperial College (1980).

12. J. Darlington, "The Structured Description of Algorithm Derivations," pp. 221-250 in *Algorithmic Languages*, ed. J. L. van Vliet, North Holland, Amsterdam (1981).

13. J. Darlington and M. J. Reeve, "Alice: A Multiprocessor Reduction Machine for Applicative Languages," *Proc. ACM/MIT Conference on Functional Languages and Computer Architecture*, Portsmouth, Massachusetts (1981).

14. I. W. Moor, "An Applicative Compiler for a Parallel Machine," *Proc. Sigplan '82 Symposium on Compiler Construction*, Boston (1982).

15. P. J. Landin, "The Mechanical Evaluation of Expressions," *Computer Journal* **6**(4), pp.308-320 (1963).

16. P. Henderson, *Functional Programming Application and Implementation*, Prentice Hall (1980).

17. T. Johnsson, "The G-Machine: An Abstract Machine for Graph Reduction," *Proc. Declarative Programming Workshop*, pp.1-19, University College, London (1983).

18. D. A. Turner, "A New Implementation Technique for Applicative Languages," *Software Practice and Experience* **9**, pp.31-49 (1979).

19. H. B. Curry and R. Feys, *Combinatory Logic*, North Holland (1958).

20. T. J. W. Clarke et al., "SKIM- The S,K,I Reduction Machine," *Proc. LISP Conference*, Stanford (1980).

21. J. Hughes, "Graph Reduction with Super-combinators," PRG-28, Programming Research Group, Oxford University (1982).

22. J. McCarthy, "Recursive Functions of Symbolic Expressions and Their Computation by Machine," *CACM* **3**, pp.184-95 (1960).

23. M. J. Gordon et al., "Edinburgh LCF," CSR-11-77, Dept. of Computer Science, Edinburgh University (1977).

24. R. M. Burstall et al., "HOPE an Experimental Applicative Language," *Proc. LISP Conference*, Stanford (1980).

25. D. A. Turner, *SASL Language Manual*, Computer Laboratory, University of Kent (1976).

26. J. Backus, "Can Programming be Liberated from the von Neumann Style? A Functional Style and its Algebra of Programs," *CACM* **21**(8), pp.613-41, Turing Lecture (1978).

27. D. T., Sanella and M. Wirsing, "A Kernel Language for Algebraic Specification and Implementation," CSR-131-83, Dept of Computer Science, University of Edinburgh (1983).

28. J., Kernighan and R. Plauger, *Software Tools*, Addison Wesley (1976).

29. M. A. Feather, "'ZAP' Program Transformation System. Primer and User Manual," Rep No. 54, Dept. of Artificial Intelligence, University of Edinburgh (1979).

30. K. Arya, "Describing Pictures using the Functional Language HOPE," *Computer Graphics Forum* **3**(1) (1984).

31. S. L. Peyton Jones, "Yacc in SASL," Indra Note 1533, University College, London (1983).

32. P. Henderson, "The LISPKIT Library," Internal Report, Programming Research Group, Oxford (1983).

33. P. Buneman et al., "A Practical Functional Programming System for Databases," *Proc. ACM/MIT Conference on Functional Programming and Computer Architecture*, Portsmouth, Massachussetts (1981).

34. J. Darlington, "Unifying Logic and Functional Languages," Internal Report, Dept. of Computing, Imperial College (1983).

35. H. Abramson, "A Prological Definition of HASL, a Purely Functional Language with Unification Based Conditional Binding Expressions," *New Generation Computing* **2**(1) (1984).

6 Logic Programming and Prolog

W. F. Clocksin

6.1 AN HISTORICAL INTRODUCTION

Logic programming has come about as a result of earlier work on mechanized theorem proving. One of the first serious studies of the mechanization of reason was carried out by the 17th Century mathematician Gottfried Leibniz, with his proposal of the *calculus ratiocinator*. The disappointed Leibniz failed in his attempt to devise the *ratiocinator,* and had to content himself with inventing (with Newton) the differential and integral calculus.

Since the work of Herbrand [1] in the 1930's, much research in mechanized theorem proving has been carried out by Davis, Putnam, Prawitz, and others. The growth of interest which has produced the field as we know it today can be traced from Robinson's paper [2] in which a description of the *resolution* principle first appeared. Resolution is a generalization of *modus ponens* and makes use of a powerful pattern matching operation called *unification*. Siekmann and Wrightson [3] give a comprehensive collection of the earlier papers in the field.

The development of logic programming as an area of study in its own right can be traced to the work of Green [4], Hayes [5], Kowalski [6], and Alain Colmerauer. Around 1970, Kowalski and Colmerauer were led to the fundamental idea of *programming in logic*: that logic can be used as a programming language. The acronym Prolog -- *Pro* gramming in *Log* ic -- was contrived at about this time, and the first Prolog interpreter was implemented by Roussel at Marseille in 1972.

The idea of using subsets of first order predicate calculus as a programming language was a significant contribution, because, until about 1970, computer scientists had used logic only as a specification language. However, Kowalski [7] and others showed that logic has a *procedural interpretation* as well, making it *possible* in principle to use logic as a programming language. The subsequent development of efficient implementations of Prolog compilers [8,9] has shown that it is also *practical* and *efficient* to use subsets of logic as a programming language. The programming language Prolog is not a pure logic programming language, but it is the first widely available language that has been inspired by logic programming concepts.

The main thesis of logic programming, as expressed by Kowalski [10] is that an algorithm can be usefully expressed in two components: the *logic* and the *control*. The logic is the statement of *what* the problem is: properties of the problem and the solution. The control is a statement of *how* it is to be solved. The ideal goal of logic programming is that the programmer need only specify the logic component of an algorithm. The control should be exercised by the computer. This ideal has not yet been achieved, but it is an interesting research methodology to determine the extent to which useful programs can be written using only logic. Several benefits could accrue if this goal is met:

(1) It is easier to reason about statements in a logic program.

(2) A large number of problem solving methodologies can be conveniently represented in logic [11].

(3) There are more opportunities for the exploitation of parallelism.

(4) Using a single uniform formal system may bear helpful consequences for software engineering.

In order to achieve this goal, two problems need to be solved. The first is the *control problem*. Currently, programmers need to provide small but undue amounts of control information, partly by ordering the clauses and goals in a program, and partly by the use of extra-logical "features" in the language. Although experienced and fluent Prolog programmers can write idiomatic and hence "better" programs having little or no control information, some control problems have still not been solved satisfactorily.

The second problem is the *negation* problem. Since only positive information can be a logical consequence of a database, special rules are needed to deduce negative information. Thus, existing interpreters cannot implement negation, but only a problematic version by means of the *negation by failure* rule. Current research is aimed at understanding negation and finding a more satisfactory implementation.

Today logic programming is a well established and quickly growing field in computer science. Although initially established in Britain and Europe, it has recently attracted considerable attention in the USA and Japan. There are now several international conferences and workshops per year, and a new journal devoted to logic programming has been founded. Textbooks on logic programming [12, 11], mathematical reasoning [13], and Prolog programming [14] are available. Prolog has been widely used in the areas of artificial intelligence and design automation, and we will survey some of these applications in this tutorial. See [15] for a recent discussion of the current major issues in logic programming: comparison with functional programming and with languages such as Prolog, and the combination of object language and metalanguage. A survey of the theoretical foundations of logic programming is available in [16]. A more comprehensive history of logic programming has been written recently by J A Robinson [17].

6.1.1 The Future

Prolog is only a first step in the practical use of logic programming. Promising areas of active interest include the following:

- *Databases.* Logic programming could make important contributions to our concepts of database systems: using logic as a uniform language for data, programs, queries, views, and integrity constraints has great theoretical and practical potential [18, 19, 20].

- *Concurrency.* We need ways of understanding and exploiting the parallelism implicit in a logic program. Recent explorations in this direction are PARLOG [21] and Concurrent Prolog [22, 23, 24]. PARLOG has a rich set of control features expressed by annotations, while Concurrent Prolog is very simple.

- *Semantics.* Improvements in how the semantics of logic programming and of Prolog [25, 26] can be expressed have been made recently by [27, 28, 29].

- *Other Logics.* Bowen [30] investigates the issues involved in programming in full first-order logic. Moszkowski and Manna [31] propose the use of temporal logic as a programming language. Deduction methods for S_5, a modal logic, have been developed [32, 33]. There is increased interest in unifying logic programming with functional programming [34]. Using many-sorted equational logic as a programming language has been proposed by [35].

- *Efficiency.* Ways of speeding up Prolog programs are under investigation. Further work on portable compilation [36] is needed; work is in progress on "intelligent" backtracking [37] and processors more suitable for running logic programs are under development [38].

- *Tools.* Logic Programming needs software engineering (and *vice versa*). One way forward is to investigate the use of logic as a specification language; logic programs can then be derived by using program transformation techniques [39]. Prolog needs a module system; many have been proposed [40]. A polymorphic type system and checker based on the work of Milner has been devised by Mycroft and O'Keefe [41]. Automatic debugging of Prolog programs has been investigated by Shapiro [42]. Software engineering of some aspects of Prolog has been investigated by Mellish [43] and Bruynooghe [44].

6.2 PREDICATE CALCULUS

6.2.1 Syntax

We begin with a quick review of the syntax for Predicate Calculus (PC). We shall use the version known as *PC with equality.* The following symbols are used:

- *variables.* Variables are written in lower-case, and are drawn from the last few letters of the alphabet (examples: x, y).

- *constant symbols.* Constant symbols are written in lower-case, and are drawn from the beginning of the alphabet and from the digits (examples: a, nil, 0, 1).

- *function symbols.* Function symbols are constant symbols having an *arity,* which is a positive number specifying how many arguments the function takes. Constant symbols can be thought of as function symbols of arity 0.

- *predicate symbols.* Predicate symbols are written with an initial upper-case letter, and have an arity. There are two reserved predicate constants **T** and **F**, which will be used to stand for "true" and "false".

Terms are constructed from applying a function symbol to constants and variables. The syntax of terms is defined recursively by three rules:

(1) Constants and variables are terms.

(2) If f is a function symbol of arity n, and $t_1,...,t_n$ are terms, then $f(t_1,...,t_n)$ is a term.

(2) A sequence of symbols is a term only on the basis of rules (1) and (2).

An *atomic formula* is a predicate symbol applied to terms. If P is a predicate symbol of arity n and $t_1,...,t_n$ are terms, then $P(t_1,...,t_n)$ is an atomic formula. The predicate symbol

'=' of arity 2 is usually written infixed between its arguments: for terms t_1 and t_2, $t_1 = t_2$ is an atomic formula.

The following are *statements* (or *Formulae*):

- *atomic formulae.*

- $\sim S$ for statement S.

- $S_1 \wedge S_2$ for statements S_1 and S_2.

- $S_1 \vee S_2$ for statements S_1 and S_2.

- $S_1 \supset S_2$ for statements S_1 and S_2.

- $S_1 \equiv S_2$ for statements S_1 and S_2.

- $\forall x.S$ the universal quantifier, for variable x and statement S.

- $\exists x.S$ the existential quantifier, for variable x and statement S.

Some examples of statements are as follows:

$$\forall x. \ \text{Number}(x) \supset \exists y. \ x = \text{succ}(y)$$
$$\forall x. \forall y. \ \text{add}(x,y) = \text{add}(y,x)$$

A *literal* is an atomic formula or a negated atomic formula. A *positive* literal is a literal without a negation sign; a *negative* literal is a negated literal.

6.2.2 Semantics

An *interpretation* of a statement S consists of a nonempty domain D, and a set of assignments to each constant, variable, function symbol, and predicate symbol occurring in S as follows:

(1) To each constant, and to each variable, we assign some element in D.

(2) To each n-ary function symbol, we assign a mapping from D^n to D.

(3) To each n-ary predicate symbol, we assign a mapping from D^n to $\{T,F\}$.

For every interpretation of a statement over a domain D, the statement can be evaluated to **T** or **F** according to the following rules:

(1) If the truth values of statements S, S_1 and S_2 are evaluated, then the truth values of $\sim S$, $(S_1 \wedge S_2)$, $(S_1 \vee S_2)$, $(S_1 \supset S_2)$, and $(S_1 \equiv S_2)$ are evaluated using the classical truth tables for these connectives.

(2) $\forall x.S$ is evaluated to **T** if S evaluates to **T** for every assignment of a member of D to x; otherwise it is evaluated to **F**.

(3) $\exists x.S$ is evaluated to **T** if S evaluates to **T** for at least one assignment of a member of D to x; otherwise it is evaluated to **F**.

If a statement evaluates to **T** in an interpretation Ψ, we say that Ψ is a *model* of S, or that S has a model Ψ. A statement S is *satisfiable* if and only if it has at least one model (that is, iff there is at least one interpretation Ψ such that S is evaluated to **T** in Ψ). A statement is *unsatisfiable* if it has no models. If a statement S evaluates to **T** in all interpretations, it is called *valid* and we write $\vdash S$. Note that if S is unsatisfiable, then $\models \sim S$. Examples of valid statements are:

$$\vdash \forall x.\ x = x$$
$$\vdash F(0) \supset \exists x.\ F(x)$$
$$\vdash (\forall x.F(x)) \supset F(0)$$

6.2.3 Proofs

A statement in the propositional logic (no variables and quantifiers) having n predicate symbols has 2^n interpretations, so it is possible (but sometimes impractical) to verify the validity of a propositional statement under all possible interpretations. However, in PC there are an infinite number of interpretations. Thus, exhaustive evaluation is not possible. We thus require the notion of proof.

A *formal system* has the following components:

(1)   Sentences, the things that can be expressed.

(2)   Axioms. These are a subset of the sentences which are postulated to be theorems.

(3)   Rules of inference. These are rules for deducing new theorems from given ones.

A *formal proof* is a sequence $S_1, S_2, ..., S_n$ of sentences such that each S_i is an axiom, or follows by a rule of inference from some subset of $S_1, ..., S_{i-1}$. The *theorems* of the formal system are those sentences which are members of proofs. The last sentence in a proof is called the theorem proved by the proof. The notation $\vdash S$ means that S is a theorem.

Collections of axioms and rules of inference for PC can be found in, for example, Manna [45]. In general, the purpose of the axioms and rules of inference is to ensure that a statement is provable (a theorem) if and only if it is valid (true in all models), that is, $\vdash S$ iff $\vDash S$. In the next section we shall show how rules of inference may be used to perform *computation*. The two rules we use are $\forall$-elimination (specialization) and the substitution of equal expressions:

(1)   if $\vdash \forall x.S$, then infer $\vdash S$, in which occurrences of x have been replaced by some expression e, where free variables in e are considered unique. The last proviso is given so that from formula $\forall x.\exists y.\ x > y$, and expression y, we cannot infer $\vdash \exists y.\ y > y$.

(2)   if $\vdash t_1 = t_2$, then infer $\vdash t[t_1] = t[t_2]$, where $t[t_i]$ means that t is a term containing t_i.

We shall not dwell here on the many different kinds of inference rules used in, for example, natural deduction systems. In later sections we shall see that one rule, the resolution rule, will suffice for our purposes.

6.3 FUNCTIONAL AND RELATIONAL FORMS, AND PROOFS

The interpreter of a logic programming language is a *theorem prover* which controls the order in which inference rules are used. There are many possible ways one might "execute" sets of statements via inference. We shall show two approaches here: an equational style related to functional programming, and a clausal form of the style generally employed in logic programming.

Consider the language with the constants nil and the integers, and with function symbols cons of arity 2, and append of arity 2. Suppose we have a theory with the following axioms:

A1. $\vdash \forall y.$ append(nil,y) = y

A2. $\vdash \forall a.\forall x.\forall y.$ append(cons(a,x),y) = cons(a,append(x,y))

If we want to compute append(cons(1,cons(2,nil)),cons(3,nil)), we can proceed to cons(1,cons(2,cons(3,nil))) by a judiciously chosen sequence of inferences as follows:

1. By A2 and $\forall$-elimination,

$\vdash$ append(cons(1,cons(2,nil)),cons(3,nil)) = cons(1,append(cons(2,nil),cons(3,nil)))

2. By A2 and $\forall$-elimination,

$\vdash$ append(cons(2,nil),cons(3,nil)) = cons(2,append(nil,cons(3,nil)))

3. By 1, 2, and the '=' rule,

$\vdash$ append(cons(1,cons(2,nil)),cons(3,nil)) = cons(1,cons(2,append(nil,cons(3,nil))))

4. By A1 and $\forall$-elimination,

$\vdash$ append(nil,cons(3,nil)) = cons(3,y)

5. By 3, 4, and the '='-rule,

$\vdash$ append(cons(1,cons(2,nil)),cons(3,nil)) = cons(1,cons(2,cons(3,nil)))

Thus, sequences of inferences constitute a kind of computation. To illustrate another style closer to that used in logic programming, we enrich the language with a *predicate* symbol Appended of arity 3 satisfying:

A3. $\vdash \forall y.$ Appended(nil,y,y)

A4. $\vdash \forall w.\forall x.\forall y.\forall z.$ Appended(x,y,z) $\supset$ Appended(cons(w,x),y,cons(w,z))

Intuitively, Appended(x,y,z) means that the result of appending y to x is z. In this formulation we can represent the problem of appending x and y as the problem of finding a z such that $\vdash$ Appended(x,y,z). For example, to append cons(1,cons(2,nil)) to cons(3,nil) we proceed as follows:

1.   Answer is z_1 where $\vdash$ Appended(cons(1,cons(2,nil)),cons(3,nil),z_1)

2.   By A4, answer is z_1, where z_1 = cons(1,z_2) and
     $\vdash$ Appended(cons(2,nil),cons(3,nil),z_2)

3.   By A4, answer is cons(1,z_2), where z_2 = cons(2,z_3) and
     $\vdash$ Appended(nil,cons(3,nil),z_3)

4.   By A3, answer is cons(1,cons(2,z_3)), where z_3 = cons(3,nil).

Thus, the answer is cons(1,cons(2,cons(3,nil))).

Although the style of logic programming illustrated by A3 and A4 may seem cumbersome compared with the functional style of A1 and A2, it does have the advantage that arguments and results are treated symmetrically. For example, in the equation append(x,y) = z, it is implicit that z is the result of appending x to y. In the statement Appended(x,y,z), the variable z is not treated specially. Thus, we can use A3 and A4 to solve problems such as:

> Given x and z, find y such that Appended(x,y,z).
> Given z, find x and y (i.e. partitions of z) such that Appended(x,y,z).

Thus, the *same* logic program can be executed in different ways to solve different problems. Doing this is not as straightforward in the functional style of A1 and A2.

In performing the above proofs, or computations, the correct rule of inference was judiciously chosen every time, to give a short and efficient computation. This came about because my colleague who performed the computation knew the answer in advance, and was able to 'guide' the computation toward the answer with a minimum of intermediate steps. Until researchers better understand the nature of theorem proving, purely mechanical methods cannot be expected to possess such oracular prowess, so special techniques must be used when performing such computations.

Most logic programming interpreters are *refutation systems*, which reason by a method the early philosophers called *reductio ad absurdum*. That is, the negation of the result to be proved is used to derive a contradiction. Working from the negated goal, the theorem prover applies rules of inference to derive successive goals. If a contradiction is eventually derived, then the original goal is a logical consequence of the program.

From a theorem proving point of view, the only interest is to demonstrate logical consequence. However, from a programming point of view, we are more interested in values that are bound to variables. Thus, when we give a goal S to a theorem prover, we are asking it to find values of the variables such that S, with these values substituted, holds. Thus, when performing a refutation proof, if a contradiction is derived, then not only have we found the contradiction to the negated goal, but we have also found a set of values that gives a counterexample, which is an instance that satisfies the original goal. This kind of proof is called a *constructive* proof.

The Resolution Rule is a rule of inference which is especially suitable for conducting formal proofs by machine. Before we discuss the resolution method, we should introduce *unification,* which is the pattern-matching mechanism by which variables are bound to values during the course of a resolution proof.

6.4 SUBSTITUTION AND UNIFICATION

Variables in a logic program are instantiated by a special process of substitution called *unification*. A *substitution* is a finite set of the form $\{t_1/v_1,...,t_n/v_n\}$, where each v_i is a variable, each t_i is a term, and the variables are distinct. Each element t_i/v_i is called a *binding* for v_i. We read this as "t_i is substituted for u_i". If ψ is a substitution and L is a literal, then $L\psi$ is the term obtained from L by simultaneously replacing each occurrence of the v_i in L by t_i. $L\psi$ is called an *instance* of L. For example, if L is the literal P(x,f(y),a) and ψ the substitution $\{f(z)/x, z/y\}$, then $L\psi$ would be the statement P(f(z),f(z),a). Note that in this case, $L\{f(z)/x, z/y\}$ means the same thing as $L\psi$. We shall use these notations interchangeably in the Unification Algorithm below.

As we shall see below, it is sometimes necessary to *combine* substitutions. Given a literal L and substitutions ψ and ξ, we need a combination operation, denoted $\bigcirc$, such that $L(\psi\bigcirc\xi)$ has the same effect as $(L\psi)\xi$. The reason we need this is to combine substitutions as they are generated, so we can delay the application of the composite substitution to L. The set union operation, $\cup$, might be used as a combiner, but is incorrect when different substitutions want to bind different terms to the same variable. The following combination method is explained fully in [13].

To combine substitutions ψ and ξ,

(1) Replace each pair t/X in ψ by $t\psi/X$ to form Ψ.

(2) Delete from ξ each pair u/Y, such that u/Y $\in$ Ψ, to form Ξ.

(3)   The combined substitution is now $\Psi \cup \Xi$.

We say that a substitution ψ *unifies* a set $\{L_1,...,L_n\}$ if $L_1\psi = ... = L_n\psi$. We call the statement L_i the *unification* of $\{L_1,...,L_n\}$ by ψ. Robinson [2] showed that for any unifiable set there is a *most general unifier*, which is unique to within a permutation of variables, and from which any other unifier can be obtained by a further substitution. For example, the set $\{P(x,f(y),b), P(x,f(b),b)\}$ has a unifier $\{a/x, b/y\}$, but the most general unifier is $\{b/y\}$.

There are a number of algorithms for unifying a set of literals and for reporting failure if the set cannot be unified. Such algorithms are found in theorem proving programs, Prolog systems, and many artificial intelligence programs. Refer to, for example [2, 46, 47, 48, 49, 13].

We now give an algorithm for unification. This algorithm contains the *occur check*, in which the algorithm reports failure if a circular (infinite) term is constructed. Because the occur check is expensive, most implementations of Prolog ignore it. The unification algorithm given below takes as its input two terms and a 'partial' substitution which is used to gather substitutions as they are discovered. The output is the set of combined substitutions giving the most general unifier. The algorithm works by searching T_1 and T_2 as expression trees, simultaneously, by depth-first search. If two corresponding nodes in T_1 and T_2 are found to be different, we call such a pair a *disagreement pair*. The nodes in a disagreement pair are actually the roots of subtrees of T_1 and T_2.

To unify terms T_1 and T_2 given ψ:

(1)   If T_1 and T_2 are identical, then succeed and output ψ.

(2)   Otherwise, search the expression trees of T_1 and T_2, looking for the first disagreement pair. Let $<t_1,t_2>$ be the first disagreement pair.

(3)   If t_1 is a variable and t_1 does not occur in t_2, then recursively unify the terms $T_1\{t_2/t_1\}$ and $T_2\{t_2/t_1\}$ given $\psi \bigcirc \{t_2/t_1\}$.

(4)   If t_2 is a variable and t_2 does not occur in t_1, then recursively unify the terms $T_1\{t_1/t_2\}$ and $T_2\{t_1/t_2\}$ given $\psi \bigcirc \{t_1/t_2\}$.

(5)   Else fail.

The unification algorithm above unifies two terms, and this is all that is required for a Prolog implementation. However, full unification as defined for the resolution method requires the simultaneous unification of a set of terms. The above algorithm can be extended to unify a set of expressions:

- T_1 and T_2 must be replaced by a set of expressions, Σ.

- As substitutions are applied to this set, it will be reduced in size. If it ever becomes a singleton (containing only one element), the algorithm terminates with success.

- The disagreement pair must be replaced with a disagreement set Δ, of corresponding subexpressions from each member of Σ.

Thus, to full-unify Σ given ψ:

(1)   If Σ is a singleton, then succeed and output ψ.

(2)   Otherwise, let Δ be the first disagreement set of Σ.

(3) If Δ contains a variable v and a term t, and v does not occur in t, then recursively full-unify $\Sigma\{t/v\}$ given $\psi \bigcirc \{t/v\}$.

(4) Else fail.

When unification is used in resolution proofs, the unification algorithm used must satisfy two properties:

- Unification must succeed in unifying Σ precisely when there is a substitution ψ such that $\Sigma\psi$ is a singleton.

- Unification must return the most general unifier, ψ, of Σ. That is, there must be no substitution ξ such that $\Sigma\xi$ is a singleton and that Σ is an instance of $\Sigma\xi$, unless $\Sigma\xi$ is also an instance of $\Sigma\psi$.

The proof that full-unify has both these properties appears in [47].

6.5 CLAUSES AND RESOLUTION

A *clause* is a disjunction of literals. A *ground* clause is one which contains no variables. The *resolution rule* [2] is a rule of inference that can be applied to clauses. When it is applicable, the resolution rule is applied to two *parent* clauses to produce a derived clause called the *resolvent*. The resolvent is computed by forming the disjunction of the two clauses and then eliminating any complementary pairs. Complementary pairs, which are clauses of the form $\sim P \vee P$, are in fact tautologies and may be deleted from any formula without any effect. Thus, from the ground clauses

$$P \vee \sim Q \vee R$$

and

$$\sim P \vee Q \vee S$$

we obtain the disjunction

$$P \vee \sim Q \vee R \vee \sim P \vee Q \vee S$$

from which, when eliminating complementary pairs, the resolvent

$$R \vee S$$

is obtained.

In order to apply resolution to clauses containing variables, we must be able to find a substitution that can be applied to the parent clauses so that complementary literals are produced. In this case, we simply check to see if the two parent clauses have a most general unifier. So, for clauses

$$P(x) \vee \sim Q(x)$$

and

$$Q(a)$$

we obtain

$$(P(x) \vee \sim Q(x) \vee Q(a))\{a/x\}$$

which simplifies to $P(a)$.

Given a predicate calculus statement S, it is possible to convert it to a conjunction of clauses by applying a sequence of transformation rules. Given S, we construct a sequence of formulas $S_1,...S_n$ such that $S = S_1$, each S_i is satisfiable if and only if S_{i+1} is satisfiable, and S_n is a conjunction of clauses. We shall summarize one algorithm for converting S to clause form. More information can be found in, for example [49, 45, 14].

(1) Eliminate equivalence symbols by substituting $(X_1 \supset X_2) \wedge (X_2 \supset X_1)$ for $X_1 \equiv X_2$. Eliminate implication symbols by substituting $\sim X_1 \vee X_2$ for $X_1 \supset X_2$.

(2) Reduce the scope of negations so that each negation symbol applies to at most one atom. Make use of DeMorgan's laws and other equivalences pertaining to negated quantifiers.

(3) Remove existential quantifiers by introducing new constant symbols called *Skolem functions* (named after Thoralf Skolem [50] who first isolated their properties).

(4) Move universal quantifiers to the outside of the formula.

(5) Distribute '$\wedge$' over '$\vee$' to put the formula in conjunctive normal form.

(6) Convert the conjunction to set form, where each argument of the conjunction is a member of some set C. Each member of set C will be either a literal or a disjunction of literals, and thus is a clause.

Let us consider the following example of conversion from a PC formula into clause form. We shall convert three axioms and a goal into clause form, and perform a resolution proof. Consider the statement, "for all x and y, if x is the father of y, and y is the father of z, then x is the grandfather of z." In PC, this is:

$$\forall x. \forall y. \ F(x,y) \wedge F(y,z) \supset G(x,z).$$

Set C contains one clause, namely our first axiom:

A1. $\sim F(x,y) \vee \sim F(y,z) \vee G(x,z).$

Now let us add the PC formulae F(Charles,William) and F(Philip,Charles), which convert into the next two clauses:

A2. F(Charles,William)
A3. F(Philip,Charles)

Now if we wish to pose the query, "Do there exist individuals x and y such that x is the grandfather of y?", we use the PC formula

$$\exists x. \exists y. \ G(x,y)$$

which, when negated (because we shall perform a refutation proof), and converted to a clause, becomes:

$$\sim G(x,y).$$

After renaming the variables of the goal clause (from x and y to u and v) to prevent clashes, the resolution proof proceeds as follows, where we produce one new theorem at each step:

T1. Resolving A1 and the goal clause, ⊢ ~F(u,y) ∨ ~F(y,v).
(with substitutions {u/x, v/z})

T2. Resolving A2 with the right-hand literal of T1, ⊢ ~F(u,Charles).
(the substitutions are {Charles/y, William/v})

T3. Resolving A3 with T2, we derive the empty clause and halt.
(the substitutions are {Philip/u}).

The substitutions relevant to our goal are {Philip/u, William/v}, so we see that
G(Philip,William) is a theorem. Thus, our above "computation" has found a
grandfather-grandson pair.

Again, the sequence of deductions was judiciously chosen. Suppose in T2 we had
decided to resolve A2 with the *left*-hand literal of T1. We would have obtained
~F(William,v), which cannot be resolved with any of our axioms or theorems, so is a
"dead-end" of the proof -- it cannot be shown that William is the father of anyone.
Similarly, resolving A3 with the right-hand literal of T1 would have given a dead-end.
The fact that just one refutation exists is sufficient to prove the goal, however.

There is considerable scope for parallelism in this example. A refutation was obtained
when A1 was reduced to the empty clause: this reduction of A1 can be achieved in one
step by simultaneously resolving A3 with the leftmost literal of A1, A2 with the centre
literal of A1, and the goal clause with the leftmost literal of A1.

The resolution algorithm for a conventional sequential computer can be written as follows. We begin with a base set of clauses (our "logic program") C:

> Until the empty clause is a member of C, repeat:
> 1.   select two distinct resolvable clauses i and j from C
> 2.   compute a resolvent r of clauses i and j
> 3.   add r to set C

What we have not mentioned is how to decide *which* two clauses to select (Step 1), and
which resolution of literals to perform (Step 2). Many strategies have been developed,
and much of the history of mechanical theorem-proving has been devoted to developing
control strategies and refinements to the resolution method. Names of typical strategies
are: breadth-first, set-of-support, unit-preference, linear-input, ancestry-filtered. Many of
these are surveyed in [47, 51, 49, 13].

Linear-input resolution is a suitable strategy for use as a logic program interpreter. In
this method we always use the previous resolvent as one of the parents of the next resolution step. The other parent must be one of the axioms, and not a derived theorem.
Thus, we can represent the refutation as a linear path; our above proof was a linear-
input resolution. In clauses which have one positive literal, linear-input resolution is
complete -- it will find a refutation if there is one. SL-resolution [52] tells us to use
linear resolution (that decides one parent), and to select one of the most recently used
literals from that parent to determine what the other parent should be (if there is one).
This narrows down the search even more. The search technique used in most Prolog
implementations is a variant called LUSH resolution, which operates over clauses that
have at most one positive literal. This is discussed in the next section.

6.6 LOGIC PROGRAMMING TERMINOLOGY

In this section we will give the terminology generally used in logic programming. In particular, the Horn clause [53] is normally used in logic programs. The predicate Appended previously defined was expressed using two Horn clauses. We begin with the syntax of logic programs.

- A *term* is as previously defined.

- An *atom* is an atomic formula as previously defined. A *literal* (positive literal, negative literal) is as previously defined.

- A *Kowalski clause* is a formula of the form $A_1,...,A_k \leftarrow B_1,...,B_n$, where each A_i ($i=1,...,k$) and each B_i ($i=1,...,n$) are atoms. The B_i are called the *antecedent,* and the A_i are called the *consequent.* The *empty clause*, denoted $\leftarrow$, is the Kowalski clause with empty consequent and empty antecedent. Such a clause is understood as a contradiction.

- A *definite clause* is a formula of the form $A \leftarrow B_1,...,B_n$, where A and each B_i ($i=1,...,n$) is an atom. A definite clause of the form $A \leftarrow$ is called a *unit clause*.

- A *goal clause* is a formula of the form $\leftarrow B_1,...,B_n$, where each B_i ($i=1,...,n$) is an atom.

- A *Horn clause* is a clause which is either a definite clause or a goal clause.

- If $A \leftarrow B_1,...,B_n$ is a definite clause, then A is called the *head* and $B_1,...,B_n$ is called the *body* of the clause. A *logic program* is a finite set of definite clauses. The collection of all definite clauses having the same predicate in the head is called a *procedure.*

It is conventional to assume that variables in clauses are universally quantified. Commas separating atoms in the antecedent denote conjunction, and commas separating atoms in the consequent denote disjunction.

Disjunctions of literals can be converted into Kowalski clauses simply by writing negative literals as positive literals in the antecedent, and writing positive literals as positive literals in the consequent. Thus,

$$\sim B_1 \vee ... \vee \sim B_n \vee A_1 \vee ... \vee A_k$$

where all the B_i are negative literals, may be written in Kowalski form as

$$A_1,...,A_k \leftarrow B_1,...,B_n.$$

A clause containing only one positive literal will contain only one literal in the Kowalski-form consequent, and this is defined above as a definite clause. To simplify matters, we shall henceforth use only Horn clauses, which contain zero or one positive literals, and thus are either definite clauses or goal clauses.

Considering our grandfather relation from the previous section, conversion of the axioms into Horn clauses yields:

H1. $G(x,z) \leftarrow F(x,y), F(y,z).$
H2. F(Charles,William) $\leftarrow$
H3. F(Philip,Charles) $\leftarrow$

Our query to "compute" a grandfather-grandson pair converts to the following goal clause:

$\leftarrow$ G(x,y).

The LUSH proof procedure was designed to conduct constructive proofs over sets of Horn clauses. The LUSH system is due to Kowalski [7], but the name LUSH was contrived by Hill [54] as the rather unlikely acronym for *L*inear resolution with *U*nrestricted *S*election for *H*orn clauses. LUSH works as follows. Given a goal clause

$$\leftarrow A_1,...,A_{i-1},A_i,A_{i+1},...,A_n$$

and some definite clause

$$C \leftarrow B_1,...,B_m$$

The LUSH method selects some literal A_i such that C and A_i have a most general unifier ψ, and infers a new goal clause

$$\leftarrow (A_1,...,A_{i-1},B_1,...,B_m,A_{i+1},...,A_n)\psi$$

Thus, the body of the definite clause is substituted for the selected literal A_i. The unifier ψ represents the variable bindings now in effect as a result of this deduction step.

It now remains to decide on a rule to select the literal A_i. The selection rule assumed by the *Prolog* language is the one that always selects the leftmost literal. The search strategy determined by this selection rule is depth-first leftmost-descendant-first. Finally we must decide the order in which definite clauses are chosen. In Prolog, the order is determined by the textual order of clauses in a program: if clauses C_1 and C_2 occur in that order and *both* match the selected literal in a goal statement, then the inferred goal clause will be obtained by matching with C_1 first.

Using our Horn clauses H1-H3 above, let us conduct a LUSH computation to answer the goal clause $\leftarrow$ G(u,v).

(1) Starting with the leftmost goal (there is only one), the only choice we can make is H1, giving the new goal clause $\leftarrow$ F(u,y), F(y,v) with variables matched as shown.

(2) Starting with the leftmost goal, we must match it with H2 (the textually earlier one). Replacing the leftmost goal by the null body and instantiating the variables, we obtain the goal clause $\leftarrow$ F(Charles,v).

(3) Matching the leftmost goal (the only one), the only choice we can make is H3, which gives $\leftarrow$, the empty goal. The substitutions {Philip/u, William/v} are now available, which satisfies the goal G(Philip,William).

Prolog's selection rule enforces a strict depth-first left-to-right search of the proof tree. More general variations of Prolog use whatever selection rule they see fit. This is exploited in (to name a few) IC-Prolog [55], PARLOG [21], LOGLISP [56], Concurrent Prolog [22], and MU-Prolog [57]. These systems are steps closer to the ideal of programming in logic. Further development will be necessary before such languages can approach the *efficiency* with which strict Prolog-style computation can be performed on conventional computers. However, *effectiveness* may be more telling: Naish [58] gives a convincing demonstration of the ability of MU-Prolog to perform a well-directed computation on problems that confound ordinary Prolog's inflexible search strategy.

6.7 DATABASES AND NEGATION

The connection between logic and databases is appealing and useful, and this is an area of active interest (see, for example [18, 59],) in the logic programming community.

Consider the relationship between a Horn clause program and a relational database. In a relational database [60] relations are regarded as tables, in which each element of an n-ary relation is stored as a row of the table having n columns. Using Horn clauses, a table can be represented by a set of unit clauses; an n-ary relation is named by an n-ary predicate symbol. Other representations, such as 2-tuples as suggested by semantic nets [61] have been considered.

According to Dahl [62] the use of Horn clause logic has a number of advantages over conventional treatments of databases:

- Rules as well as facts can coexist in the description of a relation.

- Recursive definitions are allowed.

- Multiple answers to the same query are allowed.

- There is no role distinction between input and output.

- Inference takes place automatically.

Other advantages of using logic for databases are described by Kowalski [63, 19] and Lloyd [20].

Two issues in particular arise when considering logic and databases: *monotonicity* and *negation*. The issue of monotonicity arises when considering the use of logic for the representation of knowledge [64, 65]. Most logics we consider are monotonic: if sentence S follows from a set of sentences Σ, then S follows from any set of sentences that includes Σ. Using the previous terminology, if $\Sigma \vdash S$, then $T \vdash S$, where $\Sigma \subset T$. So, the addition of "new" statements cannot lead to the repudiation of "old" consequences; once you deduce something, you can't get rid of it. This property has led some researchers to criticize logic as a means of representing knowledge. For example, consider representing the belief that "all birds can fly": if x is a Bird, then x Can Fly. If there are exceptions (such as penguins), how do we axiomize this conveniently? When new information comes to light concerning flightless birds, how do we reconcile this with previous axioms? Studying how to address these issues formally is the problem confronted by non-monotonic logic [66]. It is incorrect to criticize standard logic for its inadequate handling of non-monotonic problems, because it was never designed to deal with such problems. The issues of using logic for knowledge representation should instead focus on:

- having a better idea of what we want to represent;

- recognizing that knowledge acquisition involves more than simply adding new clauses to a database.

The next issue is negation. A Horn clause program, like a database, is incapable of representing negations of relations -- the database contains only information about *true* instances of a relation. However, processing even simple queries may reveal the need to show that certain instances of a relation are false. For example, suppose we have the following database:

The battle of Waterloo occurred in 1815.

How can we show that the battle of Waterloo did *not* happen in 1923? The above (admittedly small) database cannot tell me when the battle *didn't* happen, unless we are prepared to do one of two things:

- We can *complete* the database by adding a sentence meaning that the battle of Waterloo did not happen in any year other than 1815: we could say that the battle happened *only* in 1815.

- We can use a general rule of inference, called *negation by failure:* if what we are looking for is *not* in the database, then we conclude that it is false.

A crucial assumption is that all the information contained in the database is sufficient as a model. This is known as the Closed World Assumption (CWA) [67]. Using this assumption, if we wish to show that $\sim$P, we attempt to prove P. If every possible proof fails, then we "deduce" $\sim$P. Both PLANNER [68] and Prolog handle negation this way. This can be considered as a "negation by failure" deduction rule of the form

$$\text{from not} \vdash P \text{ infer } \vdash \sim P$$

as introduced by Clark [55]. Clark showed that the negation by failure rule was sound provided that P is ground, and that the required deductions are made from a "completed" database (CDB) obtained by replacing the "if" clauses of the database by "only if" clauses. Recent work, comparing Clark's CDB with Reiter's CWA, has been carried out by Shepherdson [69]. In particular, he has shown that there are logic databases for which the CWA and CDB may be separately consistent, but may be incompatible. However, if the database consists only of definite Horn clauses, then the CWA and CDB are mutually consistent.

6.8 PROLOG AS A PROGRAMMING LANGUAGE

Prolog is the most widely used programming language to have been inspired by logic programming research. The popularity of Prolog as a programming language stems from a number of properties:

- Powerful symbol manipulation facilities, including unification with logical variables. Programmers can consider logical variables as named 'holes' in data structures. Unification also serves as the parameter passing mechanism, and provides a selector and constructor of data objects. When combined with recursive procedures and a surface syntax for data structures, the symbol manipulation possibilities of Prolog can be compared with -- and can be considered to exceed [70] -- those of LISP.

- Automatic backtracking provides generate-and-test as a basic control flow model. This is more general than the strict unidirectional sequential flow of control in conventional languages such as LISP. Although generate-and-test is not appropriate for some applications, other control flow models can be programmed to correspond to the demands of a particular application.

- Program clauses and data structures have the same form. This is a property that Prolog shares with LISP.

- The procedural interpretation of clauses, together with a backtracking control structure, provides a convenient way to express and to use nondeterministic procedures. However, the price to pay is the occasional necessity to employ extralogical control features such as *fail* and *cut*.

- The relational form of procedures lends the possibility to define 'reversible' procedures that can be used for more than one purpose. It is the responsibility of the programmer to ensure whether or not a particular procedure is meant to completely implement a given relation.

- A Prolog program can be regarded as a relational database that contains rules as well as facts. It is easy to add and remove information from the database, and to pose sophisticated queries.

It is not the purpose of this chapter to give a tutorial on programming in Prolog in particular. For this refer to the article by Sammut and Sammut [71] and the textbooks by Clocksin and Mellish [14] and Clark and McCabe [72]. In this section we hope to convey what it is like to program in Prolog.

A Prolog *program* is a set of *procedures*. Each *procedure* defines a particular logical relationship, or *predicate*. A procedure consists of one or more assertions, or *clauses*. A clause can be either a *fact* or a *rule,* and is represented by a *term.*

A term is either a *constant,* a *variable,* or a *structure.* Constants are either *atoms* or *integers,* although some Prologs make available signed floating-point numbers and negative integers. Structures are sometimes called *"complex terms"* or *"compound terms",* and are essentially the same as atomic formulae as previously defined. Note the different use here of the word *atom,* which is used in Prolog to mean a non-numeric constant, and has nothing to do with atomic formulae as previously defined.

The exact syntax of terms varies from one variant of Prolog to another, but we will describe the so-called Edinburgh syntax, which is accepted by the most widespread of Prolog implementations. *Atoms* consist of alphanumeric atoms or sign atoms. Alphanumeric atoms are denoted as strings that begin with a lowercase character, and can include digits and the underscore character. Sign atoms are strings that consist of characters known as sign characters ($+$, $>$, ?, \$, *etc*). Integers are, as expected, strings of digits. In case it is desired to denote an atom other than the above, any string enclosed in single quotes will be treated as an atom. *Variables* are denoted as strings beginning with an upper-case character or with an underscore character. *Structures* consist of a *functor* (which is an atom) and one or more *components* (which are terms). A functor of arity N has N components. Structures are denoted by denoting the functor, followed by an opening round bracket, followed by the N components separated by commas, followed by a closing round bracket. List structures are composed from the functor '.' of arity 2, but a more convenient syntax for lists is accepted. The elements of a list may be enclosed in square brackets and separated by commas. Atoms may be nominated as *operators,* and may be assigned a priority, an associativity (right or left), and a position (prefix, infix, postfix). When used to denote functors of structures, the nominated atom may be used in the nominated operator syntax. For example, if the atom '$+$' is nominated as an infix right-associative operator, then it can be used to denote terms such as $X + 12$, which is the same as $+(X,12)$.

Note that the syntax for Prolog terms is 'upside down' from that used in logic programming -- constants are lower-case instead of upper-case, and variables are upper-case instead of lower-case. One can contrive many reasons for why this should be; perhaps the best is so that Prolog programs can never be confused with logic programs.

As stated above, clauses are either facts or rules, and are denoted by terms. Clauses can be given a *declarative* interpretation or a *procedural* interpretation. Suppose A and $B_1,...,B_n$ are terms. The rule clause

$$A :\text{-} B_1, B_2, ..., B_n$$

(in which the B_i are called *goals*) can be read in two ways:

- As a declarative statement: That A is provable follows from B_i (for all i, $1 \leqslant i \leqslant n$) being provable.

- Or procedurally, where in order to execute procedure A, then all procedures called by $B_1,...,B_n$ should be executed. Clauses that have no goals are called facts.

Notice that the above interpretations do not admit the order in which the goals should be considered. Prolog uses the LUSH strategy discussed in the previous section, in which the selection rule selects the leftmost goal for execution. Thus, the conjunction of goals acts as a stack of procedures awaiting execution -- the leftmost goal acts as the top of the stack. The order in which clauses are examined is determined by the textual order in the program.

For an example, the append relation is often used for concatenating two lists together to form a third. We define the predicate *append(X,Y,Z)* such that the list X concatenated with the list Y forms the list Z. The procedure can be defined using two clauses. The first clause represents the fact that the empty list concatenated with some list L is the same as L. The second clause represents the fact that a list with head H and tail T, when concatenated with some list L, produces a list with head H and some tail Z, provided that T is concatenated with L to produce Z. The procedure is as follows:

```
append([ ],L,L).
append([H|T],L,[H|Z]) :- append(T,L,Z).
```

Note the similarity with the relational form of the predicate Appended as defined in an earlier section of these notes. The reversible behaviour of append can be seen from a few examples. In each case, the Prolog user is posing a goal clause (prefixed by '?-') to the Prolog system, which then responds by printing the terms unified with variables in the goal clause:

```
?- append([a,b,c],[1,2,3],X).
```

X = [a,b,c,1,2,3]

```
?- append(X,[beta],[alpha,17,beta]).
```

X = [alpha,17]

```
?- append(X,Y,[a,b,c]).
```

X = [], Y = [a,b,c]
X = [a], Y = [b,c]
X = [a,b], Y = [c]
X = [a,b,c], Y = []

For the last goal, the system has computed all of the partitions of the list [a,b,c].

For another example, consider searching a graph. Given the definition of a relation arc(X,Y), meaning there is an arc from node X to node Y in the graph, let us define a relation path(X,Y), meaning there is a path of arcs from node X to node Y. The following facts will represent a graph having five nodes and five arcs:

```
arc(a,b).
arc(b,c).
arc(a,d).
arc(d,e).
arc(b,e).
```

The path predicate consists of two clauses. The fact states that any node is a path to itself. The rule states that a path from X to Y consists of an arc from X to some Z, together with a path from Z to Y:

path(X,X).
path(X,Y) :- arc(X,Z), path(Z,Y).

Such a program will work on an acyclic graph, but may not necessarily terminate if the graph has a cycle. Suppose we had added the fact arc(c,a) to the above database, and queried path(a,d). Despite the fact that arc(a,d) is part of the definition of the graph, using the built-in search strategy of Prolog would result in an endless loop searching the nodes a,b,c,a,b,c,...! This is easily mended: we simply ensure that we do not search nodes that have been visited. We redefine path to include another component: a list of the forbidden nodes. When finding an arc along which to travel, ensure that it is not a forbidden node. If it is not forbidden, then traverse the arc, adding the node to our list using list construction. If backtracking should occur at any point, the list is automatically restored to the appropriate prior value. The additional predicate legal(X,Y) succeeds if node X is not on the forbidden list Y:

path(X,X,F).
path(X,Y,F) :- arc(X,Z), legal(Z,F), path(Z,Y,[Z|F]).

legal(X,[ ]).
legal(X,[H|T]) :- X $\neq$ H, legal(X,T).

Notice the second clause of the *path* predicate. In strict Prolog we are compelled to write the *legal* goal to the left of the *path* goal. Because of the left-to-right execution strategy, we must ensure that the node is checked for legality before we find a path from it. This is an example of the way that Prolog diverges from the ideal of programming in logic. Presumably in logic programming, one would be able to write the goals in any order.

Because the basic computational mechanism of Prolog is top-down search through a tree of goals, representing parsing problems is especially suited to the Prolog approach. A grammar rule notation can be used to express the grammar of a Prolog, and the Prolog system will translate a grammar rule clause into a normal Prolog clause automatically.

The following example shows a Prolog program that can parse and generate sentences in a language, constructing a parse tree tagged with the appropriate linguistic constituents. The problem from pages 31-32 of Nilsson [49] translates into Prolog grammar rules in the following way. Let the grammar contain the following terminal symbols,

of approves new company sale director the

and the following non-terminal symbols,

s np vp pp p v dnp det a n

which will be used to labels nodes of the parse tree that correspond to linguistic constituents sentence, noun phrase, verb phrase, prepositional phrase, preposition, verb, determined noun phrase, adjective, and noun. The grammar is defined by the following Prolog program, which bears a resemblance to grammars as written in linguistics texts. Each rule expresses the decomposition of a linguistic constituent into simpler constituents. Terminal symbols (words in the sentence) are shown enclosed in square brackets. Elements of the parse tree are built up as the arguments of goals become instantiated.

sentence(s(X,Y)) --> det_noun_phrase(X), verb_phrase(Y).

verb_phrase(vp(X,Y)) --> verb(X), det_noun_phrase(Y).

prep_phrase(pp(X,Y)) --> prep(X), det_noun_phrase(Y).

prep(p(of)) --> [of].

verb(v(approves)) --> [approves].

det_noun_phrase(dnp(X,Y)) --> determiner(X), noun_phrase(Y).
det_noun_phrase(dnp(X,Y)) --> det_noun_phrase(X), prep_phrase(Y).

noun_phrase(np(X,Y)) --> adjective(X), noun_phrase(Y).
noun_phrase(np(X)) --> noun(X).

adjective(a(new)) --> [new].
adjective(a(company)) --> [company].

noun(n(director)) --> [director].
noun(n(company)) --> [company].
noun(n(sale)) --> [sale].

determiner(d(the)) --> [the].

For example, if the sentence "the company director approves the new sale" is run through the above program, the parse tree shown in **Figure 6-1** is obtained. This structure can be used in subsequent phases of a language understanding program, for example. For a real application, the grammar would require enhancement for richer syntactic and semantic constructs, for detecting number, tense agreement, etc. See [73] for more information.

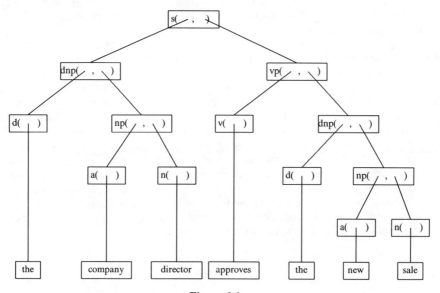

Figure 6-1

6.9 EXTRALOGICAL FEATURES

To use Prolog in "real" applications, it is currently sometimes necessary to use language features that go beyond pure logic. These features are made available as built-in (or evaluable) predicates. Dömölki and Szeredi [74] classify the extralogical language features into five categories: arithmetic, string-handling, input and output, program modification, and control of execution.

Arithmetic and string handling could in principle be represented in pure logic. Arithmetic operations could be represented extensionally as tables, and string handling could be accomplished by list manipulation. However, these operations are implemented using built-in predicates because conventional computer hardware does these operations more efficiently.

Input and output are needed for arbitrary communication with users. Input and output cause side-effects and are thus extralogical. However, some implementations provide a form of "backtrackable" input, meaning that backtracking will undo the given side effect. This is useful for implementing stream-oriented input. In this scheme, alternative versions of a procedure may access the same input stream: elements of the stream are not destructively consumed.

The built-in predicates for program modification are used for adding and removing clauses from the database. This makes possible self-modifying procedures, which can be considered dangerous programming practice. In practice, Prolog programs are factored into procedures and data, although the boundary is not often obvious. O'Keefe [75, 76] argues that much of the normal manipulation of the database is dangerous and ill-considered. In the present situation, where the database facilities had not been "designed into" Prolog, and where the semantics are complicated, O'Keefe is certainly correct. Problems can be alleviated by devising higher-level interfaces to the primitive database operations, for example "set of all solutions" predicates [77] and dependency-oriented database systems [78]. Database manipulations are also necessary for implementing programming environments [79].

The most controversial built-in predicates are for controlling the execution mechanism of Prolog. Two issues on the use of control features should be borne in mind. First, it is valuable to know the extent to which every "real" application can be written in pure logic. As mentioned before, certain advantages are thereby conferred. Second, as we show in a later section, overuse of control features can be indicative of poor programming practice. It is desirable to approach logic on its own terms rather than to write Fortran programs in Prolog. Thus, it is debatable whether control features should be made available in the first place. The *cut* operation, written as an exclamation mark in programs, removes a number of branches in the search tree by prohibiting the remaining alternative choices of the currently executing procedure. This can be used to increase efficiency without changing the meaning of the program. However, the cut is often used to deliberately change the meaning of the program. Often, such changes of meaning are unnecessary. For example, consider three alternative definitions of the *max* predicate, for which max(X,Y,Z) means that Z is the maximum of X and Y.

```
max1(X,Y,X) :- X > Y.
max1(X,Y,Y) :- X ⩽ Y.

max2(X,Y,X) :- X > Y, !.
max2(X,Y,Y) :- X ⩽ Y, !.

max3(X,Y,X) :- X > Y, !.
max3(X,Y,Y).
```

In these examples, max1 and max2 are declaratively correct. Of these two, max2 provides a more efficient program, because the cut removes the information retained for (an ultimately futile) backtracking. Regrettably, max3 is the most common rendering. When the strict Prolog execution model is used, it is procedurally correct, and is probably the most efficient because the ⩽ test is not required on the second clause. However, declaratively speaking, max3 is rubbish, and is not guaranteed to execute correctly on more general logic interpreters.

There are a number of research activities in the area of control primitives for logic programming. In particular, control can be specified by annotating variables with their intended function [55]. Also, control declarations (see [80, 58]) can be used to separate the program from the control specifications. This can be used, for example, to declare that a procedure is determinate. Control issues are most important when devising alternative execution models that exploit parallelism. We have previously mentioned a list of implementations that offer more sophisticated default control schemes.

6.10 IDIOMATIC PROGRAMMING IN PROLOG

As with any programming language, it is possible to design poorly and to program poorly in Prolog. Probably the ability to write "good" Prolog programs is a sign of fluency in the language, and it turns out that well-written programs tend to be free of extralogical features and within the purely functional logic programming methodology. To put it another way, simply because extralogical "features" exist does not mean that the programmer, with careful thought, is compelled to use them. Programmers who think in terms of global variables, iteration, and **if..then..else** tend to rely on the extralogical features. This reliance is ultimately to their cost: the resulting programs are often obscure and inefficient. Of course, it is dangerous to make pronouncements in what is regrettably an emotionally-charged topic such as programming practice. However, the advice that I offer here is not derived from some philosophy of programming, but from experience.

We can illustrate the dramatic contrast between "writing Fortran programs in Prolog" and writing idiomatic programs with the following example. The two programs given below were written independently by two different programmers, who, at the time they wrote their code, were not aware that they might attract public notice. The programs compute solutions to the "Truthteller" puzzle: Find a number, consisting of N digits, in which the first digit is the number of 0's in the number, the second digit the number of 1's in the number, The first solution, perhaps the worst Prolog program I have ever seen, is as follows:

```
init(D) :- ass_xn(D), assert(rest(D)), !.

ass_xn(0) :- !.
ass_xn(D) :- D1 is D-1, asserta(x(D1,_)), asserta(n(D1)), ass_xn(D1).

go(D) :- init(D), guess(D,0).
go(_) :- abolish(x,2), abolish(n,1), abolish(rest,1).

guess(D,D) :- result, !, fail.
guess(D,N) :- x(N,X), var(X), !, n(Y), N = < Y, N*Y = < D, ass(N,Y),
              set(D,N,Y), N1 is N+1, guess(D,N1).
guess(D,N) :- x(N,X), set(D,N,X), N1 is N+1, guess(D,N1).

ass(N,X) :- only(retract(x(N,_))), asserta(x(N,X)), only(update(1)).
ass(N,_) :- retract(x(N,_)), asserta(x(N,_)), update(-1), !, fail.

only(X) :- X, !.

set(D,N,X) :- count(N,Y), rest(Z), !, Y = < X, X = < Y+Z, X1 is X-Y, set1(D,N,X1,0).

set1(_,N,0,_) :- !.
set1(D,N,X,P) :- n(M), P = < M, x(M,Y), var(Y), M*N = < D, ass(M,N),
                 set(D,M,N), X1 is X-1, P1 is M, set1(D,N,X1,P1).

count(N,X) :- bagof(M,M^(x(M,Z),nonvar(Z),Z=N),L), length(L,X).
count(_,0).

update(Z) :- only(retract(rest(X))), Z1 is X-Z, assert(rest(Z1)).
update(Z) :- retract(rest(X)), Z1 is X+Z, assert(rest(Z1)), !, fail.

result :- print(-->), n(N), x(N,M), print(M), fail.
result :- nl.
```

The above program uses nearly every extralogical feature available: use of the database for side-effects, cut, fail, var, and metacalls. By contrast, the following program is much shorter. It is easier to understand, and runs about 100 times faster. Extralogical features are used sparingly (in fact, a simple modification to the program obviates any need for them) for obvious reasons.

```
go(N,L) :- guess(N,N,0,0,[ ],L), print(L), nl, fail.

guess(1,Total,S,SS,L,[T|L]) :- !, T is Total-S, count(0,[T|L],T).
guess(Val,Total,S,SS,L,List) :-
         V1 is Val-1,
         n(A),
         SS2 is V1*A+SS,
         SS2 = < Total,
         S2 is S+A,
         guess(V1,Total,S2,SS2,[A|L],List),
         count(V1,List,A).

count(N,[ ],0).
count(N,[N|A],B) :- !, B > 0, C is B-1, count(N,A,C).
count(N,[A|B],C) :- count(N,B,C).

n(0). n(1). n(2). n(3). n(4). n(5). n(6). n(7). n(8). n(9).
```

For more discussion along these lines, this time using an example from theorem proving, refer to the paper by O'Keefe [75] for an entertaining and informative study of comparative programming in Prolog. Also, other issues in this area are discussed by Bruynooghe [81].

6.11 PRACTICAL APPLICATIONS OF PROLOG

In this section we shall survey a number of applications to which Prolog has been put. We concentrate on four areas -- expert systems, interface to databases, design automation, and scientific tools -- giving two or three examples from each area. For more discussion of the experiences of using Prolog in practice, refer to [74]. A survey of Prolog applications in Hungary appears in [82].

6.11.1 Scientific Tools

The Press system [83] is a Prolog program for deriving the analytic solutions of simultaneous transcendental equations. Press was originally designed as a component of Mecho [84], but increased interest in computer-aided algebra led to the development of Press in its own right. Examples of equations that can be solved in a few second include the following (in each case, solve for x):

$$4^{2x+1} \times 5^{x-2} = 6^{1-x}$$

$$\cos(x) + \cos(3x) + \cos(5x) = 0$$

$$3\tan(3x) - \tan(x) + 2 = 0$$

$$\log_2(x) + 4\log_x(2) = 5$$

$$3\text{sech}^2(x) + 4\tanh(x) + 1 = 0$$

$$\log_e(x+1) + \log_e(x-1) = 3$$

$$e^{3x} - 4e^x + 3e^{-x} = 0$$

$$\cosh(x) - 3\sinh(y) = 0 \ \& \ 2\sinh(x) + 6\cosh(y) = 5$$

For more information about using logic programming and Prolog as tools for the mathematician, refer to [13].

Designing drugs is an expensive business, and it would be helpful to predict the performance of experimental substances before they are synthesised. A group in Budapest [85] has devised a program for automatic derivation of regression models as used in biochemical problems. Their system can predict the activity of unsynthesised drugs on macromolecular receptor sites. A specific example is the calculation of qualitative structure-activity relationships for antifungal nitroalcohols [86] which is important in the development of pesticides. Also see [87] for an application in predicting the interaction of pharmacological compounds.

6.11.2 Expert Systems

An expert system is, like Gaul, thrice divided: it consists of an inference engine, a database of facts and rules, and an interface to the user. An expert system must satisfy these criteria:

(1)   It must be easy to examine, change, and extend the knowledge in the database;

(2)   The system must be able to 'explain' its deductions by responding to "why" questions from the user;

(3)   The system should be able to reason judgmentally, using confidence factors or some other system.

Clark and McCabe [88] sketch some techniques for implementing such portions of expert systems in Prolog.

A group at Lisbon University [89] has developed an expert system for environmental resource evaluation. Called ORBI, the system can answer questions stated in Portugese concerning whether, for example, a particular map reference is suitable for intensive agriculture. ORBI gives an answer in Portugese based on information in the database such as climate, soil characteristics, planning permission, and geological data. The authors of ORBI state that Prolog is "an excellent language for expert system implementation", and gave three reasons:

(1)   The same simple formalism (clauses) can be used uniformly for natural language processing, the knowledge base, the explanation facility, *etc.*

(2)   Prolog offers compactness of expression together with efficient implementation, and this makes it possible to implement ORBI in a minicomputer.

(3)   The dual semantics, declarative and procedural, facilitates system development.

An expert "garden centre assistant" system has been implemented by Walker and Porto [90]. It can answer questions stated in English about a variety of garden pests and pesticides. Typical questions it can answer are as follows:

> What products do you sell?
> What can I use to kill snails?
> Is there anything I can use that will fertilize my lawn?
> What can I use to kill weeds around my fence?
> Do I need a sprayer to use Product A?
> Does Product A kill dandelions in less than 20 days?
> What are the weeds?
> When should I use Product F?
> What precautions should I show when using Product A?
> What is the response time of each product that kills annual weeds?
> What can I use on dandelions that will kill them in less than 2 days?

When the normal facilities of Prolog are not sufficient for an expert system, it is possible to write a layer of software in Prolog to provide the extra facilities needed. Such an expert system "shell" has been developed [91] to provide a system for embedding expert systems. This system provides facilities for forward as well as backward chaining, confidence factors, and various methods for controlling the session.

6.11.3 Design Automation

Forrest and Edwards [92] describe a Prolog program that can translate algorithmic finite-state machines (AFSMs) into programmable logic array (PLA) programs. AFSMs are procedural programs, rather like Algol programs, that specify the desired behaviour of a component -- for example, the toy traffic light controller of Mead and Conway [93]. Translating such programs into PLA programs is one step toward automatic generation of VLSI from behaviourial specifications.

Barrow [94] has developed a Prolog program that can prove the correctness of digital hardware circuits. Circuits are represented hierarchically, with a component name at the top and NMOS FETs at the bottom. One such circuit consists of 23,448 components, of which 14,432 are transistors. Designs consisting of about 18,000 transistors have been verified, but the DEC-10 begins to run out of space at about this point.

A design-for-testability (DFT) system has been developed by Horstmann [95] The purpose of a DFT system is to verify that certain rules in circuit design have been observed. If a violation is detected, the system will change the circuit to preserve the design rules. An advantage of this system is the ease in which it can be interrupted to "explain" how it arrived at a particular violation (or non-violation). According to Horstmann, Prolog is a good language for this application, and other Computer Aided Design problems that can take advantage of logic programming are design verification, design transformation, and certain forms of design analysis that require non-algorithmic solutions.

A group in Edinburgh [78] has devised a system for maintaining consistent architectural databases. This aids the architect in carrying out modifications to an architectural design by automatically checking and enforcing predetermined constraints. Other work on using Prolog for computer-aided architectural design is reported in [96, 97, 98]

6.11.4 Interface to Databases

CHAT-80 [73] is a system that can answer questions about world geography stated in English. The system knows about cities, populations, countries, continents, rivers, and oceans. Examples of questions that can be answered by CHAT include:

> Does Afghanistan border China?
> Which country's capital is Ouagadougou?
> Which is the ocean that borders African countries and that borders Asian countries?
> What is the capital of each country bordering the Baltic?
> What are the latitudes of the countries north of the UK?
> Which country is bordered by two seas?
> How many countries does the Danube flow through?
> From what country does a river flow into the Persian Gulf?
> What is the total area of countries south of the Equator not in Australasia?
> What is the average area of the countries in each continent.
> How many countries are there in each continent?
> Is there some ocean that does not border any country?
> What does border the ocean that does not border any country?
> Which are the continents no country in which contains more than two cities whose
>   population exceeds two million?
> Which country bordering the Mediterranean borders a country that is bordered by
>   a country whose population exceeds the population of India?

All of these questions are answered in a few seconds or less on a DECsystem-10.

If you need to access CODASYL databases using relational queries, then you must translate the queries into a program that will efficiently traverse the CODASYL database. Gray and Moffat [99] describe a Prolog program to do this translation, and interestingly enough, it outperforms the original PASCAL program for this task.

6.12 ACKNOWLEDGEMENTS

I thank Mike Gordon for encouraging and commenting on an earlier draft, and for permitting me to plunder his teaching notes. I am grateful to John Lloyd for permission to adapt material for the first section from [16]. I am also grateful to Alan Bundy for kind permission to adapt material from his discussion of unification which appears in his book *Computer Modelling of Mathematical Reasoning*, Academic Press, 1983, for section 6.4.

6.13 REFERENCES

The following abbreviations are used in this list:

CACM*Communications of the Association for Computing Machinery*

ECAI *1982 European Conference on Artificial Intelligence,* Orsay, France

ESMEA*Expert Systems in the Micro Electronic Age,* ed. D Michie, Edinburgh University Press, 1979

FFG　*From Frege to Gödel* ed. J van Heijenoort, Harvard University Press, 1967

IJCAI *International Joint Conference on Artificial Intelligence*

JACM *Journal of the Association for Computing Machinery*

LPC1 *Proceedings of the First International Logic Programming Conference,* Marseille, France, 1982

LPW　*Proceedings of Logic Programming Workshop '83,* Albufeira, Portugal

1.　J. Herbrand, "Recherches sur la théorie de la démonstration," Thesis at the University of Paris (1930). English translation in FFG pp. 525-581

2.　J. A. Robinson, "A machine-oriented logic based on the resolution principle," *JACM* **12**, pp.23-41 (1965).

3.　J. Siekmann and G. Wrightson, *Automation of Reasoning,* Springer-Verlag (1983).

4.　C. C. Green, "Application of theorem proving to problem solving," *IJCAI* **1**, pp.219-239 (1969).

5.　P. Hayes, "Computation and deduction," *Proceedings 2nd MFCS Symposium,* pp.105-118, Czechoslovakian Academy of Sciences (1973).

6.　R. Kowalski, "Search strategies for theorem proving," pp. 181-201 in *Machine Intelligence,* ed. B. Meltzer and D. Michie, Edinburgh University Press (1970).

7.　R. Kowalski, "Predicate logic as a programming language," *Proc IFIP 74,* pp.569-574 (1974).

8.　D. H. D. Warren, "Implementing Prolog," Research Reports 39, 40, Department of Artificial Intelligence, University of Edinburgh (1977).

9.　D. H. D. Warren, "Prolog on the DECsystem-10," *ESMEA,* pp.112-121 (1979).

10.　R. Kowalski, "Algorithm = logic + control," *CACM* **22**, pp.424-436 (1979).

11.　R. Kowalski, *Logic for Problem Solving,* North Holland (1979).

12. J. A. Robinson, *Logic: Form and Function,* Edinburgh University Press (1979).

13. A. Bundy, *The Computer Modelling of Mathematical Reasoning,* Academic Press (1983).

14. W. F. Clocksin and C. S. Mellish, *Programming in Prolog,* Springer Verlag (1981).

15. R. Kowalski, "Logic programming," pp. 133-145 in *Information Processing 83,* ed. R. E. A. Mason, North-Holland (1983).

16. J. Lloyd, "Foundations of logic programming," Technical Report 82/7, Department of Computer Science, University of Melbourne (1983).

17. J. A. Robinson, "Logic programming -- past, present, and future," *New Generation Computing* 1, pp.107-124 (1983).

18. H. Gallaire and J. Minker (eds), *Logic and Data Bases,* Plenum Press, New York (1978).

19. R. Kowalski, "Logic as a database language," Department of Computing, Imperial College, University of London (1981).

20. J. Lloyd, "An introduction to deductive database systems," *Australian Computer Journal* 15, pp.52-57 (1983).

21. K. L. Clark and S. Gregory, "PARLOG: A parallel logic programming language," Research Report DOC 83/5, Department of Computing, Imperial College University of London (1983).

22. E. Shapiro, "A subset of Concurrent Prolog and its interpreter," Technical Report TR-003, Institute for New Generation Computer Technology, Tokyo, Japan (1983).

23. E. Shapiro and A. Takeuchi, "Object oriented programming in Concurrent Prolog," *New Generation Computing* 1, pp.25-48 (1983).

24. A. Takeuchi and K. Furukawa, "Interprocess communication in Concurrent Prolog," *LPW*, pp.171-185 (1983).

25. K. Apt and M. H. van Emden, "Contributions to the theory of logic programming," *JACM* 29, pp.841-862 (1982).

26. M. H. van Emden and R. A. Kowalski, "The semantics of predicate logic as a programming language," *JACM* 23, pp.733-742 (1976).

27. N. Jones and A. Mycroft, "Stepwise development of operational and denotational semantics for Prolog," Datalogisk Institute, Copenhagen University (1983).

28. A. Mycroft, "Logic programs and many-valued logic," Institutionen för Informationsbehandling, Chalmers Tekniska Högskola, Göteborg, Sweden (1983).

29. D. A. Wolfram, M. J. Maher, and J-L. Lassez, "A unified treatment of resolution strategies for logic programs," Technical Report 83/12, Department of Computer Science, University of Melbourne (1983).

30. K. A. Bowen, "Programming with full first-order logic," pp. 421-440 in *Machine Intelligence*, ed. J. Hayes, D. Michie and Y-H. Pao, Ellis Horwood (1982).

31. B. Moszkowski and Z. Manna, "Temporal logic as a programming language," *Proceedings of Parallel Computing '83*, Freie Universitaet, West Berlin (1983).

32. F. M. Brown, "A sequent calculus for modal quantificational logic," *Proceedings of the AISB/GI Conference on Artificial Intelligence*, pp.56-65, Hamburg (1978).

33. L. Farinas-del-Cerro, "A deduction method for modal logic," *ECAI*, pp.60-61 (1982).

34. J. Darlington, "Unification of logic and functional languages," Department of Computing, Imperial College, University of London (1983).

35. H. Sawamura, T. Takeshima, and A. Kato, "Towards a descriptive language based on many-sorted equational logic," Research Report 42, International Institute for Advanced Study of Social Information Science Numazu, Japan (1983).

36. D. Bowen, L. Byrd, and W. F. Clocksin, "A portable Prolog compiler," *LPW*, pp.74-83 (1983).

37. S. Matwin and T. Pietrzykowski, "Intelligent backtracking for automated deduction in FOL," *LPW*, pp.186-191 (1983).

38. M. Yokota, A. Yamamoto, K. Taki, H. Nishikawa, and S. Uchida, "The design and implementation of a personal sequential inference machine: PSI," *New Generation Computing* 1, pp.125-144 (1983).

39. C. J. Hogger, "Derivation of logic programs," *JACM* 28, pp.372-392 (1981).

40. P. Szeredi, "Module concepts for Prolog," *Prolog Programming Environments Workshop*, Linköping, Sweden (1982).

41. A. Mycroft and R. O'Keefe, "A polymorphic type system for Prolog," *LPW*, pp.107-122 (1983).

42. E. Shapiro, *Algorithmic Program Debugging*, MIT Press (1983).

43. C. S. Mellish, "Automatic generation of mode declarations for Prolog programs," DAI Research Paper 163, Department of Artificial Intelligence, University of Edinburgh (1981).

44. M. Bruynooghe, "Adding redundancy to obtain more reliable and more readable Prolog programs," *LPCI*, pp.129-133 (1982).

45. Z. Manna, *Mathematical Theory of Computation*, McGraw-Hill (1974).

46. J. A. Robinson, "Computational logic: The unification computation," pp. 63-72 in *Machine Intelligence*, ed. B. Meltzer and D. Michie, Edinburgh University Press (1971).

47. C-L. Chang and R. C-T. Lee, *Symbolic Logic and Mathematical Theorem Proving*, Academic Press (1973).

48. A. Martelli and U. Montanari, "An efficient unification algorithm," *ACM Transactions on Programming Languages and Systems* 4, pp.258-282 (1982).

49. N. Nilsson, *Principles of Artificial Intelligence*, Springer Verlag (1982).

50. T. Skolem, "Uber die mathematische Logik," *Norsk matematisk tidsskrift* **10**, pp.125-142, English translation in FFG pp. 508-524 (1928).

51. D. W. Loveland, *Automated Theorem Proving: A Logical Basis*, North-Holland (1978).

52. R. Kowalski and Kuehner, "Linear resolution with selection function," *Artificial Intelligence* **2**, pp.227-260 (1971).

53. A. Horn, "On sentences which are true of direct unions of algebras," *Journal of Symbolic Logic* **16**, pp.14-21 (1951).

54. R. Hill, "LUSH resolution and its completeness," DCL Memo 78, Department of Artificial Intelligence, University of Edinburgh (1974).

55. K. L. Clark and F. G. McCabe, "The control facilities of IC-PROLOG," *ESMEA* (1979).

56. J. A. Robinson and E. E. Siebert, "LOGLISP: An alternative to Prolog," *Machine Intelligence* **10**, pp.399-419, Ellis Horwood (1982).

57. L. Naish, "MU-Prolog Reference Manual," Department of Computer Science, University of Melbourne (1983).

58. L. Naish, "Automatic generation of control for logic programs," Technical Report 83/6, Department of Computer Science, University of Melbourne (1983).

59. "Special issue on knowledge representation," *Computer* **16**(10) (1983).

60. E. F. Codd, "A relational model for large shared data bases," *Communications of the ACM* **13**, pp.377-387 (1970).

61. A. Delyanni and R. A. Kowalski, "Logic and semantic networks," *Communications of the ACM* **22**, pp.184-192 (1979).

62. V. Dahl, "Logic programming as a representation of knowledge," *Computer* **16**(10) (1983).

63. R. Kowalski, "Logic for data description," in *Logic and Data Bases*, ed. H. Gallaire and J. Minker, Plenum Press, New York (1978).

64. D. J. Israel, "The role of logic in knowledge representation," *Computer* **16**(10) (1983).

65. J. McCarthy and P. J. Hayes, "Some philosophical problems from the standpoint of artificial intelligence," in *Machine Intelligence*, ed. B. Meltzer and D. Michie, Edinburgh University Press (1969).

66. "Special issue on non-monotonic logic," *Artificial Intelligence* **13**(1,2) (1980).

67. R. Reiter, "On closed world databases," in *Logic and Data Bases*, ed. H. Gallaire and J. Minker, Plenum Press, New York (1978).

68. C. Hewitt, "Description and theoretical analysis (using schemata) of PLANNER," AI-TR-258, Artificial Intelligence Laboratory, MIT (1972).

69. J. C. Shepherdson, "A comparison of Clark's completed database and Reiter's closed world assumption," School of Mathematics, University of Bristol (1984). To appear in Journal of Logic Programming

70. D. H. D. Warren, L. M. Pereira, and F. C. N. Pereira, "Prolog -- the language and its implementation compared with LISP," *Proceedings of the Symposium on AI and Programming Languages*, pp.109-115, reprinted in SIGPLAN Notices/ SIGART Newsletter (1977).

71. R. A. Sammut and C. A. Sammut, "Prolog: A tutorial introduction," *The Australian Computer Journal* 15(2), pp.42-51 (1983).

72. K. L. Clark and F. McCabe, *Programming in Logic: MicroProlog*, Prentice-Hall (1984).

73. D. H. D. Warren and F. C. N. Pereira, "An efficient easily adaptable system for interpreting natural language queries," *American Journal of Computational Linguistics* 8, pp.110-122 (1982).

74. B. Dömölki and P. Szeredi, "Prolog in practice," *Information Processing 83*, pp.627-636, North-Holland (1983).

75. R. O'Keefe, "Prolog compared with Lisp?," *SIGPLAN Notices* 18, pp.46-56 (1983).

76. R. O'Keefe, "Some thoughts on assert and retract," *Prolog Digest* 1(29), Prolog@SU-Score.ARPA (24 September 1983).

77. D. H. D. Warren, "Higher-order extensions to Prolog -- Are they needed?," in *Machine Intelligence*, ed. J. Hayes and D. Michie, Ellis Horwood (1981).

78. P. S. G. Swinson, F. C. N. Pereira, and A. Bijl, "A fact dependency system for the logic programmer," *Computer Aided Design* 15, pp.235-243 (1983).

79. P. Köves, "The MPROLOG programming environment: Today and tomorrow," *Prolog Programming Environments Workshop*, Linköping, Sweden (1980).

80. K. L. Clark and S-A. Tärnlund, *Logic Programming*, Academic Press (1982).

81. M. Bruynooghe, "Some reflexions on implementation issues of PROLOG," *LPW*, pp.1-6 (1983).

82. E. Sántáne-Tóth and P. Szeredi, *Logic Programming*, Academic Press (1982).

83. L. Sterling, A. Bundy, L. Byrd, R. O'Keefe, and B. Silver, "Symbolic reasoning with PRESS," in *Computer Algebra*, ed. J. Calmet, Lecture notes in Computer Science 144, Springer Verlag (1982).

84. A. Bundy, L. Byrd, G. Luger, C. Mellish, and M. Palmer, "Solving mechanics problems using meta-level inference," *ESMEA*, pp.50-64 (1979).

85. F. Darvas, K. Bein, and Z. Gabanyi, "A logic-based expert system for model building in regression analysis," *LPW*, pp.229-239 (1983).

86. A. Lopata, F. Darvas, K. Kalkó, G. Mikite, E. Jakucs, and A. Kis-Tamás, "Structure-activity relationships in a series of new antifungal nitroalcohol derivatives," *Pesticide Science* 14, pp.513-520 (1983).

87. F. Darvas, I. Futó, and P. Szeredi, "A logic-based program system for predicting drug interactions," *International Journal of Biomedical Computing* 9, pp.259-271 (1978).

88. K. L. Clark and F. G. McCabe, "PROLOG: A language for implementing expert systems," in *Machine Intelligence*, ed. J. Hayes and D. Michie, Ellis Horwood (1980).

89. L. M. Pereira, P. Sabatier, and E. de Oliveira, "ORBI -- An expert system for environmental resource evaluation through natural language," *LPC1*, pp.200-209 (1982).

90. A. Walker and A. Porto, "KBO1: A knowledge-based garden store assistant," *LPW*, pp.252-270 (1983).

91. M. Merry, "APEX3: An expert system shell," *GEC Journal of Research* **1**, pp.39-47 (1983).

92. J. Forrest and M. D. Edwards, "The automatic generation of programmable logic arrays from algorithmic state machine descriptions," *Proceedings of VLSI '83*, pp.183-191, Tronheim, Norway (1983).

93. C. Mead and L. Conway, *Introduction to VLSI Systems,* Addison-Wesley (1980).

94. H. Barrow, *Proving the correctness of digital hardware designs,* Fairchild Laboratory for Artificial Intelligence Research (1983).

95. P. W. Horstmann, "Expert systems and logic programming for CAD," *VLSI Design* (November 1983).

96. Z. Márkusz, "Design in logic," *Computer Aided Design* **14**, pp.335-343 (1982).

97. P. S. G. Swinson, "Logic programming -- a computing tool for the architect," *Computer Aided Design* **14**, pp.97-104 (1982).

98. P. S. G. Swinson, "Prolog: a prelude to a new generation of CAAD," *Computer Aided Design* **15**, pp.335-343 (1983).

99. P. M. D. Gray and D. S. Moffat, "Manipulating descriptions of programs for database access," Technical Report, Department of Computer Science, University of Aberdeen (1983).

7 The 'Language First' Approach

J. R. Kennaway and M. R. Sleep

7.1 MOTIVATION FOR CHANGE

Technology has advanced considerably since the first computers were built. Very Large Scale Integration (VLSI) techniques make it possible to produce huge numbers of single chip computers at low cost. In spite of such advances, the basic organizational principles on which computer design is based have remained largely static, with the following key features:

(1) sequential, centralized control of computation via a unique sequence control register.

(2) a centralized random access memory.

These 'von Neumann' features have served us well for over 30 years, particularly with the use of clever engineering ideas like pipelining, virtual memory, and Single Instruction Multiple Data (SIMD) extensions. These ideas, when carefully integrated and realized using the most advanced technology, have led to very powerful computers like the Cray and the ICL DAP. Before considering more novel forms of architecture, an obvious first question is: why not stick with von Neumann architectures?

The clearest motivation for re-examining the basic principles is sheer speed. Given VLSI technology, we can produce cheaply huge armies of chips to attack problems in parallel. Provided we can work out some way of organizing these chips to do the work required, we can 'buy speed' from VLSI. But - particularly if we wish to exploit a Multiple Instruction Multiple Data (MIMD) approach to parallelism - new organizational principles are needed.

A less obvious motivation is the software crisis. We want to produce high-quality software at reasonable cost. Backus [1] has argued that conventional languages are unnecessarily difficult to program in, and that many of the difficulties stem from a 'von Neumann' orientation of the languages concerned. The underlying concern of a conventional programmer is to guide a single locus of control through a cunningly designed maze of assignment, conditional and repetitive statements (ie the program). At each step the programmer has (perhaps quite unconsciously) as a major concern the details of *how* things are done rather than getting right *what* is done.

Because much of our civilization manages to stagger along using programs developed in this imperative style, it may be judged reasonably successful - at least for programming von Neumann machines with a single locus of control. Even here, however, the software crisis indicates there is something wrong with conventional languages and suggests we should examine alternatives. When 5th generation architectures [2] with perhaps thousands of chips working in parallel are considered, the prospect of programming each chip individually becomes unthinkable, and the case for a new approach which does not require the programmer to consider individual control loci in detail becomes overwhelming.

In this chapter and the next we present one view of the growing body of work on novel architectures for declarative languages. Such work is motivated by the following beliefs:

(1)   Architecture should be language oriented.

(2)   The most harmful feature of conventional languages after the *goto* statement is destructive assignment.

(3)   Declarative (zero assignment) languages not only facilitate the reading and writing of programs by people, but also enable automatic program transformation techniques [3].

(4)   Banishing destructive assignment from the programmers vocabulary has the interesting side effect of making declarative programs naturally amenable to parallel execution. In particular, sub-expressions can be evaluated safely in parallel.

7.2 THE 'LANGUAGE-FIRST' APPROACH

Although the following quote from Dijkstra [4] is taken out of context, it neatly summarizes the general approach of novel architects: *It used to be the program's purpose to instruct our computers; it became the computer's purpose to execute our programs.*

The architects' starting point is now the language rather than some fiendishly clever engineering idea which takes no account of programmability. A possible disadvantage of this approach is that each language may lead to a quite individual architecture which is unsuited to other languages. In the event, just two families of declarative languages have been considered seriously by novel architects, the *lambda-based* languages, for example Burge's language [5], HOPE [6], SASL [7], FFP [1], ML [8] and VAL [9]; and the *logic-based* languages, for example Prolog [10]. Operationally, lambda-based languages require only simple (non-backtracking) pattern matching facilities and are therefore easier to support. Perhaps for this reason, and the fact that logic languages are fairly recent, the bulk of the work so far on novel architectures has focussed on lambda-based languages.

There are now signs that logic and lambda languages (and perhaps process-oriented languages too) can be integrated in a natural manner. While this does not simplify the problem, it does suggest that work on lambda-oriented architectures provides useful guidelines for parallel architectures which support more advanced languages.

7.2.1 An Example of Declarative Programming

Both logic and lambda languages are *declarative*. The most striking feature of these languages for a conventional programmer is the total absence of assignments as well as goto statements. Programming in a declarative language is much closer to writing a set of mathematical equations than conventional programming. Earlier chapters present excellent introductions to lambda and logic languages. Here we give only a simple example intended to highlight operational and architectural issues. We use SASL rather than HOPE because it illustrates nicely the lazy evaluation issue.

The problem we consider is a simplified form of the Hamming problem discussed in [4]. We want to generate and print in ascending order integers of the form $(2^i)*(3^j)$ where i and j range from 0 upwards.

Our basic approach is to write equations which define the required infinite list, which we will call ans. There are many equations which have the desired solution. Because we want to feed the equations to some machine which we expect to produce the answer, we must be careful to make sure our equations have a workable *procedural* (machine oriented) reading as well as the *declarative* (equational) reading.

In lambda languages, the procedural interpretation of equations is to regard them as rewrite rules which permit the machine to replace elements of an expression which match the left hand side of an equation with the corresponding right hand side.

For example, in order to define a function which accepts a (possibly infinite) list of integers, and returns a new list in which every element has been doubled, we may write in SASL:

> DEF DoubleAll ( ) = ( )
> DoubleAll (h:t) = (2*h):(DoubleAll t)

The first equation says that given an empty list the result is also an empty list. The second equation deals with the more general case of a list with head h and a tail called t, using the infix ':' operator to represent the LISP constructor CONS. In procedural terms, the equation says that we can produce a doubled version of a list by doubling the first element and then applying the function DoubleAll to the tail. Given the list (1:(2:( ))) we can ask a SASL system to print a doubled version by typing:

> DoubleAll (1:(2:( ))) ?

First, the SASL machine will see that the form as input cannot be printed because it is a function application. It now searches the 'database' of equations, and recognizes that the second equation can be used as a rewrite rule, matching h with 1 and t with the list (2:( )). This produces the revised form:

> 2:(DoubleAll (2:( )))

Because this is (in LISP terms) a CONS, the machine now attempts to print the head, and succeeds immediately because it is the integer 2, which is directly printable. The machine will now process the tail, whose form is currently:

> (DoubleAll (2:( )))

After further deductions like those illustrated above, the system will print the required result and then stop. Notice that although the equations were written in terms of infinite lists, this does not present a problem because of the printer-driven nature of the SASL machine. It is perfectly possible (and very useful) to write equations which define real infinite objects in SASL. For example,

> DEF PosInts = (from 1) WHERE from n = n:(from(n + 1))

defines the list of natural numbers. SASL progams written using this infinite list will of course use only part of it if they terminate.

Although we have interpreted the equations procedurally as rewrite rules, each operational step represents a change of *form* in keeping with the equations. Each change preserves the meaning. Because of this fact, unlike programmers, architectures for declarative languages may actually overwrite old forms with equivalent ones, using destructive assignment. This is the basis for *graph reduction* described in more detail below.

Returning to our problem, we can also define a function called TrebleAll which is similar to DoubleAll except that it uses 3 as a multiplier instead of 2. We can now write:

> DoubleAns = DoubleAll(ans)
> TrebleAns = TrebleAll(ans)

and observe that if we merge DoubleAns with TrebleAns we obtain (with some repetitions) ans with the first element (1) missing. This is the critical observation which allows us to solve the problem and write:

> DEF ans = 1:(RemoveDups(Merge(DoubleAll(ans)),(TrebleAll(ans)))))
>   WHERE
>   DoubleAll ( ) = ( )
>   DoubleAll (h:t) = (2*h):(DoubleAll(t))
>   TrebleAll ( ) = ( )
>   TrebleAll (h:t) = (3*h):(TrebleAll(t))
>   Merge (( ),( )) = ( )
>   Merge (x ,( )) = x
>   Merge (( ), x) = x
>   Merge (x , y) = IF head(x)<head(y)
>   THEN head(x):(Merge((tail(x)),y))
>   ELSE head(y):(Merge(x,(tail(y))))
>   FI
>   RemoveDups ( ) = ( )
>   RemoveDups (h:(h:t)) = RemoveDups (h:t)
>   RemoveDups (h:t) = h:(RemoveDups(t))

Having input these equations to a SASL system, we can ask for the whole (infinite) sequence to be printed, or select some finite portion using an appropriate function.

Note the use of pattern matching to define the auxiliary functions Merge and RemoveDups. The ordering of the equations for the different cases is significant, because the machine will try the cases in the order presented. In the interests of clarity, we have deviated slightly from real SASL syntax by using the IF.....FI form of conditional, and using the selectors head and tail which should really be hd and tl in runnable SASL.

The major points to note from this example are:

(1) Running a declarative program changes its *form* but never its *meaning*.

(2) The declarative programmer must have a good understanding of the procedural interpretation of the equations he writes if he is to produce good programs.

(3) The basic idea in declarative programming is to conceive of the result as some complex data structure, and then to devise defining equations which, besides their mathematical interpretation also have a machine oriented (procedural) interpretation.

(4) Printer-driven control of the use of equations as rewrite rules. This makes it possible to write equations involving infinite objects without necessarily producing non-termination.

Not all declarative languages have the final property, which perhaps emphasizes the fact that declarative languages, like conventional languages, require the programmer to think operationally. But the declarative framework constrains the programmer to a world in which *form* but not *meaning* can change. This means that if the equations are right, a wrong answer will never be produced, although termination may be affected. This property makes declarative programming much more like writing specifications than conventional programming. Resulting programs are much easier to read, write and prove. The new approach adds new problems, however. In particular, updating a single element of a huge data structure requires in principle a complete copy of the whole object, and clever implementation techniques are needed to deal with this.

7.2.2 The Design Process

For a given language, an idealized machine can be designed which defines operationally the semantics of the language. This *computational model* usually makes unrealistic assumptions - for example an idealized Algol machine supports arrays of unbounded size and no real computer can deal with this. The job of the computer architect is to devise a *physical model* which, within its limitations, behaves exactly like the computational model. The process of designing a language oriented architecture starts with the rather high level computational model and progressively refines it until it becomes physically realisable at which point it is a physical model. By the time this stage is reached, the set of programs which the model will deal with satisfactorily will be considerably smaller than the set of programs which the idealized computational model supports. Finally, the physical model is mapped onto existing technology using all the clever engineering ideas around to yield a *real machine*.

Given a single computational model, a huge number of differing physical models may be derived using the top-down methodology. The physical models may be distinguished both in performance terms (sheer speed) and also in terms of the restrictions placed on the programmer. A good physical model leads to real machines which run fast, and perhaps more important, do not unduly force the user to 'program round' their limitations.

No real architect uses a pure top-down methodology. In practice, there is a strong temptation to let 'efficient' instructions on the real machine find their way into a language implementation, often changing the language semantics dramatically. Thus 'real' LISPs support destructive assignment, and most language implementations provide 'hooks' which allow the user to get at a relatively naked form of the raw machine.

Novel architects are not immune from this bottom-up influence, especially if they support an active user community. But the novel architect feels guilty when he succumbs to such pressures, and asks the language designer for help.

7.3 DESIGN ISSUES FOR LAMBDA MACHINES

Because functional languages such as HOPE and SASL are based on the lambda calculus, the starting point for a 'top down' architect is the lambda calculus core of such languages. From this core we now develop some of the central architectural issues.

7.3.1 The Lambda Calculus

The following remarkably simple syntax captures the essence of all the classical functional languages:

$$E ::= \quad \text{identifier}$$
$$\lambda \text{ identifier . E}$$
$$@ \ E \ E$$

The first production allows us to introduce names for objects, the second production gives the power of abstraction, and the third production expresses the application of one function to another. The (usually invisible) symbol @ is read APPLY. This very sparse notation is in fact very general, but we will follow [11] and use a richer notation which allows atoms representing constructors, integers, integer operations etc. in what follows. We will also use the conditional form of expression.

In most conventional languages, the function which triples its argument is (give or take minor syntactical details) written in the following form:

$$f(x) = x*3$$

In lambda languages, we write instead:

$$f = \lambda \ x. \ (x*3)$$

or without the infix sugar:

$$f = \lambda \ x. \ @ \ (@ * x) \ 3$$

This allows us to talk about f without worrying about naming its arguments. In particular, we can now write equations defining functions in which just one identifier appears on the left hand side. We 'call' functions in the lambda calculus by applying them to an argument, eg

$$@ \ f \ 5$$

will 'send' 5 to f, to produce the result 15 which - because it is exactly equivalent to the original expression - can replace it.

At first sight the lambda calculus with an explicit symbol for application looks rather horrid; for example $f(x) = 2*x + x/3$ turns into

$$\lambda \ x. \ (@ \ (@ + (@ \ (@ * 2) \ x) \ (@ \ (@ / x) \ 3)))$$

However, the unsugared (machine) form has advantages: in particular, functions which both accept and return functions may be defined. (@ * 2) is the function which doubles its argument. In general, the 'equal civil rights' property of the lambda calculus is a powerful mechanism for developing - in conventional terms - program forming programs, the advantages of which have been amply illustrated elsewhere [12].

Usable ('sugared') lambda languages allow the user to adopt conventional infix notation, to pre-name values of expressions using LET, and to post-name values using WHERE. Structured data types can be made available by adding a few built-in functions and constants. Programming in a pure lambda-based language can be done in a purely descriptive fashion: we imagine the output (presumably some complex data structure) and describe it in terms of the input, as illustrated in section **7.2.1**. Aside from the capability to write 'program forming programs' (which takes some practice), the most notable feature of programming in a lambda-based notation is the total absence of the assignment statement. This means, for example, that the usual 'loop counting' variables must be replaced by recursive calls. The reward is *referential transparency*: within its scope, any mention of an identifier denotes the same value *throughout the run of the program*. This key property makes life easier for both the human reader and the machine reader (e.g. some architecture expected to run the program).

7.3.2 From Semantics to Architectural Issues

The basic formal rule for evaluating lambda expressions is *beta-conversion*:

$$@ (\lambda x. E) F \rightarrow [x \leftarrow F] E$$

where the right hand side means (a copy of) the expression E with all free occurrences of x replaced by (a copy of) the expression F, possibly with name changes to avoid free variables in F being captured by abstractions in E. This rule appears simple to state, is incredibly powerful, but is very difficult to implement efficiently. It is also very ambiguous: in particular, given a large expression containing many reducible sub-expressions, *no evaluation order is specified*.

All usable lambda languages considerably extend the core syntax, for example by allowing arithmetic operators and numeric atoms. Although such extensions lead to many new reduction rules (e.g. $3*4 \rightarrow 12$) besides beta-conversion, there are two central issues in developing lambda-oriented architectures:

(1)   What evaluation order should we use?

(2)   How should beta conversion be done?

Very roughly, in conventional terms the questions are: (1) when should we evaluate parameters? and (2) how should parameters be passed? In the sections which follow we illustrate and discuss both issues.

7.3.2.1 Evaluation Order

In conventional (control flow) languages, the order in which statements are executed usually has a dramatic effect on the outcome. A major result of the lambda calculus (see e.g [5]) states (roughly) that the choice of order makes no difference to the value, although it may affect termination. Evaluation of a lambda expression proceeds by identifying one or more reducible sub-expressions (or *redexes*), and replacing them with equivalent, but simpler expressions using the reduction rules. This *reduction* process is repeated until there are no more redexes, when the expression is in *normal form*. For example, $((3*4)+(5*6))$ contains 2 redexes: $(3*4)$ and $(5*6)$. These may be reduced in any order (or in parallel) to 12 and 30 respectively. The original expression has now been reduced to the form $(12+30)$ which may be further reduced to the normal form 42. Essentially, *computation is viewed as controlled deduction* rather than a sequence of apparently meaningless state changes. This change of viewpoint is perhaps the most fundamental aspect of 'novel architecture' work.

It looks at first sight as if exploiting parallelism gains speed and loses nothing. Why not 'data drive' the computation so that all redexes are reduced in parallel? Unfortunately, an injudicious choice of evaluation order may have undesirable consequences:

(1)   it may lead to non-termination, most obviously when the two arms of a conditional statement are evaluated in parallel. Most interesting computations depend on conditional statements to prevent fruitless (and possibly infinite) computation.

(2)   however many chips are used, any real machine has a finite capacity for realizing parallelism. Once this limit is reached, further attempts to exploit parallelism simply clog up the system queues.

(3)   in a distributed architecture, the communication costs involved in distributing sub-expressions to other processing elements may outweigh the time saved.

Thus the choice of evaluation order affects performance in a marked manner, and the issues noted above provide a useful checklist for evaluating novel architectures. One attractive solution is to pass the buck to the user by introducing annotations to the language which he may use to specify the evaluation order, and perhaps the form (ranging from string to pointer) in which arguments are passed. This is reminiscent of pre virtual-memory days when every programmer worth his salt had his optimal overlay scheme for memory management. The alternative approach is to make the architecture take the decisions in a dynamic manner. This is the ideal approach, but it is much harder. At present, we cannot be sure that the distributed equivalent of virtual memory 'magic' will appear, and certainly annotations are useful in the short term.

7.3.2.2 Beta-conversion

Methods of implementing beta-conversion can be divided into several classes.

(i) String Reduction

Whenever a function is applied to an argument, a copy is made of the function body with a copy of the argument substituted for each occurrence of the formal parameter. Using an 'outermost first' evaluation order, the following expression:

f(sqrt(4)) WHERE f(x)   =   IF x = 1
                                THEN h(x)
                                ELSE g(x*5)
                                FI

is beta-convertible to:

IF sqrt(4) = 1 THEN h(sqrt(4)) ELSE g(sqrt(4)*5) FI

Here we have used *string reduction* to realize beta-conversion, making 3 complete copies of the argument. Because the new form is a conditional, and the argument occurs in both arms, one of the copies will certainly be thrown away. Further, because of the evaluation order, two evaluations of sqrt(4) are involved assuming both h and g force evaluation of their arguments.

For this reason, systems using string reduction generally evaluate expressions in applicative order, reducing arguments to normal form before supplying them to functions. This loses the software engineering advantages of being able to handle infinite data structures in a uniform way. It is interesting to note that HOPE [6] though having predominantly applicative order semantics, includes a non-strict list-constructor for precisely this purpose. Furthermore, some functions - such as conditional, mentioned above - should not be evaluated with applicative order.

(ii) Graph Reduction

We can save much of the unnecessary work of string reduction by copying *pointers* to sub-expressions rather than the full text. This *graph-reduction* approach is described in detail for the pure lambda-calculus in [13]. The basic idea is that the current form of the expression being evaluated is stored not as a string or a parse-tree, but as a graph, in which common subexpressions may be shared. As an example, the expression

IF sqrt(4) = 1 THEN h(sqrt(4)) ELSE g(sqrt(4)*5) FI

might be represented in graphical form as in **Figure 7-1**, where the subexpression sqrt(4), which occurs three times in the linear representation, occurs but once in the graph, with three references to it.

To perform the beta reduction of an expression @ (λx.f) g (where f and g are expression graphs) we make a new copy of f in which all occurrences of the formal parameter x are replaced, not by copies of g, but by pointers to g. Notice that we cannot simply substitute pointers to g for x in f itself, as there may be other references to f. We must 'peel off' a new copy to make the substitution in.

The great advantage of this method is that when g is eventually evaluated, every reference to g will have the benefit of the work performed. g will be evaluated at most once, however many times its value is needed. And if we perform reductions in normal order, then if the value of g is never needed it will never be evaluated at all. Thus we obtain normal order semantics without the overhead of multiple evaluation which we saw for string reduction.

This method may still require some unnecessary copying. Whenever a function is applied, we must peel off a copy of its body. Some of this can be avoided. Any subexpressions of the body in which the formal parameter does not occur need not be copied, but can be shared between the original and all peeled off copies. It is not clear, however, that the cost of storing the information necessary to recognize these subexpressions does

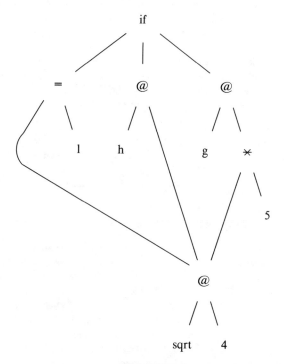

Figure 7-1

not outweigh the benefits gained. Another possibility is that if there are no references to the function body other than through one particular application of it (and a reference counting scheme could be used to recognize this) then substitution for the formal parameter can be done in the original, without copying. But in general there may be substantial parts of the function body which a graph reducer cannot avoid copying, and which (because they lie on unselected arms of conditionals) may be thrown away.

(iii) Environmental Schemes

Moving from string to graph reduction involves being progressively lazier about making copies, in the sense that we copy pointers instead of strings of arbitrary length. The standard *environmental* scheme for realizing beta-substitution takes this process to its logical conclusion by doing no copying at all. Instead, beta-substitution is simply 'remembered' by adding an (identifier,expression) pair to an *environment*. In the example above, the pair would be (x,sqrt(4)). When the identifier x is needed for further evaluation, (e.g. in the conditional test x = 1) it is looked up in the environment, and future lookups can share the benefit of forced evaluation if we take some care in the implementation.

At first sight, the environmental scheme wins hands down because copying is never done unless it is needed. In this sense, it is a purely *demand-driven* scheme. On closer examination, however, the picture is not so clear:

(1)   The basic drawback of the environmental mechanism is that in order to understand an expression fully the environment in which it was created must be consulted. In a correct implementation which supports functions which can accept and return functions, this means that each expression must contain at least a reference to the environment in which it was created. In a simple-minded environmental scheme, in which every beta-conversion is remembered, a considerable amount of excess baggage may be accumulated in the form of environmental entries which will never be consulted. Schemes which minimize excess baggage tend to destroy the basic point of the environmental approach by complicating the remembering process.

(2)   Even if the excess baggage problem can be cured, efficient lookup mechanisms are needed. The larger the environment, the higher the cost of entry and lookup. In an expression with a huge environment and many free occurrences of a variable x, it might be cheaper to perform the lookup once and distribute copies (possibly as pointers) rather than do many lookups.

(3)   In a highly parallel machine access to the environment acts as a bottleneck.

(iv) Lazy Graph Reduction and Combinators

The newest approach to beta-substitution is to use *lazy* graph reduction. In Wadsworth's original scheme [13] every beta substitution involved a 'full peel' of a copy of the original graph. It would be better to only do the copying in response to the demands of the rest of the computation. One method of achieving this is to introduce environments, though in a way rather different to the previous section. When we encounter a beta-redex @ (λx.f) g, we merely replace it with the pair (f,{x=g}), where {x=g} is the environment which associates x with g. Such a pair is called a *closure*. We then continue by attempting to evaluate f. If we discover further redexes, we reduce them. But if we find an occurrence of x whose value we need before proceeding further, then we 'push' the environment {x=g} down through f to that occurrence of x, peeling off a copy only of the path traversed. At the end of the path we substitute for x a pointer to g, and continue looking for the next redex to reduce. In general, when we find a redex we reduce it; when we find a variable we look for the closure where it is defined and peel off a copy of the path from that closure down to the variable.

The evaluation method we have just described can be programmed directly. Another way of obtaining lazy graph copying is by the use of *director strings* [14]. We examine the program at compile time and translate it into a variable-free form which replaces a tree consisting of interior nodes and leaf nodes which mention variables by a tree of interior *director* nodes which will switch incoming arguments to exactly the places specified by the variables. The 'switches' encode the information in the variables, which may now be replaced by anonymous holes which notionally wait to be filled by the switching process.

For example, the expression:

$$f(5) \text{ WHERE } f(x) = 2*x + x*(3*4)$$

may be replaced by the tree shown in **Figure 7-2**.

The *distribution sub-tree* for x has been marked with double lines: it indicates that in order to evaluate the expression, the argument 5 may (in this case will) have to be sent both left and right at the uppermost + node in the tree, and that this + node should distribute copies both right and left. Copies (string or pointer) now arrive at the * nodes in the diagram, to be further distributed right (by the leftmost * node) and left (by the rightmost * node). Intuitively, we imagine the incoming value for x being distributed to

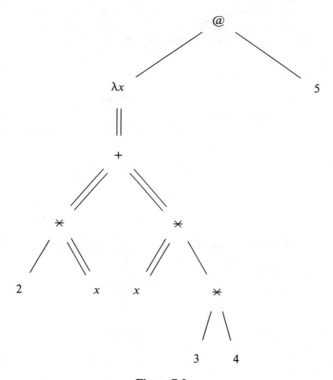

Figure 7-2

just the places it is needed in the expression via the distribution sub-tree. An obvious encoding for distribution sub-trees is to tag each *apply* with a *director* from the set $(\wedge, \backslash, /)$ representing the distribution instructions 'send both ways, send right, send left' respectively. Multiple abstractions produce strings of directors. Using this idea, **Figure 7-2** translates to the variable-free form shown in **Figure 7-3**, where the boxes represent 'holes' for the missing argument values. The directors guide an argument to just the places required in an expression, in a number of small steps *which may be realized concurrently* when 'both-ways' directors are involved. Conditional expressions effectively represent directors which are determined dynamically, switching an argument left or right depending on whether the condition is true or false. Director strings provide a simpler means of obtaining lazy graph copying than the environmental scheme, but at the cost of some loss of flexibility of reduction order.

The practicability of this technique was first suggested by Turner [7] who introduced the S1, B1, and C1 *combinators* (switches) which closely correspond to the three directors. A fuller description of the director approach is available in [14, 15].

7.3.2.3 Choice of computational model

It would be nice if the architect could select a preferred evaluation order and a scheme for beta-substitution in the secure knowledge that the decisions are independent. Unfortunately, this is not the case. For example, selection of outermost (lazy) evaluation favours some pointer scheme (graph reduction, lazy graph reduction or environment) as against string reduction to reduce the amount of copying. In general, string reduction is only practicable for innermost (eager) evaluators.

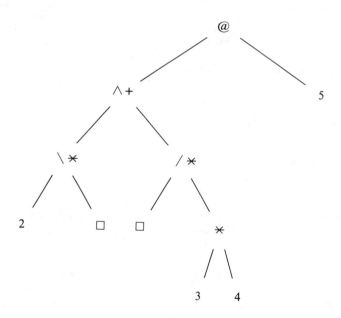

Figure 7-3

To complicate matters further, use of 'lazy' evaluation   [16] (which corresponds to outermost evaluation) extends significantly the class of programs which terminate: in particular, the programmer can define his output using functions which operate on 'folded up' versions of infinite lists. Because this is an extremely useful tool in the programmer's kit, the expressive power of the language adds another dimension to the problem of choosing a computational model.

7.4 THE IMPORTANCE OF THEORY

In the last section, we saw that the choice of evaluation order and method for beta substitution are not independent. This suggests that we may be working at too high a level. Lazy beta substitution breaks a single potentially large beta substitution into a number of bounded operations, and allows the evaluator to order these so as to optimize some measure of performance.

Although some theoretical results have emerged from recent U.K. work in this area, notably on the space complexity of translation to combinator form [17, 18] a powerful theoretical handle on the basic pragmatic issues is needed.

The recent work of Staples may provide such a handle. In a series of papers [19, 20, 21] Staples develops a general theory of optimal reduction orders in graph rewriting systems, of which lambda calculus with beta reduction, combinators, and directors are examples. In particular he develops a key requirement of the 'basic reductions' provided by a machine which ensures that there exists a simple optimal reduction order. For 'pure' combinators and directors (i.e. without any built-in operators such as addition, multiplication, etc.) this optimal order is just the leftmost-outermost ordering. When arithmetic operators are added this algorithm only has to be augmented with 'demand forking' at such operators. In [22] he develops a form of lambda-calculus in which beta-reduction is broken down into small steps in a way similar to the environmental scheme of section **7.3.2.2(iii)**. For this system too, leftmost-outermost reduction is optimal.

Because Staples' work applies to any 'reduction' machine, it provides important clues to the designers of novel architectures. More generally, it illustrates the importance of theory in a new and exciting area.

7.5 REFERENCES

1.   J. Backus, "Can Programming be liberated from the von Neumann style?," *Comm. ACM* **21**(8) (1978).

2.   Uchida, "Towards A New Generation Computer Architecture," ICOT report TR/A-001, Tokyo (July 1982).

3.   R.M. Burstall and J. Darlington, "A transformation system for developing recursive programs," *JACM* **24**(1) (Jan.1977).

4.   E.W. Dijkstra, *A Discipline of Programming.*, Prentice-Hall. (1976).

5.   W.H. Burge, *Recursive Programming Techniques,* Addison-Wesley (1975).

6.   R.M. Burstall, D.B. MacQueen, and D.T. Sannella, "HOPE: An Experimental Applicative Language," Internal Report CSR-62-80, University of Edinburgh, Department of Computer Science (1980).

7.   D.A. Turner, "A New Implementation Technique for Applicative Languages," *Software, Practice and Experience* **9**(1) (1979).

8.   M.J. Gordon, A.J. Milner, and C.P. Wadsworth, "Edinburgh LCF.," *Lecture Notes in Computer Science*, Springer-Verlag. (1979).

9.   W.B. Ackerman and J.B. Dennis, "VAL - Preliminary Reference Manual," Report TR-218., MIT Lab. for Computer Science (1979).

10. W.F. Clocksin and C.S. Mellish, *Programming in Prolog*, Springer Verlag (1981).

11. P.J. Landin, "The next 700 programming languages.," *Comm.ACM* **9**(3, 157-166) (1966).

12. D.A. Turner, "The Semantic Elegance of Applicative Languages.," *Proc. ACM Conf. on Functional Programming Languages and Computer Architectures*, New Hampshire (Oct. 1981).

13. C.P. Wadsworth, *Semantics and Pragmatics of the Lambda Calculus; D.Phil. thesis*, Univ. of Oxford (1971).

14. J.R. Kennaway and M.R. Sleep, *Director Strings as Combinators.*, University of East Anglia. (1982).

15. E.W. Dijkstra, "A Mild Variant of Combinatory Logic.," EWD735. (1980).

16. P. Henderson and J.M. Morris, "A Lazy Evaluator.," *3rd. Symp. on the Principles of Programming Languages*, Atlanta (Jan. 1976).

17. F.W. Burton, "A linear space translation of functional programs to Turner combinators," *Inf. Proc. Letters* **14**(5), pp.201-204 (1982).

18. J.R. Kennaway and M.R. Sleep, *Efficiency of counting director strings*, University of East Anglia (1983).

19. J. Staples, "Optimal reductions in replacement systems," *Bull. Austral. Math. Soc.* **16**, pp.341-349 (1977).

20. J. Staples, "Computation on graph-like expressions," *Th. Comp. Sci.* **10**, pp.171-185 (1980).

21. J. Staples, "Optimal evaluations of graph-like expressions," *Th. Comp. Sci.* **11**, pp.39-47 (1980).

22. J. Staples, "A graph-like lambda calculus for which leftmost-outermost reduction is optimal," *Lecture Notes in Computer Science* **73**, Springer-Verlag (1978).

8 Towards a Successor to von Neumann

J. R. Kennaway and M. R. Sleep

8.1 PHYSICAL MODELS

An effective physical model acts as a conceptual bridge between the computational model and the hardware. At the highest level, the physical model specifies the general organization of the architecture which can be realized in hardware.

At this level, a von Neumann machine consists in essence of a processing element with one or more registers, a special sequence control register, and a global random access memory with completely destructive update. This efficiently supports sequential control flow.

Parallel evaluation of declarative programs appears to require radical changes to von Neumann architectures, which will be developed and illustrated in this chapter.

8.2 EVOLUTIONS OF THE VON NEUMANN PHYSICAL MODEL

Before considering alternatives to von Neumann architecture at the physical level, it is worth considering ways in which its performance could be improved, and how it could be used to support a declarative style of programming.

8.2.1 Increase Clock Speed

This has the enormous advantage that *every* program experiences the same speedup: exploitation of parallelism is irrelevant. But for a given technology improvements in this direction are limited, and the basic concern of the programmer continues to be navigating the von Neumann control locus through a complex maze of imperative statements. Thus, even if it were possible to increase clock speed at will, the von Neumann contribution to the software crisis would remain.

8.2.2 Increase Granularity of Instruction

This can be done by (in extremis) providing a single instruction for each program, and/or making instructions operate on much larger data items. The first approach is not practicable (although 'special purpose' instructions are good for some applications). The second approach leads to SIMD (single instruction stream/multiple data stream) generalizations of the original von Neumann design such as the CRAY and the DAP. Such machines require great skill to program well.

8.2.3 Use Pipelining

A basic characteristic of the von Neumann machine is that *each instruction appoints a unique successor*, which is most often the instruction stored in the immediately following location. Pipelined architectures exploit this fact by performing speculative work on future instructions which is lost when a jump takes place. For sound statistical reasons, commercial exploitation of pipelining involves a small (e.g. 4) number of stages, and good compilers are needed to utilize pipelining effectively.

8.2.4 Parallel Composition of von Neumann Chips

VLSI allows us to make whole von Neumann machines on single chips. Provided we can find out how to exploit, in a programmable manner, large-scale hookups of such chips we should be able to 'buy speed', at least for some applications. This route is attractive, especially when coupled with a good programming methodology. occam on the Transputer [1] is the best example around at present. Transputer-like devices may yield many GIPS (billions of instructions per second) per cubic foot if correctly programmed for specialist applications, for example ones amenable to systolic algorithms [2]. A very important use of large scale transputer hookups is to provide usable simulations of novel architectures such as ALICE [3] which are very slow on sequential machines.

8.2.5 Exploiting von Neumann for Declarative Languages

Computational models such as the SECD machine for ISWIM [4] the combinator machine for SMALL [5] and the APM machine for extended Prolog all give simple state transition models for supporting particular styles of declarative programming.

A very fruitful approach in the short term to realizing high performances for declarative languages is to decompose an abstract machine such as SECD or APM into a small set of specialist functions which can be realized as a finite network of communicating von Neumann devices.

The precise decomposition of the overall functionality of a machine which supports declarative languages into a finite number of subfunctions, each of which can be realized by bounded von Neumann chips, is a subject of considerable commercial interest at the time of writing. This interest makes it reasonably safe to say that 'super von Neumann' machines will be making money around 1990, and that such machines will typically involve a smallish number (say 10-20) of communicating chips. A good machine will yield better than one million LIPS (logic instructions per second) for logic languages around 1990, and will cost about 100 pounds at 1984 prices. Dramatic improvements on these figures are conceivable given the discovery of a truly novel machine design.

8.3 A GENERAL MODEL OF A VON NEUMANN SUCCESSOR

From the above discussion of von Neumann machines, a key characteristic which emerged was that *each instruction appoints a unique successor*. A secondary, but (particularly if we have distributed computing in mind) important characteristic of a von Neumann machine is the assumption of a *large, flat* address space for the main memory.

From the requirements of both lambda and logic formalisms, it is clear that the 'unique successor' attribute of the von Neumann machine is inadequate. For example, evaluation of

$$x*y \text{ WHERE } x = \text{sqrt}(4) \text{ AND } y = \text{sqrt}(9)$$

means the simultaneous creation of two demands, one for the integer form of sqrt(4), the other for the integer form of sqrt(9).

In logic languages, each goal to be proved may appoint several subgoals, all of which are to be proved. A successor to von Neumann machines must be capable of appointing more than one instruction to succeed the current one. Formally, the state transition function for the new machine must support the concept

$$\text{subexpression} \rightarrow \text{SET OF subexpressions}$$

But not only must the architecture be able to appoint more than one successor, it must also be able to remember that, when all the successors have finished, the parent expression may be reducible. Thus the simple 'goto' nature of the von-Neumann architecture is inappropriate, and recursive call is the basic mechanism for transferring control.

We concentrate in what follows on the lambda language case, mainly because it is much easier. A very general organization is shown in **Figure 8-1**.

It consists of an (extensible) number of PE's (processing elements) and two 'task pools'.

Notionally at least, each task fully describes a sub-expression of the overall computation, together with a *destination* specifying where the evaluated form is to be placed. For the original expression which began the computation, this will be an output device. For sub-expressions, the destination will specify a field within some other task held in the *waiting pool*.

Each processing element picks any task from the *selected pool* and examines it to see if it requires sub-expressions to be evaluated. If so, the relevant sub-expressions are extracted and added as tasks to the *selected pool*. The original task, which now has holes in it, is added to the *waiting pool*. These holes will be filled by returning results. If the original task does not need sub-evaluations, it is evaluated and the result used to fill a hole (either in one of the tasks in the waiting pool or in the output device). Filling in

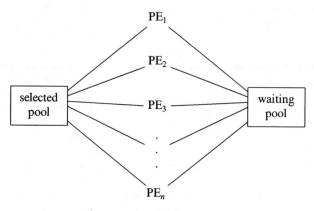

Figure 8-1

the last hole in a waiting task moves it to the selected pool.

This simple picture is the basis for nearly all novel architectures to date, which however differ greatly in detail. The basic idea is to replace the single sequence control register in a von Neumann machine by a set of tasks selected for execution at each time step. The choice of computational model specifies a scheme for beta-substitution. If we can devise an efficient, extensible, highly parallel, random access implementation of the task pools required in the general organization, there is no reason not to use pointer schemes for beta substitution. If on the other hand this proves tricky, it may be better to risk some unnecessary copying to avoid bottlenecks in accessing the pools.

8.4 PARTICULAR ORGANIZATIONS FOR DISTRIBUTING WORK

The general organization shown above represents a rather high level model which lacks a considerable amount of important detail. It is obviously possible to simulate the model directly using a uniprocessor. It is much more difficult to invent a scheme which distributes the computation over real parallel hardware without creating communication bottlenecks. This is the *distribution* problem, which is the main issue at the physical level. We now examine some approaches to this problem.

8.4.1 Pipelined Ring Architectures (PRAs)

Rather than let tasks sit passively in a pool as the general model proposes, and making the processing elements pick them out, we might reverse the idea and make selected tasks move to the processing elements. Each processing element now processes a stream of incoming tasks and emits a stream of results. These results can be merged and the resulting stream processed by a *task former* which, in terms of the general model has access to the *waiting* pool and employs it to create a stream of new tasks. The ring is closed by feeding all the result streams to a fan-out mechanism which distributes the tasks to the processing elements as they become available. The PRA scheme is shown in **Figure 8-2** in diagrammatic form.

At this level of abstraction, no decision has been made about the representation of tasks, nor about their *granularity*. Note that the PE's do not have direct access to the *waiting* pool in the PRA model, so that each executable task must include all the information (code and data) needed to perform the task. Perhaps for this reason tasks in working prototypes tend to be fine grain, eg $(3 + 4)$.

In contrast to most of the other models of distribution, several prototype PRA's are running now, notably the Manchester Dataflow Machine [6]. By clever decomposition of the task former, the ring may be heavily pipelined, and many rings may be interconnected using an *exchange switch* for inter-ring communication. MIT's Jack Dennis [7] pioneered this approach, but continues to advocate a more static approach than the Manchester group. If inter-ring traffic can be kept low, multi-layered dataflow machines promise very high performances. By clever - perhaps seminal - use of the 'colouring' facilities in the Manchester machine, it is possible to support higher order functions [8].

The PRA model was originally proposed by Dennis, who has been a prime mover towards a 'top-down' approach to architecture. Dennis has now been joined by Arvind [9] who is currently planning to build a 64-ring prototype using available chips within the next 3 years. Arvind's proposal follows closely the Manchester work, but adds a special *I-structure* unit to each ring to handle large data structures. This alleviates the problem of having to physically process huge data structures each time an element is examined.

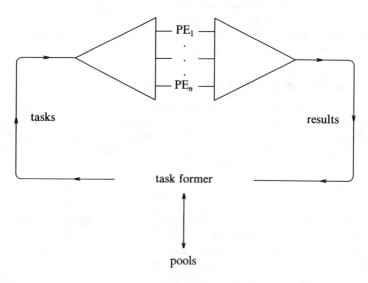

Figure 8-2

8.4.2 Packet Circulation Ring Architectures (PCRAs)

The most obvious bottlenecks in the PRA scheme are the input and output streams to and from the processing elements. One way of increasing throughput is to use many rings, and both Manchester and MIT are following this path. One alternative approach is to use a *slotted ring* for communication to distribute resources to processing elements. A slotted ring is simply a circular conveyor belt divided into slots. A sender places a message in the first empty slot he sees. A receiver looks out for a message addressed to him, and removes it to create a new empty slot. The practicality of the slotted ring concept has been amply illustrated by the Cambridge ring project [10].

The general idea behind PCRA's is to place a number of PE's in a circle and serve them with resources using one or more slotted rings. Messages, represented by 1 or more packets may denote for example a task, a global address, or data. A single slotted ring may be used for all communication, as with the real Cambridge ring, or a number of specialized rings may be used to distribute particular resources. Similarly, the *ring servers* may be highly specialized or more general purpose, eg processing elements with some local memory.

An advanced machine is being constructed at Imperial college by the ALICE (Applicative Language Idealized Computing Engine) group [3]. Although the present (1984) design of ALICE has evolved considerably (it now has both VTA and SDMA aspects), the original ALICE proposal used two slotted rings, one for distributing tasks from the *selected* pool and one for distributing memory for new tasks. Both rings act as distribution agents for a global *packet pool* which merges the functions of the selected and ready pools in the general model. To avoid the merged packet pool becoming a bottleneck, use of a multi-ported memory with an advanced topology is proposed.

A particularly interesting feature of ALICE is that it can support traditional control flow concepts as well as reduction semantics. This is because the Compiler Target Language (CTL) [11] retains some von Neumann features, supporting random access to a global packet memory and destructive update of packets. The early development of CTL allows software tools for ALICE to be developed in parallel with hardware construction.

A precursor of ALICE is the Newcastle GCF (Generalized Control Flow) architecture proposed by Treleaven et al [12]. An earlier (hardware) use of the slotted ring idea is seen in the Texas Instruments Distributed Data Processor [13] which effectively used a slotted ring to link several dataflow uniprocessors.

8.4.3 Physical Tree Architectures (PTAs)

Rather than use a slotted ring for communication, we might use a more advanced topology. Many proposals adopt a binary tree which is perhaps the simplest topology that gets everything close (O(log n)) together. Some proposals for example AMPS [14] use the tree structure solely for communication and load balancing purposes, with all the work being done at the leaves. Other proposals for example DDM1 [15] and Mago's machine [16] use more intelligent interior nodes.

In the AMPS proposal [14] each leaf of the tree is a processor/memory element which is capable of executing tasks sequentially or in parallel, and also capable of allocating storage for new tasks. There is no global memory, although there is a uniform global address space. The internal nodes in the physical tree perform the routing required for access to non-local memory, and external communication is via specialized leaf nodes. Although the root node of a binary tree is in principle a potential bottleneck, the load balancing takes place at the lowest possible interior node so that the root node is only employed when one half of the tree is full loaded. AMPS supports outermost evaluation of the lambda language FEL [17] which includes many pragmas/annotations for user control of parallelism. FEL supports a wide range of syntactic sugar. At present, AMPS exists as a sophisticated simulation vehicle.

Because the evaluator for a lambda language is essentially recursive, the idea of building a physical tree structure of processor/memory/routing elements which recursively decomposes an expression into its primitives is attractive. An early example of this approach is the DDM1 hardware at Utah [15] which evaluates simple data-driven nets. A basic difficulty with this very direct approach is that whilst work can be distributed down the tree, there appears to be no counterpart of the AMPS mechanism for passing work from one leaf to another.

A quite different way of using a tree is the *Mago machine* [16]. This represents a simultaneous head-on attack at all the difficult problems. The machine is unashamedly string reduction - pointers are not used. Storage management is dealt with by including it in the basic machine cycle. Expressions (written in Backus's FFP notation [18]) are stored in a linear array of *lcells* which are the leaves of a physical binary tree. Each lcell contains processing power as well as memory, and lcells are connected to immediate neighbours to facilitate data movement within the lcell array. The interior nodes of the physical binary tree, called *tcells*, co-operate with their neighbours in a largely asynchronous fashion to achieve distributed string reduction. A computational cycle is realized by a number of waves which sweep down from the root node of the physical tree and are reflected upwards by the leaves. The wavefront may carry control and data information. During its passage up and down the tree, the wavefront encounters tcells and lcells with which it exchanges control and data information. A number (which is variable) of sweeps is required to execute a basic Mago cycle, which can be split into the following three phases:

(1)   The *partitioning* phase. This examines the lcell array to determine the innermost (reducible) sub-expressions, and allocates tcells to each such expression. An important result of Mago's work is that each tcell will never be allocated to more than 4 sub-expressions during this phase. Microcode for the operators discovered during

this phase is distributed to appropriate places.

(2) The *execution* phase. The lcells which contain a reducible expression, and the tcells sitting above them, now operate in concert to achieve distributed reduction. If the result requires more lcells than the original expression (eg if a named operator is replaced by its FFP text), further processing is delayed until the next cycle.

(3) The *storage management* phase. Although this is achieved in a distributed fashion, involving several sweeps, it is best thought of as a global operation which entirely rearranges the text stored in the lcells to leave room for sub-expressions which grow with reduction, and to compact those which shrink. When the whole expression represented in the array of lcells outgrows its physical bounds, some of the expression overflows into virtual memory, presently via the leftmost cell [Darn82]. During the storage management phase, all execution is suspended. Once storage management is complete, another Mago cycle begins.

The whole scheme (as Darlington once commented) is rather like a petrol engine: first the reducible expressions are determined, then 'fuel' in the form of microcode is distributed, next actual reductions (computational work) takes place, and finally (during the 'exhaust' phase) unwanted lcells are reclaimed.

The Mago machine is a unique and highly original proposal. Its major features are:

(1) A global machine cycle synchronized by the physical root.

(2) Inclusion of storage management in the basic cycle.

(3) A direct 'string reduction' approach.

Although not realized in hardware, the well known planar layout scheme for a binary tree makes the Mago machine attractive for direct VLSI realization. Considerable effort has been made to develop analytic techniques for performance prediction [19]. This work suggests that by clever microcoding of suitable primitives an $O(n*n)$ time for matrix multiplication is possible.

8.4.4 Virtual Tree Architectures (VTAs)

Parallel evaluation of a lambda-based language requires the architecture to recursively decompose an expression into its component parts (eg arithmetic operations), evaluate some of the components, and combine the results. The whole evaluation process may be regarded as growing an 'evaluation tree' which first expands and then collapses to yield the final result. The structure of the evaluation tree is defined by the original expression, together with the evaluation order selected in the computational model. Innermost first evaluation in its purest form completely expands the process tree until all nodes represent primitive expressions (eg $(3+4)$) which can be directly reduced. Outermost (lazy) evaluation reduces each node until further reductions necessitate the (lazy) evaluation of sub-expressions, and only then instructs the necessary sub-trees to grow.

If the expression at the root node of the evaluation tree determined that (say) 5 sub-expressions should be evaluated in parallel, we could in principle create 5 new physical evaluators, give one sub-expression to each, and wire the 5 new evaluators to allow them to send the results to the root node. Similarly, each new evaluator might be recursively endowed with the same powers to create and wire in new evaluators as and when they are needed.

Direct hardware implementation of this scheme is unrealistic, but it is possible to simulate it using a finite, strongly connected set of physical evaluators each of which can support many nodes in the evaluation tree. Each evaluator has primitive off-loading and memory management capability. The basic idea behind the Virtual Tree approach is to wrap a possibly huge evaluation tree around a much smaller physical network. A good VTA will initially grow the evaluation tree as fast as it can, and when all the physical evaluators are busy restrict further growth of the evaluation tree to avoid overloading the physical resources (eg system queues).

Because it entirely avoids complex compile time analysis of expressions, the simplest approach to realizing a VTA is to implement some sort of *diffusion mechanism*, which uses only local communication between physical evaluators to make decisions regarding offloading and memory management. One basis for such a scheme is a physical evaluator which, left to its own devices, simulates depth-first priority parallel evaluation. When new nodes are created in the evaluation tree they are placed on a stack in local memory, and the uppermost node is then considered by the evaluator. Suitable modifications are made to the parent node which remains stacked and will be reconsidered when its children return results. An important feature of this simple scheme (which can be seen in [20]) is that the memory required to support it is related to the maximum depth of the evaluation tree rather than (as with very eager schemes) the total size of the evaluation tree. For a balanced evaluation tree, this is O(log N) which perhaps suggests that a means of *dynamic* rebalancing during evaluation is desirable.

To introduce the possibility of parallel evaluation, we connect our single physical evaluator (which simulates lots of virtual evaluators) to a small number of immediate neighbours, each of which we endow with the power to *steal* work from the stacks of immediate neighbours. In general, allowing neighbours to steal work from the uppermost part of the stack results in *fine grain* diffusion, whilst the choice of lower elements on the stack corresponds to *coarse grain* diffusion. Note that rather than add extra work to an already overloaded physical processing element by asking it to take responsibility for offloading, we make inactive neighbours actively seek to *steal* tasks. In order to make good offloading decisions, each physical evaluator needs a fairly recent picture of the workload in its vicinity. This may be maintained by forcing physical neighbours in the architecture to exchange loading information regularly.

VTA work is particularly active in the UK. The University of East Anglia has developed a simulation vehicle with full-colour graphics instrumentation, which shows clearly how a simple diffusion mechanism leads to rapid and even spread of work across the physical topology and yet governs undue exploitation of parallelism which leads otherwise to huge system queues [21]. The University of Bath [20] have been developing similar ideas although with considerably more emphasis on compile-time analysis. Bath have recently reported a working hardware configuration [22]. The idea of preventing communicating processes from getting separated in a physical architecture has been traced to [23]. Both East Anglia and Bath devoted much attention in their early work to developing physical topologies which are intuitively well suited to supporting evaluation trees. In retrospect, this effort may be unnecessary: first, every architecture must in the end be realized in 3-space, and second, given locality-preserving offloading, fancy topologies really only help the initial 'infection' stage of the computation, during which a big problem placed at a single node diffuses throughout the network. For interesting (huge) problems, this represents a decreasing fraction of the run time: it is conjectured that even a ring would support many Virtual Tree applications.

8.4.5 Shared Distributed Memory Architectures (SDMAs)

In a Shared Distributed Memory Architecture, a large number (eg 4K) of processing elements access a large number of memory elements via an advanced multistage switching network. Schwartz [24] develops a family of extensible computers based on this idea, and illustrates a large number of applications. The NYU (New York Ultracomputer) project [25] is examining this SDMA approach in considerable detail, for example [26] discusses the wireability problem and proposes a solution for 4K processing elements.

Because previous SDMA work has largely been concerned with particular applications, its potential for lambda-based languages remains largely unexplored. There appears to be considerable potential, especially for graph-reduction schemes where efficient support of sharing is very important. Recent changes to ALICE make it look increasingly like an SDMA machine.

8.4.6 Novel Sequential Architectures (NSAs)

In the short term at least, the best way to 'buy speed' might be to realize some novel approach to beta-substitution directly in conventional hardware. The SKIM [27] project takes just this view, by implementing Turner's combinator approach [28] to beta substitution directly in hardware. The performance outpaces most conventional implementations, with notable exceptions such as the Chalmers VAX implementation [29] which directly compiles equations into VAX machine code, and Cardelli's ML compiler [30].

An early direct hardware realization of beta-conversion is the GMD lambda machine [31] which uses several hardware stacks. A parallel variant, which may fairly be considered a VTA, has recently been developed by Kluge [32]. A joint ICL/Oxford project has recently produced a rather fast microcoding of the PERQ which supports Henderson's LISPKIT LISP [33]. Turner at Kent is currently engaged on a similar microcoding exercise for his KRC [34] language using an Orion. KRC is notable in supporting *set abstraction* which, as Turner has demonstrated [35] is a very powerful language feature.

8.5 A NOTE ON LOGIC MACHINES

Programming in a lambda-based language is accomplished by writing down an expression which denotes the desired result, and requiring the implementation of the language to transform it into normal form. Thus, writing times(4,5), the implementation is expected to replace this by 20. Logic-based languages such as Prolog depend on relations rather than functions. The simple example of a multiplication would be written as times(4,5,z), and the implementation is expected to deduce that $z = 20$. But relational programming gives much greater generality: the multiplication predicate can just as easily be used 'in reverse' as a factorization predicate. Writing times(x,y,20), the implementation is required to deduce that (1,20), (2,10), (4,5), (5,4), (10,2), and (20,1) are possible values of x and y. In general, a relation may be 'programmed' by writing down a set of *clauses* which specify what must be proved in order to prove an instance of the relation. Each clause specifies, for some class of instances of the relation, a set of subgoals, all of which must be satisfied in order to prove some instance of the relation. A simple example is list concatenation, which may be programmed in Prolog as:

```
concat(NIL,x,x)    :- .
concat(x.y,z,x.w)  :- concat(y,z,w) .
```

The first clause says that the concatenation of NIL with any list x is the same list. The second says that to show that x.w is the concatenation of x.y and z, we may show that w is the concatenation of y and z. (In LISP terms, x.y means CONS x y so that '.' is the Prolog infix operator for CONS.) Suppose we supply the Prolog system with the above program and the goal concat(1.2.NIL,3.NIL,x). It will match the goal against the head of the second clause (as the first clause does not match), and will make the following associations between the variables of the clause and those of the goal:

$$x \Leftrightarrow 1$$
$$y \Leftrightarrow 2.NIL$$
$$z \Leftrightarrow 3.NIL$$
$$x.w \Leftrightarrow x$$

Note that the x which occurs in the goal is a different x from that which occurs in the clause. It now finds that to produce an x making the original goal true, it should find a w such that concat(2.NIL,3.NIL.w) is true, and take x = 1.w. This in turn will give rise to a new goal concat(NIL,3.NIL,v), with w = 2.v. This goal matches the first clause for concat, giving v = 3.NIL, and by a series of back-substitutions, x = 1.2.3.NIL.

The computation proceeds very much as it would in a lambda-based language such as HOPE [36] where we would define a concat function by:

$$concat(NIL,x) = x$$
$$concat(x.y,z) = x.concat(y,z)$$

But there the similarity ends. There is a complete symmetry between the three argument-places of the concat predicate. It can be used not just for concatenation, but for splitting a list in two. concat(1.2.NIL,x,1.2.3.NIL) will be executed by Prolog to bind x to 3.NIL, and concat(x,y,1.2.3.NIL) will split the list 1.2.3.NIL into two parts in every possible way. Similarly, one predicate can do the work of both multiplication and factorization, or both addition and subtraction.

In the example program, the right hand sides of the clauses consisted of at most one literal (i.e. a relation symbol applied to a set of arguments). In general they may contain several, and a set of values is sought for the variables of the clause which makes all the literals true together. For each literal, there may be several clauses whose left hand sides contain the same predicate as the literal. These are alternatives which must each be matched against the literal in turn until one succeeds. The clauses of a Prolog program thus define a tree-structured search space which the implementation must explore. This tree has two sorts of branching: AND branching, where each of a set of sub-goals must be completed, and OR branching, where any one must be.

We can distinguish between the purely logical core of the language and the control structures, implicit or explicit, which direct this exploration [37]. Examples of implicit control in sequential implementations are the ordering of literals in a clause (they are executed from left to right) and the ordering of all the clauses having a given predicate on their left-hand sides (they are attempted in sequence). Additionally, there is a powerful mechanism, CUT, allowing the programmer to discard parts of the search space, and it is possible for a program to add or remove clauses from itself as it runs. Some implementations add further control facilities [38].

Logic programs provide obvious opportunities for parallelism. Expansion of the descendants of any node in the search tree may be done simultaneously. The problem is to decide what the appropriate control structures for directing a parallel search should be. There have been several proposals for parallel versions of Prolog [39, 40] but this area of research is as yet not so well developed as for lambda-based languages.

A key issue here is probably what clauses constitute 'reasonable' input for a logic machine. Warren [41] has shown that 'reasonable' logic programs can be compiled into efficient code for a DEC-10 and in principle an army of chips should be able to work fast on large logic programs. But we are much further from knowing how to 'buy speed' for logic languages than we are for lambda-languages. Pollard [42] has considered the problem in some detail, and the Stockholm group [43] has several active logic machine projects. The largest single co-ordinated effort at building logic machines is currently in Japan [44] where much of the 5th generation programme is devoted to producing efficient logic machines, both sequential and parallel, in short order.

8.6 CONCLUSION

There is still some mileage to be gained from further developments of von Neumann architectures. But the main conclusion must be that the increasingly active dialogue between the designers of languages and machines evidenced above will produce a new generation of machines which will be largely programmed in declarative style. If it turns out that we can 'buy speed' from VLSI for declarative languages, performance considerations alone will force a change. If, on the other hand, this proves to be a hard problem, the undeniable software engineering advantages of the declarative approach will be the major force for change.

Factors which militate against the general adoption of declarative languages include the following:

(1) Current implementation techniques for declarative languages are relatively slow, although the adoption of good compiling techniques, see for example [29, 30, 41] has brought the factor down to 2 to 4.

(2) It is difficult with the current breed of declarative languages to express detailed control information which is critical in some applications such as real-time process control and database update.

In the short term, we foresee the development of 'super von-Neumann' machines specifically designed to produce high performance for one or more declarative languages. Such machines will follow the route taken by specialist LISP machines, and employ pipelining and caching extensively. Within the next few years, such super von-Neumann machines will rapidly reduce the perceived performance gap between classical and declarative languages.

Concurrently with these developments, we anticipate within a decade real speedups from novel, highly parallel architectures for declarative languages. In our view the question is no longer if such techniques will win, but when.

8.7 ACKNOWLEDGEMENTS

Thanks are due to all the workers in the field who gladly took time off to explain what they were doing, and to the United Kingdom Science and Engineering Research Council via the Distributed Computing Systems panel for supporting many discussions with the most active groups. Chapters 7 and 8 are heavily based on [45]. The permission of IEE to revise [45] for a more general audience is gratefully acknowledged. Special thanks are due to Phil Treleaven et al. whose recent survey paper [46] provided an excellent starting point for this work. Roy Dowsing's many useful comments are gratefully acknowledged.

8.8 REFERENCES

1.   INMOS, *occam Programming Manual,* Prentice-Hall (1984).

2.   H.T. Kung, "Let's Design algorithms for VLSI," CMU-CS-79-151, Carnegie-Mellon University (1979).

3.   J. Darlington and M. Reeve, "ALICE: A Multi-Processor Reduction Machine for the Parallel Evaluation of Applicative Languages.," *Proc. ACM Conf. on Functional Programming Languages and Computer Architectures,* New Hampshire (Oct. 1981).

4.   P.J. Landin, "The mechanical evaluation of expressions," *Computing Journal* **6**(4), pp.308-320 (1964).

5.   A.C. Norman, *Pure Programming,* Computer Laboratory, Cambridge University (1979).

6.   J. Gurd and I. Watson, "A Data Driven System for High Speed Parallel Computing," *Computer Design* (June, July 1980).

7.   J.B. Dennis, G.A. Boughton, and C.K.L. Leung, "Building blocks for data flow prototypes," *Proc. 7th Ann. Symp. Computer Architecture,* La Baule (May 1980).

8.   C. Kirkham, *The Implementation of Functions on the Manchester Dataflow Computer,* Univ. Manchester. (1982).

9.   Arvind and V. Kathail, "A Multiple Processor Data Flow Machine That Supports Generalised Procedures," *Proc. 8th Ann. Symp. Computer Architecture* (May 1981).

10.   R.M. Needham, "System Aspects of the Cambridge Ring," *Proc. 7th. Symp. on Operating System Principles* (1979).

11.   M. Reeve, *An Introduction to the ALICE Compiler Target Language,* Dept. Comp. and Control, Imperial College.

12.   E.P. Farrell, N. Ghani, and P.C. Treleaven, "A Concurrent computer and ring-based implementation," *Proc. 6th Ann. Symp. on Computer Architecture,* New York (April 1979).

13.   M. Cornish, "The TI data flow architectures: The power of concurrency for avionics," *Proc. 3rd. Conf. Digital Avionics Systems,* Fort Worth (Nov. 1979).

14.   R.M. Keller, G. Lindstrom, and S. Patil, "A loosely-coupled applicative multiprocessing system," *Proc. 1979 AFIPS NCC* (1979).

15.   A.L. Davis, "A dataflow evaluation system based on the concept of recursive locality," *Proc. 1979 NCC,* New York (June 1979).

16.   G.A. Mago, "A Network of Microprocessors to Execute Reduction Languages, Parts 1 and 2," *Int. J. Comp. Inf. Sci.* **8**(5 and 6) (1979).

17.   R.M. Keller, *FEL - Function Equation Language - users manual,* Univ. of Utah (1982).

18.   J. Backus, "Can Programming be liberated from the von Neumann style?," *Comm. ACM* **21**(8) (1978).

19. G.A. Mago, D.F. Stanat, and A. Koster, *Program Execution on a Cellular Computer: Some Matrix Algorithms,* Univ. North Carolina at Chapel Hill. (1981).

20. A. Bowyer, P. Willis, and J. Woodwark, "A multiprocessor architecture for solving spatial problems," *Computer Journal* **24**(4) (1981).

21. F.W. Burton and M.R. Sleep, "Executing Functional Programs on a Virtual Tree of Processors," *Proc. ACM Conf. on Functional Programming Languages and Computer Architectures,* New Hampshire (Oct. 1981).

22. J. Marti and J. Fitch, *The Bath Concurrent LISP machine,* School of Maths., Univ. of Bath (Dec 1982).

23. A.J. Martin, "A Distributed Implementation Method for Parallel Programming," Memo 3-090 1, Phillips research lab, Eindhoven (July 80).

24. J.T. Schwartz, "Ultracomputers.," *ACM TOPLAS* **2**(4) (1980).

25. A. Gottlieb, R. Grishman, C.P. Kruskal, K.P. McAuliffe, L. Rudolph, and M. Snir, *The NYU Ultracomputer -- designing a MIMD, Shared-Memory Parallel Machine,* Courant Institute, New York University. (1982).

26. R. Bianchini, "Wireability of an Ultracomputer," Ultracomputer note 43, Courant Institute, New York University (1982).

27. T.J.W. Clarke, P.J.S. Gladstone, C.D. Maclean, and A.C. Norman, "SKIM - the S,K,I reduction machine.," *Proc. LISP-80 Conf.,* Stanford (Aug. 1980.).

28. D.A. Turner, "A New Implementation Technique for Applicative Languages," *Software, Practice and Experience* **9**(1) (1979).

29. L. Augustsson, "Functional Compiler Status Report No.1," LPM memo 24, Chalmers University, Goteborg, Sweden (1982).

30. L. Cardelli, "The Functional Abstract Machine," *Polymorphism* **1**(1) (January 1983).

31. K. Berkling, "Reduction Languages for Reduction Machines," *Proc. 2nd. Int. Symp. Computer Architecture,* Houston (Jan. 1975.).

32. W.E. Kluge, private communication, 1982.

33. P. Henderson, *Functional Programming: Application and Implementation,* Prentice-Hall. (1980).

34. D.A. Turner, *KRC Language Manual.,* Computer Lab., Univ. of Kent. (1981).

35. D.A. Turner, "The Semantic Elegance of Applicative Languages.," *Proc. ACM Conf. on Functional Programming Languages and Computer Architectures,* New Hampshire (Oct. 1981).

36. R.M. Burstall, D.B. MacQueen, and D.T. Sannella, "HOPE: An Experimental Applicative Language," Internal Report CSR-62-80, University of Edinburgh, Department of Computer Science (1980).

37. R. Kowalski, "Algorithm = Logic + Control," *Comm.ACM* **22**(7), pp.424-436 (1979).

38. K.L. Clark and F.G. McCabe, "The Control Facilities of IC-Prolog," in *Expert Systems in the Microelectronic Age*, ed. D. Michie, Edinburgh University Press (1979).

39. K.L. Clark and S. Gregory, "PARLOG: a parallel logic programming language," Research Report DOC 83/5, Imperial College, London (1983).

40. E. Shapiro and A. Takeuchi, "Object oriented programming in Concurrent Prolog," *New Generation Computing* 1(1), pp.25-48 (1983).

41. D.H.D. Warren, "Implementing Prolog.," DAI report nos. 39,40, Dept. Artificial Intelligence, Univ. of Edinburgh (1977).

42. G.H. Pollard, *Ph.D. Thesis,* Dept. Comp. and Control, Imperial College (1982).

43. L. Thorelli, "CSALAB Progress Report.," TRITA-CS-8201, Royal Inst. Tech., Stockholm, Sweden. (1982).

44. Uchida, "Towards A New Generation Computer Architecture," ICOT report TR/A-001, Tokyo (July 1982).

45. J.R. Kennaway and M.R. Sleep, "Novel architectures for declarative languages," *Software & Microsystems* 2(3), pp.59-70 (June 1983).

46. P.C. Treleaven, D.R. Brownbridge, and R.P. Hopkins, "Data-Driven and Demand-Driven Computer Architecture," *ACM Computing Surveys* 14(1) (1982).

Part III

Loosely - Coupled Systems

K. H. Bennett
I. C. Wand
A. J. Wellings

9 Architectures

I. C. Wand

9.1 INTRODUCTION

It is generally agreed that distributed computing has been made possible by the dramatic change in the price/performance of computing elements resulting from the recent rapid advances in VLSI technology, and by the development of effective communications, both over local area (LAN) and wide area networks (WAN).

Semi-conductor technology has advanced at a bewildering rate over the last 15 years. It is now possible to buy processors for a few pounds which will outperform most of the mainframes that were available in the 1960's. Clearly it is tempting to connect a number of these relatively cheap processors together to achieve increased processing power, geographical separation and increased reliability. To do this, wide area and local area networks are required.

Wide area computer networks have been available to some researchers for several years, although their availability to UK workers is quite recent following the establishment of PSS and SERCnet. However special purpose networks have been available for some time (e.g. banking). To date most wide area computer networks have used packet switching technology.

Local area networks, which are intended to provide wide bandwidth over a limited distance, have developed rapidly in recent years. Such networks make use of relatively cheap methods of interconnection such as co-axial cable, twisted pairs, fibre optics, etc. Unfortunately there is no agreed international standard for LANs and no single technology yet dominates the market. Loosely coupled systems, the subject of this tutorial, are usually connected via LAN systems.

Distributed computing systems are well suited to organizations which do not exhibit a centralized structure. Such structures have become more common as companies have devolved responsibilities away from the central office towards semi-independent subsidiaries. Clearly the computing systems used within such an organization must reflect this devolved structure or an artificial distortion in commercial practice will develop. Local tasks can be run and controlled by the people who understand them best; they are then fully responsible for the results.

If processing is installed at the locations where the computing power is required, then communications costs are reduced. Many different system architectures are possible ranging from the use of intelligent terminals connected to a central mainframe, to placing powerful workstations on the desks of each worker. There are many intermediate arrangements which might involve clusters of computers and a number of different network technologies.

9.2 OBJECTIVES

LeLann [1] has listed the objectives that users expect from distributed systems:

1. *Increased performance.* This can be obtained by the use of multiple processing elements, although contention and bottlenecks are present in conventional multiprocessors with shared store or busses. Decentralized techniques of overall system control are probably the only ones that can achieve greatly enhanced performance. Short response time and high throughput are probably best achieved by the partitioning of global system functions.

2. *Extensibility.* Such systems must adapt to a changing environment, although the overall design of the system should not be changed. Alterations to the environment might include the modification of performance requirements and the modification of functional requirements. Any extensibility will require some kind of modular architecture, which will provide a simpler system design and ease installation (and subsequent maintenance).

3. *Availability.* Hardware has become more reliable as technology has advanced; furthermore reliability can be enhanced by duplicating or triplicating vital hardware. Similar progress is now being made with software [2] by providing checkpoints, roll-back, and other specialized recovery mechanisms. Clearly distributed or multi-processor systems can be used for consistency checking so that failsoft computing is available.

4. *Resource Sharing.* A resource may be a low-level physical device such as a peripheral or it may be a complex item such as a filing system. Such resources may be allocated statically (at system generation time) or they may be allocated dynamically. The system requires a mechanism whereby optimal and dynamic resource allocation can be achieved with associated optimal sharing.

9.3 A MODEL FOR DISTRIBUTED SYSTEM ARCHITECTURES

Watson [3] has described a model for distributed systems architecture which contains three dimensions. One axis is concerned with a set of logical layers, where each layer and sublayer has design and implementation issues of its own. In addition there are a set of issues common to all layers. Watson describes this axis as being perpendicular to that describing the individual layers. The third axis is said to describe global interactions of various parts of the system. It is the first and second axes which we describe here.

9.3.1 Layers, Interfaces and Abstract Objects

The concept of layers of design or levels of abstraction has long been accepted as good software engineering practice. Layers have a number of advantages, including:

1.   The internal structures, including the algorithms, are not visible to other layers. Therefore we have separation of concerns.

2.   Complex systems can be broken down into simpler pieces.

3.   Testing and analysis can proceed a layer at a time.

The service provided at any particular layer can be further decomposed into modules. The decomposition of a system into layers and modules is somewhat arbitrary, although guidelines are suggested in the ISO Reference Model [4]. This decomposition requires the identification of interfaces both between adjacent layers and between modules within a given layer. An interface consists of:

1.   A set of visible abstract objects, together with operations and parameters.

2.   The rules governing the legal sequences of these operations.

3.   The encoding and formatting required for operations and parameters.

Distributed systems provide access to real and abstract objects or to resources where the distributed nature of the system is often hidden as much as possible. Real objects are entities such as processors, I/O devices, etc., whereas abstract objects are entities such as files, directories, etc. Abstract objects can be used as basic building blocks for creating higher level objects. A particular object type is implemented by a group of modules together called an object manager or server. Note that the implementation details of a resource representation are only of concern to a particular server.

Two kinds of object are possible:

1.   *Active,* where the distributed system model is of a process which can be thought to be executing on a real or virtual processor.

2.   *Passive,* such as an I/O device, a communications channel or a file.

All communication is between processes via interprocess communication (IPC) using messages as requests and replies. Even when the remote procedure call model is used, it can be described in terms of messages being exchanged. A particular process can be a server or a customer/client at different times. Messages that contain directives are called *control messages;* these can be distinguished from *data messages,* which contain information that is simply passed on or is used. As Watson [3] points out, data messages are logically just parameters of requests and replies, which because of their size, are sent separately.

9.4 THE MODEL LAYERS

The model is made up of several basic layers, each of which is discussed in turn.

9.4.1 Applications Layer

The services provided by this layer depend upon the particular application being considered. In turn it will determine the services to be provided by the lower layers.

As Watson remarks, there are few distributed applications in the true sense, although the following design areas can be identified as important.

1. *Application structure,* in which the important questions are: how should processing be distributed? How should application processes be organized for control and communication? How should data be distributed? What mechanisms are required to support different data and processing organizations?

2. *Language issues,* in particular what language features are necessary to support distributed processing beyond those required in languages that are used in uniprocessor systems. One possible objective of any such languages would be to provide a view from which the system appears to be non-distributed to the user. A further requirement may be to give the user the ability to specify the placement of data and its visibility hence providing both control and performance.

9.4.2 Distributed Operating System

This layer will provide all the services needed by the distributed servers. The layer will build upon kernel component drivers, and will communicate with higher level objects via the message-based IPC.

The characteristics of distributed operating systems are quite similar to those of non-distributed systems, and the relationship between the application program and the operating system is likely to be roughly similar in the two environments. The major new issues are those of internal organization and implementation.

Important issues in the design and construction of a distributed operating system layer are:

1. The resource model.

2. The server model, together with the Customer-Server Interaction Model.

3. The distributed system kernel, including the IPC service and interface, the network and the associated protocols.

9.4.3 Hardware/ Firmware Components

Most components used in computing systems have been designed for use in single processor or closely coupled non-distributed systems. Of course most can be used in distributed systems, although their design is not always suited to a message-orientated distributed environment. Many aspects of low-level components could be improved when used in a distributed environment including: structures that will deal with efficient IPCs and the representation/encoding of the related data; structures that will support system state information; and mechanisms to provide access control, security, etc.

9.5 ISSUES WITHIN EACH LAYER

9.5.1 Naming

An identifier is a symbol used to designate or reference an object; it can be used for a wide variety of purposes, including protection, error control, resource management, locating resources, and as a way to build composite objects from simpler components. Furthermore, identifiers can be used at all levels in a system; at the bottom level they will be machine addresses. Names can often be used within a local context; other names will be unique within the whole system.

9.5.2 Error Control

Error control is used to detect and to attempt to recover from errors at all levels in the system. No single error control mechanism would appear to be appropriate for all layers in a system. There are particular problems in a distributed environment, namely:

1. Names may be re-used.

2. Error control must be maintained during periods of delay, message errors, system crashes, etc.

3. The communications medium may cause damage to the error control information, including mis-sequencing.

Clearly protocols supporting the IPC mechanism via end-to-end protocols require mechanisms to guard against lost information. One obvious mechanism is the retry.
    A full discussion of these reliability issues is given in Anderson and Lee [2].

9.5.3 Resource Management

Each layer in a system is responsible for the appropriate management of buffer space, communication channel access, address space, etc. Allocation and scheduling is usually carried out locally because allocation on a global basis is not well understood. Watson concludes that the mechanisms which will achieve both low delay and high throughput will require long term retention of some state information and some preallocation of resources and functionality in various layers. Cacheing and demand allocation strategies are possible ways of achieving the appropriate delay-throughput balance. Clearly some form of flow control will required to prevent congestion.

9.5.4 Synchronization

The term synchronization is usually used to describe mechanisms by which cooperating processes share resources or share events. In a non-distributed system, the problem is straightforward as all processes see the same system state. This is not the case in a distributed system, even when there are no errors or node failures in the associated network.
    When errors, including message damage or mis-sequencing, are introduced, the problem becomes much more difficult. Clearly there is a strong interaction between error control and synchronization; the problem becomes more difficult when the number of nodes exceed two.

9.5.5 Protection

The same degree of protection will be required in a distributed and a non-distributed system, although in the former case these will be much complicated by the problems of physical distribution and heterogeneity.
    Within a single processor, either all processes are equally trustworthy or they can access each other through a well defined, reliable interface such as an IPC mechanism. Assuming that the kernel operating system running on each node and the servers can be trusted, then encryption can be used at all levels to protect the information and the overall system.
    An alternative system uses capability techniques [5] where the possession of a capability gives the right of access. In a uni-processor system these can be administered by the kernel alone, although in a distributed system they can no longer be kept in a trusted

place. Of course, servers can encrypt capabilities or use passwords to protect them against forgery.

9.5.6 Object Representation

At each level in the system, objects will be defined. These may be files, processes or directions at the higher-level or they may be packets at the IPC level. Usually type information will be passed to indicate the form of translation required with a header/body structure being required. Communication objects can be considered to be either data or control information.

9.6 GLOBAL ISSUES

Important global issues include:

1. What is the relationship between local scheduling and resource allocation on global performance?

2. How and when should objects be moved from node to node?

3. When multiple copies of files exist, how can global consistency be maintained?

4. Are global name servers required?

5. What is the correct layering of the overall system architecture and what are the interfaces?

9.7 REFERENCES

1.   G LeLann, "Motivations, objectives and characterization of distributed systems," pp. 1-9 in *Distributed systems - architecture and implementation. Lecture notes in Computer Science Vol 105*, ed. B W Lampson, M Paul and H J Siegert, Springer-Verlag (1981).

2.   T Anderson and P A Lee, *Fault Tolerance: Principles and Practice,* Prentice-Hall (1981).

3.   R W Watson, "Distributed system architecture model," pp. 10-43 in *Distributed systems - architecture and implementation. Lecture notes in Computer Science Vol 105*, ed. B W Lampson, M Paul and H J Siegert, Springer-Verlag (1981).

4.   ISO, "Reference model of open system interconnection," ISO/TC97/SC16 N 227, International Standards Organisation (1979).

5.   R M Needham and R D H Walker, "The Cambridge CAP computer and its protection system," *Proceedings of the 6th Symposium on Operating System Principles* (1977).

10 Communications

K. H. Bennett

10.1 INTRODUCTION

A physical data link between computers is a prerequisite of many distributed computer system architectures. During the last few years, local area network technologies have provided the means to access a remote computer with latency and transfer rates commensurate with those provided by a local hard disc. Although we shall see in this chapter that higher-level protocols usually hide the implementation details of the physical link layer, the potential communications performance opens up opportunities for cooperative working between computers that would be infeasible with slow links.

In this chapter we shall concentrate on the Cambridge Ring local area network [1, 2]. A brief review of other local area network technologies is presented, but a more detailed description of alternative approaches can be found in [3]. Cambridge Rings are installed in a number of U.K. Universities and companies; components are available commercially; and development is being supported by the UK Science and Engineering Research Council. The Ring work undertaken at the University of Kent is particularly notable both for its pioneering role in a service environment and its contribution to software and hardware products.

We shall adopt a bottom-up presentation of the Cambridge Ring, starting with the physical level and discussing subsequently the design of higher level protocols. Two approaches to protocol design will be described; the first is based upon the adoption of international standards, and the second based upon remote procedure calls. We shall then discuss the performance of the ring, including both theoretical and practical results.

Over the last few years, several variants of the Cambridge Ring have appeared. In an attempt to discourage further divergence, the Science and Engineering Research Council with the Joint Network Team of the Computer Board and Research Councils, have published a recommended standard specification for Ring hardware interfaces and for certain protocols [4, 5]. In this chapter, these recommendations will be described unless stated otherwise.

The Ethernet [6] was developed at Xerox Palo Alto Research Centre from about 1972 onwards; related designs have also appeared e.g. [7]. A cooperative effort involving Digital Equipment Corporation, Intel and Xerox has produced an "Ethernet Specification" [8], in effect as an intended standards proposal. More recently, Subcommittee 3 of IEEE Committee 802 has dealt with what is generally known as "Ethernet". In practice, it is likely that the recommendations of this Subcommittee will be accepted as the standard; for example certain changes proposed by this group have now been adopted in commercial integrated circuit designs.

The Ethernet uses a shared passive communications channel (the "ether") for which stations wishing to transmit must contend. To acquire the ether, a station listens until the ether is quiet (i.e. no other transmissions are in progress), when it immediately begins to transmit. It is possible nevertheless for a collision to occur for two reasons: first an erroneous station may start to transmit at any time; and second, two stations may start to transmit on a quiet ether at approximately the same time. Due to electrical propagation delays, each only detects the collision (by detecting signal distortion) a little later. The maximum time interval is called the collision window. As soon as a collision is detected, the stations abort their transmissions, and each reschedules theirs a pseudo-random interval later. Stations recognize transmissions intended for them by inspecting the packet addresses. Higher level protocols will (as usual) deal with errors, corruption, receiver not listening etc. A number of performance studies and measurements of Ethernets (and Ethernet-like systems) have been undertaken; see for example [9, 10].

Token passing rings represent an important class of networks. A token (usually a distinctive header) circulates a ring-organized network. Any node wishing to transmit must capture the token (i.e. alter the header); it then has exclusive use of the network until it releases the token. Care must be taken to ensure that the loop contains exactly one token.

A further category of network topology is the store and forward mesh. This is more commonly found in wide area networks but can be used locally. An example is a campus network based on X25. Such systems have been installed in several UK Universities, and Universities have contributed to X25 developments. For example, the research group at University College London under Prof. Kirstein was influential in the early design of X25 and implementations were undertaken. At the University of Kent, X25 to Ring gateways were produced, and at the University of York an implementation of X25 under UNIX has been released.

10.2 THE CAMBRIDGE RING

10.2.1 Hardware Mechanisms

At the lowest level, the communications link consists of a number of repeaters connected by a cable, the complete link forming a closed loop (**Figure 10-1**). The cable uses two twisted pairs to carry the signal unidirectionally. The modulation scheme is a form of phase modulation. Each balanced pair carries a nominal rectangular wave; when a change in both signals is present, a logical '1' is indicated, while a change in only one pair indicates a logical '0'. The direction of the change is not relevant, and to avoid long periods of D.C. when sending continuous logical '0's, the single change is alternated between the pairs (**Figure 10-2**).

The data is transmitted at 10Mbits per second, and since each bit is denoted by a change on at least one pair, the modulation code is 'self-clocking', i.e. a 10 MHz clock is carried with the signals. The two twisted pairs operate at a potential difference of 28 volts, which is maintained at several sites around the ring by simple D.C. power supplies. The repeaters obtain their D.C. power from the ring, thereby being independent of the mains supply in the building in which they are housed. The basic operation of the ring is thus ensured as long as sufficient 28V power supplies remain active (**Figure 10-3**).

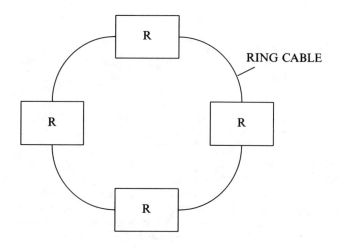

R = REPEATER

Figure 10-1

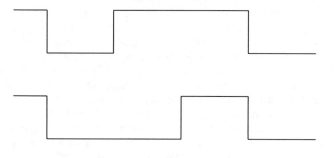

2 changes =   "1"
1 change   =   "0"   - alternating

Rate = 10 Mbits sec^{-1} (self - clocking)

Figure 10-2

At this level, the ring behaves as a large shift register, with storage provided by the cable and repeaters. The repeaters perform two functions: first they regenerate the signals; and second they provide the means of injecting data into the ring and extracting data from it, in demodulated bit-serial form (i.e. NRZ with separate clock). Using ordinary telephone cable, runs of up to 200m between repeaters are possible, although at Keele University the use of high quality signal cable has enabled runs of up to 400m without problems.

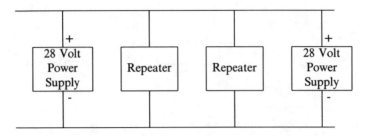

Figure 10-3

A minipacket structure is imposed on the underlying circulating data by stations inter-posed between repeaters and host computers. Data is always transmitted in fixed-length minipackets of 40 bits, and there are a fixed number of minipackets in a ring (deter-mined by the electrical length of the ring installation). A special station called a monitor ensures a clean start-up of the ring, as well as detecting a limited class of errors. A ring will not operate if this critical component fails (so in practice it is important to hold a second monitor station for rapid substitution when problems arise).

10.2.2 Minipacket Operation

Each station in a ring is given a unique integer address in the range 1 to 254. When a station wishes to transmit, it awaits an "empty" minipacket; this minipacket is set to "full", and two bytes of data are inserted. The minipacket travels to the destination where the data is copied (usually) and the minipacket returns to the sender. The transmitting station now sets this minipacket to "empty" again as well as comparing the incoming minipacket contents with that sent out (raising an error if corruption is detected). A station cannot immediately re-use a minipacket and no station can swamp the ring with traffic. In addition, the minipacket after the one just emptied cannot be used either (because the station cannot react to the full/empty bit so soon after the response bits of the previous packet), so for an S-minipacket ring, the maximum point-to-point data rate is $4/(S+2)$ Mbits per second. Note that a transmitter has at most one minipacket in flight at any time. The minipacket structure is :

```
type byte = 0..255;
type minipacket = record
                header : 0..1; {permanently "1"}
                full/empty : 0..1;
                monitor passed : 0..1;
                destination : byte;
                source : byte;
                data high : byte;
                data low : byte;
                response : 0..3;
                type : 0..3;
                parity : 0..1      {even parity}
        end
```

The header bit exists for synchronization purposes. The full/empty bit indicates the state of the minipacket as described above. The ordering of fields is chosen carefully so that minipackets may be transmitted and received "on the fly". The destination byte, as well as the high and low data bytes and the type bits, are filled under program control from the host computer. The source byte is inserted by the transmitting station and may be read at the receiver by the host. Several facilities are included for low-level error detection (e.g. monitor passed and parity bits).

Each station has as part of its receive function a source select register (SSR) which is set under host control to one from three sets of values. The SSR determines, in part, the response of the receiver to an incoming minipacket.

Value	Meaning
0	listen to no-one
1-254	listen to named station
255	listen to all

The response bits in the minipacket indicate the action at the station identified by the 'destination' field as follows

Response bits		Meaning
1	1	ignored (as sent out)
1	0	rejected (due to SSR)
0	1	accepted
0	0	busy

If there is no station with the specified address, the response will be "ignored". Otherwise, if SSR is set to exclude the transmitter the response will be "rejected". Third, the receiver station may not yet have emptied its buffer, and a response of "busy" will be returned. In some station designs, the transmitter will automatically retry the minipacket, with some form of back-off to avoid using excessive ring bandwidth. Finally, the minipacket may be "accepted".

10.2.3 Node Structure

The station provides a parallel data interface to the host computer. Since direct connection is unlikely, an interface unit (sometimes called an access logic unit) is interposed (**Figure 10-4**). Two types of station interface are in common use; these are referred to as "Type 1" and "Type 2" and are distinguished by the details of the electrical signals. The station interface provides signals for both data and gating, so that information required to transmit a minipacket and information from a received packet may be transferred.

The Type 1 interface permits the connection of a typical 8-bit bus-structured minicomputer to a ring station using only a few TTL chips; see for example [11]. The registers of the station are mapped into the address space of the microprocessor allowing simple control from software.

10.3 PROTOCOLS

In distributed computer systems, two approaches to the design of communications protocols are taken. The first follows the route of standardization, and is heavily influenced by the ISO-OSI seven layer model. Thus at the level of the transport layer interface, local area networks will not be distinguishable from wide area networks (apart perhaps from their performance). We shall not consider this approach in detail here; Tanenbaum [12] for example gives a good introduction to the ISO-OSI model and terminology, and [5] shows how the transport level interface [13] may be mapped onto the Cambridge Ring. Also, the ISO protocols have generally been designed to optimize the use of

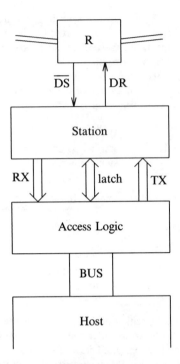

Figure 10-4

networks characterized by low bandwidth, low throughput and high error rate and these protocols may notably and unnecessarily affect performance in a local area network, giving a poor throughput under ideal conditions.

In the second approach, the requirements for a distributed system are identified, and appropriate protocols are designed to fulfil them. An important class of requirements is demanded by inter-process communication and we shall spend some time discussing these. In both approaches, a simple data link level of protocol called "P-layer" protocol is in popular use, so we shall describe this briefly first of all.

10.3.1 P-layer Protocol

The P-layer protocol is derived from an older "Basic Block" protocol which is similar in principle, but differs in detail e.g. in the length of some of the fields. A packet is defined by:

```
type    octet   = 0..255;
type    16-bit  = 0..2^16-1;
type    packet  = record
                  header: 16-bit = Hex 9C99;
                  size:   16-bit;
                  port:   16-bit;
                  data:   [1..size + 1] of octet;
                  pad:    octet; (only if size is even)
                  checksum: 16-bit
                  end
```

The checksum is an end-around-carry sum, not a cyclic redundancy remainder. The semantics of the P-layer packet are "best effort to deliver". Although the returning mini-packets provide a mechanism for flow control and acknowledgement, extra minipackets may erroneously arrive at the receiver; a block may escape the checks of the sumcheck; recognition of headers may present difficulties, and so on.

10.3.2 Inter-process Communication

In a wide class of distributed systems, processes are executed on a collection of computers. It is necessary for the processes to communicate with each other to transmit data and to synchronize. It is not the intention here to discuss process models in distributed systems. However, Lauer and Needham [14] have argued that many operating system designs fall into one of two broad categories: message-passing or procedure-orientated. They then argue that each characteristic of a message-passing system has a dual in the procedure-based system. In this chapter we shall consider in more detail the procedure-orientated model, concentrating in particular on the provision of a remote procedure call (RPC) facility. The discussion will be based heavily on the work of Panzieri and Shrivastava [15, 16] although the scheme described by Blair [17] is also acknowledged. In both cases, distributed operating systems were being constructed on top of an existing local operating system, UNIX [18], which provided a procedure call mechanism to all services. It thus made sense to provide a uniform interface to both local and remote services - in other words to provide a remote procedure call which was indistinguishable from a local call.

Although our description of protocol design is top-down, starting from the requirements to provide an RPC, it is important to note that this can be taken one stage further in the so-called 'end-to-end argument'. Saltzer [19] suggests that efficient protocol designs can only be justified by considering the applications for which they are required. A layered approach may replicate checks in each layer, yet more are required by the application. For example, if a user wishes to read a file, the only message sent to the target site could be a read request. The acknowledgement is implied in the arrival of the requested data. In the LOCUS system [20], the use of protocols based on the above argument is supported by its authors.

10.3.3 Remote Procedure Calls

In this section, the caller is termed the "client" and the called object is termed the "server". An RPC basically involves sending the client's request (the procedure parameters) to the appropriate port identifying the service at the appropriate server. The server performs some work, and later returns the results to the client. During the call, the client's execution is suspended. Issues of naming (i.e. to identify the server/port) are not discussed here; for further details, see for example [21].

A distributed system is characterized by the possibility of partial failure; either the client or the server (or both) may crash during the call. In addition there will in general be errors on the communications link, requiring multiple transmission of the same message. In [16] the reliability requirements are defined:

R1:   The client's request message must include a sequence number which must match that of the corresponding result message (note : all retries of the message contain the same sequence number).

R2:   Sequence numbers must survive node crashes.

The sequence numbering allows the server to detect and reject duplicated messages. Additionally if the client crashes during a call an "orphan" execution continues at the server. In order to effect an 'exactly once' RPC semantics, a third requirement in addition to R1 and R2 must be met:

R3:   A server must detect an orphan, and undo the work done before accepting a new call.

The design in [16] does not meet requirement R3 at the RPC level; instead orphans are handled at a higher level which deals with the atomicity of user programs. The implementation of the RPC is now quite straightforward, using the P-service (for example) of the Cambridge Ring. The semantics are thus "at most once".

The only remaining problem is that of generating sequence numbers. A combination of the unique node number (e.g. ring station address) and the current clock value is suggested; a broadcast algorithm is required to keep clocks in the required degree of synchronization whilst coping with "runaway" clocks. Each node maintains a list of the latest sequence numbers from every active mode.

10.3.4 Multiple Networks

In the previous section, the application level requirement for remote procedure call was provided in terms of the Cambridge Ring P-layer service. A realistic distributed system should not be tied to one network technology, and in the general case there may be more than one network between the client and the server. Different networks may be used to call a different server, and may include local and wide area networks.

Panzieri and Randell have recently [22] proposed an interface for use within UNIX user programs which hides the actual communications protocols used over each network. The approach is of wider interest than UNIX (United) however. At the higher level, remote procedure calls are implemented in terms of lower level network-specific drivers e.g. for X25, simple serial lines, Ethernet etc. The P-level service for the Cambridge Ring also is regarded as a network-specific driver. Each of these lower level drivers has an associated adaptor program which maps the network-specific interface into a single network-independent interface (the kernel interface). Note that at this kernel level, the different networks are still visible, but we now have a single synchronous procedure call mechanism for all of them.

Thus the adaptor interface provides simple primitives for sending and receiving (possibly large) datagrams, using a simple standardized network addressing scheme based on a <host number, port number> pair (**Figure 10-5**).

An attractive feature of the Newcastle design is that it includes a specific well-defined programming interface to the network adaptors. Also, it is a top-down approach in which the various issues are separated and dealt with at different levels. Thus the

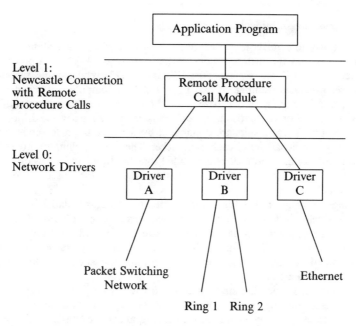

Figure 10-5

application program is concerned with the issue of transaction units and atomicity. The application could employ a server whose actions are idempotent, thus simplifying the handling of orphan servers.

At the next level, the RPC handler provides an 'at most once' call to the remote process, independently of the underlying network. The RPC is implemented in terms of a network-independent datagram service. Communications issues particular to the network are dealt with by the network-specific driver, which also provides a network-specific programming interface. The adaptor then maps the network-independent interface into this. For example, if a network specific driver provides access to an X25 packet switching network, it may incorporate an X25 driver whose interface supports virtual circuits between pairs of host computers. The adaptor for this driver provides to higher levels the abstraction of a uniform datagram service.

Note that the adaptors do not attempt to unify many networks; each network is still visible at the level of service provided by the adaptors, although a single naming convention is used for all networks. A remote service is thus identified by the triple (adaptor, host number, port number).

10.4 PERFORMANCE ISSUES

It was noted at the start of this chapter that high speed local area networks were an "enabling technology" for distributed computer systems. The performance offered in practice by local area networks is thus of considerable importance and has been the subject of a number of studies. The results of some of these concerned especially with the Cambridge Ring are presented in this section. It will become apparent that to measure or model the ring performance in isolation is not of great interest. The characteristics of the hardware and software at the transmitter and receiver must be incorporated in order to achieve results of importance.

10.4.1 Interrupt-per-minipacket Access Logic

The simplest way to connect a host computer to a Cambridge Ring Station is to map the station registers into the memory space of the host (e.g. [11]). All processing of the minipackets is carried out by the host. Brereton [23] reported measurements taken between user processes running on two LSI11/02 host computers attached to a ring by such interfaces. For a block size of 512 bytes, the transfer rate was 1.45 kilobytes/second. For comparison, a local transfer of a similarly sized block gave 26.3 kilobytes/second. These results are dominated by the time taken to service an interrupt from the arrival or departure of each minipacket. The use of polling improves the performance (but not dramatically). It is concluded that hardware and software techniques of commensurate performance to the ring must be used in the hosts to exploit its high speed potential.

Following the above rather discouraging measurements, simulation studies were carried out at Keele [24] to explore the high-performance limitations of the ring. The rationale for the simulation is based on the contention caused not by the ring itself but by the receiver, due to SSR being set. Three queue scheduling policies at the transmitter were investigated : cyclic; longest queue first; and oldest queue first. One queue per destination station was assumed.

It was concluded from the study that the cyclic queue policy is best. For a small number of hosts, the ring should provide a satisfactory communications system even at high demand rates. At low demand rates, the ring under the "basic block" protocol performs an order of magnitude faster than a disc transfer with head movement, under the (possibly unrealistic) assumption that a node can receive at maximum rate.

An alternative strategy at the receiver is to omit setting SSR on receipt of a header. The receiver must then be responsible for inspecting each incoming packet and adding it to an appropriate buffer ("unzipping"). This now introduces contention on a minipacket basis. Singleton and Peake [25] modelled this strategy under the cyclic transmit queue policy. Briefly it was concluded that at low ring utilization there is no significant difference; it is only at very high utilization that the unzipping method becomes superior. However the model did not include any extra overhead for processing the minipacket at the receiver, which may be unrealistic. Additionally, the 'SSR' method is well suited to special hardware support using an outboard processor to implement the P-level protocol; the hardware for the unzipping approach looks much more complex. DMA techniques to handle basic blocks in some form of outboard processor are essential to reach the performance levels suggested in this section. Calculation of the checksum on the fly, repeated retry on "busy" status etc. are relatively straightforward to achieve.

10.4.2 Other Work

In [26] Temple reports on measurements made on the ring installed in the Computing Laboratory at Cambridge, in particular concerning the number of minipackets circulating the ring. In [27], it is argued that the optimum size for minipackets is around 8 bytes, offering a trade-off between an increase in effective bandwidth and fragmentation. It is reported that at Cambridge University a prototype ring provides a means of altering the minipacket size to between 1 and 8 data bytes. Mayne [28] describes a model for Basic Block timeouts, which shows the importance of choosing the values correctly to avoid lock-out.

In [29] a comparison of the performances of the Cambridge Ring and Ethernet is described, based on a simulation model. The protocol assumed the 'Basic Block' scheme described earlier. A Poisson distribution for the message arrival is used, with uniform distribution amongst the receiver stations. Details of the queueing discipline are not given. As with the Keele simulation, blocking actually within the receiver is not modelled, and conventional use of the SSR with the Cambridge Ring is assumed.

The first set of experiments take a 16-byte block and investigate the delay provided for a given offered load. A speed of 10MHz is assumed for both the Ring and Ethernet. The Ring is much less sensitive to the number of stations than Ethernet. Generally however the Ethernet offers lower average delays. In further experiments, the effect of varying the message size is investigated. The Ethernet offers much greater efficiency for the transmission of 128 byte blocks, measured by the average delay time. However for the Ring, the transmission efficiency of 16 byte and 128 byte blocks is almost the same, as measured by the normalized delay (=delay/message length). This is due to the effect of the fixed length 2 byte minipackets.

It is concluded from economic arguments that it is reasonable to compare a 10MHz Ring with a 3MHz Ethernet. It would seem that, according to the model, the mean delay of the Ring is significantly better than that of Ethernet. At Strathclyde University, a local area network configuration has been established [7] which incorporates both a Cambridge Ring and "Strathnet", an Ethernet-like network. This will allow direct comparison of performance, though no results have yet been published.

Work by King and Mitrani [30] on modelling the Cambridge Ring has led to interesting results. The first part of the paper models the basic Ring hardware using a closed loop queueing network with 2 nodes and N jobs, where N = number of stations. The paper discusses appropriate functions for the server, and results from analytical solutions are compared with simulation studies. King and Mitrani also model the Ring at the Basic Block level, again using a closed queuing network. Good agreement is found between the results of this model and a simulation. An interesting comparison is made between the model and a model of a token-passing ring. For a two station Ring, response times are plotted against the coefficient of variation of the message length distribution. The Cambridge Ring has a constant response time, which is worse than the token ring when the coefficient of variation is small, but better for a larger coefficient.

10.5 DEVELOPMENTS

A number of developments of the Cambridge Ring have been proposed, though not all have been published. It is hoped that the Ring station, and repeater can be implemented on a very small number of special purpose chips, thereby reducing the node cost considerably. The technology of the Cambridge Ring (TTL) could be enhanced, and in conjunction with fibre-optic links it is possible that much higher speeds than 10MHz are attainable. The minipacket length could be extended; in one proposal that is understood to be under investigation in Cambridge, the current 40 bit minipacket would coexist alongside "long minipackets" which could be used (for example) to send complete disc blocks. This would move the Ring towards the 'token-passing' type of architecture, which could improve latency and transfer rates for large blocks, though the Ring would lose its attribute of a predictable lower limit on point-to-point bandwidth as well as an upper limit.

As the use of local area networks grows, the problems of internetworking, including connections to wide area networks, become of importance. In the UNIVERSE project [31], several Cambridge Rings in the UK were connected via 1Mbit/second satellite links. At the London site, four rings were used, with inter-ring bridges among them, and also bridges to the PSS and SERCNET wide area networks. For further details of this project, see [32].

10.6 CONCLUSIONS

Attention has been concentrated on local area networks and especially on the Cambridge Ring. A top-down approach to protocol design has been described, motivated by the requirements of a distributed operating system incorporating communicating distributed processes. Other applications may have different requirements (e.g. distributed process control) but the strategy of top-down design may still be valid. An important advantage of this approach is that it has kept network-dependent issues separate from network-independent issues. However the applications have all been concerned with homogeneous systems. The problem of heterogeneous linked systems is regarded as another separate issue, which layers 5 to 7 of the ISO-OSI model address; they have not been considered in this chapter.

The top-down approach does not however argue that the method of communication is irrelevant and that performance can be ignored. If the high bandwidth of current technologies (let alone higher speed derivatives) is to be exploited fully, the performance of all communications hardware and software must be considered. This remains a challenging development area.

10.7 REFERENCES

1.   M. V. Wilkes and D. J. Wheeler, "The Cambridge Digital Communications Ring," *Local Area Comms. Network Symp.*, Mitre Corp. and National Bureau of Standards (May 1979).

2.   R. Needham, "System Aspects of the Cambridge Ring," *ACM Seventh Symp. on Operating Systems Principles*, pacific Grove, California (December 1979).

3.   B. K. Penny and A. A. Baghdadi, "Survey of Computer Communications Networks," Research Report 78/42, Imperial College of Science and Technology, London (1978).

4.   W. P. Sharpe and A. R. Cash , *Cambridge Ring 82 Interface Specifications,* Science and Engineering Research Council, Rutherford Appleton Laboratory (1982).

5.   J. Larmouth (Ed.), *Cambridge Ring 82 Protocol Specifications,* Joint Network Team, Science and Engineering Research Council, Rutherford Appleton Laboratory, (1982).

6.   R. M. Metcalfe and D. R. Boggs, "Ethernet: Distributed Packet Switching for Local Computer Networks," *Comms. A. C. M.* **19**(7) (July 1976).

7.   D. Hutchinson and W. D. Shepherd, "Strathnet - A Local Area Network," *Software & Microsystems* **1**(1) (October 1981).

8.   Ethernet, *The Ethernet, A Local Area Network: Data Link Layer and Physical Layer specifications, Version 1.0,* Xerox Corporation Inc. (September 30, 1980).

9.   G. J. Almes and E. D. Lazowska, "The Behaviour of Ethernet-like Computer Communication Networks," *Proc. Seventh ACM Symp. on Operating Systems Principles*, pp.61-81 (December 1979).

10. J. F. Shoch and J. A. Hupp, "Measured Performance of an Ethernet Local Area Network," *Comms. A. C. M.* **23**(12), pp.711-721 (December 1980).

11. K. H. Bennett and P. Singleton, "A Simple Access Logic for the Cambridge Ring," *J. Microcomputer Applications* **to appear** (1984).

12. A. S. Tanenbaum, *Computer Networks,* Prentice Hall , Englewood Cliffs, NJ (1981).

13. British Telecom PSS User Forum (Study Group 3), *A Network Independent Transport Service,* Data Communication Protocols Unit, Department of Industry (Feb. 1980.).

14. H. C. Lauer and R. M. Needham, "On the Duality of Operating System Structures," *Operating Systems Review* **13**(2), ACM (April 1979).

15. S. K. Shrivastava and F. Panzieri, *The Design of a Reliable Remote Procedure Call Mechanism,* IEEE Trans. Computers (1982).

16. F. Panzieri and S. K. Shrivastava, "Reliable Remote Calls for Distributed UNIX: an Implementation Study," *Proc. 2nd. Symp. on Reliability in Distributed Software and Database systems,* pp.127-133, Pittsburgh (July 1982).

17. G. S. Blair, "Distributed Operating System Structures for Local Area Network based Systems," *Ph. D. Thesis,* University of Strathclyde (1983).

18. D. M. Ritchie and K. Thompson, "The UNIX Time-sharing System," *Comm. ACM* **17**(7), pp.365-375 (July 1974).

19. J. Saltzer, D. Reed, and D. Clark, "End-to-end Arguments in System Design," *Notes from IEEE Workshop on Fundamental Issues in Distributed Systems,* Pala Mesa, IEEE (1980).

20. G. Popek, B. Walker, J. Chow, D. Edwards, C. Kline, G. Rudisin, and G. Thiel, "LOCUS: A Network Transparent, High Reliability Distributed System," *ACM Operating Systems Review* **15**(5), pp.169-177 (1981).

21. D. R. Brownbridge, L. F. Marshall, and B. Randell, "The Newcastle Connection or UNIXes of the World Unite!," *Software - Practice & Experience* **12**, pp.1147-1162 (1982).

22. F. Panzieri and B. Randell, "Interfacing UNIX to Data Communications Networks," SRM/354, Computing Laboratory, University of Newcastle upon Tyne (July 1983).

23. O. P. Brereton, "Performance Figures for Message-passing over a Cambridge Ring," *Software - Practice & Experience* **12**(1) (January 1982).

24. K. Lunn and K. H. Bennett, "Message Transport on the Cambridge Ring - A Simulation Study," *Software - Practice & Experience* **11**, pp.711-716 (1981).

25. P. Singleton and P. J. Peake, "Simulation of the Low-level Behaviour of the Cambridge Ring," *Report of the Cambridge Ring Modelling & Simulation Special Interest Group,* pp.3-5(e), Univ. of Cambridge, (UK Science & Engineering Research Council) (April 1981).

26. S. Temple, "Measurements on the Cambridge Ring," *Report of the Cambridge Ring Modelling & Simulation Special Interest Group,* pp.11-12(j), Univ. of Cambridge, (UK Science & Engineering Research Council) (April 1981).

27. G. S. Blair, "A Performance Study of the Cambridge Ring," *Computer Networks* **6**(1) (February 1982).

28. A. J. Mayne, "A Simple Model of Multi-station Time-outs on a Ring using the Basic Block Protocol and Byte Stream Protocol," INDRA Note 1002, Department of Computer Science, University College London (March 1981).

29. G. S. Blair and D. Shepherd, "A Performance Comparison of Ethernet and the Cambridge Ring Digital Communication Ring," *Computer Networks* **6**(2) (May 1982).

30. P. J. B. King and I. Mitrani, "Modelling the Cambridge Ring," *Performance Evaluation Review* **11**(4), pp.250-258 (1982).

31. P. T. Kirstein and S. R. Wilbur, "The UNIVERSE Project," *IUCC Bulletin* **5**(2), pp.86-90 (Summer 1983).

32. C. J. Adams et al, "Protocol Architecture of the UNIVERSE Project," *Proc. Int. Computer Comms. Conf.*, pp.379-383, ONLINE, (several other papers in these Proceedings are concerned with UNIVERSE) (1982).

11 Distributed Filestores

K. H. Bennett

11.1 MOTIVATION

In any computer system, secondary storage performs three key functions, as a repository for data, as an extension of main memory and as a means of inter-user communication. The user view (how it performs, how reliable it is, for example) is critical to the success not only of the filestore but of the whole system. This is no less true of a distributed computer system than of a single stand-alone machine. The ability on one machine to access a file stored on another is often considered to be an important facility of a distributed system.

We shall begin this chapter by defining terms and then discussing important issues in filestore design. We shall then examine several filestore designs representing different approaches and emphases. The general issue of reliability will receive particular attention. The early sections of this chapter and the description of the Keele filestore are largely based on [1].

11.1.1 Filestores, Fileservers and Files

A *filestore* will be considered as a repository for data, providing a mnemonic (user-arbitrary) naming scheme for files. There will be some means of protecting data from unauthorized access, plus some means of allowing clients of a shared file to ensure consistent update of data. A *file* will be taken to be a user-arbitrary sequence of bytes which is stored by the filestore under a given name (or names), and not interpreted by the filestore.

A *fileserver* will be taken to mean a repository, where files can be stored, and which provides an index address for files contained in it. This address may contain authorization information. A *directory server* will provide a mapping from user-arbitrary mnemonics to the fileserver index, and provide data protection, perhaps using any authorization facilities provided by the fileserver.

11.1.2 Naming

The naming of files in a filestore (and in a fileserver) is an issue of great importance; many of the new problems in a distributed filestore are concerned with naming. In this section the basic concepts are introduced, using the approach of [2].

A *name* is an identifier, typically a character string or integer, used to refer to an object. An object may have more than one name; a name may refer to more than one object but this can lead to ambiguities which must be resolved in practice. A *context* is defined as a mapping from a set of names to a set of objects. A common example is a directory in a UNIX-style filestore which maps filenames to files. A context may well map a name to another context. For example, a directory in a filestore may name other directories, often referred to as subdirectories. In this case we have a naming network. This allows reference to an object indirectly via a path name. A *path name* is a sequence of names, where all but the last name is the name of a context; this is illustrated by the UNIX filestore, where /usr/fs/keith/myfile refers to the file myfile in the directory /usr/fs/keith. If there is a particular context in a naming network from which all objects can be named then that context is called a *root*. The instantiation of a mapping in a context is called *binding*. The time at which binding is performed has a large impact on the properties of the system. A *static binding*, applied when the object is declared, is often efficient, but restricts relocation and other system changes. *Dynamic binding* is performed when the object is used allowing greater flexibility but at the cost of applying the binding at each use. Since several contexts may be involved in the mapping of a name to the eventual object, a spectrum of binding possibilities exists.

By an *address*, we mean a name which is system generated. Intuitively, an address refers to the location of an object, but this is not always the case. An example of an address in UNIX is an i-node number, which refers to a file on disc. The i-node number itself is not sufficient to locate the data in a file and it is necessary to use the i-list as a mapping from i-node to blocks of data on the disc. The i-node number is not usually referred to directly by a user, but is obtained from a directory which maps names to i-node numbers. In practice the implementation of a context, such as a directory in a filestore, may not provide a direct mapping from name to object, but from name to address (which is but another name). That address may have to be interpreted in another context in order to access the object. For example, UNIX directories map names to i-nodes, which in turn map to files.

There is widespread use of the idea of a *unique identifier* (example: a CPU serial number). A unique identifier is a name in a single global context which names all objects in the system. Its advantage is that it provides an unambiguous way of identifying any object in the system. Typically, a unique identifier is a fixed length integer chosen to be large enough to exceed the number of objects ever likely to be created by the system.

Shoch [3] has further categorized identifiers into names, addresses and routes. A name refers to an object; an address refers to its location; a route refers to the means of finding the address once we know what it is.

At a given layer in the architecture of a system, contexts can be hierarchical or flat (unique identifier). The latter is simple, but there are problems in a distributed system of generating system-wide unique identifiers. (How does one ensure that the serial numbers of CPUs are indeed unique?). Context tables can become very large. Hierarchical contexts have an important advantage in that they are readily extensible.

11.1.3 Protection

In a system which is shared among a number of users, the issue of data protection is important. Individuals should be limited to the data they are permitted to access. This is to prevent reading of confidential data, to prevent inadvertent update of another person's data or, in extreme circumstances, to prevent malicious update of another person's data.

11.1.4 Consistency

A filestore is said to be *consistent* if it satisfies a set of conditions called *consistency constraints*. These constraints are arbitrarily chosen, but intuitively state that the filestore (or database) behaves sensibly. Consistency constraints can be considered to form part of the specification of the filestore. It is often the case that a filestore must pass through inconsistent states. For example, a transfer of money between accounts may leave a ledger file inconsistent between the times of debiting one account and crediting of the other.

To overcome this, operations are usually grouped into "logical transactions" which are similar to atomic actions with the added property that they transform the filestore from one consistent state to another. Atomicity includes the property that an operation succeeds completely, or has no effect at all, so that inconsistent intermediate states are not important (the recoverability property). A second atomicity property ("serializability") is that two independent transactions operating on the same data concurrently will have the same effect as if one transaction had completed operations on the data before the other commenced. Techniques to implement atomic transactions are discussed later.

11.2 ISSUES IN DISTRIBUTED FILESTORE DESIGN

11.2.1 Data Placement

If the distributed filestore consists of a fileserver on a single computer then data placement is simply concerned with disc space management. In a filestore in which data is (in some way) spread across several linked computers, mechanisms must be designed to place data according to some policy decision. For example, the optimization of performance is a sensible objective which might be met by trying to keep a process and its data as "near" as possible to each other. However, physical proximity is not necessarily an adequate definition of nearness. On a high speed local area network, accessing a remote file may be little slower than a local file, and there is unlikely to be much difference in accessing two files on two similar remote nodes. Where the physical network provides significant delay either on latency or on transmission rate, then a distinction between local and remote is useful. A further aspect of performance could be the relative loading on the nodes which contain the filestore. If two copies of a file exist, it would be advantageous to access the file copy on the node with the lesser loading.

Reliability may be achieved by holding multiple copies of files; it is then necessary to place files in such a way as to minimize the likelihood of loss and to maximize availability. There is clearly no sense in placing two copies of a file on the same volume if it is possible to split them across two volumes. If volumes are on distinct nodes, then all the better.

11.2.2 Consistency

There are a number of consistency constraints that one might place on a filestore:

1. Any two copies of the same file shall appear to be identical to a user.

2. Any process which does not successfully complete an operation on a file shall have no effect on the contents of the file.

3. Between user-generated operations on a file, the contents of the file shall not change.

4. Two independent concurrent operations on the same file shall be serializable.

The first constraint is clearly vital. At worst, a user process ought to be informed if two copies of a file are not identical, but then the process is left with a difficult decision. The second constraint implies some form of recoverable atomic action or transaction. The third point might well be an integrity constraint (i.e. the system models the real world). The fourth point again implies some form of atomic transaction.

In a distributed system, which can exhibit partial failures, the second and fourth constraints are of overriding importance. It is interesting to note that several centralized filestores, notably UNIX, do not guarantee either.

Verhofstad [4] has written a useful review of recovery techniques in database systems; most of these use replicated copies of data either in full or in the form of side files, audit trails etc.

11.2.3 Shared Access

Users need to share data storage for reasons of economy. However, much more fundamental is the need to access and update shared data due to cooperative working, i.e. the data is used for communication between users. Two important issues must be resolved, namely the protection of data from illegal access and the control of concurrent accesses.

The former problem may be alleviated by holding purely personal data physically separate from shared data. Nevertheless a mechanism to protect confidential shared data should also cope with personal data. Two approaches to protection are feasible: we can protect the interface, and we can protect access to the data. Interface protection is difficult in a distributed system where malicious users may tap the communication line. This may require encryption techniques, but implemented at the user level rather than as an integral part of the filestore. Davies [5] gives further details of cryptography. Discussion of the protection of the access to data is also based on this source. We postulate a set of objects O_i to be protected, and a set of subjects S_j who wish to access objects. A matrix A is set up such that A_{ij} contains the access rights of subject j to object i (**Figure 11-1**).

An entry A_{ij} may contain rights such as read, write, execute, change rights etc. It is impractical to store the matrix as such in a computer as it is very sparse, so techniques must be adopted of representing it compactly yet allowing fast lookup.

A column in the matrix represents what is termed the access control list of that object. In practice, the list (of subjects) can be stored in association with the object and checked on access. Thus each subject S_j must have a unique identifier, which (as we have seen) is difficult to accomplish in a distributed system. In UNIX, only three subjects for a file are recognized: the owner, the group and everyone else.

A row corresponding to one subject represents the capabilities of that subject. When a subject requires access to some object, it presents a capability for the object which is then checked for validity. The checking is simple since no extra data is required.

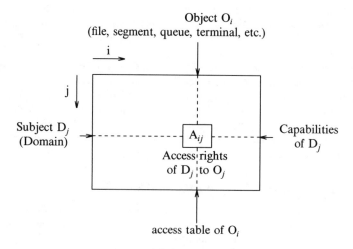

Figure 11-1

However, capabilities must not be forgeable, and although this is often accomplished in centralized systems by tagging the address, in distributed systems some form of encryption may be used instead.

Filestore facilities and protection are separate issues, in the sense that access control mechanisms should not make the filestore restricted in application nor intolerable to users. For example, filestores which attempt to provide protection by limitations on naming tend to be unsatisfactory in practice.

11.2.4 Shared Update

The problems of implementing serializable and recoverable atomic transactions are described in the next section. We note here that serializability requires some method of implementing mutually exclusive access to files, and a common method of doing this is by means of a lock. Before a process accesses a file it must lock that file, and on completion of the activities of that file, unlock it. One problem with locks is that of deadlock. Another problem is how to deal with a process which does not relinquish a lock, either by oversight or because of some partial failure. Performance can be degraded because concurrency is limited. In a loosely coupled system the detection of such problems is not easy.

11.2.5 Naming

The naming scheme for files and contexts depends very much on the style of secondary storage required. The provisions of the Cambridge fileserver, and the UNIX United filestore (two systems reviewed later) are very different. In this section we shall concentrate on filestores, because of the extra requirements posed by file sharing.

The naming in a filestore is largely for the benefit of users of the system. The naming is typically mnemonic, and ideally arbitrary strings of characters should be permitted (though practical limitations often exist). Apart from allowing individual users to retrieve files, the naming scheme should allow users to share files. This means that any file can be accessed (via a global context) by any user on the system. UNIX achieves this by allowing any user to use the pathname of any file in the system. The separate access control mechanism is used to provide protection. A useful facility of a filestore is the ability to switch contexts. For example, if user1 wishes to access the files of user2, it is useful if user1 can use the same names (i.e. the same context) as user2.

Two possible ways of implementing a filestore are discussed by [2]. The first technique effectively requires access to a file for read and write using the filename each time. The second technique, called "direct access", is to use the name of a file to obtain an address, and that address is used for accessing the contents of the file. The choice of technique depends on a number of issues in the design of the system. The direct access method is most common (e.g. it is used in UNIX). However the address must remain valid during the period of activity of the file. Finally, any dependency of a file name on its location (or on the client) is highly undesirable.

11.3 REVIEW OF DISTRIBUTED FILESTORES

In this section we describe three different approaches to providing filing facilities in a distributed computing system. The first of these, the Cambridge fileserver [6, 7], is motivated by application in a server-based operating system. It is used, for example, in the Cambridge Model Distributed System (CMDS) [8, 9]. Briefly the fileserver must provide a service to a range of clients' machines which do not necessarily wish to operate identical filestores, and may not possess their own discs. The machines in the CMDS are connected via a Cambridge Ring network.

The second system to be described is the UNIX United system developed at Newcastle University. This is an homogeneous environment, in that all machines support the UNIX version 7 kernel interface. The literature contains a number of examples of attempts to link UNIX machines, in particular their filestores. UNIX United is probably the most elegant of these.

The third system is the KUDOS filestore developed at Keele University. This has different objectives again, stressing the increase in availability that potentially can be gained through the redundancy that is often present in distributed systems. Thus files may be kept as multiple copies, but algorithms must be incorporated to ensure consistency between them.

11.4 THE CAMBRIDGE FILESERVER

11.4.1 Operations

The design objectives of this fileserver include high speed transfer to random-access word-addressed files, and a high degree of crash resistance. Objects stored are either files or indices, each identified by a unique identifier (UID) which is 64 bits long including 32 "random" bits. A file is a sequence of 16-bit words on which random-access read and write operations are available to clients. Note that the fileserver keeps no state information between operations (apart from the files and indices of course). An index is a list of UIDs, on which preserve, retrieve and delete operations are available. Finally files and indices may be created.

Naming in the fileserver is in terms of UIDs; moreover a client can set up a general directed storage graph where nodes are files and indices. Thus there is a single global context in which file UIDs are unique, but it is implemented by stepping through indices whose UIDs are known. The UID is also used as a capability for protecting access to files and indices. A client must remember the UID of the node given as its root;

subsequently the client may construct directed graphs and exchange UIDs with others knowing only this root UID. No delete operations are provided in the fileserver. A special system "root" index is designated and a periodic asynchronous garbage collector is invoked [10] to remove all objects not accessible from root. If a client wishes to use its own naming scheme (e.g. a UNIX-style directory scheme) it may do so in terms of the fileserver interface. The fileserver itself has no knowledge of this higher level structure. Thus UNIX directories would be implemented using files.

11.4.2 Crash Recovery

A single write operation can cause changes to many data and map blocks, and failure part way through can leave the storage in an inconsistent state (note that transactions involving more than one fileserver operation are the responsibility of the client). When a file is created, it is defined by the client to be normal or special. In the former case no provision is made for recovery; update may be in place. Special files in the Cambridge fileserver are updated using an "intentions list" mechanism [11] which permits a single operation comprised of several block operations to be carried out atomically. The block allocation tables for special files contain the following state information:

    i) allocated/deallocated

    ii) intending to allocate/intending to deallocate

The intentions list algorithm is:

```
for all blocks to be updated do
        choose a deallocated block and mark it "intending to allocate";
        change old block to "intending to deallocate";
        write to the new block
od;
set commit bit; {on stable storage}
for all relevant blocks do
        change all intending to allocate blocks to "allocated";
        change all intending to deallocate blocks to "deallocated"
od;
reset commit bit;
```

Up to the setting of the commit bit, all changes can be done. After setting the commit bit, the changes will be done (eventually). On a crash, the commit bit indicates whether to go forward or back. In the forward case, all "intending" blocks must be definitely allocated or deallocated. Clearly a crash part way through setting the commit bit or intention bits will invalidate the above algorithm. The fileserver uses a form of stable storage (see Chapter 12) comprising map blocks and cylinder blocks. Should one or other be unreadable, it can be reconstituted from the other. Various performance optimizations are described, for example holding a modest cache of frequently used disc blocks which tends to favour the retention of cylinder and objects map blocks.

11.4.3 Conclusions

The fileserver combines high performance with a simple interface. Under light loading conditions, typical access times for a 512 byte block in a file are 50 milliseconds (read) and 65 milliseconds (write) including communications overheads. Matters of locking are left to clients.

The Xerox WFS system (e.g. [12, 13]) is not dissimilar from the Cambridge fileserver; a comparative review is given in [14]. The Xerox DFS [11] is implemented on a cooperating set of server computers, and to give the illusion of a single logical system, the additional complexity of multiple server operations must be catered for. The DFS provides special operations as well for start transaction and end transaction, between which there may be more than one simple file operation involving multiple clients.

11.5 UNIX UNITED

The UNIX United system [15] is much more than just a distributed filestore. In this chapter we shall concentrate on the filestore aspects. Before examining the system itself, we shall discuss the notion of recursive structuring which has in part motivated the UNIX United development [16]. Several other systems incorporate linked UNIX machines; see for example [17, 18, 19, 20, 21, 22, 23, 24, 25].

11.5.1 Recursively Structured Distributed Systems

The basic thesis of Randell's paper is that a distributed computing system should be functionally equivalent to the individual computing systems of which it is composed. Thus UNIX United, which is composed of several UNIX systems, aims to be functionally equivalent to a conventional UNIX system. All the standard UNIX features including naming, protecting and accessing devices, files and directories are provided. Hence issues of inter-processor communication are completely hidden from users and programs.

Randell emphasizes the distinction between recursive structuring and "flat transparency". We shall illustrate this by comparing the UNIX United naming scheme for files with that of the Apollo system [26]. Both are based upon UNIX.

Figure 11-2 shows a typical UNIX name space. Files are named relative to either of two movable "pointers", the current root and the current working directory. If the root is "/" and the current working directory is keith, then /fs/cs/keith/x and x both refer to the same file, using a pathname scheme as described earlier. Also the convention ".." is

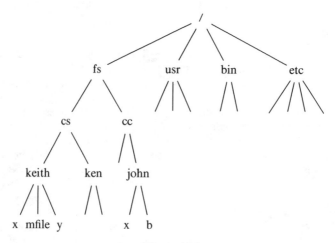

Figure 11-2

used to indicate the parent of a context, so ../../cc/john/x and /fs/cc/john/x name the same file. To construct a larger system out of several such name spaces, the above properties (with others) must be unchanged. **Figure 11-3** shows a UNIX United name space. This larger namespace is constructed from **Figure 11-2**, and two subtrees "bung" and "bbc". This in fact is the UNIX United namespace that is used at Keele University and bung and bbc correspond to specific hardware systems. (this need not be the case however). Thus files on the bbc machine can be referred to from bung, assuming a root directory pointer at bung, by e.g. /../bbc/bin/who. The systems at Newcastle and Keele could be united, say, as shown in **Figure 11-4** so that a user on bbc could access a file at Newcastle using the name /../../Newcastle/U1/bin/date.

In the Apollo Domain system, a special system-wide root, designated by // provides a single global context for UNIX system names, e.g. as shown in **Figure 11-5**.

The name // provides an absolute starting point so that e.g. //machine1/bin/who uniquely identifies the named file. Clearly extra machines (or UNIX namespaces) can be added to the Apollo system. However two separate Apollo systems cannot be linked so that they function as one; a single // is required (two machines must have unique names).

11.5.2 Naming

The major requirement in a recursively structured system is that all names are context-relative. There is no such thing as an absolute name since this would conflict with the ability to extend the namespace. Today's base directory is tomorrow's subdirectory in some larger namespace. It is thus evident why UNIX has proved a suitable system for a recursively structured distributed system. The hierarchical file naming scheme makes it easy to combine systems without name clashes. Standard mechanisms for file protection and controlled sharing of files carry over directly (although the problem of user identifiers must be recognized and solved). The use of relative addressing, based on movable current working and root directories is of particular importance.

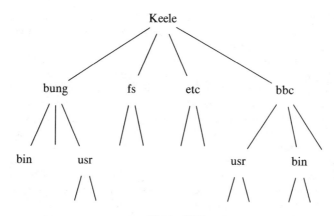

Figure 11-3

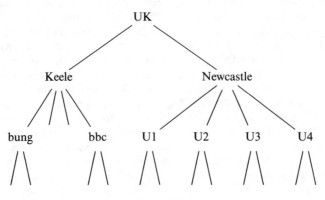

Figure 11-4

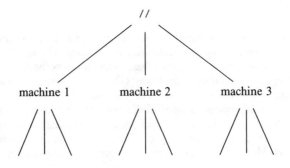

Figure 11-5

11.5.3 Implementation

UNIX United is implemented by imposing an extra layer of software, called the Newcastle Connection, between the kernel on each participating system and the rest of the operating system as in **Figure 11-6**.

System calls (to the kernel) are intercepted; those that are to be handled locally are passed to the local kernel, while those that are to be handled remotely are passed to the appropriate machine. To user and operating system programs this is invisible; put differently, no changes to existing user and operating system programs are required to participate in a UNIX United system. The Connection layer is implemented as a library, and programs using system calls are relinked to that library (programs not so linked therefore are purely local).

The mechanism used for the inter-machine communication is the remote procedure call described earlier. On a remote machine, a spawner process, which runs continuously, initially receives an "open file" request and spawns a fileserver process as a result. Subsequently the originator communicates directly with the fileserver, using the name returned by the spawner. When the file is opened the Connection makes an entry in a per-process table indicating whether or not the file descriptor (an integer used to refer to the file between open and close calls) refers to a local or remote file. This table also holds the corresponding remote node addresses, so that at a read or write, remote

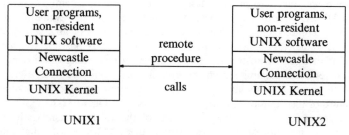

UNIX1

UNIX2

Figure 11-6

accesses are routed immediately.

11.5.4 Other Issues

Protection in UNIX United uses the facilities provided by UNIX. Each system has its own list of approved users, set up by the system manager. In a UNIX United system, a manager must decide additionally on a list of permitted remote users, together with a mapping from remote to local name. Remote and local user names are not confused. No new mechanisms are introduced for shared access to files. Work is proceeding at Newcastle to implement a triple modular redundancy layer, and primitives to support atomic transactions, above the UNIX kernel, but few details are yet available.

The performance of UNIX United is difficult to quantify, and little numeric information is available. The system at Keele University consists of three PDP/LSI11 type machines connected by a Cambridge Ring. Recompilation of programs to link in the Connection library increases the code space, sometimes by a few Kbytes. Access to local facilities seems unimpaired. The time taken for a remote operation would appear to be dominated at Keele by the limitations of the Cambridge Ring access logic hardware on each host. In qualitative terms, the Connection was accepted with great enthusiasm by users at Keele, who were happy to put up with the communication delays because of the extra facilities offered.

The confluence of the recursive structuring principle and UNIX results in a distributed filestore which, at Keele at least, has proved highly successful in a Computer Science user environment. The decision of the UNIX United designers to retain the UNIX Version 7 kernel interface as their "standard" means that the system is straightforward to bring up on a machine which conforms to this interface. The Connection layer then deals with the issue of "distributedness".

Finally, we note that certain nodes could offer specialised UNIX services - fileservers, terminal switches etc., by offering just the appropriate kernel calls.

11.6 THE KEELE DISTRIBUTED FILESTORE

The project at Keele (called KUDOS) had complementary objectives to the two systems described earlier. An important aim was to explore the costs and benefits of using redundancy - and in particular multiple file copies - to achieve high reliability and availability of file service. The main part of the design is thus a distributed directory system, which uses one or more fileservers to construct a filestore of greater reliability than its components. A fileserver provides the ability to create, delete, read and write random-access rows of bytes. Protection is by means of capabilities. Any pointers within a file must be kept by clients. Unlike the Cambridge fileserver there are no atomic operations.

Rather such matters are regarded as the responsibilities of clients.

The decision was taken to provide a sensible text naming scheme along the lines of that used in UNIX. Additionally it was decided to increase the availability of files by holding multiple copies of them. Thus a named file is a level of abstraction at which a single object is actually implemented as several copies. It is possible to hide multiple copies at different levels of abstraction (for example by replicating disc drives on a controller). However a text naming scheme permits sharing readily between users, and there is a strong incentive to hold the multiple copies on different machines if possible.

The structure of the filestore as a whole is described by **Figure 11-7**.

The name server is an important component of the Keele system. It implements a mapping from a logical namespace to a network address. Although the diagram shows it as a single process, a distributed algorithm is used (full details are given in [27]). Logical names include volume names and directory managers but not files.

The directory server implements a mapping from file names to volume/file identifier pairs. A file name may refer to a number of copies and the directory server resolves

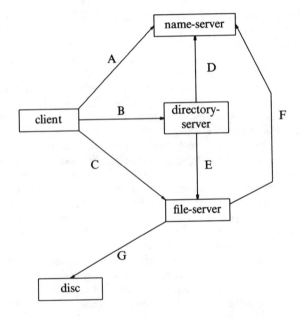

A	-	locate directory-server
B	-	locate/add/delete files
C	-	file I/O, file creation/deletion
D	-	catalogue location of directory-server
E	-	file I/O, file creation/deletion
		(for storage of directories and copies of files)
F	-	catalogue location of volumes
G	-	physical I/O

Figure 11-7

inconsistencies between copies of the same file.

11.6.1 The Directory System

KUDOS provides a system-wide single hierarchical filestore; the naming scheme is similar to that of UNIX (without links). A root directory exists, which is replicated in all volumes. The root directory contains subdirectories (not necessarily replicated on all volumes). Each subdirectory can have subdirectories of its own. All directories can also contain files. To access a file, it is necessary to "activate" all directories in the path to that file. Activation of a directory involves creating a process to handle operations on files in that directory. Such a process is called a directory manager, and is created on behalf of a client by the parent directory's manager. The manager of root is permanently active. The manager of a directory is responsible for all operations on files in that directory, for ensuring consistency of file copies and for deactivating itself. Also it is responsible for multiple client access to the directory. Only one manager is allowed to exist for any one directory at one time.

We shall call the *active filestore* the hierarchy of directories and their contained files which have currently active managers. The dormant filestore is all the rest. Files can only be accessed through the active filestore. It is only necessary to ensure that the active filestore is consistent and up-to-date. Inconsistencies can be permitted in a dormant part of the filestore until that part is activated. It is likely that only a small fraction of the filestore will be active at any time.

11.6.2 Replication Management

Each directory has a set of *associated volumes*, which are exactly those volumes on which any file or subdirectory in that directory is replicated. The set of associated volumes of a directory must be a subset of the associated volumes of its parent directory. Thus the root directory has, as its associated volumes, all volumes in the system (see **Figure 11-8**). A command interpreter could hide the details of the associated volumes if required, simply offering different levels of reliability (possibly at different costs). The above scheme is called "overlay mount" to distinguish it from the UNIX-style subtree mount.

The notation x(v1v2) means that file or directory x has associated volumes v1 and v2. Thus a volume contains the full path name to any files stored on it, and if the volume is

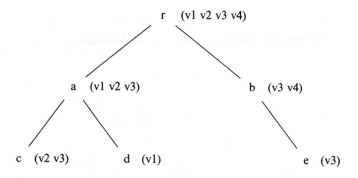

Figure 11-8

active, all files with copies held by it are accessible. Volumes are thus independent of one another and this is the basic mechanism for achieving high availability. Mounting a volume is straightforward; its name must be identified to the name server. The directory manager detects its presence and acts accordingly.

11.6.3 Directory Resolution

We assume temporarily a strictly increasing timestamp universally available throughout the system (this problem is discussed in more detail in Chapter 12). When a file is stored through the directory system, the filename plus a timestamp are stored in each copy of the directory. On activation all on-line copies of the directory are inspected and any out-of-date file copies are identified using their timestamps. All copies are brought up-to-date by copying files (and timestamps). A problem can occur when a file is deleted from one copy of a directory while another copy is off-line. An "assassin" is placed in the directory entry in this case, together with a timestamp. The entry can then be removed when the volume comes on-line and the directory is activated. Since only one manager for a directory is permitted in KUDOS, provided that manager always consults the same clock, and that clock is accurate to a few seconds, there should be no problems of timestamping. In KUDOS a clock was simulated by a simple counter incremented on each read.

11.6.4 Other Features

The basic protection mechanism used is capabilities; users may also provide a read and write capability on file creation. A simple mapping can be provided (by clients) from a mnemonic password to a capability.

The directory scheme provides a multiple readers or single writer type of locking. A lock will timeout unless refreshed; this is the mechanism for deadlock breaking. A lock is on a whole file.

11.6.5 Results

Suppose that a disc is on-line with probability p. If discs are independent, and if there are n copies of a file, the probability that the file is available in KUDOS is:

$$1-(1-p)^n$$

This of course ignores faults in other parts of the system. If C is the probability that the communications system is working, and N is the probability that a node is operating, then the file is available with probability

$$1-(1-pNC)^n.$$

The KUDOS system was implemented on two LSI11/02 machines, with two UCSD Pascal workstations acting as clients. The communication mechanism was a Cambridge Ring network. The performance of this scheme was totally dominated by hardware limitations, so performance was analysed in terms of disc accesses and messages passed. The consistency algorithms are O(N) in time, where N = number of file copies.

KUDOS constructs a virtual filestore from several physical fileserver machines. More recently at Keele, Brereton has been using the "overlay mount" concept to provide highly available files in UNIX United. A replication layer is interposed above the Newcastle Connection but below user and operating system code. System calls are intercepted; if they do not involve replicated files, they are passed to the Connection layer below. If the call is an operation on a replicated file, the layer carries out the required actions, using the facilities provided by the Connection to access both local and remote resources transparently. The layer thus maps a single user textname onto several UNIX United textnames. A majority consensus algorithm is used to vote on replicated operations. It is envisaged (but not yet implemented) that the name tree supporting highly available files could form part of a larger UNIX United name tree. Users access all the name space in a unified way. This does not of course mean that the files are highly available to "remote" users (since there will probably be unreliable components interposed). For further details see [28, 29].

11.7 OTHER WORK

This chapter has examined three different solutions to providing filestores in a distributed computing system, based on the design issues outlined in section 11.2. There are, of course, a number of other filestore projects of interest as well as those referenced in the text. An example is the Network Filing System developed at Edinburgh University [30]. This provides a coherent filing system to client processes, using a UNIX-style textnaming scheme. The filing system will typically incorporate several servers. Consistency of files is preserved across concurrent access and server crashes; this is accomplished by an atomic transaction mechanism which uses a two-phase commit tailored to the requirements of a file store. The reference also includes an excellent review.

The Felix file server [31] has as its principal aims the support of workstation virtual memory, the sharing of data and the secure storage of data. In the referenced paper only the "first layer" of services is described; higher level facilities such as a conventional file system with user defined directories are not discussed but are promised for the future. However a set of locking and begin/commit/end transaction management primitives are provided. Careful replacement is used to provide atomic updates on files; no stable storage is used.

The Swallow project [32] at M.I.T. contains interesting ideas for reliable data storage, especially concerning transaction management. The "data repository", possibly distributed over several machines, is designed to offer long term reliable storage and to support sharing of data amongst a distributed system of highly autonomous machines. Atomic transactions are permitted which can update data stored on several machines. Each client machine must run a program called a "broker" which mediates all accesses to data in the repositories. The data repository is designed so that the principal long term storage can be provided by (write-once) optical discs. Tanenbaum [33] describes the Amoeba distributed system incorporating a directory system which provides UNIX-style textnaming. All pathnames are relative and the server maps them to ports. These are used to access the file itself.

Another system of particular interest is the PULSE project at the University of York [34]. This is described in more detail in 13.3.2 below.

It has been shown that different applications and different objectives can result in very different designs for distributed filestores. In which direction, then, are such filestores likely to develop? One strong possibility is for filestores to be superseded, at least at the application level, by database systems. Even in a multi-access operating system there is a requirement for structured files, locking on file records and an avoidance of the multiple occurrence of data items. Often files have many more attributes than those explicitly catered for in existing filestores, and there need to be mechanisms to express the relationship between these attributes. Whether the high efficiency of filestores can be retained with a database (possibly distributed) is less clear, but the arguments sound strangely familiar to those of the 1960's regarding high level languages.

11.8 REFERENCES

1. K. Lunn, "Reliable File Storage in a Distributed Computer System," Ph. D. Thesis, University of Keele (1983).

2. J. H. Saltzer, "Naming and Binding of Objects," pp. 99-208 in *Operating Systems - an Advanced Course*, ed. G. Seegmuller, Springer Verlag, Berlin (1979).

3. J. F. Shoch, "Inter-network Naming, Addressing, and Routing," *Compcon*, IEEE (Spring 1978).

4. J. S. M. Verhofstad, "Recovery Techniques for Data Base Systems," *Computing Surveys* **10**(2), pp.167-195 (1978).

5. D. W. Davies, "Protection," pp. 211-245 in *Distributed Systems - an Advanced Course*, ed. H. J. Siegert, Springer Verlag, Berlin (1983).

6. J. Dion, "The Cambridge Fileserver," *ACM Operating Systems Review* **14**(4), pp.26-35 (October 1980).

7. J. Dion, "Reliable Storage in a Local Network," Technical Report 16, University of Cambridge Computing Laboratory (February 1981).

8. A. Herbert, "The User Interface to the Cambridge Model Distributed Computer System," *Proc Second Int. Conf. on Distributed Computer Systems* **81CH1591-7**, pp.503-508, IEEE (April 1981).

9. M. V. Wilkes and R. M. Needham, "The Cambridge Model Distributed Computer System," *ACM Operating Systems Review* **14**(1), pp.21-28 (January 1980).

10. N. H. Garnett and R. M. Needham, "An Asynchronous Garbage Collector for the Cambridge File Server," *ACM Operating Systems Review* **14**(4), pp.36-40 (October 1980).

11. H. Sturgis, J. Mitchell, and J. Israel, "Issues in the Design and Use of a Distributed File System," *ACM Operating Systems Review* **14**(3), pp.55-69 (July 1980).

12. D. Swinehart, G. McDaniel, and D. Boggs, "WFS: A Simple Shared File System for a Distributed Environment," *Proc. 7th. Symp. on Operating System Principles*, Pacific Grove, Ca., ACM (10-12 December 1979).

13. W. Paxton, "A Client-based Transaction System to Maintain Data Integrity," *Proc. 7th. Symp. on Operating System Principles*, Pacific Grove, Ca., ACM (10-12 December 1979).

14. J. Mitchell and J. Dion, "A Comparison of Two Network-based File Servers," *Proc. Eighth Symp. on operating Systems Principles*, pp.45-46, ACM (December 1981).

15. D. R. Brownbridge, L. F. Marshall, and B. Randell, "The Newcastle Connection, or, UNIXes of the World Unite!," *Software - Practice & Experience* **12**, pp.1147-1162 (1982).

16. B. Randell, "Recursively Structured Distributed Computing Systems," Report srm/346, Computing Laboratory, University of Newcastle upon Tyne (May 1983).

17. G. L. Chesson, "The Network UNIX System," *ACM Operating Systems Review* **9**(5), pp.60-66 (1975).

18. K. Hwang, W. J. Croft, G. H. Goble, B. W. Wah, F. A. Briggs, W. R. Simmons, and C. L. Coates, "A UNIX-based Local Computer Network with Load Balancing," *Computer* **15**(4), pp.55-66 (1982).

19. G. W. R. Luderer, H. Che, J. P. Haggerty, P. A. Kirlis, and W. T. Marshall, "A Distributed UNIX System based on a Virtual Circuit Switch," *ACM Operating Systems Review* **15**(5), pp.160-168 (1981).

20. P. M. Lu, "A System for Resource Sharing in a Distributed Environment - RIDE," *Proc. IEEE Computer Society 3rd. COMPSAC*, New York, IEEE (1979).

21. J. C. Kaufeld and D. L. Russell, "Distributed UNIX System," in *in Workshop on Fundamental Issues in Distributed Computing*, ACM SIGOPS and SIGPLAN (15-17 December 1980).

22. G. Popek, B. Walker, J. Chow, D. Edwards, C. Kline, G. Rudisin, and G. Thiel, "LOCUS: A Network Transparent, High Reliability Distributed System," *ACM Operating Systems Review* **15**(5), pp.169-177 (1981).

23. B. Walker, G. Popek, R. English, C. Kline, and G. Thiel, "The LOCUS Distributed Operating System," *ACM Operating Systems Review* **17**(5), pp.49-70 (December 1983).

24. L. A. Rowe and K. P. Birman, "A Local Network based on the UNIX Operating System," *IEEE Trans. Software Eng.* **SE-8**(2), pp.137-146 (1982).

25. E. Lazowska, H. Levy, G. Almes, M. Fischer, R. Fowler, and S. Vestal, "The Architecture of the EDEN System," *ACM Operating Systems Review* **15**(5), pp.148-159 (1981).

26. Apollo Computer Inc., *Various Sales and Information Literature*, 1981.

27. K. Lunn and K. H. Bennett, "An Algorithm for Resource Location in a Distributed Computer Network," *ACM Operating Systems Review* **15** (April 1981).

28. O. P. Brereton, "Improving File Availability on a UNIX United System," Computer Science Report DCP/WD/102, University of Keele (January 1984).

29. O. P. Brereton, "The Management of Replicated Files in a UNIX Environment," Computer Science Report DCP/WD/114, University of Keele (March 1984).

30. P. M. McLellan, "The Design of a Network Filing System," CST-12-81, Computer Science Department, University of Edinburgh (November 1981). Ph. D. Thesis

31. M. Fridrich and W. Older, "The FELIX Fileserver," *ACM Operating Systems Review* **15**(5), pp.37-44 (December 1981).

32. L. Svoboda, "A Reliable Object-oriented Repository for a Distributed Computer System," *ACM Operating Systems Review* **15**(5), pp.47-58 (December 1981).

33. A. S. Tanenbaum and S. Mullender, "An Overview of the Amoeba Distributed Operating System," *ACM Operating System Review* **15**(3), pp.51-64 (July 1981).

34. D. Keeffe, G. M. Tomlinson, I. C. Wand, and A. J. Wellings, "PULSE Project 1983," YCS.67, Computer Science Department, University of York (1984).

12 Mechanisms for Distributed Control

K. H. Bennett

12.1 REVIEW OF PROBLEMS

In loosely-coupled distributed systems, there are two problems which lie at the heart of many of the new difficulties in system design. The first problem is that of unpredictable delays in the communications mechanism. The second is the possibility of partial failure.

A communications system can be made as reliable as required, but then unpredictable delays may become very considerable and widely distributed. Jensen [1] has suggested a useful model in which he defines the production of a signal, and its manifestation; the relationship between the two, including ordering, latency and completeness, is defined as the signal observability. In a centralized system, or tightly coupled distributed computing system with shared memory, signal observability is very high. In a loosely-coupled system it is poor, and conventional centralized techniques of synchronization do not carry over. The reason is that the overall system state (represented by values in memory) is spread round several machines. No process operating on one machine can have a consistent view of the total system state. Assume for example that a process on machine A reads from store on machines B and C. By the time the values get back to the process (probably at different times) the values in the store locations on B and C may well have changed (and possibly the manifested signal is now of little use).

In this section we shall base our approach on the work of Anderson and Lee [2] and LeLann [3]. Systems will be regarded as constructed as a number of levels of abstraction, in which an operation at level i is composed of one or more actions at level j, where $j < i$. With knowledge of the specification of each operation and its constituent actions, we are in a position to prove the correctness of the system. It is evident that the specification of an action must not be invalidated in practice by unanticipated concurrent activities, and this may be ensured by insisting that all actions be executed strictly serially. In a distributed system, which can offer opportunities for parallelism, this is very inefficient. Two actions can proceed concurrently if they do not read from or write to any data objects in common (the correctness proofs are independent). However, of more interest is the problem: how do we organize access to shared data objects in such a way that the specification is preserved, yet maximum concurrency is attained? Control of the order in which actions are carried out is a vital requirement for the implementation of atomic operations, and therefore for correctness proofs. The need to coordinate the executions of cooperating sequential processes may be satisfied by mutually exclusive access to a common data object; we therefore regard this as another manifestation of the ordering problem. The example now given is due to Lelann [3].

Let a set of data objects $X = [X_1, X_2, ... X_n]$ be updatable by two concurrently executing operations $A = [A_1, A_2, ... A_n]$ And $B = [B_1, B_2, ... B_n]$. Here A_i and B_i represent the actions belonging to A and B respectively which manipulate data object X_i. According to the order in which the actions A_i and B_i are executed and interleaved, different final states of X will result. For each data object X_i, one of two orderings of actions is possible; either A_i is before B_i or B_i is before A_i. More formally, either $X_i(A,B) = B_i(A_i(X_i(0)))$ or $X_i(B,A) = A_i(B_i(X_i(0)))$. Suppose that the specification allows only two valid final states; either

$$X(A,B):[X_i(A,B) \text{ for all i}], \text{ or}$$
$$X(B,A):[X_i(B,A) \text{ for all i}]$$

These two final states would result from serialized actions; either all A happen before all B or vice-versa. This can be achieved by ensuring that for all i either A_i happens before B_i, or B_i happens before A_i. This is the only interleaving that is valid. Let us consider a specific example; suppose we have two data objects X_1 and X_2, such that $X_1 = X_2$. Two operations A and B are defined as follows:

A:	$X_1 := X_1 + 100$		B:	$X_1 := X_1 * 5$
	$X_2 := X_2 + 100$			$X_2 := X_2 * 5$

Serial execution of these operations (in either order) maintains the truth of the predicate. So does the interleaved execution:

$$X_1 := X_1 + 100$$
$$X_1 := X_1 * 5$$
$$X_2 := X_2 + 100$$
$$X_2 := X_2 * 5$$

which conforms with the condition defined above. However the order:

$$X_1 := X_1 + 100$$
$$X_2 := X_2 + 100$$
$$X_2 := X_2 * 5$$
$$X_1 := X_1 * 5$$

does not, and does not maintain the truth of the predicate.

An interleaved ordering of actions can thus be equivalent to a strictly serial ordering; for further details see [4, 5]

12.1.1 Partial Failure

The second problem, of partial failure, occurs when a task is delegated as an set of subtasks to several concurrent processes on distinct processors. Conventional implementations of atomic actions rely on the execution being performed on a single machine. If this crashes, the recovery manager has access to the system state with high observability. In a distributed system, the subactions of an atomic operation are executing on several machines, and a crash of one machine part way through the operation must be handled both by the issuing site and by the recovery manager(s) at the crashed site(s). The issuing site may itself crash as well.

This chapter comprises three parts. The first examines synchronization mechanisms in distributed computing systems and describes two solutions, based on timestamps and on locking. The second part discusses atomic transactions and introduces the two phase commit protocol for their implementation. Finally the multiple copy update problem is considered. Some of the results described are well established and have been available in the literature for some time. Nevertheless they remain an important contribution to understanding distributed control mechanisms.

12.2 SYNCHRONISATION IN DISTRIBUTED SYSTEMS

12.2.1 Introduction

Imagine that two processes P and Q are communicating via messages. We require that messages are processed by Q in the order that they were sent by P. However, the communications mechanism between the two may well be unable to guarantee to preserve ordering (due to alternative routing, lost messages etc). The usual solution to this is to append a sequence number to each message, so that Q can detect and recover from out-of-order messages.

Now consider three processes, P, Q and R. P sends a message to Q. P then sends a message to R, which itself sends a message to Q as a result. How do we now guarantee that the messages received by Q are in the same order they left P?

A number of solutions have been proposed to solve the problem of synchronization in a distributed computing system. These are often divided into "centralized" and "distributed" solutions; an example of the former is a central physical clock. Thus a producer (say) may read the time from this clock, and append it to messages to act as a sequence number. An example of such a clock is the 60kHz signal broadcast in the U.K. with an encoded time signal. This seems straightforward but there are significant problems. It is essential that at all times the correct value of the clock is read. Also account may have to be taken of the finite propagation speed of radio waves in a widely separated distributed system.

Another class of solutions relies on centralized decision making within a single process. This leads to problems of single points of failure and performance bottlenecks.

12.2.2 A Distributed Implementation

The system we shall discuss in more detail in this section is a decentralized scheme based on multiple clocks. The solution was originally described by Lamport in [6]. A decentralized scheme has the potential advantage of greater reliability and better performance.

The object of the algorithm is to provide a consistent total ordering of events (thus we we can always determine if event a is before event b for all events). This provides us with the precise control over event ordering needed for synchronization. We assume that a signal always manifests itself after its production. If x causes action y, and p (issued after x) causes action z, we cannot define the relationship between the times of y and z. This is an example of a partial ordering. The basis of Lamport's algorithm is that each process which issues messages has a local counter (incrementation is always positive); the value of this counter is attached to each issued message at the instant it is issued. The counter is incremented between messages, and on receipt a receiver advances its counter so that it is greater than the timestamp in the incoming message. The notation "a→b" is defined, meaning a happened before b. We now state the condition for a system of clocks to be correct (where $C_i(z)$ is the value from the clock C_i assigned in process i to event z):

Clock condition: for any events a,b, if a $\rightarrow$ b then $C_i(a) < C_i(b)$

The clock condition is satisfied if

C1:   if a,b are events in process P_i and a $\rightarrow$ b, then $C_i(a) < C_i(b)$

C2:   if a is the sending of a message by process P_i and b is the receipt of the message by process P_j, then $C_i(a) > C_j(b)$

Lamport shows that the following algorithms ensure C1 and C2:

R1:   each process P_i increments C_i between any two successive events

R2:   interprocess messages are timestamped with the value $Tm = C_i(a)$. On receipt of the message, P_j sets C_j greater or equal to its present value, and $C_j > Tm$

To impose total order, we order events by the time (i.e. value of C_i) at which they occur. If $C_i(a) < C_j(b)$ there is no problem; if $C_i(a) = C_j(b)$ i.e. the events are concurrent, then the process identifier may be used as the ordering criterion. This does of course assume that we are able to identify processes uniquely. This is a significant problem, as is the management of failure and anomalous behaviour due to external events. Lamport shows how several clocks, running approximately at the same rate, may be synchronized to give a total ordering.

Other related solutions to distributed synchronization include circulating privileges and circulating sequencers [3]. A good review article may be found in [7]. The total ordering of events in a distributed computer system has wider applications, for example in some multiple copy update algorithms.

12.2.3 Locking

The simplest form of lock provides exclusive access by the process holding that lock to a data object or objects. If the object is already locked, the process must wait until the lock is released (or abort, or preempt, the other process). Locking may lead to deadlock, when no process can proceed; this may be avoided in the first place, or detected and one or more processes rolled back. More complex locks, such as "multiple readers - single writer", potentially offer higher concurrency.

Locking enables us to maintain serializability without going to the extreme of serialising all operations. Eswaran [4] has shown that the following two phase locking scheme is correct i.e. will ensure consistency. Once an operation has started, any use of a resource causes that resource to be locked. During this first phase, no locks are ever released. When all actions in the operation are complete, the operation is committed. In the second stage, all the operations in the first phase are actually carried out; when a resource is finished with, the lock on it is released. The second phase may be done concurrently with the subsequent execution.

Either the caller or the system may issue an abort instruction. This can only be done before the commit. The operation will be rolled back by releasing all locks - no updates have been undertaken at this stage.

The main example of a system-generated abort is at a detected deadlock. Furthermore, an incomplete transaction must not reveal results to others at a higher level, in order to avoid causing aborts if it subsequently must be undone. A distributed locking protocol is usually implemented within some structure such as an atomic transaction (see below). Local lock managers on participant sites are responsible for issuing and checking locks on local data objects (possibly abstracting physical resources).

12.3 ATOMIC TRANSACTIONS

12.3.1 Introduction

An *atomic transaction* is composed of one or more actions, the transaction having the following properties:

P1:   the transaction is executed entirely or not at all (failure atomicity).

P2:   If two or more concurrently executing transactions access shared data, then the effect is as if the transactions had been obeyed one after the other (serialization atomicity).

We can see immediately that atomic transactions are concerned both with recoverability and error control, and with synchronization. Their attraction lies in the property that they transform the system from one consistent state to another. In between, the state may become temporarily inconsistent, but that does not matter as long as P1 and P2 above hold. The implementation of atomic transactions becomes of particular interest when the actions within are executed on several systems in a distributed computing environment. If any one (or more) actions do not complete for any reason, the whole transaction must be aborted.

As a very simple example, consider a banking system in which the total amount of cash paid in must equal the sum of the balances. If a customer withdraws 1000 pounds from the branch at A, and the appropriate account on the head-office computer in B is debited by 1000 pounds, then either both or neither of these action must take place. To solve this type of problem (with high probability), we shall describe a technique called the two phase commit protocol; as a preparatory stage we will describe how operations on a disc may be made strongly atomic using stable storage. Then we shall describe how atomic transactions fit into the general structure of distributed systems. These techniques are well established, though less frequently implemented.

12.3.2 Stable Storage

The problem that this aims to solve is that a single sector disc operation is only weakly atomic. The operation can crash part way through, and a recovery manager cannot determine whether the operation succeeded or not. In stable storage each block is stored twice on "separate" areas of the disc: (say Block 1, Block 2). It is assumed that the disc unit will indicate if a single write operation which completes is successful (using CRC checks etc). Possibly the operation may have to be repeated until successful (or a crash). It is also assumed that a write to block 2 is not started until the write to block 1 has succeeded. Note that 'crash' does not include a disc head crash, with which stable storage (on one disc) cannot cope.

The crash recovery algorithm works as follows:

```
read block 1 and block 2;
if both are readable and block 1 = block 2
then
    nothing {crash did not affect stable storage}
else
    if one block is unreadable {a crash or other fault has occurred}
    then
        copy from good block to bad block
    else
        if both readable but different
            {a crash occurred between writing the 2 blocks}
        then
            choose either block and copy it to the other
        fi
    fi
fi
```

This algorithm works even if there are subsequent crashes during its execution.

12.3.3 Two Phase Commit

An operation does not meet property P1 if one (or more) of its component actions fails. The two phase commit resolves this as follows. The site receiving the client request becomes the commit coordinator [8]. At the start of the transaction, the cooperating sites start their sub-actions, such that they can be rolled back if required. This is the first phase. Locks are acquired if necessary as described above.

The coordinator is then requested to commit by the client. The coordinator sends "request commit" messages to all participating sites. These respond indicating their willingness to commit. If a site indicates "no" (or cannot be contacted) the coordinator aborts. If all vote "yes" then the coordinator records the commit (atomically, on stable storage) and broadcasts a "commit" message to all participants. From now on, the transaction will proceed to completion regardless of crashes of the coordinator or participants. At the very end the coordinator unsets its commit bit. Note that the decision to commit is centralized and is stored in one place.

The vital component to ensure completion is the recovery manager which is started after a crash, before any user activities. If the transaction is not yet committed, the recovery manager will roll it back (by broadcasting "abort"). More interestingly, suppose that the coordinator crashes after setting the commit bit but before the end of transaction. The recovery manager will repeat the broadcast of the "commit" message; all participants must by this time be in a position to complete or roll back, so the recovery manager waits for a positive acknowledgement. The following Algol 68-like code describes the protocol more precisely:

Coordinator:

```
        vote := commit;
        for all participants while vote = commit do
                send request commit message;
                if reply ≠ agree
                then vote := abort
                fi
        od;
        if vote = commit
        then
                COMMIT;
                for each participant do
                        send commit message;
                        wait for yes-acknowledge
                od;
                if timeout on above then repeat it fi
        else{ abort if any aborts }
                for each participant do
                        send abort message;
                        wait for yes-acknowledge
                od;
                if timeout on above then repeat it fi
        fi;
        reset COMMIT;
```

In the poll, the reply may not be "agree" because the participant cannot be contacted.

Participant:

```
        wait for request commit message;
        ensure undo-redo;
        if for any reason we cannot ensure
        then reply abort
        else reply agree
        fi;
        wait for verdict;          { phase 2 }
        if verdict = commit
        then   release resources and locks;
                instantiate update;
                reply yes-acknowledge
        else
                undo participant;
                reply yes-acknowledge
        fi
```

Initially, the participant is asked to go into a state in which it can either redo or undo the transaction. This information must be carefully recorded (ensure undo - redo). The undo and redo must be idempotent operations. The participants themselves do not "commit". They have to ensure a weaker condition, that they can be undone or that the change can be instantiated. A typical transaction participant may write to many blocks; there are techniques (e.g. the intentions mechanism) for implementing redo-undo quite simply, by never updating in place. In a database system, this may not be practical, so update in place is accompanied by a careful log of the change of state. A useful discussion can be found in [9] including a description of an implementation.

The above protocol in the absence of crashes needs 4N messages for N participants (i.e. it is O(N)). A modified version based on linear ordering requires (2N) messages but there is less opportunity for concurrency. Neither method is completely water tight - for example if the communications links fail.

12.4 TRANSACTION STRUCTURES

We have seen that the two phase commit protocol will (within an unbounded time) ensure that after a crash a transaction will be restored to a consistent state, either by rolling back or rolling forward (transaction not done/done). The issue is thus closely related to the more general topic of fault-tolerant computing, and the purpose of this section is to examine how transactions contribute to this. Much of the description is based on the results of the reliability project at Newcastle University, especially [2, 10].

One diagram in Anderson and Lee's book succinctly summarises the structuring approach to fault tolerant systems developed at Newcastle (**Figure 12-1**). Note that this structure is inherently recursive; Randell expresses this as "Fault tolerant systems should be composed out of generalized fault tolerant component systems."

Briefly, a layer of abstraction is presented with service requests. If these are outside the specification, an interface exception is immediately raised. Hopefully, the layer will eventually return a normal response. Possibly, faults will be detected locally, resulting in

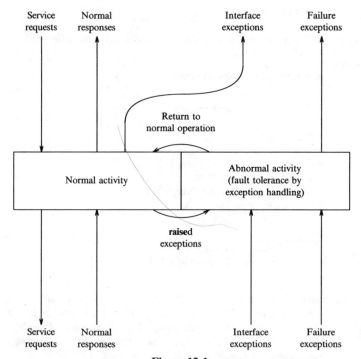

Figure 12-1

entry to code to handle this abnormal activity. Again, it is desirable for the fault to be tolerated leading to a return to normal activity. This may not be possible, in which case a failure exception is raised to the layer of abstraction above.

An important technique for providing fault tolerance in a distributed system is through recoverable atomic actions. It follows from the above arguments that provision for nested atomic actions will be required.

12.4.1 Transactions in UNIX United

At Newcastle, additions are proposed to add support for atomic actions in UNIX (and therefore UNIX United) [10]. The research is based partly on the earlier work by Jegado [11] on a distributed recoverable filestore. The main aim of this was to study the incorporation of the general recovery mechanisms for fault tolerance into a filestore rather than just transactions. The basis of the recovery structure in this design is three system calls

1. establish recovery point (erp): start state-saving and locking files

2. discard recovery point (drp): discard saved state, unlock files

3. restore recovery point (rrp): go back to state at recovery point.

The first 'erp' operation returns a recovery point number for use by drp and rrp. The act of restoring to a recovery point amounts to rolling back the execution. Discarding a recovery point is a commit operation, because we can then no longer recover backwards to the (now non-existent) recovery point.

When a user establishes a recovery point, the distributed file manager broadcasts an 'erp' message to all participants, who establish their own recovery points. A similar action occurs when the user does a restore or discard operation. A recovery cache mechanism provides the means of recovery. Note that the above scheme does not support a two phase commit protocol; some but not all of the participants may discard their recovery points. It is proposed to add a fourth system call to the UNIX (United) implementation called "prepare to discard recovery point", corresponding to the first part of the two phase commit. The structure of a system now appears as in **Figure 12-2**.

It is seen that this structure involves a clear separation of issues; the issue of distributedness is handled in the Connection layer. This provides an illusion of a single commit operation, which the Connection implements in a two phase manner on all the participant machines. Thus above the Connection the appearance of a single system is maintained.

12.5 MULTIPLE COPY UPDATING

12.5.1 Problem Area and Objectives

This section summarises a design for managing multiple copies of files within the UNIX United operating system. It represents a development of the scheme first implemented in the Keele University KUDOS distributed filestore. Multiple copy updating of files includes the problems of synchronization, naming, atomicity, recovery and performance.

Replicating copies of files is an example of increasing reliability through fault tolerant techniques, and the facilities of a loosely coupled distributed system offer novel opportunities for increasing reliability. The advantages of providing high file availability and reliability will not be re-examined here, except for stressing the importance of their use with shared files.

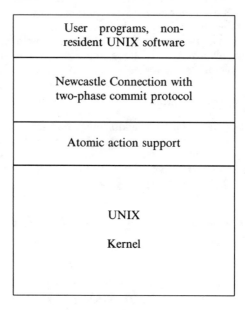

| User programs, non-resident UNIX software |
| Newcastle Connection with two-phase commit protocol |
| Atomic action support |
| UNIX

Kernel |

Figure 12-2

The requirement of multiple copy techniques could be to achieve mutual consistency i.e. all copies identical. This decreases reliability - not all copies may be on-line. Thus we relax the condition to be in terms of all on-line copies, and in the algorithm to be described there must be a majority of such copies available. We must cope with off-line copies when they reappear (or are referred to). During a multiple copy update, the copies may become temporarily inconsistent, but this must not be visible to the client process. A second requirement is to accommodate crashes which can occur at any time in the participants.

The objective of the project described here was also to examine the UNIX United interface as a means of supporting a multiple copy layer, with particular emphasis on performance, naming and crash recovery issues. This assumed that no modifications to the UNIX kernel were acceptable.

12.5.2 Related Work

The KUDOS algorithm described earlier updated whatever on-line file copies were available. No facilities for atomic actions or crash recovery were incorporated, although volumes reintroduced to the system were handled. Consistency control was achieved by timestamping file copies.

Multiple copy updating has been explored and implemented in database systems, often in conjunction with the synchronization and transaction techniques described earlier. A good introduction may be found in [12]. A set of algorithms is described which are based mostly upon voting; the participating sites intercommunicate to decide if the update can proceed. For example, in synchronous voting the participants broadcast to each other so that each can come to a decision on whether to proceed with the transaction. Then the transaction is executed (or not). The algorithm relies on a total order of events to handle concurrent transactions. This is a good example of a distributed control algorithm - there is no central coordinator site.

In a majority consensus voting scheme [13] a majority of participants must vote 'yes' for a transaction to proceed. Gifford [14] describes a variation in which a copy is assigned some number of votes. An operation must have a minimum number of votes to proceed, allowing reliability and performance characteristics of a file to be modified on both read and write. It has been implemented within the Xerox Violet system.

The LOCUS system [15, 16] supports the management of multiple file copies, and allows updates when a majority is not present (which may happen for example when the network partitions). The system then attempts to merge several updates undertaken in separate partitions, when the network reforms. In general there is no solution to this problem, but specific cases can be solved.

12.5.3 The Keele Replicated File Implementation

UNIX United provides a process model indistinguishable from that of UNIX itself. In particular, user and operating system programs make system calls for both local and remote I/O, file manipulation etc. In the Keele system, a layer is inserted between user and operating system programs, and the Newcastle Connection, to intercept system calls as described in the previous chapter. This layer presents to programs above it the illusion of single (but highly available) files, which are actually implemented as several copies.

The algorithm for consistency management requires that a majority of up-to-date copies of the file are present for an update to proceed. This means that successive updates to the same file always have at least one file copy in common, and a local version number can be used to identify consistent copies. Also at most one set of copies can take part in an update, eliminating separate updates to disjoint partitions. Note that not all on-line copies may have the same version number. The naming of replicated files is based on the KUDOS "overlay mount" scheme.

The description of the algorithm separates two quite distinct issues: the voting algorithm itself, and mechanisms for dealing with recovery from crashes of any of the participant sites. The work is derived from that presented in [17].

12.5.4 Majority Consensus Algorithm

A set of replicated copies of a file are distributed over several UNIX systems linked by the Newcastle Connection. Each copy has associated with it a version number, the location of other copies, and status information (available to the recovery manager). We shall concentrate on the update operation which is undertaken on the UNIX *write* system call. The algorithm has been described more formally by Brereton in terms of Nutt nets.

Before an update request can proceed, a single coordinator site must be established to handle the update. This is achieved by inspecting the status of the file copy marked as "master". If an update to the file is in progress, its "master" copy will be locked for the duration of the write, and the new update must be rejected or queued (the former is actually implemented). If no update is in progress, the local file copy is locked and marked as "master", and the old master is marked as "fellow". This must be performed atomically to prevent more than one master existing. The coordinator process must now locate and communicate with at least half of the remaining copies of the file. Details of the operation and the associated data are sent to each remote machine. The remote copies are locked and the updates performed as intentions (see previous section). The version numbers are also incremented using a similar mechanism. Thus the participants reach an undo-redo state. It can be seen that the "master" and "fellow" states act as the lock on the file which is held centrally.

The participants then reply to the coordinator on the success of the update. The coordinator collects votes, and then broadcasts an update message. If insufficient votes are collected, the intentions are never instantiated. The coordinator also instantiates its own update and unlocks its file. Note that all remote operations are undertaken using procedure calls. The similarity with two-phase commit mechanisms is apparent, though crash recovery is handled differently.

12.5.5 Crash Recovery

Recovery procedures are implemented for two types of failure:

(1)   failure of a participant during an update, so that a majority while initially established is no longer available.

(2)   failure of coordinator site

The above may also occur because communication fails. In either case, each remaining copy of the file is marked as "recluse" indicating "possibly out-of-date". The basis of most recovery schemes is to ensure that sufficient state information exists at the time of the crash for the recovery manager to bring up the system into a well-defined and consistent state. This is a function of the "status" associated with each file copy.

If a machine crashes, its recovery manager marks all file copies with "recluse" status on reinitialization. File copies for which a majority set is found to exist (and which is accessible) are brought up-to-date (by copying), using the master as source.

If the coordinator crashes, the recovery mechanism is invoked at the next update operation from a recluse site to establish an operational set of copies. The most recent version is used as source. The algorithm copes with simultaneous attempts to coordinate the reconstitution of an operational (up-to-date) set, and failure during the reconstitution.

12.5.6 Analysis and Performance

Deadlock is avoided when requests are in conflict by a centralized scheme for request acceptance, with distributed recovery. A possibility of starvation exists when a site repeatedly fails to become coordinator for a request. This could be overcome by queueing requests, but the overheads are undesirably high in an environment where simultaneous updates to shared files are rare.

A weak consistency is maintained between file copies so that copies are not all guaranteed to be up-to-date. However an out-of-date copy is always restored to the most recent on-line version before update. The system as implemented is not totally crash resistant because it assumes that the underlying software layers will provide support for atomic operations. This is not yet the case.

Some early performance figures have been taken for the Keele implementation. The UNIX filestore does not allow extra file attributes to be stored with the file, so explicit separate files have been used (and those associated with a directory e.g. file copy locations) are themselves replicated. Thus the overhead on file operations is dominated by the time taken to open files. A read of a local copy of a replicated file takes approximately the same time as a read on a non-replicated local file. It is hoped to report on more detailed measurements elsewhere.

12.6 SUMMARY

Synchronisation and atomicity in distributed systems pose new problems compared to centralized operating systems. Mechanisms have been presented in this chapter for achieving consistent behaviour in the face of partial failure and unreliable communications. The management of replicated copies of objects brings together several of these difficulties which must be solved coherently to give an adequate system design. There is a need to obtain further experience of implementing the type of mechanisms described in this section, and assessing their performance in everyday use.

12.7 REFERENCES

1.   E. D. Jensen, "Distributed Control," pp. 175-190 in *Distributed Systems: Architecture and Implementation*, ed. M. Paul, Springer Verlag, Berlin (1983).

2.   T Anderson and P A Lee, *Fault Tolerance: Principles and Practice,* Prentice-Hall (1981).

3.   G. LeLann, "Synchronization," pp. 175-190 in *Distributed Systems: Architecture and Implementation*, ed. M. Paul, Springer Verlag, Berlin (1983).

4.   K.P. Eswaran, J. N. Gray, R. A. Lorie, and I. L. Traiger, "The Notions of Consistency and Predicate Locks in a Database System," *Comm. ACM* **19**(11), pp.624-633 (November 1976).

5.   C. H. Papadimitriou, "Serializability of Concurrent Database Updates," *J. ACM* **26**(4), pp.631-653 (October 1979).

6.   L. Lamport, "Time, Clocks and the Ordering of Events in a Distributed System," *Comm. ACM* **21**(7), pp.558-565 (July 1978).

7.   W. H. Kohler, "A Survey of Techniques for Synchronisation and Recovery in Decentralised Computer Systems," *Computer Surveys* **13**(2), pp.149-184 (June 1981).

8.   J. N. Gray, "Notes on Database Operating Systems," pp. 393-481 in *Operating Systems: an Advanced Course*, ed. G. Seegmuller, Springer Verlag, New York (1979).

9.   P. M. McLellan, "The Design of a Network Filing System," CST-12-81, Computer Science Department, University of Edinburgh (November 1981). Ph. D. Thesis

10.   B. Randell, "Recursively Structured Distributed Computing Systems," Report srm/346, Computing Laboratory, University of Newcastle upon Tyne (May 1983).

11.   M. Jegado, "Recoverability Aspects of a Distributed File System," *Software - Practice & Experience* **13**(1), pp.33-44 (January 1983).

12.   E. Holler, "Multiple Copy Update," pp. 175-190 in *Distributed Systems: Architecture and Implementation*, ed. M. Paul, Springer Verlag, Berlin (1983).

13.   R. H. Thomas, "A Majority Consensus Approach to Concurrency Control for Multiple Copy Databases," *ACM Trans. Database Systems* **4**(2), pp.180-209 (June 1979).

14. D. K. Gifford, "Weighted Voting for Replicated Data," *Proc. Seventh Symp. on Operating Systems Principles*, pp.150-162, Pacific Grove, Ca., ACM (December 1979).

15. G. Popek, B. Walker, J. Chow, D. Edwards, C. Kline, G. Rudisin, and G. Thiel, "LOCUS: A Network Transparent, High Reliability Distributed System," *ACM Operating Systems Review* **15**(5), pp.169-177 (1981).

16. B. Walker, G. Popek, R. English, C. Kline, and G. Thiel, "The LOCUS Distributed Operating System," *ACM Operating Systems Review* **17**(5), pp.49-70 (December 1983).

17. J. Seguin, G. Sergeant, and P. Wilms, "A Majority Consensus Algorithm for the Consistency of Duplicated and Distributed Information," *J. Digital Systems* **5**(1/2) (Spring/Summer 1981).

13 Distributed Operating Systems

I. C. Wand and A. J. Wellings

13.1 THE DISTRIBUTED SYSTEM MODEL

Flynn [1] has divided computer architectures into four types:

(1) single instruction acting on a single item of data (SISD); for example, a conventional uni-processor system;

(2) single instruction acting on multiple data items (SIMD); for example, parallel processors;

(3) multiple instructions acting on a single data stream (MISD); for example, pipeline computers; and

(4) multiple instructions acting on multiple data items (MIMD); for example, multiprocessor systems and computer networks.

It is possible to classify MIMD architectures further according to their interconnection structures [2]; however, for the purpose of this tutorial, two types of MIMD systems are considered: those where the processor elements share access to a common memory and those where they do not. These two types of system are referred to as tightly-coupled and loosely-coupled distributed systems. Clearly a system where each element consisted of multiple processors could still be viewed as a loosely coupled distributed system but unless otherwise stated this tutorial assumes that each element is a uni-processor. It also assumes that processor elements are identical in that they execute the same order code. The problems associated with connecting heterogeneous processor elements together are not addressed here.

13.1.1 Tightly Coupled Distributed Systems

In a tightly coupled system, processors have access to a common memory, although each may have private memory as well. They usually take the form of multi-processor systems, such as CM* [3] and CYBA-M [4], or special systems for fast specialized computations such as vector or array processors.

Enslow and Saponas [5] list four reasons to explain why the improvements in performance expected with tightly coupled systems have not been obtained.

(1)   The direct sharing of resources such as memory and I/O devices often results in access conflicts and delays.

(2)   User programming languages that support the effective utilization of tightly coupled systems have not been developed adequately.

(3)   The development of "optimal" schedules for the utilization of the processors is very difficult except in straightforward or static situations.

(4)   Any inefficiencies present in the operating system appear to be greatly exaggerated by the distribution of the executing code.

13.1.2 Loosely Coupled Distributed Systems

In loosely coupled systems processors do not share access to a common memory although they may share peripheral devices. Communication between processors is done at the input/output level.

Two types of loosely coupled systems can be considered: those which operate over a wide area network, such as the Arpanet [6] or PSS [7], and those which operate over a local area network (LAN) such as the Cambridge Ring [8] or the Ethernet [9]. However, the nature of the distributed system is essentially independent of the type of network technology used.

Logically, a loosely coupled distributed system can be considered to be collection of processes running on various processor elements (or nodes). Although processes running on the same node can communicate using shared memory, processes running on separate nodes must communicate via messages (or their equivalent).

13.1.3 Static and Dynamic Systems

A static system is one whose structure remains unchanged as long as the system exists. It may have built-in redundancy to cope with failures in particular elements of the system but the overall operational requirements will demand a system that is unchanging as a function of time. Static systems tend to be associated with special purpose applications and often run on dedicated hardware. A typical example is an Embedded Computer System, which may be a uni-processor, a tightly coupled or a loosely coupled system. An example of a static loosely coupled system is the Demos-86 Multi-microcomputer [10].

Dynamic systems have changing operational requirements so their structure must be able to adapt to possible changes. This may take the form of adding extra nodes to the systems or it may be the dynamic creation or destruction of processes. General purpose operating systems are dynamic systems. Examples of dynamic tightly coupled operating systems include STAROS [11], Hydra [12], Medusa [13] and MUNIX [14]. Examples of loosely coupled operating systems are Arachne [15], Series One distributed operating system [16], Accent [17], LOCUS [18], the Rings-Star system [19] and PULSE [20].

13.1.4 Fully Distributed Systems

The term distributed system has been used, so far, to denote the physical distribution of hardware. However, as Enslow [21] points out, at least four components of a system might be distributed: hardware or control logic, data, the processing, and control. He defines a "Fully Distributed Processing System" [5] as being characterized by the following:

(1)   multiplicity of general resources, including processors;

(2)   loosely coupled physical interconnection;

(3)   a unity of control such that the system must define and support a unified set of policies governing its operation;

(4)   system transparency: users must be able to request services without being aware of their physical location; and

(5)   component autonomy: components operate in an autonomous fashion, requiring cooperation with other components to exchange informations.

Another description has been given by Jensen [22]. He describes a "Fully Distributed Computer" to be

"a multiplicity of processors that are physically and logically interconnected to form a single system, in which overall executive control is exercised through the cooperation of decentralized system elements. It is not sufficient that the processors appear to the user as a virtual single system - they must constitute an actual single system at all levels of abstractions."

13.2 CLASSIFICATION OF DISTRIBUTED OPERATING SYSTEMS

We present below an informal classification of Distributed Operating Systems. It is based upon a presentation given by Keeffe et al [20].

(1)   **A Network of Autonomous Systems**

The main characteristic of this division is that the network is used explicitly. No attempt is made to hide the underlying system from the user. In order that machines of widely differing architectures, and consequently different operating systems, may communicate, there must be protocols for all projected activities. Two such systems are well known: one is **uucp** [23], whereby different UNIX systems may transfer files; the other is represented by implementation of the JNT "Blue Book" file transfer protocol [24]. At command level, both these systems require the user to express the communication in terms of "machine name" and "operation name". The user must know the "address" of the remote machine.

(2)   **A Network of Autonomous Systems with the Network Hidden**

Systems within this category are broadly similar to those described above, except that the presence of a network is hidden from the user. This is usually achieved by introducing a further layer of software between the user and the network. The most important characteristic is that the user must know the location of the resource within his name space, but he may not know whether that name denotes a remote or local object. It does not follow that the name space for the overall "super-system" appears the same from different points within it, with the possible result that a resource may have different names from different nodes in the network. Examples that fall within this category are the National Software Works [25], the Newcastle Connection [26], and Cocanet [27].

(3)   **Integrated Loosely Coupled Systems with Autonomous Nodes**

This category is characterized by the presentation of a uniform name space to all users, but where individual nodes of the system may function alone, albeit with only a subset of that name space available to them. Any given resource will have the same name, irrespective of the source of the request. Additionally, the name may denote a resource which, depending on conditions, may be either local or remote. We place our own work on the PULSE system in this category, along with the LOCUS project [18].

(4)   **Integrated Loosely Coupled Systems but with Non-autonomous Nodes**

Systems within this division are similar to those in the previous one, except that the nodes are not capable of operating alone. A machine removed from the network will no longer be operable, but the remainder will continue to function. Examples are Arachne [15], the Cambridge Distributed Computing System [28], the New Mexico State University Ring-Star system [19], and the Edinburgh Domain Structure for Distributed Computer Systems [29].

(5)   **Tightly Coupled Distributed Systems**

Unlike the systems described above, this category applies to several processors sharing memory on a common bus. One such system is StarOS: [11] there are many others.

The categories above are not exhaustive. For instance, we have not included the Demos system [10], where processes are allocated to machines at link time. Furthermore, we have not attempted to categorize the network nodes themselves, so that no mention has been made of the homogeneity or power of the processors, or whether there is local file storage.

A further classification of distributed UNIX operating systems based upon the naming structures of distributed file systems is given by Wupit [30].

13.3 DESCRIPTION OF TWO DISTRIBUTED OPERATING SYSTEMS

13.3.1 Cambridge Distributed Computing System

The Cambridge system is built around a Ring local area network, to which terminals are connected via a concentrator; a set of processors; and various servers which are responsible for allocating services upon receipt of an appropriate request. The Cambridge system is essentially different from other distributed operating systems where the computing power are dispersed to the individual terminals (which are then called Personal Computers or Workstations).

In this system each user has a private terminal which can be connected as a remote terminal to some other machine on the network. The computers are provided in a so-called Processor Bank, where the individual machines in the bank are not committed in advance to any particular user. When a request is made by a user at a terminal for a computer then the processor bank acts as a processor server and will allocate a machine if one can be made available.

The Processor Bank is organized by a Resource Manager and the user's interface to it is controlled by a Session Manager. Other servers in the system are the File Server, the Ancilla (for loading programs into individual machines), the Time Server, and the Name

Server (which relates names to locations).

This system, by contrast with other systems such as PULSE, concentrates all of the disk storage in the File Server and the individual machines do not have private, local disks. From the point of view of data sharing, this has some benefits as it has enabled several other systems, such as TRIPOS, to be implemented on top of it.

One innovative feature of the system is that authentication and protection mechanisms are built in at the lowest level. This is done by building authentication into even the most basic protocols; this means that once the user has identified himself to the system, unique identifiers can be passed around the system without further user involvement.

13.3.2 The PULSE Distributed Operating System

PULSE [20] is an experimental system designed and implemented at the University of York with support from the SERC DCS programme since early in 1980. It is intended to operate on a high speed local area network of loosely coupled powerful personal computers. A prototype system running on two LSI/11-23 based personal computers connected by a Cambridge Ring is currently operational.

The PULSE project is a development of the results of earlier research [31, 32] which explored various ways of distributing the UNIX operating system [33]. It has two major goals:

(1) To investigate how a system may be constructed to give the benefits of a self-sufficient personal computer to each user, whilst not losing the facilities for communication and sharing of data inherent in centralized systems. In particular a distributed file system has been built which provides a single global UNIX-like hierarchy.

(2) To assess the suitability of the programming language for the development of distributed systems in general and distributed operating systems in particular. This work is discussed further by Wellings et al [34].

The system has two main features. First, each machine in the network is capable of running "stand-alone" without logical or physical connection to the network. Second, the filing system has a consistent appearance when accessed from any machine.

Each PULSE machine runs at least a kernel and a file server. The kernel supports the requirements of the Ada language, as well as allowing several programs to run concurrently and to communicate. An important result of using Ada is that all interprogram communication is achieved through task rendezvous: kernel objects called "Mediums" act as buffer tasks, which accept and forward messages. The kernel also provides basic management facilities for the allocation and manipulation of new program images.

The file system is implemented by an instance of a file server program running on each PULSE machine. This program is written in Ada, and makes full use of the language's tasking facilities. Each server is responsible for all access to, and management of, files on its machine. This includes the loading of programs, and the association of particular IPC channels with file names.

In order to improve the availability and speed of access to files, a primary copy [35] scheme of file replication has been adopted. The file servers co-ordinate access to multiple copies of the same file and ensure their mutual consistency. A fuller description is given by Keeffe et al [20].

The PULSE project has now reached the point where truly distributed programs can be loaded and run, where a distributed filing system is operational, and where the operational characteristics of the system can be measured. One significant result has be the discovery of major problems in the use of the Ada tasking model. These difficulties have been caused both by the complexity of Ada (giving a slow implementation, and, in particular, very long task switching times) and by fundamental problems with the language when it is used for resource control [36].

13.4 REFERENCES

1. M. Flynn, "Some Computer Organisation and their Effectiveness," *IEEE Transactions on Computers* **C-21**(9), pp.948-960 (September 1972).

2. G. Anderson and E. D. Jensen, "Computer Interconnection Structures: Taxonomy, Characteristic and Examples," *ACM Computing Surveys* **7**(4), pp.197-213 (December 1975).

3. A. Jones and E. Gehringer, "The CM* Multiprocessor: A Research Review," CS-80-131, Department of Computer Science, Carnegie-Mellon University (July 1980).

4. E. Dagless, *A Multimicroprocessor - CYBA-M,* IFIP North Holland (1977).

5. P. Enslow and T. Saponas, "Distributed and Decentralised Control in Fully Distributed Processing Systems - A Survey of Applicable Models," GIT-ICS-81/02, Georgia Institute of Technology (February 1981).

6. L. Roberts and B. Wessler, "Computer Network Development to Achieve Resource Sharing," *AFIPS Conference Proceedings, Vol 36.*, pp.543-549 (June 1970).

7. British Telecom, "Packet Switchstream (PSS) Technical Guide," (1983).

8. M. V. Wilkes and D. J. Wheeler, "The Cambridge Digital Communication Ring," *Local Area Communication Networks Symposium*, Mitre Corp. and National Bureau of Standards, Boston (May 1979).

9. R. Metcalfe and D. Boggs, "Ethernet: Distributed Packet Switching For Local Computer Networks," *CACM* **19**(7), pp.395-404 (July 1976).

10. M. Dowson and et al., "The Demos 86 Multimicrocomputer," Scicon Technical Report (1980).

11. A. K. Jones and et al., "StarOS, a Multiprocessor Operating System for the Support of Task Forces," *Proceedings of the Seventh ACM Symposium on Operating System Principles*, pp.117-127, Pacific Grove, California (December 1979).

12. W. Wulf, R. Levin, and C. Pierson, "Overview of the Hydra Operating System Development," *Proceedings Fifth ACM Symposium on Operating System Principles*, pp.122-131 (1975).

13. J. Ousterhout and et al., "Medusa: An Experiment in Distributed Operating System Structure," *CACM* **23**(2), pp.92-105 (February 1980).

14. J. Hawley and W. Meyer, "MUNIX, A Multiprocessor Version of UNIX," Masters Thesis, Naval Postgraduate School, Monterey, California (June 1975).

15. R. Finkel, M. Solomon, and R. Tischler, "Arachne User Guide," MRC-TSR-2066, Mathematics Research Center, University of Wisconsin (April 1980).

16. W. D. Sincoskie and D. J. Farber, "The Series/1 Distributed Operating System: Description and Comments," *Proceedings of the COMPCON 80 Fall Distributed Computing Conference*, pp.579-584, Washington DC (September 1980).

17. R. F. Rashid and G. G. Robertson, "Accent: A communication oriented network operating system kernel," *Proceedings of the Eighth ACM Symposium on Operating Systems Principles*, pp.64-75, Pacific Grove, California (December 1981).

18. G. Popek, B. Walker, and et al., "LOCUS A Network Transparent, High Reliability Distributed System," *Proceedings of the Eighth ACM Symposium on Operating Systems Principles*, pp.169-177, Pacific Grove, California (December 1981).

19. A. Karshmer, D. DePree, and J. Phelan, "The New Mexico State University Ring-Star System: A Distributed UNIX Environment," *Software Practice and Experience* **13**(12), pp.1157-1168 (December 1983).

20. D. Keeffe, G. M. Tomlinson, I. C. Wand, and A. J. Wellings, "PULSE - An Operating System for a Network of Personal Computers," PULSE Project 1983, YCS.67, Department of Computer Science, University of York (February 1984).

21. P. H. Enslow, "What is a 'Distributed' Processing System?," *Computer* (January 1978).

22. E. D. Jensen, "The Honeywell Experimental Distributed Processor - An Overview," *Computer* **11**(1) (January 1978).

23. D. A. Nowitz and M. E. Lesk, "Implementation of a Dial-Up Network of UNIX Systems," *Proceedings of the COMPCON 80 Fall Distributed Computing Conference*, pp.483-486, Washington DC (September 1980).

24. File Transfer Protocol Implementors Group, *A Network Independent File Transfer Protocol*, National Physical Laboratory, Teddington (February 1981).

25. E. Holler, "The National Software Works (NSW)," pp. 421-442 in *Distributed Systems - Architecture and Implementation*, ed. B. W. Lampson, Springer-Verlag (1981).

26. D. Brownbridge, L. Marshall, and B. Randell, "The Newcastle Connection," *Software Practice and Experience* **12**(12), pp.1147-1162 (December 1982).

27. L. Rowe and K. Birman, "A Local Network Based on the UNIX Operating System," *IEEE Transactions on Software Engineering* **SE-8**(2), pp.137-146 (March 1982).

28. R. M. Needham and A. J. Herbert, *The Cambridge Distributed Computing System*, Addison-Wesley Publishing Company, London (1982).

29. L. M. Casey and N. Shelness, "A Domain Structure for Distributed Computer Systems," *Proceedings of the Sixth ACM Symposium on Operating System Principles* (November 1977).

30. A. Wupit, "Comparison of UNIX Network Systems," *1983 ACM Conference on Personal and Small Computers*, pp.99-108, San Diego, California (December 1983).

31. G. M. Tomlinson, I. C. Wand, and A. J. Wellings, "Distributed UNIX Project 1980," YCS.40, Department of Computer Science, University of York (December 1980).

32. A. J. Wellings, I. C. Wand, and G. M. Tomlinson, "Distributed UNIX Project 1981," YCS.47, Department of Computer Science, University of York (21 December 1981).

33. D. M. Ritchie and K. Thompson, "The UNIX Time-Sharing System," *Bell Sys. Tech. J.* **57**(6), pp.1905-1929 (1978).

34. A. J. Wellings, D. Keeffe, G. M. Tomlinson, and I. C. Wand, "Programming Distributed Systems in Ada," *Actes Des Journees Europeennes D'Etude Sur Les Systemes Informatiques Distribues*, pp.99-109, Le Mont Saint-Michel, INRIA (September 1983).

35. P. A. Alsberg and J. D. Day, "A Principle for Resilient Sharing of Distributed Resources," *Proceedings of the Second International Conference on Software Engineering*, pp.562-570 (October 1976).

36. A. J. Wellings, D. Keeffe, and G. M. Tomlinson, "A Problem with Ada and Resource Allocation," *Ada Letters* **3**(4) (January, February 1984).

14 Programming Languages

I. C. Wand and A. J. Wellings

14.1 INTRODUCTION

The techniques underlying distributed systems implementation draw heavily upon those used in operating systems for controlling concurrent access to shared resources; in many cases the related concepts have been incorporated in programming languages.

Although languages for concurrent programming differ considerably one from another, they must have three features in common [1]

(1)   the ability to express concurrent execution,

(2)   process synchronization, and

(3)   inter-process communication.

There has been much experimentation with new methods for concurrency and resource control by extending a programming language with suitable library facilities. Generally, when the techniques have been understood they are brought into the language domain, thereby extending the security of the mechanism by including, for example, strong typing. Examples of such methods include concurrent (or parallel) processing, exception handling, and more recently atomic transactions. Language research into atomic transactions is being carried out in the US by Liskov at MIT [2, 3, 4] and at Rochester [5], and in the UK at Newcastle [6, 7].

We now discuss concurrent programming techniques and the associated programming language features; where appropriate, examples from operating systems are given. Subsequent sections discuss how these techniques are extended to particular forms of distributed computing.

14.2 CONCURRENT EXECUTION

There are four basic mechanisms for achieving concurrent execution. First and simplest of these is the *coroutine* which has been included in languages such as Simula [8] and Modula-2 [9]. Secondly, the *fork and join* notation, which is used in the UNIX operating system [10], and can be found in the Mesa language [11]. Thirdly, the *Cobegin* or *Parbegin*, first introduced by Dijkstra, has appeared in Communicating Sequential Processes [12], Edison [13], and more recently in occam [14] and Argus [4]. Finally, explicit *process declarations* can be found in Concurrent Pascal [15], Modula [16], Distributed Processes

[17], Parlance [18], Pascal-M [19], the RED language [20], starmod [21] and SR [22].

14.2.1 Process Synchronization and Communication

Synchronization and communication can be achieved either by reading and writing shared data or by the sending and receiving of messages between processes which do not share data. In general it is difficult to separate synchronization from communication. If a process is to synchronize with another it must detect an action performed by that process; this requires a flow of information between the processes which can take the form of a simple message called a *signal*. Furthermore some ordering of events is required if two processes are to communicate with each other sensibly.

14.2.2 Shared Variables

Andrews and Schneider [1] distinguish two types of synchronization when communication is based upon the use of shared variables. The first is *mutual exclusion*, which ensures that a sequence of statements is treated as an indivisible operation. The second is *condition synchronization*, to coordinate execution of concurrent processes when a shared object is in a state inappropriate for executing a particular operation.

Various methods of achieving synchronization and communication using shared variables are now discussed.

Test and Set

If the hardware provides a single *test and set* instruction, then synchronization can be achieved using a *busy wait* protocol. To provide mutual exclusion a process uses *test and set* on a shared variable. If the test indicates that the variable was previously zero then the process may enter the mutually exclusive routine; at the end of the routine it must set the variable back to zero. If a process finds as a result of using *test and set* that a variable was previously set, then it can deduce that another process is currently executing the routine. Condition synchronization is now required so that the process can wait until the routine is cleared for entry. This is achieved by continually testing and setting the variable until the result indicates that the variable is now clear. This is usually known as *busy waiting*.

Semaphores

Semaphores are another simple mechanism for providing synchronization. They are integer-like variables whose values can only be altered by the operation P and V. If S is a semaphore, when a process executes the operation P(S), then S is decremented by one. If S is greater than or equal to zero then the process continues execution. However, if S is less than zero then the process is blocked and put on a queue associated with S. It remains blocked until a V(S) operation releases it. When a process executes the V(S) operation, S is incremented by one. If S is greater than zero it continues, if S is less than or equal to zero a process waiting on the queue associated with S is released. Both the releasing and the released process are now free to continue.

Semaphores can be used to program almost any kind of synchronization although they lead to an unstructured form of programming. For example, if a process omits a P or applies such an operation to the wrong semaphore, then the result can be chaotic.

Conditional Critical Regions

Condition Critical Regions [23, 24] are an attempt to overcome some of the problems with semaphores. A *critical region* is a section of code that is guaranteed to be executed in mutual exclusion. A conditional critical region provides mutual exclusion and condition synchronization. Variables which are to be shared between processes are grouped together in *resources* where a shared variable is only allowed in one resource and can only be accessed by a conditional critical region naming that resource. Processes executing different regions naming the same resource are also mutually exclusive. Condition synchronization is provided by allowing a boolean variable as a guard to that conditional critical region. If a process attempts to enter a conditional critical region and the associated guard evaluates to false, then the process is delayed until the guard evaluates to true. Processes must re-evaluate their guards every time a conditional critical region naming the resource is exited. Brinch Hansen [24] introduced the *await* and *cause* constructs to increase the efficiency of this language mechanism; when a condition is tested in a conditional critical region, if that condition is false then the process *awaits* an *event*, where an event is a variable of type event on which processes can be queued. When a process exits a conditional critical region it can wake up up all processes waiting on an event by issuing a *cause* on that event. Conditional Critical regions have been implemented in Edison [13].

Monitors

The main problems with conditional critical regions are that they can be dispersed throughout the programs and that they are costly to implement [1]. Monitors [25, 26] are intended to alleviate these problems. The critical regions are written as procedures and are encapsulated together with the data into a single program unit called a monitor in which associated procedure calls are guaranteed to be mutually exclusive. Condition synchronization is provided by a variety of methods depending on the particular type of monitor being used. In Hoare's [25] monitors condition variables are used with the operations *wait*, including an optional priority, and *signal*. When a process issues a wait operation on a condition variable it is blocked and placed on a queue associated with that variable; the queue is ordered according to the priority of the wait operation. If no priority is given, then they are queued in *first-in-first-out* order. The monitor lock is then released allowing further monitor procedure calls. When a process executes a signal operation on a condition variable, then, if no other process is blocked, it continues. However, if there are processes waiting, the process which issued the signal operation is suspended and the first process in the queue associated with the condition variable is reactivated. A process blocked on a signal is resumed when no other process has the monitor lock; they are given priority over all other processes attempting to obtain the lock to execute a monitor procedure. Pascal Plus [27] is an example of a language which uses Hoare's monitors. Modula [16] provides very similar facilities using interface modules and signals.

In Concurrent Pascal [15], condition variables are replaced by *queue* variables; they differ in that only one process can be waiting on a queue variable at any one time. The operations *delay* and *continue* are analogous to wait and signal, the main difference being that a continue causes the invoking process to return from the monitor procedure whereas the signal does not. The process activated by the continue resumes execution of the monitor procedure within which it was delayed.

So far it has been assumed that a process resumes its execution after being delayed if the condition causing it to block initially is no longer true. An alternative approach is to provide a *conditional wait* [25] where a boolean expression is associated with the operation. The process is blocked until this expression evaluates to true. This approach is potentially inefficient because it requires the evaluation of all conditional waits every time a process exits from a monitor.

In Mesa [11] a different approach is taken. There is no conditional wait, but processes cannot assume that the condition causing a block is removed. The *notify* operation (comparable to a signal) merely indicates that the blocked process should re-evaluate the condition. A *broadcast* operation is also provided to notify all the processes waiting on a particular condition variable. Mesa provides external procedures in a monitor; these are procedures which are logically outside the monitor but are declared within the same module for reasons of packaging. However these procedures may access only unchanging read-only global variables inside the monitor and must not call any internal procedures, or use any of the condition variable operations. These restrictions are checked at compiler time.

The problems associated with the use of monitors have received much attention in the literature with particular interest in the semantics of nested monitor calls [28, 29, 30, 31]. Andrews and Schneider [1] have discussed this controversy in detail. Various approaches to the nested monitor problem have been suggested [29, 32, 31]. The most popular one, adopted by Concurrent Pascal [15] and Mesa [31], is to maintain the lock. Other approaches include prohibiting nested procedure calls altogether [33], providing a special purpose construct [34] or providing constructs which specify that certain monitor procedures may release their mutual exclusion during procedure calls [32].

Path Expressions

Path Expressions [35] provide synchronization of a shared variable by specifying the allowed ordering of procedures which manipulate that variable. The following is an example of the notation used:

> selection   " , "
> sequencing   " ; "
> concurrency " {} "

For instance the path

> path {read},(openwrite;write) end

denotes permitted read/write access to a shared variable; a choice is made between an arbitrary number of readers or a single write which must first issue an open write request.

This approach provides a mechanism for denoting mutual exclusive access to a shared resource while not preventing access when mutual exclusion is not required. However conditional synchronization is difficult. Problems occur when access to parameter information is required before attempting synchronization [36, 1].

Ada Tasking

In all of the techniques described above mutual exclusion and synchronization are controlled by separate mechanisms. *Ada tasking* [37] attempts to amalgamate these requirements into a single language feature.

Ada tasking is a complex set of language features which are interconnected with most other aspects of the language. Ada tasks can be declared at the start of any scope and are initiated either by virtue of their declaration or by their use via the storage allocator. The lifetime of a task is intimately bound up with its dependent tasks and no block will be left until all dependent tasks have completed. The Ada tasking model assumes that all of the tasks in a program run in the same address space; in other words it presumes a shared store model. As will be seen later it is difficult to construct an implementation of Ada tasking for a loosely coupled system that reflects the Ada tasking semantics and is reasonably efficient.

Communication between Ada tasks can be achieved by two different mechanisms. First, by the use of variables which are global to the tasks which want to communicate, and second, by the use of procedure-like entries into tasks. When a task wishes to pass information to another it calls the entry in that task; the sender will wait until the called task has dealt with the call. In Ada this interaction is called a rendezvous. It is important to note that, although the caller must know the name of the task entry it is calling, the called task is unaware of the identity of the caller. The called task will receive the entry calls in a FIFO order. Several facilities are provided for further control over the calling entry sequence including timed calls, a method of specifying alternative entry points, families (arrays) of entries, etc. Furthermore, there is a complicated interaction with the exception mechanism in Ada.

Wellings et al [38] has shown that the Ada tasking mechanism has serious shortcomings when it is used for resource allocation.

14.2.3 Message Passing

Message passing is an alternative to the use of shared data when providing a communication and synchronization mechanism between processes. Gentleman [39] has suggested that there are four issues which determine the semantics of message passing:

(1)   process naming,

(2)   blocking or non-blocking send,

(3)   representation of a message, and

(4)   communication failures.

Furthermore, Liskov [3] has suggested four properties that the communication primitives should provide:

(1)   User programs need not deal with the underlying form of messages. For example, users should not need to translate data into bit strings suitable for transmission or to break up the message into packets.

(2)   All messages received by user programs are intact and in good condition. For example, if messages are broken into packets, then the system only delivers a message if all packets arrive at the receiving node and are properly reassembled. Furthermore, if the bits in a message have been scrambled, the message either is not delivered or is reconstructed before delivery; clearly some information is required for error checking.

(3)   Messages received by a module are the kind that module expects. Support for this property requires type checking which may be performed either at compile-time or run-time. Performing such type checking is analogous to the type checking of procedure calls.

(4)   Modules are not restricted to communicating only in terms of a predefined built-in set of types. Instead, modules can communicate in terms of values of interest to the application. In particular, if the application is defined using abstract data types, then values of these types can be communicated in messages.

14.2.3.1 Process Naming

In many programming languages the process receiving the message does not know the identity of the sending process. In others both identities must be known. For example, in CSP [12] explicit naming is required; in DP [17] the calling task, must name the called task, but the called task is unaware of who is calling and can receive from anyone; and in Parlance [18] neither task names each other, the connection being done by another process. By contrast in DP the calling task not only has to name the called task but also an associated procedure. In SR the caller need only name the entry, termed an operation, because each entry is directly associated with a process.

If processes name each other indirectly then some form of medium is required for inter-process communication. This medium is called a channel in occam, a mailbox in RED and Pascal-M, an exchange in the Series One Distributed Operating System [40], a link in the Arachne (formerly called Roscoe) distributed operating system [41], and a port in the extensions to CLU [3] and the SPICE kernel [42]. With indirect naming and using some forms of interconnection medium, it is possible to have many processes sending messages and many processes reading messages, although some systems restrict this to many senders and a single reader. For example the Arachne link allows only a single reader whereas Pascal-M allows many readers and many writers.

It is important to decide whether the names used for communication are interpreted locally or globally. For example in the Accent kernel [42] ports cannot be manipulated or named by a process as they are local capabilities; this protects a port against accidental or malicious access. However, in Pascal-M a mailbox is named by a global number which identifies the processor on which the mailbox resides. Protection is provided by having a large scattered range of identifiers with a random number component.

14.2.3.2 Blocking or Non-blocking Send

Liskov has suggested three possibilities for message operations: [2]

(1)   a no-wait send,

(2)   a synchronized send, and

(3)   a remote invocation send.

In the no-wait send, the sender continues execution immediately the message has been sent. This implies some buffering mechanism between the communicating processes. If there is an unbounded buffer then the sending process will never be blocked. However, the sending processes can then queue more messages than the receiving process can handle. A bounded buffer means that the system must provide a means of controlling the flow of data between processes which have mismatched speeds.

Rashid and Robertson [42] have listed three alternative actions that can be taken when the buffer is full.

(1)   The process is blocked until the message can be placed in the queue. This is useful if the sending process does not care if it is blocked and it is only interested in sending the message. An example of this can be found in the RED language.

(2)   The process is notified after suspending itself for a specified period while waiting for the message to be sent. This approach would be convenient where the process is sending a wakeup message to another process.

(3)   The message is accepted by the kernel but the data is left in the process' address space until it can be queued. The process is notified when this has happened. The most likely use for this option is that a server process is attempting to reply to a message but the client's queue is full. In this case the server does not wish to block but does want the data to be sent and furthermore wishes to be notified when this has been done.

An alternative action, not mentioned by Rashid and Robertson, is for the system to throw the message away. If the message was important then the sending process will wait for a reply; if an acknowledgement has not arrived within the specified time, the message can be repeated.

With the synchronized send the sender waits until the message has been received, as for example in CSP, Pascal-M and Parlance. In the remote invocation send the sender waits until it has received a reply as in the SR language and the Thoth operating system [43].

So far a blocking receive has been assumed. However some languages provide an option for a non-blocking receive and a means whereby a process can block while waiting for one of several messages to arrive. In Pascal-M this is provided by the *select* statement. CSP and SR use this form of message. In the more general case the selection may be between either send, receive or both message operations, and each one may be preceded by a guard [44]. Andrews [45] gives details of how guards function within selective message operations.

When selection is applied to receiving messages further control may be provided. In PLITS [46], a transaction key may be attached to a message when it is sent and the receiving process can delay until a message with the specified transaction key arrives. In SR a process can supply a Boolean condition with the receive operation which may include information in the message itself. This allows a process to look at the contents of a message before it receives it. If the Boolean condition is true, then the 'receive' is complete, otherwise another message is tried. If all messages queued on that 'receive' do not satisfy the boolean expression, then the statement blocks or another guard is evaluated.

14.2.3.3 Message Formats

The form of message can be thought of as being similar to a function call where the parameters to the send or receive contain the data to be sent in the message. DP and SR are examples of this syntax. The alternative notation is where a message is treated as a single object which may be compound in structure. Operating Systems with message passing primitives view messages in this way, as do Pascal-M and the RED language.

The messages can be of fixed or variable length. The Arachne [41], Thoth [43] and GEC 4000 operating systems allow only a fixed size message to be sent. Pascal-M allows variable length messages to be sent through different mailboxes but they must be fixed for a particular one. The RED language allows variable length data to be sent through its mailboxes in the form of variable length arrays. If variable length data transmission is allowed then there is the problem of allocating the space in the receiving process. This may be solved by allocating a maximum size buffer for the message, by allowing a preview of the message to determine its size and then preallocating the space, or by using virtual memory techniques to map the message into the receiver's address space.

14.2.3.4 Communications Failure

There are several failures which may occur when processes are communicating. They include the following: the destination is absent; the destination is unable to accept the communication; or the communication subsystem has garbled, lost or duplicated a message. Two protocols [47] have been proposed for communication in an environment where errors may occur: a Virtual Circuit and a Datagram.

A Virtual Circuit is a logical connection set up between communicating processes. All errors are masked out by the supporting software which must be able to cope with garbled communication and sequencing problems. Only when the connection is broken are the processes informed. A Datagram is a packet of information which is carried to its destination without reference to any other packet. No guarantee is given of their arrival, whether they are intact or whether they are lost or duplicated. The programs using the datagram service must provide their own error detection and correction.

14.3 TASKS ON LOOSELY COUPLED DISTRIBUTED SYSTEMS

In a loosely coupled distributed system there is no shared memory between the processors, so tasks in separate machines cannot run efficiently if they share data.

Clearly the difficulty of sharing data efficiently between tasks gives rise to problems in the efficient implementation of existing (uni-processor) multi-process (task) programming languages on loosely coupled distributed systems. Languages in this class include Modula, and Pascal-Plus.

14.3.1 Ada

Downes and Goldsack [48] have discussed the difficulty of using preliminary Ada in a loosely coupled system. They have introduced the concept of a *zone* which is a package containing a static task with other (possible) internal subtasks. All tasks within a zone may communicate using the full language features; however, communication between zones can only use the rendezvous mechanism and is restricted further by not allowing pointers to be passed as parameters. It is intended that a particular zone should be considered as a virtual node in a network. (A more detailed discussion of the virtual node concept when applied to Ada is given by a feasibility study commissioned by the European Communities and carried out by SPL International [49].) This virtual node concept is similar to language constructs designed specifically for distributed programming, for example the guardian of extended CLU [3] and Argus [4], and the "network module" of starmod [21],

Jessop [50] states that for a language to be effective in a distributed environment, as well as providing a suitable model for process communication and synchronization, it must also provide the following.

(1)   The separate compilation of modules and support for program libraries

(2)   The exceptions encountered when attempting to communicate.

(3)   The dynamic instantiation of nodes in the network without reinitialising the entire virtual network system.

An Ada task satisfies two of these requirements but, because it is unable to encapsulate data the same way as a package and cannot be a library unit, it is unsuitable as a virtual node. (In the early version of Ada called Green, tasks could satisfy (1) and (2) but not (3).) A package on the other hand is static.

For a static distributed system, such as those found in embedded computer systems, Jessop's requirement for dynamic instantiation of nodes can be relaxed. A *network package* as a virtual node can be introduced, which is a restricted form of a normal package. Only tasks specifications and type declarations may be visible from this package; in addition, access variables may not be declared as parameters to entries.

Even with this simple approach, certain assumptions have been made about the underlying communication network. For example it assumes that the request "to enter a rendezvous" arrives at the site of the called task. Although the language does provide a timed entry call, if the delay time expires it is assumed that the called task could not respond within the stated period, although it is assumed that the entry call was received. Furthermore, once a rendezvous has been entered, the language assumes it will complete eventually or the entered task is aborted. In addition, the language assumes that the called task will be able to return any result to the calling task immediately the rendezvous has finished. Consequently, if the communication subsystem fails, there is no way for the calling task to withdraw from the rendezvous, and the called task must wait until the calling task has received the results. Once a connection is broken, either the tasks must wait for the communication network to be repaired, or assume that the task has been aborted. The problems of remote entry call are very similar to the problems of remote procedure calls. A fuller discussion of the problems and possible solutions is given in the literature [51, 52, 53]. A further complication is caused by the replication of the network package at many nodes in the network. If a change is made to the package (for example, to the static data), then the new package must be made available to all of the nodes simultaneously.

Even if we accept the restrictions of the virtual node concept, the problems associated with the actual synchronization primitives, already outlined in these notes, become more difficult. In a distributed system, machines can go down and therefore tasks will be aborted arbitrarily. There can be long delays when communication takes place across the network, and so race conditions may occur in this circumstance.

14.3.2 occam

occam [14] is a small language designed to exploit the architecture of a number of loosely coupled processors connected by communication channels; such an architecture is realised by the forthcoming INMOS Transputer. The language is modelled on CSP, although the detailed method of synchronization is very similar to that of Ada. In particular, input can be awaited on a number of channels, the input being taken from the first channel which provides data. One important difference from Ada is that an occam concurrent process must state the name of the channel in use and the provider of data must also name the same channel. Communication can be thought of as a distributed assignment. For example:

```
PAR
    c ! x
    c ? y
```

is the same as the distributed assignment

```
y := x
```

The behaviour of a process is only visible from the messages which pass along its channels. The internal structure of a process is hidden, providing modularity when constructing large programs.

The language provides explicit mechanisms for the construction of sequences of sequential statements (SEQ) and for sets of statements that may be executed in parallel (PAR). For example the following is a simple double buffer:

```
WHILE TRUE
     VAR x, y :
     SEQ
         PAR
             buffer.in ? x
             buffer.out ! y
         PAR
             buffer.out ! x
             buffer.in ? y
```

The language contains a restricted set of statements consistent with its philosophy of simplicity. It is interesting to note that the initial version of occam is typeless, the single data type being the "word". Furthermore, occam programs will execute on one or more processors with identical semantics, although there will be performance gains when further processors are added to the network.

14.3.3 Pascal-m

Pascal-m [19] is a dialect of Pascal designed to allow type-secure programming of systems of communicating processes, designed at QMC under a DCS SERC grant. It is based upon synchronized message-passing, without the use of shared memory, using so-called mailboxes, which are separated from processes; thus allowing non-deterministic pairings of senders and receivers.

Pascal-m programs are structured using modules which allow the programmer to describe the constraints on the initial interconnection of processes, and to control the lifetime of mailboxes. The association of types with mailboxes means that the Pascal rules of strong typing apply across the entire system. Mailbox identifying values may be transmitted, thus allowing the specification of dynamically extensible patterns of interconnection.

As an example of the use of Pascal-m, the following program fragment is a solution to the producer-consumer problem using an intermediate buffer to solve the problem of the producer and consumer running at unequal speeds.

```
CONST Tmax = ...

MAILBOX P, C: mt;

PROCESS producer (X: mt as send);
BEGIN ... send data to X ... END;

PROCESS buffer(U: mt as receive; V: mt as send);
TYPE Tindex = 1..Tmax;
VAR T: ARRAY[Tindex] of t;
    nextin, nextout: Tindex;
    count: 0..Tmax;

BEGIN
    count := 0; nextin := 1; nextout := 1;
    REPSELECT
        IF count < Tmax THEN receive T[nextin] from U:
            BEGIN
            nextin := (nextin mod Tmax)+1; count := count+1
            END;
        IF count<>0 THEN send T[nextout] to V:
            BEGIN
            nextout := (nextout mod Tmax)+1; count := count-1
            END
    END {repselect}
END; {buffer}

PROCESS consumer(Y: mt as receive);
BEGIN ... receive V from Y ... END;

INSTANCE p = producer(P); b = buffer(P, C); c = consumer(C);
```

In this program, the producer sends its data to the mailbox P and the consumer process receives its data from mailbox C. The buffer process between them receives from P and sends to C. The REPSELECT statement, which never terminates, offers to receive from the producer whenever there is room in the buffer array, and, simultaneously, to send to the consumer whenever there is something in the buffer array.

Any number of intermediate buffer processes can be inserted between the producer and the consumer processes. Note that the designers of the producer or consumer processes need take no notice of the inclusion of buffer processes. The following program fragment interposes two buffer processes between producer and consumer.

```
MAILBOX P, B, C: mt;

INSTANCE p= producer(P);
    b1 = buffer(P, B); b2 = buffer(B, C);
    c = consumer(C);
```

The designers of Pascal-m have now described the extended semantics that are necessary for the use of the language in a distributed environment [54]. Their basic assumption is that no distinction should be made between local and remote communication in the linguistic structure of the language. Furthermore they make a assumption of *fairness* when several communications are possible, in the sense that if a process is willing to communicate and there continue to be potential partners for it, then there must be a time in the future by which that process will have communicated. The designers of Pascal-m have now defined a protocol which will ensure the appropriate semantics, with the basic communication taking place using datagrams over the underlying network. The protocol does not demand a completely reliable network, but requires a *transmission-truthful network;* by this they mean that if the sender is told that the message was received, then it definitely was received; although if he is told that the message wasn't received, then the position is uncertain. Such a network property can be implemented by using suitable checksums in each packet transmitted. Fairness is ensured by associating a counter with each select guard.

At present the QMC group are putting their ideas on distributed Pascal-m to the test by implementation. So far no results have been reported.

14.3.4 CONIC

CONIC [55] provides an integrated set of techniques and tools for constructing and managing large distributed computer control systems. The original architecture evolved during a project, funded by the National Coal Board, on the use of microprocessors for monitoring and control in coal mines. The project has been funded subsequently by the SERC DCS programme.

The CONIC system provides a two level language: one for the programming of individual software components (module definitions), and the other for the configuration management of a distributed system built from instances of these modules.

The module definition language has some similarity to Ada, in that it separates the interface specification of a module (or package) from the operational part. A major concern has been the definition of an interface specification technique which does not include behavioural aspects of the module. Each module or group of modules may contain one or more tasks; this program is then placed in the distributed system using the configuration language. The inter-task communication is achieved by message passing, using send-wait and receive-reply primitives.

The configuration language enables modules to be interconnected to form a system. The language insists that ports and their associated messages are strongly typed; furthermore, it enables the mapping, of groups of modules on to hardware structures of stations and subnets, to be specified. In addition, it permits the naming of groups of modules so that they can be associated to reflect a particular application structure.

The implementation work has investigated the problems of dynamic reconfiguration, an important problem in any environment which requires continuity of service.

14.4 REFERENCES

1.   G. R. Andrews and F. Schneider, "Concepts and Notations for Concurrent Programming," *ACM Computing Surveys* **15**(1), pp.3-44 (March 1983).

2.   B. Liskov, "Primitives for Distributed Computing," *Proceedings of the Seventh ACM Symposium on Operating System Principles*, pp.33-43, Pacific Grove, California (December 1979).

3.   B. Liskov, "On Linguistic Support for Distributed Programs," *IEEE Transactions on Software Engineering* **SE-8**(3), pp.203-210 (May 1982).

4. B. Liskov and R. Scheifler, "Guardians and Actions: Linguistic Support for Robust, Distributed Programs," *ACM Transactions on Programming Languages and Systems* **5**(3), pp.381-404 (July 1983).

5. C. Ellis, J. Feldman, and J. Heliotis, "Language Constructs and Support Systems for Distributed Computing," TR102, Department of Computer Science, University of Rochester (May 1982).

6. S. Shrivastava and J. Banatre, "Reliable Resource Allocation Between Unreliable Processes," *IEEE Transactions on Software Engineering* **SE-4**(3), pp.230-240 (May 1978).

7. S. Shrivastava, "Structuring Distributed Systems for Recoverability and Crash Resistance," *IEEE Transactions on Software Engineering* **SE-7**(4), pp.436-447 (July 1981).

8. W A Whitaker, "Ada - The New DoD Standard High Order Language," *1979 Summer Computer Simulation Conference*, pp.832-834 (16-18 July 1979).

9. N. Wirth, "Modula-2," Nr.36, Institut fur Informatik, ETH (December 1978).

10. D. M. Ritchie and K. Thompson, "The UNIX Time-Sharing System," *Bell Sys. Tech. J.* **57**(6), pp.1905-1929 (1978).

11. J. G. Mitchell, W. Maybury, and R. Sweet, "Mesa Language Manual Verson 5.0," CSL-79-3, Palo Alto Research Center, Xerox (April 1979).

12. C. A. R. Hoare, "Communicating Sequential Processes," *CACM* **21**(8), pp.666-677 (August 1978).

13. P. Brinch-Hansen, "Edison: A multiprocessor language," *Software Practice and Experience* **11**(4), pp.325-361 (April 1981).

14. D May, "occam," *SIGPLAN Notices* **18**(4), pp.69-79 (April 1983).

15. P. Brinch-Hansen, "The Programming Language Concurrent Pascal," *IEEE Transactions on Software Engineering* **SE-1**(2), pp.199-206 (June 1975).

16. N. Wirth, "Modula: a Language for Modular Multiprogramming," *Software Practice and Experience* **7**(1), pp.3-35 (January-February 1977).

17. P. Brinch-Hansen, "Distributed Processes: A Concurrent Programming Concept," *CACM* **21**(11), pp.934-941 (November 1978).

18. P. F. Reynolds, "Parallel Processing Structure: Languages, Schedules, and Performance Results," Ph.D Thesis, University of Texas, Austin (1979).

19. S. Abramsky and R. Bornat, "Pascal-m: A Language for Distributed Systems," QMC CSL 326, Queen Mary College Computer Systems Laboratory (December 1982).

20. J Nestor and M Van Deusen, *Red Language Reference Manual,* Intermetrics Inc IR.310.2 (8 March 1979).

21. R. P. Cook, "*MOD - A Language for Distributed Programming," *Proceedings of the 1st International Conference on Distributed Computing Systems*, pp.233-241, Huntsville, Alabama (October 1979).

22. G. R. Andrews, "Synchronising Resources," *ACM Transactions on Programming Languages and Systems* **3**(4), pp.405-431 (October 1981).

23. C. A. R. Hoare, "Towards a Theory of Parallel Programming," pp. 61-71 in *Operating Systems Techniques*, Academic Press (1972).

24. P. Brinch-Hansen, "Structured Multiprogramming," *CACM* **15**(7), pp.574-578 (July 1972).

25. C. A. R. Hoare, "Monitors - An Operating System Structuring Concept," *CACM* **17**(10), pp.549-557 (October 1974).

26. P. Brinch-Hansen, *Operating System Principles,* Prendice-Hall, New Jersey (July 1973).

27. J. Welsh and D. Bustard, "Pascal-Plus - Another Language for Modular Multiprogramming," *Software Practice and Experience* **9**(11), pp.947-957 (November 1979).

28. A. Lister, "The Problem of Nested Monitor Calls," *ACM, Operating Systems Review* **11**(3), pp.5-7 (July 1977).

29. B. Haddon, "Nested Monitor Calls," *ACM Operating Systems Review* **11**(4), pp.18-23 (October 1977).

30. D. Parnas, "The Non-Problem of Nested Monitor Calls," *ACM, Operating Systems Review* **12**(1), pp.12-14 (January 1978).

31. B. Lampson and D. Redell, "Experience with Processes and Monitors in Mesa," *CACM* **23**(2), pp.105-117 (February 1980).

32. G. R. Andrews and J. R. McGraw, "Language Features for Process Interaction," *Proceedings of the ACM Conference on Language Design for Reliable Software, SIGPLAN Notices* **12**(3), pp.114-127 (March 1977).

33. W. Kaubisch, R. Perrott, and C. A. R. Hoare, "Quasiparallel Programming," *Software Practice and Experience* **6**(3), pp.341-356 (July-September 1976).

34. A. Silberschatz, R. Kieburtz, and A. Bernstein, "Extending Concurrent Pascal to Allow Dynamic Resource Management," *IEEE Transactions on Software Engineering* **SE-3**(3), pp.210-217 (May 1977).

35. R. Cambell and A. N. Habermann, "The Specification of Process Synchronisation by Path Expressions," pp. 89-102 in *Lecture Notes in Computer Science, vol 16*, Springer-Verlag, New York (1974).

36. T. Bloom, "Evaluating Synchronisation Mechanisms," *Proceedings of the Seventh ACM Symposium on Operating System Principles*, pp.24-32, Pacific Grove (December 1979).

37. U.S. Department of Defense, "Reference Manual for the Ada Programming Language," ANSI/MIL-STD 1815 A (January 1983).

38. A. J. Wellings, D. Keeffe, and G. M. Tomlinson, "A Problem with Ada and Resource Allocation," *Ada Letters* **3**(4) (January, February 1984).

39. W. M. Gentleman, "Message Passing Between Sequential Processes: the Reply Primitive and the Administrator Concept," *Software Practice and Experience* **11**(5), pp.435-466 (May 1981).

40. W. D. Sincoskie and D. J. Farber, "The Series/1 Distributed Operating System: Description and Comments," *Proceedings of the COMPCON 80 Fall Distributed Computing Conference*, pp.579-584, Washington DC (September 1980).

41. M. H. Solomon and R. A. Finkel, "The Roscoe Distributed Operating System," *Proceedings of the Seventh ACM Symposium on Operating Systems Principles*, pp.108-114 (December 1979).

42. R. F. Rashid and G. G. Robertson, "Accent: A communication oriented network operating system kernel," *Proceedings of the Eighth ACM Symposium on Operating Systems Principles*, pp.64-75, Pacific Grove, California (December 1981).

43. D. Cheriton, M. A. Malcolm, L. S. Melen, and G. R. Sager, "Thoth, a Portable Real-time Operating System," *CACM* **22**(2), pp.105-115 (1979).

44. E. W. Dijkstra, "Guarded Commands, Nondeterminacy, and Formal Derivation of Programs," *CACM* **18**(8), pp.453-457 (August 1975).

45. G. R. Andrews, "Distributed Programming Languages," *ACM'82 Conference Proceedings*, pp.113-117, Dallas (October 1982).

46. J. A. Feldman, "High Level Programming for Distributed Computing," *CACM* **22**(1), pp.353-68 (June 1979).

47. L. Pouzin, "Virtual Circuits vs Datagrams - Technical and Political Problems," *Proceedings of the National Computer Conference, AFIPS*, pp.483-494 (June 1976).

48. V A Downes and S J Goldsack, "The Use of the Ada Language for Programming a Distributed System," in *Real Time Programming*, ed. V H Hasse, Pergamon Press, Oxford (1980).

49. R. Stammers and et al., "A Feasibility Study to Determine the Applicability of Ada and APSE in a Multi-Microprocessor Distributed Environment," SPL International, Research Centre, The Charter, Abingdon, OX14 3LZ, UK (March 1983).

50. W H Jessop, "Ada packages and distributed systems," *SIGPLAN Notices* **17**(2), pp.28-36 (February 1982).

51. B. J. Nelson, "Remote Procedure Call," CMU-CS-81-119, Department of Computer Science, Carnegie-Mellon University (May 1981).

52. B. Lampson, "Remote Procedure Calls," pp. 365-370 in *Lecture Notes in Computer Science, Vol. 105*, Springer-Verlag (1981).

53. S. K. Shrivastava, "On the Treatment of Orphans in a Distributed System," *Proceedings of the 3rd Symposium on Reliability in Distributed Software and Database Systems*, Florida (October 1983).

54. S Cook, "The Distributed Implementation of Pascal-m," *QMC internal report* (24 June 1983).

55. J Kramer, J Magee, M Sloman, and A Lister, "CONIC: An integrated approach to distributed computer control systems," *IEE Proceedings* **130 Part E**(1), pp.1-10 (January 1983).

Part IV

Closely - Coupled Systems

D. Aspinall
R. L. Grimsdale
F. Halsall

15 Architecture

D Aspinall

15.1 INTRODUCTION

Parallel computation, or the concurrent operation of separate processing units, has for a long time been used as a technique to derive better performance from a given technology. The first step, taken some thirty years ago, was to move from bit-serial computers to word-serial or parallel computers to achieve an order of magnitude improvement in performance. Various styles of concurrency within a monolithic computer system then evolved to enable several operations to occur at once. These styles were identified and classified by Flynn [1]

SISD	Single Instruction Single Data (Conventional Computer)
SIMD	Single Instruction Multiple Data (e.g. ICL-DAP)
MISD	Multiple Instruction Single Data (e.g. CRAY-205)
MIMD	Multiple Instruction Multiple Data (e.g. CMU-C.mmp)

In the first (SISD) the instruction cycle is executed as one sequential procedure. In the second (SIMD) a plurality of data operations may be invoked to occur concurrently during one instruction cycle, whilst in the third (MISD) actions within an instruction cycle may be overlapped with different actions of consecutive instruction cycles to achieve a higher rate of instruction execution. The MIMD organisation allows several computers to operate separately,concurrently and in concert so that several instruction cycles may be occurring simultaneously, to give an instruction execution rate which is directly proportional to the number of active computers in the assemblage. It is this organization which is the basis for the architecture of closely coupled systems. In these systems, we are concerned about methods of interconnecting computers to enable communications between them to occur within the conventional instruction cycle, to achieve the rapid transfer of working variables and control information between concurrent processes acting as parts of a total process. The interconnection method itself places certain requirements on the instruction set and hence the architecture of the individual computer [2].

In this chapter we will consider strategies for the interconnection of computers and the basic properties of the instruction set to enable reliable connections. The direct shared memory, implemented as a multiport memory in the CYBA-M or as part of a Multibus system will be described in some detail before indirect methods of coupling computers are discussed, which lead on to loosely coupled distributed systems, or to the realization of very large parallel computing systems utilising a vast number of transputers [3].

15.2 INTERCONNECTION STRATEGIES

A study of the possible methods of interconnecting computers was carried out by Anderson and Jensen [4], which was later analysed to identify the most likely methods to be used for closely coupled systems [5]. It is appropriate to revise this analysis in the light of experience.

In closely coupled systems the implementation of the algorithm to be executed can be seen as a network of co-operating sequential processes **Figure 15-1**. Each sequential process occupies a single microcomputer or processor/memory pair and the co-operation involves an arc which links computer to computer. It is in the nature of co-operation that during a transaction one process will send data to a second process which receives it. Thus, each arc can be viewed as a buffer register which is written to by the execution of a *store* order in the sending processor and subsequently read from by a *load* order obeyed in the receiving processor. As far as each processor/memory pair is concerned, the real memory address space is apportioned between conventional memory, output ports and input ports. The output ports connect to arcs for sending by *store* orders and the input ports for receiving from arcs by *load* orders. The physical provision of the memory elements which enable these ports and hence the arcs (which link the processes) depends upon the interconnection structure to be used. The most obvious structure is by direct wire links. In this each arc is physically provided by an individual buffer memory and appropriate connections into the memory space of both the sending and receiving processor. The problem is not unlike that faced by the designer of a product based upon a single microprocessor, several input/output devices and different types of RAM and ROM. Each new problem to be solved is described by a new network of

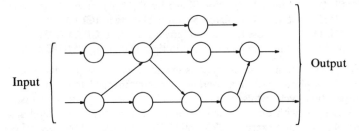

Input   Output

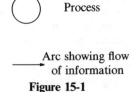

◯   Process

⟶   Arc showing flow of information

Figure 15-1

processor/memory pairs, which in turn specifies the memory arrangement for each processor and the physical routing of the wires which become the arcs. Modifications to the network require physical changes at both the sender and receiver, as well as the change of the buffer memory and the interconnections.

The network of arcs between the processor/memory pairs are programmed by a physical process not unlike that of a patchboard of the early analogue computers. The setting up of a new problem by patching a different set of interconnections for an assemblage of processor/memory pairs creates many difficulties and it is worthwhile to consider an electronically programmed method of interconnection. One obvious method is the cross bar employed in the CMU-C.mmp system [6]. The alternative which has been adopted on a wide scale is to provide a direct shared memory as in CYBA-M [7], or as in Multibus [8].

15.3 INSTRUCTION SET PRIMITIVES

The basic method of transferring data between the processor and the buffer of the arc is to use the *load* and *store* instructions, which effectively transfer between a central register in the processor and a location in the memory space designated as the address of the buffer. Each processor is assigned address locations for its own private memory, and for the shared memory space which provides the arc buffers. It is possible for all the shared memory to be accessible from all the processors attached to it. Conflicts arise when two or more processors attempt to access the shared memory simultaneously. This connection for access must be dealt with by the circuits of the multiport memory or the shared bus. The way in which the contention is resolved is transparent to the process running in the processor/memory pair and does not affect the instruction set, it merely affects the timing of the interaction between processor and shared memory. Synchronisation of the instruction cycles of the various processors is achieved within the logic circuits of the shared memory controllers, and is no concern of the programmer when preparing the instruction sequences. However, incorrect software synchronization can lead to indeterminacy deadlock. Many of these processes are at a high level and will be dealt with in Chapter 16, but there is one problem which must be solved by special facilities in the hardware which affect the instruction set [9].

15.4 TEST AND SET OF LOCK

So far in this discussion the shared memory has been the location of the private arc buffers, which are essentially only ever written to by a single sender and read by a single receiver. The shared memory may include locations which are used as working space by several processors, or correspond to buffers for shared peripheral devices. The sharing of these resources amongst several concurrent processes can lead to confusion if two or more use the shared resource simultaneously. Special semaphore arrangements must be made to ensure that one and only one process has sole use of the resource until it has dealt with it. The form of the semaphore could be a byte in the shared memory, termed a *lock* byte, which is associated with each shared resource. If the *lock* is set, or closed, then the particular resource is currently the property of a process, and all others are locked out from it and denied access to it. If the *lock* is not set, or open, then the resource is free and waiting to become the property of the first process which attempts to stake a claim. The protocol requires a process to examine the *lock* byte before attempting to have its way with the shared resource behind the *lock*. If the *lock* is set as closed, then the resource is already seized by another process, and the interrogating process must proceed no further, but must delay access to this resource until the *lock* is open. If the *lock* is open, then the interrogating process must first close the *lock* before proceeding to access the resource. The action of reading from the shared memory, then checking the status of the *lock* byte, can take several memory cycles, during which time other processors may read the same *lock* byte and believe they have also found an open *lock*. They will then close the *lock* and proceed as if they had sole rights of access. The use of the simple *load* and *store* instructions with the *lock* byte cannot guarantee correct working of the protocol.

It is necessary to make special provision in the hardware either to ensure that the reading of a *lock* byte will immediately set the *lock* to closed [10], or to provide special instructions [9]. The 6800 instruction set includes a test and set instruction. When this is obeyed, the *lock* byte is read from shared memory into the processor; all other accesses to the shared memory are held up until the processor has examined the value of the *lock*, and written back a new value into the byte in shared memory. At the end of this Read-Modify-Write memory cycle the shared memory is again released to accesses from any processor through the bus. In the 8086 a special prefix *lock* may be inserted before any instruction. When inserted before an *exchange* instruction, the action is similar to the Read-Modify-Write sequence of the Test and Set instruction.

15.5 MATCHING OF PROCESSOR AND MEMORY SPEED

In the early days of computing, the technology of the processor was based solely on electronic components whilst the memory devices relied upon acoustic or magnetic phenomena. The electronic components could operate at a higher rate then the memory devices, and extra delays were introduced at the interfaces where the transducers converted between electronic signals and acoustic or magnetic effects. The processor became much faster than its associated main memory. Whilst the memory technology was predominantly based upon the magnetic core the time of an instruction cycle was determined by the cycle time of the read (destroy) - write (restore) cycle of the memory. Within the instruction cycle there would be one memory cycle for instruction fetch and usually a second memory cycle for operand fetch or store.

In those days, the circuits of the processor were waiting for the memory and their potential for doing work was not fully exploited. The efficiency of the combined processor/memory pair could be increased by partitioning the memory into a small number of sections, and allowing for a separate access mechanism to each section; so that the access for an instruction in one section might be interleaved with the operand access of the previous instruction located in another section of the memory [11]. Such an arrangement, as shown in **Figure 15-2**, resulted in several similar separate memory components being attached to one processor component.

The advent of semiconductor memory technology changed the situation. Gradually, as the semiconductor technology developed, the time devoted to accessing a memory component became similar to that of the time required for actions within the processor. Indeed, when the first microprocessors were released in the early 1970s, the instruction cycle time of the processor was longer than the access time of the associated memory components. An arrangement as shown in **Figure 15-3** became possible in which four microprocessors could be interleaved with one memory, giving a structure in which each processor could operate at full speed; a factor of four improvement in raw instruction speed could be achieved. This increase in instruction execution rate can be exploited if the program can be subdivided into four separate procedures, which run concurrently on the four separate processing elements. This is a rare possibility, and should not be used as the basis for achieving an increased performance for execution of a conventional sequential program. It is far easier to achieve a better overall instruction execution rate

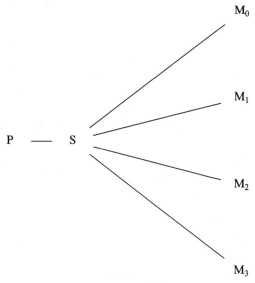

Figure 15-2

for a given program by using a single processor to match the speed of the memory component. This is seen in the development of bi-polar bit slice microprocessor components to match the uni-polar memory components.

However, there are few information processing tasks which rely on the execution of a single sequential procedure. It is more common to find several concurrent processes making up the total processing activity. A single processing element may be time-shared amongst these processes, or each process may be assigned to its own processing element, which co-operate with other processes by communicating through a shared memory as shown in **Figure 15-4**.

The shared memory may also include common data or program areas and memory mapped input/output devices to be shared among the processing elements.

15.6 SHARED MEMORY IMPLEMENTATION

There are two extreme requirements which govern the choice of shared memory implementation technique. At one extreme is a requirement for a high rate of response by the shared memory to requests for access by individual processes. These are situations where performance is important, and there is a desire to achieve an overall speed which is proportional to the number of processing elements involved.

At the other extreme there is less desire for a high response rate, but more desire for flexibility in the number and type of processing elements and memory components to be shared.

The first requirement suggests a multi-port memory approach, **Figure 15-5**, in which the number of ports is fixed at the outset by the problem, to allow optimizing the design of the access circuitry to achieve a high rate. The second requirement suggests a bus structure, **Figure 15-6**, which can be flexible both in the number and type of devices attached to it. In this case emphasis is on the development and adoption of a bus standard to support this type of activity, over a long period of time, involving many

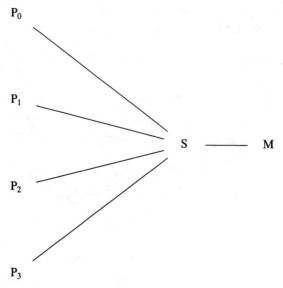

Figure 15-3

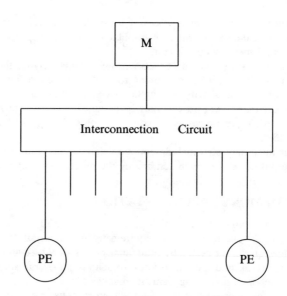

PE :- Processing Element = P-S-M

Figure 15-4

manufacturers. Such a standard must be a compromise which sacrifices performance to some extent.

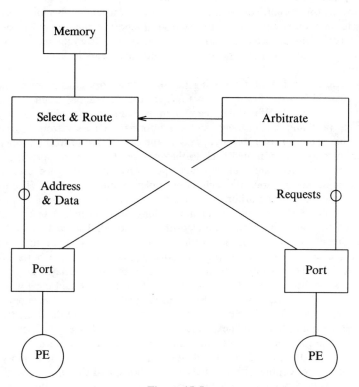

Figure 15-5

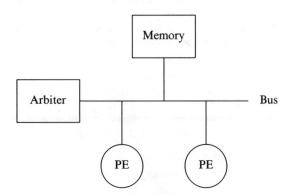

Figure 15-6

15.7 COMMON FEATURES OF SHARED MEMORY ACCESS MECHAN-ISMS

First we have the ports at the interface between the individual processing element and the shared memory interconnection mechanism. Next we have the arbitration circuit which receives signals from each of the ports, and delivers acknowledgements to these when they are allowed to proceed to access the memory. The arbitration circuit must also control the method of selecting the route between the port and the global memory. The route is the next important component. In the case of the shared memory, this is a basic *and/or* gate for routing data and addresses from the port to the memory access mechanism, and a basic fan-out mechanism for the routing of data from the memory to the individual ports. Finally, we have the memory component and its own individual access mechanism.

The sequence of actions for accessing the shared memory is as follows, and is numbered in **Figure 15-7**. The first action is to signal the arbitration circuit and to wait for permission to proceed. When the permission is granted, the routes are established between the port and the memory, and the information passes from the port to the memory. The memory is then accessed, and, in the case of a read from memory, the data read from memory is then routed back to the appropriate processor port. It is important to remember that there are four separate operations involved, since each one has a different time depending upon the method of implementation employed. The first action, that of negotiating with the arbitration circuit and receiving permission to proceed, can be either a very short time interval or a very long one, depending upon traffic to the memory and the particular arbitration algorithm employed. The next action, of actually moving address (and data) from the port to the memory depends upon the particular circuit technique employed and the physical wire delays between the ports through the routing circuit to the memory itself. In the case of a bus these delays can be quite long since the bus has been designed to cover a fairly long distance and cope with a diverse number of processor ports attached; whereas in the multi-port shared memory, the routes have been very carefully engineered to be as short as possible, and the delay from port to memory can be quite short. The next time is the access to the memory itself. Where performance is important, it is assumed that this memory is of high speed and of only one type. However, in the case of the bus situation, it is assumed that the memory may well be of different types coping with a variety of situations, and that the actual time to this memory may vary depending upon the type. The final action is routing data from the memory to the port. The time taken for this in the case of the bus is similar to the time for routing from the port to the memory component, since the circuitry is very similar. In the case of the multi-port memory, the mechanism is different, since here the memory is providing fan-out to all the individual ports; only one of the ports will, in fact, get the output from the memory into its own buffer registers. This is a different mechanism to

$$
\begin{array}{l}
1 \left\{ \begin{array}{l} \text{Signal request to arbitration} \\ \text{circuit and wait for permission.} \end{array} \right. \\
2 \left\{ \begin{array}{l} \text{Route Address (\& Data) Between} \\ \text{Port \& Memory} \end{array} \right. \\
3 \left\{ \begin{array}{l} \text{Access Memory} \\ \text{for read (or write)} \end{array} \right. \\
4 \left\{ \begin{array}{l} \text{Route Data from} \\ \text{Memory to port} \end{array} \right.
\end{array}
$$

Figure 15-7

the *and/or* combination required for routing data and address from the ports into the memory.

The main difference between the two implementation mechanisms can be seen in the discussion on the timing sequence. In the case of the multi-port memory, the times are all short and can all be well controlled, suggesting the possibility of a highly synchronized access mechanism. In the case of the bus approach, the delays can vary depending upon the particular application, since the number of processing elements attached to the bus can vary, the number of memory components attached to the bus can vary, and so on. It would seem, therefore, sensible to assume that the bus interconnection mechanism would lend itself to a more asynchronous approach, where time is less predictable. It is not intended to look at the bus system in any fine detail, since this information can be readily obtained from the manufacturers of microprocessor components. The detailed considerations of the direct shared memory access mechanisms used in the CYBA-M are given in Chapter 19. The CYBA-M interconnection mechanism is able to achieve a very high performance from the shared memory. The rate of executing instructions in a processor, where the memory accesses are made to the shared memory, is only reduced by a very small percentage, even when 16 processors are simultaneously in contention for the one shared memory.

15.8 POINT-TO-POINT INTERCONNECTIONS : THE TRANSPUTER

So far in this chapter, we have considered the ways in which we may programme the interconnections between processing elements by the use of shared memory to represent the arcs. An alternative approach would be to provide processing elements with appropriate communication facilities, so that they may be directly connected as indicated in **Figure 15-1**. Before we pursue this alternative, it is as well to note that the directionality indicated in **Figure 15-1** may represent the general behaviour of processes which transmit input into outputs. In practice, however, the arcs between processing elements are usually bidirectional, if only to enable the backward acknowledgement from the receiver to the sender. It is therefore obvious that, in designing a node to support directly arcs for interconnection purposes, these arcs must be bidirectional, and the node must cope with this bidirectional feature. In agreeing the specification of such a processing element, it is important to decide upon the number of arcs which need to be provided in the physical structure of the device. It is clear that a transputer with one bidirectional port attached to it may, in certain circumstances, be used to implement a unidirectional ring. However, this is a special case which is hardly worthy of further discussion. A transputer which has two bidirectional ports can be used to implement a bidirectional ring. It is necessary to provide three bidirectional ports to enable anything other than these structures. With three bidirectional ports, it is possible to provide random nets of processing elements, which allow streams to merge onto one node or to be fanned out from a node. Such a component is, of course, a natural for the implementation of a tree of processing elements which may have application for reduction machines. The next step would be to provide four bidirectional arcs on such an element. By this technique, it is possible to have two orthogonal bidirectional rings, providing a structure as shown in **Figure 15-8**, as well as a tree structure or a wider set of random structures. A transputer proposed by the INMOS Company does indeed provide a capability of implementing four simultaneously active arcs [12]. Each arc can support a transfer of 1.5Mbytes per second each way. The internal processing element of the transputer is a 32-bit system providing 10 million instructions per second processing power, with memory as well as these link capabilities. It also provides facilities for interfacing local peripherals.

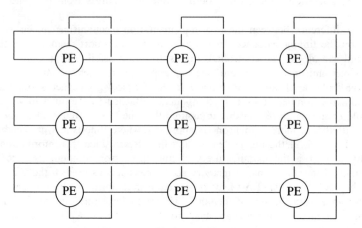

Figure 15-8

15.9 CONCLUSIONS

The architecture of Closely-Coupled Systems is based primarily upon the direct shared memory. There are two possible ways in which to implement interconnections to this memory. One is by a multi-port approach with special circuitry to obtain a high rate of access to the memory, which has the constraint of providing a fixed number of ports, and there is some loss of flexibility. The other extreme is the multi-bus approach, which allows for a variety of processing elements to gain access through a shared bus to the shared memory components which may, themselves, be of a variety of devices.

It is essential when considering the processing element to be included in such closely-coupled systems to ensure that there are certain basic facilities to enable synchronization of processes. The recent advent of the transputer has made it possible to contemplate a regular array of processing elements linked via high performance arcs. Such elements, which have a capability of four links, also make it possible to contemplate other irregular structures suited to the particular needs of a problem. In the case of the transputer, the programming of arcs must be achieved by an indirect method superimposed upon the regular structure, or by direct physical connections using direct links between the processing elements involved. There is clearly going to be much interest in future in the role of the transputer in closely-coupled systems.

15.10 REFERENCES

1.   M. J. Flynn, "Very High Speed Computing Systems," *Proceedings of the IEEE* **12**, pp.1901-1909 (December 1966).

2.   D. Aspinall, "Multi-microsystems'," *Proceedings of INFOTECH State of the Art Conference*, pp.47-62, Future Systems, London (1977).

3.   I. M. Barron, "A Transputer," pp. 343-357 in *The Microprocessor and its Application*, ed. D. Aspinall, Cambridge University Press (1978).

4.   G. A. Anderson and E. D. Jensen, "Computer Interconnection Structures; taxonomy, characteristics and examples," *ACM Computing Surveys* **5**(14), pp.197-213 (December 1975).

5. D. Aspinall, "Systems of Many Processing Elements," pp. 295-311 in *The Microprocessor and its Application*, ed. D. Aspinall, Cambridge University Press (1978).

6. W. A. Wulf and C. G. Bell, "C.mmp - A multi-miniprocessor," *AFIPS Conference Proceedings, FJCC 1972* **41**(2), pp.765-777.

7. E. L. Dagless, "A multi-processor - CYBA-M," pp. 843-848 in *Information Processing 77*, ed. B. Gilchrist, North Holland (1977).

8. *Intel Multibus Specification No. 9800683,* Intel Corporation, California, USA (1978).

9. D. Aspinall, "Microcomputer Systems Design," pp. 135-175 in *Lecture Notes in Computer Science No. 126*, ed. McCarthy, Springer-Verlag (1982).

10. D. Aspinall and E. Dagless, "Overview of a Development Environment," *Microprocessors and Microsystems* **3**(7), pp.301-305 (September 1979).

11. R. N. Ibbett, *The Architecture of High Performance Computers,* McMillan (1982).

12. INMOS Ltd, *IMS T424 Transputer - Advance Information,* INMOS. Bristol (November 1983).

16 Programming Languages

R. L. Grimsdale

16.1 INTRODUCTION

The type of system with which we are concerned has been identified in the previous chapter as a member of the MIMD class. The architecture is characterized by an arrangement in which two or more processors have shared access to a memory module. Another important characteristic is the degree of granularity of the software modules. An important property of multi-processor systems is their ability to perform operations in parallel. In the present type of system there is coarse granularity and moderate size tasks execute in parallel. Each task includes a block of instructions which are executed in sequence. At certain points in the sequence of execution of the tasks there is a requirement for data exchange between the tasks. A task which is due to receive data cannot proceed until the supplying task is able to deliver. This arrangement should be compared with the Data Flow class of machine which exhibits fine granularity. Processing units perform operations on, typically, two operands. Before the operation can commence, both the operands must have been supplied. The coarse grain system with which we are concerned requires careful design of the inter-task communication facilities, because the user has a considerable degree of freedom in the design of the individual modules. Good support from a programming language is thus very desirable. The physical path over which processor pass data from one to another has been identified as a register, which may be a single separate physical unit, or exist with others in a memory module. An objective of a programming language which supports multi-tasking is to hide such details from the user, and to provide safe methods of inter-task communication.

In addition to the special requirements noted above, a good programming language should provide control constructs for structured programming, with the ability to define data types and to provide run-time type checking. The task of creating a large system benefits enormously from a modular language permitting partial compilation and testing.

16.2 CONCURRENCY SUPPORT MECHANISMS

Certain basic requirements to support concurrency can be identified. First, it is necessary for the results produced by one task to be used as an input to another task, therefore some satisfactory mechanism of data transfer between tasks must be provided.

Second, there is normally a need to synchronize the operation of tasks. Because of mutual interdependence, one task cannot proceed beyond a certain stage without some action occurring in a dependent task. Similarly the dependent task cannot continue beyond a particular stage until the previous task has accomplished certain operations. Summarizing, there is a need to pass data between tasks, and a requirement to synchronize mutually dependant tasks.

Before the advent of programming languages which supported concurrency it was necessary to employ a multi-tasking operating system to perform the inter-tasking operations. This provided a way of binding together a number of separate sequential programs to form a multi-task system. A common arrangement was to provide a bounded buffer for inter-task communication. The operation 'put(item)' and 'get(item)' respectively stored a data item in the buffer and retrieved an item from the buffer. The functions 'full' and 'empty' were used to test the current state of the buffer. To prevent simultaneous access to the buffer it was necessary to employ a semaphore [1]. There are objections to the use of a semaphore because such a low-level mechanism can be easily misused or even omitted. Because of this, various high-level constructs have been incorporated in programming languages, having the advantage of a degree of compile-time protection.

16.3 THE MONITOR CONCEPT

The *monitor* [2, 3] is an arrangement in which shared data is encapsulated with a set of procedures which perform operations on that data. The data cannot be accessed except through the use of these procedures. The monitor is activated by a process (external to the monitor) making a call on one of the monitor procedures. Only one process at a time may be actively executing a monitor procedure. The monitor construct therefore provides exclusive access to shared data, and has the advantage of encouraging careful programming of the monitor procedures - thereby safeguarding the monitor data structures against misuse. If no process has made a call on a monitor procedure, then when a process makes a call on a procedure of that monitor, that call will be serviced immediately. The execution of the calling process will be suspended until the procedure has completed its operation and returns control to the calling process. However, if a monitor procedure is in execution, then any other call on a procedure of that monitor will not be serviced immediately, the calling process will be suspended, and the request will be placed in a queue. When the activated procedure completes its execution, the process which called it leaves the monitor; the queue is inspected, the waiting request is serviced and, on completion of the associated procedure call, the calling process leaves the monitor and resumes its independent execution. In this way, the processes access the shared data in mutual exclusion.

The monitor thus provides a mechanism for accessing shared data in an exclusive and therefore safe manner; it does not directly synchronize the processes which call it, but a signalling mechanism is provided whereby this may be accomplished. A process which gains access to a monitor procedure can, within that procedure, issue a 'wait' signal. The process is then suspended and another process is allowed to enter the monitor. The waiting process will be resumed when another process enters the monitor and sends a signal for that waiting process. The monitor is an elegant concept, and can ensure that the states of the processes which use it are deterministic. It can be implemented very effectively on a multi-processor system which uses shared memory, since it is inherently a mechanism for gaining controlled access to a block of shared data. It not so convenient to use in a distributed system. An example now follows of the use of the monitor, the 'consumer-producer' problem in which a producer process generates a sequence of values which are to be subsequently processed by a consumer process. The consumer process must accept values from the producer, one by one, such that the rate at which the values are consumed matches the rate at which they are generated by the producer process. If the two processes were free running they could get out of step. The relative timing of the processes must therefore be enforced by synchronization, which implies that the faster process must be caused to wait for the slower.

```
program producer_consumer;
    monitor bounded_buffer;
        var b:buffer;
            not_full,not_empty:signal;
        procedure entry transmit(in item:data);
            begin
                if full then wait(not_full) end if;
                put(item);
                send(not_empty)
            end;
        procedure entry receive(out item:data);
            begin
                if empty then wait(not_empty) end if;
                get(item);
                send(not_full)
            end;
            begin
                    { initialize b }
            end; {monitor}
    process producer;
        var item:data;
        begin
            repeat
                produce(item);
                bounded_buffer.transmit(item)
            until false
        end;{producer}
    process consumer;
        var item:data;
        begin
            repeat
                bounded_buffer.receive(item);
                consume(item)
            until false
        end;{consumer}
    parallel begin
            producer;
            consumer
    parallel end.
```

The program consists of the monitor module, the producer process and the consumer process. Within the monitor is the data structure b which is a buffer acting as a temporary receptacle for transporting the 'item' of data, together with the two procedures transmit and receive which are the only means of accessing b.

The program body simply initializes the two processes, setting them into concurrent operation. On completion of 'produce' the 'producer' process calls the monitor procedure 'transmit' with 'item' as the parameter of the call. Similarly the 'consumer' process will issue a call to the 'receive' procedure at the appropriate time. Normally, the mutual exclusion rule applies to monitor procedures - only one process can be executing a monitor procedure at any one time. However, to allow synchronization within a monitor, a signalling mechanism is provided. If a process gains access to a monitor procedure, then issues a 'wait' on a signal, that process will be caused to wait until the signal is suitable. During this period the mutual exclusion rule is waived to allow the other process to enter the monitor. This other process calls a monitor procedure, which, as the last operation, issues a 'send' on the signal, thereby activating the waiting process.

16.4 THE RENDEZVOUS

The requirements for inter-process communication are, firstly, a mechanism for data exchange, which in the monitor system is provided by the sequential use of a shared data structure by the communicating processes. The second requirement is for a scheme for synchronizing processes. This need for a synchronizing mechanism arises because communicating processes must keep in step with one another. The rendezvous mechanism, introduced by Hoare [4] and Brinch Hansen [5] combines the operations of data transmission and sychronisation in one mechanism.

In the scheme as introduced by Hoare [4], if a process A wishes to transmit data to a process B then each process must announce its intention to communicate. Process A will include, within the sequence of instructions it executes, a request to transmit to process B. Similarly process B includes in its sequence a request to receive from A. If x is the datum to be transmitted from A and y is the name of the variable of B which is to receive it, then process A includes the statement

    B ! x

and process B has the statement

    A ? y

If process A executes the statement B!x first it is suspended until B reaches the statement A?y. Similarly, if B arrives at the request first it will be caused to wait until A arrives at its request. When both processes have reached the rendezvous the data is transferred and the processes resume their respective executions. The mechanism is symmetric, in that the caller announces the name of the receiver and vice versa. This symmetry is not practical if the receiver is a library process which might be required to be called by several processes unknown to it.

The alternative, proposed by Brinch Hansen [5] and adopted in Ada is asymmetric; in this the caller announces the name of the server (receiver) process, but the callers remain anonymous to the receiver. The server process includes an 'accept' statement within the body of its code. This accept statement is very similar to a procedure statement. The reserved word 'accept' is followed by the name of the entry and after this comes the list of formal parameters; finally there is the sequence of statements which is executed when the rendezvous occurs. Through the use of parameters, data can be passed from the caller to the called process and vice versa. It is not always convenient to require that a called process should only respond to a particular entry call. A non-deterministic arrangement has therefore been introduced whereby a called process can, at a particular point in its operation, respond to a number of different entries. The classical example is the case in which the called task is the manager of a bounded buffer; the alternative responses it must be able to make are: to receive an item into the buffer or to deliver one. Furthermore, guards can be associated with the alternatives, so that, for example, a request to deliver an item will only be serviced if an item is present in the buffer. The bounded_buffer task for the consumer-producer problem in Ada simplified form is:

```
task bounded_buffer is
    entry append(item: in data);
    entry take(item: out data);
end bounded_buffer;
task body bounded_buffer is
    b:buffer;
    full,empty:boolean;
begin
    empty: = true; full: = false;
    loop
    select
        when not full  = >
                accept append(item: in data) do
                put(item);
                end append;
                {update count of number of items in buffer and set
                empty = false and full = true if appropriate};
    or
        when not empty  = >
                accept take(item: out data) do
                get(item);
                end take;
                {update count of number of items in buffer and set
                full = false and empty = true if appropriate}
        end select;
        end loop;
    end bounded_buffer;
```

The execution of a select statement begins by evaluating all the guard conditions. Then one of the 'open' alternatives (ones with true guards) is selected. Suppose that the producer process had made an 'append' entry call: it would be blocked until bounded_buffer executes the select statement. If both guards are open, then either entry could be the next to be executed; however, the select will choose the alternative which will lead to an immediate rendezvous. If, on the other hand, the select statement has been reached and both alternatives are open, bounded_buffer will wait at this point for the first rendezvous to occur.

For certain real-time applications a broadcast facility may be required. This will be non-deterministic, because there is no certainty that all processes have received the message, or that a particular process has received all the messages that have been sent. Although this non-determinacy appears unsatisfactory, it may be acceptable for particular applications, because information may be sent repeatedly, with no importance being attached to the loss of an individual message.

16.5 SYSTEM DEADLOCK

Programming languages do not normally give any protection against deadlock. Deadlock can arise, for example, in a system in which there are two resources: a printer and a disc drive. If only one process at a time is allowed to access each device, then it is possible for a system to deadlock, even though the locks which ensure exclusive access to each device are operating correctly. For example process P1 may gain exclusive access to the printer while process P2 gains exclusive access to the disc. Suppose now that P1 requests access to the disc, and P2 to the printer, while still holding access to the original devices. Process P1 must wait for P2 to give up its exclusive access to the disc. Similarly P2 is waiting for P1 to give up its access rights to the printer. Hence P1 is blocked by P2, and P2 is blocked by P1. A solution to this problem is to put both resources (printer and disc) under the control of a third process P3, and insist that P1 and P2 can only obtain access to the resources by making a request to P3. P3 then acts as a resource manager, and allocates the pair of resources to either P1 or P2. This solution which is an example of 'Deadlock Avoidance', however, assumes that the pattern of resource requests is known in advance for all processes.

The situation is more complex if there are a number of processes and resources. For example: a process P1 is forced to wait on a process P0. This in turn causes P2 to wait for P1, and so on, until a chain of waiting processes is set up, with P0 waiting on Pn. Hence a cycle is established, and a deadlock condition results, with P0 waiting on itself. An unsatisfactory solution, but one which is often suggested, is to employ time- outs so that, P0, for example, relinquishes its request and dies. However, this is unsatisfactory in most applications, and leads to an indeterminate state of the system. An alternative is to employ on-line deadlock detection. This mechanism operates at run-time every time a request for a resource is made, and therefore must be very fast. Each process calls a deadlock avoidance process before attempting to get access to a resource.

16.6 REFERENCES

1.   E. H. Dijkstra, "Co-operating Sequential Processes," pp. 43-111 in *Programming Languages*, ed. F. Genuys, Academic Press (1968).

2.   C. A. R. Hoare, "Monitors: An Operating System Structuring Concept," *Comm ACM* **17**(10), pp.549-557 (1974).

3.   P. Brinch Hansen, *Operating System Principles,* Prentice Hall (1973).

4.   C. A. R. Hoare, "Communicating Sequential Processes," *Comm ACM* **21**(8), pp.666-677 (1978).

5.   P. Brinch Hansen, "Distributed Processes: A concurrent programming concept," *Comm ACM* **21**(11), pp.934-941 (1978).

6.   R. L. Grimsdale, F. Halsall, F. Martin-Polo, and G. C. Shoja, "MARTLET: A Programming Language for a Distributed Multiple Microprocessor System," *Proc.ICS., 6th Euro.Reg.Conf. on Systems Architecture*, pp.403-414 (1981).

7.   R. L. Grimsdale, F. Halsall, F. Martin-Polo, and G. C. Shoja, "POLYPROC II - The University of Sussex Multiple Microprocessor," *Proc. IEEE 2nd. Int. Conf. on Distributed Computing Systems*, pp.95-104 (1981).

8.　H. Ledgard, *ADA - An Introduction and Ada Reference Manual,* Springer-Verlag (1981).

9.　R. L. Grimsdale, F. Halsall, F. Martin-Polo, and S. Wong, "Structure and Tasking Features of the Programming Language Martlet," *Computers and Digital Techniques, Proc.IEE* **129**(2), pp.63-69, Pt.E (1982).

10.　G. C. Shoja, F. Halsall, and R. L. Grimsdale, "A control kernel to support Ada intertask communication on a distributed multiprocessor computer system," *Software and Microsystems* **1**(5), pp.128-134 (1982).

11.　M. Dowson, B. Collins, and B. McBride, "Software strategy for multiprocessors," *Microprocessors and Microsystems* **3**, pp.263-266 (1979).

12.　G. C. Shoja, F. Halsall, and R. L. Grimsdale, "Some experiences of implementing the Ada concurrency facilities on a distributed multiprocessor computer system," *Software and Microsystems* **1**(6), pp.147-152 (1982).

17 Run-time Support

R. L. Grimsdale

17.1 THE CONTROL KERNEL

The function of a Control Kernel is to transform the individual processors of a closely-coupled system into a set of virtual machines which provide facilities for implementing the concurrency requirements of the system. Task switching, task and processor scheduling, queue handling and the implementation of inter-task communication and synchronization primitives are just some component parts of a multi-processor control kernel.

This chapter, after first discussing the overall structure of a control kernel which is suitable for use in a multi-processor computer system, describes the implementation details of a control kernel which has been produced for a multi-processor system constructed from commercially available processing units, and which supports most of the inter-task communication facilities of the concurrent programming language Ada.

17.1.1 Control Kernel Sructure

The particular architecture [1] for which the control kernel has been designed includes a number of nodes or stations which are linked together by means of a high-bandwidth communications sub-network. To meet the requirement for high data-processing rates a multi-processor shared memory architecture is used within a station.

When deciding on the overall structure of the control kernel for such systems, an important consideration is whether the local kernel associated with each processor should have the right to access and manipulate global data structures related to tasks, queues, etc. which are resident in different processors. Also, each local processor must normally handle its own I/O interrupts, and so must execute some code in an uninterrruptible state. This can clearly create access rights conflicts which must be resolved in addition to the normal communication and synchronsiation concurrency requirements.

The preferred structure for the overall control software in a multi-processor system of the type just outlined, therefore, is to utilize separate autonomous control kernels for each station in the system. Each control kernel then manages all the resources (both hardware and software) within that station, and all communications with other stations in the system. Then, if a multi-processor architecture is required within a station, each local processor contains a small slave kernel which operates under the overall control of the master control kernel within that station. The overall control software is therefore modular, and functions in a clear and consistent way.

17.1.2 Control Kernel Design

A single master control kernel within each station, controlling perhaps several local (slave) processors, results in a number of advantages, especially when implementing inter-task communications. For example, since the control kernel is the sole owner of all vital and critical data structures, such as task activation records and task queues, contention and mutual exclusion problems associated with access rights to these data structures are greatly reduced. Also, this eliminates the need for low-level access rights control primitives, and so enables the control kernel to be written entirely at a high level, resulting in a more flexible and secure design.

Another important aspect of the design of the control kernel is the uninterruptable environment in which it must be executed. Execution of tasking commands involves the updating of variables and queues which must be carried out as indivisible operations, and so the execution of the associated control kernel routines must be logically uninterruptible. However, as the control kernel manages all I/O interrupts for the station, and assuming that these are to be processed by high-level services tasks, it is not possible to allow a low-level interrupt service routine to initiate directly the execution of a high-level service task. This means, therefore, that the low-level routine can only signal to the control kernel that an interrupt has occurred, and it is the control kernel which actually maps this into a call to the high-level service task, and schedules the latter to run.

To implement this scheme, each device interrupt is first served by a linked low-level routine which runs on the associated local processor. This simply satisfies the real-time constraints of the I/O device being serviced, and the routine then sets a flag to signal to the control kernel that the interrupt has occurred. The control kernel then detects that the interrupt has occurred when it polls this flag, and, in turn, maps it into a call to the task which will eventually process the data. After setting an interrupt flag, the local processor simply resumes executing the task it was executing prior to the interrupt, without any regard to the consequences of setting the interrupt flag, and it is the control kernel which decides when the data should be processed. This ensures that the logical progress of the tasks currently being executed is not interrupted, and also that the control kernel retains control of the complete system.

17.2 CONTROL KERNEL IMPLEMENTATION

The control kernel described in this section has been designed to control and manage the resources of the multi-processor shared memory node or station which is in turn a component of a larger multiple station system. The architecture of the overall system is as shown in **Figure 17-1**. A station is constructed from a number of standard Intel 86/12A single-board computers which execute the tasks allocated to the station, and which communicate with each other using a Multibus-compatible shared memory board. The control kernel also runs on an Intel 86/12A specifically dedicated to that purpose, in order to relieve the burden of control from the remaining local processors within that station. In an attempt to maximize parallelism within the station, inter-station communication is controlled by a separate Intel 8O88 based communications control processor, which performs the necessary inter-station communications protocol, but presents a standard interface to the control kernel. The protocol may be changed, therefore, with minimal effect on the overall application and control kernel software.

The system is intended primarily for real-time embedded applications. A complete application program for the system is thus written as a suite of task modules, each of

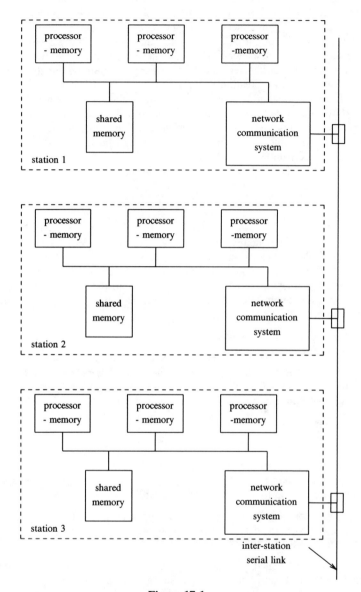

Figure 17-1

which performs a selected system processing function. Task modules are subsequently distributed and statically assigned to the individual processors comprising the system using an interactive system configuration program. The latter takes as input the output from the language compiler, and in turn produces a memory image for each processor within the system together with associated data structures for use by the run-time kernel software to effect inter-task communication.

The application programming language used with the system is called Martlet [2], and this has also been used to write the control kernel. The sequential part of Martlet is essentially Pascal, but to achieve concurrency many of the structural and tasking facilities of Ada have been incorporated. For example, task modules each contain a specification and a body, and tasks communicate with each other using the rendezvous concept. The concurrency primitives supported include the rendezvous primitives entry call, accept, end-accept and also the associated select and delay statements. Martlet also provides facilities for instancing, parameterisation, and exception handling, but there are no facilities in Martlet for dynamic creation of tasks or the use of packages, as are available with Ada. In addition, the language contains a facility - the port statement - which allows absolute I/O device ports to be manipulated and also the mapping of interrupts directly into external entry calls. Also, memory registers can be addressed directly. It is possible, therefore, to write the control kernel entirely using Martlet, resulting in a structured, and hence more easily understood, design.

The control kernel is composed of two parts: the kernel data structures and the kernel routines. Each will now be considered.

17.2.1 Data structures

The control kernel data structures consist of a suite of task activation records (one per task module resident in the station), a set of processor status records (one per local processor), a station directory containing the names and locations of each task, an interrupt map table to allow interrupts to be mapped into calls to the correct service tasks, and a set of interrupt and communications channel flags, the latter being used to control inter-station communication.

Task activation record

All the runtime information associated with each task in the system is maintained in an associated task activation record (TAR), as shown in **Figure 17-2**. A task activation record is created and initialized at the time the task is assigned to a specific local processor. In addition to information such as the name of the task, its priority, and processor identity, the task activation record also includes some fields that are used by the control kernel to implement the inter-task communication primitives at run-time. These are listed below together with a brief description of their function.

ACCEPTED_TASK: A pointer to the last task which has been accepted for a rendezvous. Because more than one task can be accepted for the same entry they are linked in a LIFO queue pointed to by the ACCEPTED_TASK.

DELAYED: A record which contains the wake-up time of the task when placed in the delay queue and also a transfer address which shows where the task should continue executing after the lapsed time has expired.

CONTEXT: A record which contains the processor registers and other run-time status information on the task, and must be saved during a context switch.

Q_STATE_SET: This field shows the entry queues which are non-empty; i.e. at least one calling task is waiting on the entry queue for which the corresponding entry index bit has been set. Q_STATE_SET is accessible by the control kernel only.

E_STATE_SET: This set shows the indexes of the entries for which calls can be accepted. E_STATE_SET is also only accessible by the control kernel.

MAILBOX: This record represents the task-system communication exchange. When a local kernel encounters a task communication opcode, e.g. entry call, accept etc., it places the opcode together with the related parameters in the MAILBOX of the

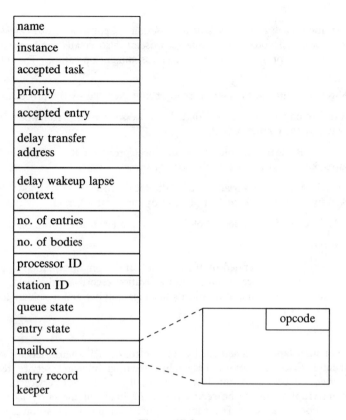

Figure 17-2

associated task activation record. It then sets a flag (REQ_FLAG) so that the control kernel can switch the processor to a new task and execute the opcode placed in the MAILBOX. The control kernel subsequently returns any variable parameters to the local tasks via the MAILBOX.

ENTRY_RECORD: This is a pointer to the entry descriptor of the task. The entry descriptor is an array of records which hold information about the entries of a task, and therefore its size depends on the number of entries of the task. Each record contains the following information:

(1) TRANSFER_ADDRESS: This is the address of the entry point to the entry's code section. When an entry call is accepted in a select statement, the processor starts executing form this TRANSFER_ADDRESS of the called entry.

(2) ENTRY_Q: All tasks calling the entry are linked to this FIFO queue which is defined as a record containing a pointer to the first and a pointer to the last task in the queue.

Processor status record

Information about each local processor in a station is kept in a record called the processor status record. The processor status records are also created and initialized by the system configuration program during the task assignment operation. The different fields are as follows:

RUN_TASK: A pointer to the task currently being executed by the processor.

NEW_TASK: A pointer to the task that the processor wil next run when forced into a context switch by the control kernel.

REQ_FLAG: A Boolean variable set by the local processor that wishes to be switched by the control kernel. It is reset by the control kernel.

ACKN_FLAG: A Boolean variable set by the local processor to acknowledge an interrupt invoked by the control kernel. It is reset by the control kernel.

READY_Q: Array of FIFO queues holding tasks that are ready to run on the processor.

Station Directory

The station directory is generated by the control kernel from information available in the processor status records of each station and activation records of the tasks. Each directory record contains the name of a task, its instance number and a pointer to the activation record of the task.

Interrupt Map Table

The interrupt map table is generated by the control kernel when interrupt service tasks identify themselves to the control kernel by executing interrupt service requests. An interrupt service request is executed at the start of an interrupt service task, and, as a result, the interrupt vector to be serviced and the index of the entry to be called are passed to the control kernel. The control kernel then initializes a corresponding map table record with the following information:

(1)   the interrupt vector

(2)   a pointer to the interupt service task

(3)   the index of the service entry to be called

17.2.2 Control Kernel Routines

The control kernel contains procedures for:

(1)   general FIFO, LIFO, and random queue management

(2)   clock and time-out management

(3)   mapping interrupts as entry calls

(4)   directory generation and search

(5)   task scheduling and processor switching

(6)   implementation of inter-task communication and synchronization opcodes

(7)   station initialization

(8)   polling the specified flags and calling the appropriate procedure when a flag is set

(9)   exception handling

The main body of the kernel then simply initializes the various data structures and then commences polling of the various flags to determine the next action to be performed. Some of the kernel routines are now discussed.

Handling of Run-time Queues

Four types of run-time queues are managed by the control kernel:

(1)   the ready queues (FIFO)

(2)   the entry queues (FIFO)

(3)   the accepted tasks queues (LIFO)

(4)   the delay queue (random).

The control kernel is the owner of all the run-time queues, and therefore has the sole right to manipulate them. A schematic diagram showing the various types of queue which the control kernel must handle is shown in **Figure 17-3**.

Each ready queue is associated with a priority level of a particular processor in the staion. Tasks are allocated and placed in the appropriate ready queue at the time the task is assigned to that processor.

Each task entry has a waiting FIFO queue which is initialized in the entry's descriptor, and all tasks calling an entry are linked to its waiting queue by the control kernel.

The accepted tasks queue is a LIFO queue which is formed by linking the tasks which have been accepted by a given task. The accepted task field in the task activation record of the called task points to this queue. The task that has been accepted last is placed at the head of the queue and is released first.

The delay queue holds all the tasks which have executed a delay statement and whose time-outs have not expired. Depending on the duration of their delays, tasks are inserted at the appropriate point within a delay queue. Sometimes it becomes necessary to remove a task from the delay queue before its delay lapse time has expired. This can happen, for example, as a result of an entry call; a rendezvous becomes possible for a task which has been placed on a delay queue during execution of a select statement. The delay queue is sorted so that the task with the least amount of delay is first in the queue.

Task Scheduling

Tasks in the system can be in one of five states: running, ready, halted, suspended or delayed, as shown in **Figure 17-4**.

The priority based scheduler is generally invoked when a task is made ready and added to a processor ready queue, or when a local processor requests the current task it is running to be suspended. The scheduler simply selects the highest priority task from the processor's ready queue and interrupts the local processor, forcing it to switch to the selected task. The latter then performs a context switch, and sets the acknowledgement flag to inform the control kernel the switch is complete. Then, if the local processor requested the switch, the control kernel accesses the opcode from the mailbox of the

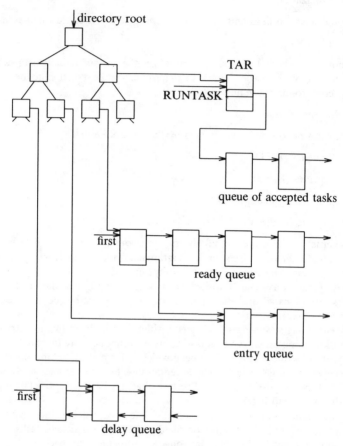

directory root

TAR

RUNTASK

queue of accepted tasks

first

ready queue

entry queue

first

delay queue

Figure 17-3

suspended task and executes the corresponding routine.

Implementation of Tasking Opcodes

A major function of the control kernel is to implement the tasking opcodes passed to it by the local kernel in the mailbox of the switched task. There are five opcodes passed from a local processor to the control kernel: suspend (opcodes accept, select and delay are all mapped as suspend), entry call, end-accept, connect-tasks and request-interrupt-service. Each is handled by a separate procedure, as follows:

Suspend The suspend routine first determines the entries which can accept a call and have also received a call from other tasks. If there are several possibilities, then one entry is selected at random. The address of the parameter block in the mailbox of the calling task at the head of the corresponding entry queue, is then transferred to the mailbox of the now suspended called task. The called task is then placed in the appropriate ready queue, and the scheduler is re-called. If, however, there is no call for any of the entries which are in a position to accept one, then the suspended task is placed in the delay queue.

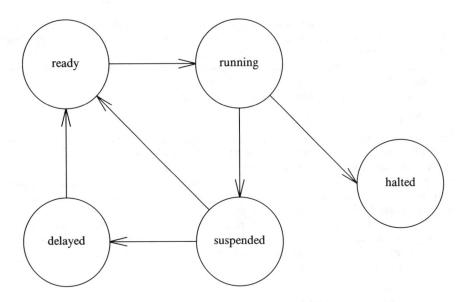

Figure 17-4

Entry-call The entry-call routine first checks if the called task is currently suspended awaiting a call. If so, the entry call can be accepted immediately, and so the suspended task is placed in the appropriate ready queue, and the scheduler is called. If, however, the entry call cannot be accepted immediately, then the caller is placed in the corresponding entry queue of the called task, and the set indicating the state of the entry queue is updated to include the new entry call.

End-accept Each accept statement is terminated by an end-accept command which signals that the statements associated with the rendezvous have been executed. The end-accept routine first checks if the call originated from an interrupt. If it did, the appropriate interrupt level is re-enabled; otherwise the task making the call is placed in its ready queue for re-scheduling. In both cases the called task is then placed in its own ready queue, and the scheduler is called to allow both tasks to continue independently of each other.

Connect-tasks The connect-task opcode is executed once only for each called task at the start of execution of the calling task. The connect-task routine searches the station directory for the called task, and returns the address of the called task to the mailbox of the calling task. The calling task is then re-scheduled.

Request-interrupt-service The request-interrupt-service command is issued by a device driver task pending receipt of an interrupt. The associated routine first removes the interrupt vector address and entry index from the mailbox of the driver task, and enters these, together with the task name, into the interrupt map table. These are then used to map the actual interrupts into dummy entry calls. The driver task is then suspended.

Exception Handling

The exception handling in Martlet follows very closely that proposed in Ada. The predefined exceptions include those normally provided with sequential Pascal, such as case error, arithmetic overflow etc., and also two associated with the tasking feature: guard closed and tasking error.

If an exception is raised during a rendezvous, the local kernel informs the control kernel via the mailbox of the task, which is then suspended. The control kernel then releases the accepted task(s) for this block, and raises the task error exception. If the tasking error flag is found to be true when a task involved in a rendezvous runs after rescheduling, then the local kernel unwinds the procedures, starting with the innermost level at which the exception was raised, until a handler is found.

I/O Interrupt Handling and Synchronisation

The run-time control kernel maintains an interrupt-enabled set which is used to synchronize servicing of the interrupt flags set by the low-level interrupt routines. The enabled set indicates those interrupts that can actually be accepted; i.e. an end-accept for a previous entry call, made on behalf of a corresponding I/O interrupt, has already been issued. When a request-interrupt-service opcode is executed, the corresponding interrupt is also enabled, by updating the interrupt enabled set.

Only when the intersection of the interrupt-flags-set and the interrupt-enabled-set is non-empty is one interrupt selected from the intersection, at random, and mapped as a dummy entry call. This ensures that an interrupt is serviced before a new interrupt is accepted for entry call mapping.

17.2.3 Memory Management

Local memory, as well as the shared memory space required for the parameter area of a task, is allocated when the task is assigned to a specific local processor at system configuration time. Run-time management of the local memory is therefore concerned simply with the dynamic requirements for stack and memory space during the execution of each task. This is managed by the local kernel of each processor.

Hence, requests by tasks for run-time memory are made to the local kernel using the external call 'acquire'. Similarly, memory is released using the 'release' call. The local kernel allocates the requested memory on a first-fit basis, and re-links any released blocks to the pool of available memory. The memory and stack requirements for each procedure within a task are produced by the compiler and stored after the code of each task. This information is therefore available to the local kernel at run-time.

17.3 INTER-PROCESSOR COMMUNICATIONS MECHANISMS

The control kernel may wish, as a result of a scheduling decision, to force a local processor to switch to a new task. Similarly, a local processor may reach a point in the execution of a task that needs the services of the control kernel (e.g. as a result of executing a tasking command).

Obviously a safe and deadlock-free method of communication between control and local processors has to be utilized. The solution adopted is for the control processor to interrupt the local processors when it requires their attention, but for the latter to get the attention of the control processor by setting a corresponding request-flag that is polled by the control processor at periodic intervals. The sequence of actions taken in a dialogue between the control kernel and a local processor is shown in **Figure 17-5**.

The preceding discussion relates to communications within a single station. In a configuration with multiple stations, however, communications between tasks located in different stations are transparent to the control kernel. A compiled suite of tasks can be assigned arbitrarily to any available processor or station at system configuration time, taking into account the available hardware, and any possible constraints concerning

TIME	*LOCAL PROCESSOR*		*CONTROL KERNEL*
↓	-encounter tasking opcode *updates mailbox *sets REQFLG *enables interrupt *halts	*-executing in parallel-*	polling flags or executing (previous) local processor requests
↓		*-local processor suspended-*	-polls REQFLG: if set a new task assigned to local processor, which is interrupted
↓ ↓	-receives switch interrupt *context switch to new task *set ACKNFLG *continue with task	*-continue in parallel-*	-await ACKNFLG *reset REQFLG and ACKNFLG *access mailbox of suspended task and execute opcode.

Figure 17-5

allocation of peripheral devices to processors. The connect-task routine of the control kernel connects tasks which are in the same station. The control kernel itself is not aware of the existence of other stations, and treats all tasks as if they existed in their own stations. This ensures a uniform handling of all entry calls in the system, irrespective of their physical location.

To realise this objective, and make the location of caller and called tasks transparent to each other (as well as to the control kernel), two intermediate transport tasks are created: a pseudo-called task, which is assigned to the same station as the calling task, and a pseudo-calling task which is assigned to the same station as the called task. The two pseudo-tasks present a standard interface with the calling and called task, respectively, and also interface with the low-level network communications system. Thus, on receipt of a call from the calling task, the control kernel simply reschedules the pseudo-called task within its own station in the normal way, and it is the latter which performs the necessary inter-station call using the network communications system. Similarly, on receipt of the incoming call, the pseudo-calling task makes the call to the called task in the normal way, and this is again handled transparently by the control kernel. This is shown diagramatically in **Figure 17-6**.

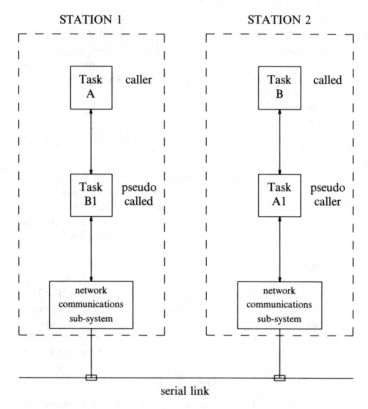

STATION 1   STATION 2

serial link

Figure 17-6

17.4 REFERENCES

1.   R. L. Grimsdale, F. Halsall, F. Martin-Polo, and G. C. Shoja, "POLYPROC II - The University of Sussex Multiple Microprocessor," *Proc. IEEE 2nd. Int. Conf. on Distributed Computing Systems*, pp.95-104 (1981).

2.   R. L. Grimsdale, F. Halsall, F. Martin-Polo, and S. Wong, "Structure and Tasking Features of the Programming Language Martlet," *Computers and Digital Techniques, Proc.IEE* **129**(2), pp.63-69, Pt.E (1982).

18 Development Aids

F. Halsall

18.1 INTRODUCTION

The widespread availability of a range of powerful and relatively inexpensive single board computers means that an increasing number of system builders are now considering the use of multiple such units in their system designs. Typically, designs containing multiple processing units are considered in order to improve throughput or to enhance the reliability of a system. However, although the hardware to implement these systems is now readily available, the associated software tools required to aid their development are, on the whole, relatively primitive and still in an evolutionary phase.

This chapter describes the range of software development facilities which have been implemented for use with an experimental multi-microprocessor development system (M-MDS). The latter is now operational and is currently being used to investigate a variety of problem areas associated with multiprocessor-based system designs. The facilities provided include not only the software tools necessary for program development - run-time diagnostic aids for example - but also the tools used to aid the performance-evaluation of operational systems.

The chapter is organized into five sections. Following the introduction, section 18.1.1 outlines a typical software development cycle for a multiprocessor-based product and identifies the role of the various software tools necessary to aid the debugging and testing of a system under development. An overview of the M-MDS which has been implemented in the laboratory is then presented in section 18.2 and section 18.3 describes implementation details of the various software tools developed. Examples illustrating the facilities are described at appropriate points, and the paper concludes with a discussion of the experiences gained, and some suggestions for additional facilities such systems might contain.

18.1.1 The Software Development Cycle

From conception to installation, the development cycle of a multiprocessor-based product can be both long and complex. Normally, the cycle starts with a detailed analysis of the overall system requirements, which results, after a number of iterations and refinements, in a formal specification for the system. The next phase is to convert this document into a working system. Typically, this commences with an analysis of the range of hardware necessary to support the application, and the selection of an appropriate software approach - programming languages, development support tools etc.

Once this system-level design is complete, the application programming phase is then entered. Essentially, this is concerned with converting the detailed requirement specification into actual program code suitable for running on the selected target hardware configuration; this process is strongly influenced by the environment within which software development is to take place. Next, the system must be debugged and thoroughly tested. Finally, the resulting product must be commissioned and installed whereupon the software commitment is reduced to maintenance and, for long-life-cycle products, upgrading.

18.1.2 Software Development Tools

This chapter is concerned specifically with a description of the various software tools necessary for the debugging and testing phase of the development cycle for multiprocessor-based products. The tools which are to be described can be partitioned into two parts: program development aids, and performance monitoring and evaluation facilities.

Program development aids are necessary to allow the application software being implemented to be debugged. They include, therefore, the language compiler, linking and loading utilities and, of particular interest here, run-time error and diagnostic facilities. A good programming language compiler will, of course, detect many of the basic syntactic errors in a program during compilation but it is equally important to provide good run-time diagnostic aids. Indeed, this is especially true for multiprocessor-based systems in which there can be many concurrent and inter-related sub-systems in operation at any one time.

The run-time testing of the application software for a multiprocessor-based product can be carried out in one of two ways. For a small, uniprocessor based system for example, it is usual to test application software on the actual target hardware with the various controlled devices attached by means of a microprocessor development system. For more sophisticated multiprocessor-based designs, the limited high-level view presented by such an approach is too restrictive and the current trend is towards the use of development "testbeds" [1, 2, 3]. In practice, the configuration of such a facility comprises a separate front-end machine, to host the development tool-set, linked to the target system. The front-end machine is normally a general purpose uniprocessor machine and the aim is to provide users with a high-level interface to the system under development.

Although the additional flexibility offered by a multiprocessor design - in terms of architecture and performance - can be of significant benefit, it must be remembered that the complexity of such systems can be great. Hence, it is essential that any development system should allow users to change aspects of the target system under consideration and to assimilate readily the effects of these changes upon the overall operation of the software. Thus, the performance monitoring and evaluation facilities to be described include utilities to monitor and display the concurrent execution of individual program modules ("tasks") running anywhere within the target hardware, both qualitatively and quantitatively.

18.2 THE LABORATORY M-MDS

The software facilities to be described have been implemented for use with a specific multi-microprocessor development system known as Polyproc [4, 5]. Although much of the run-time software to support these facilities is inevitably influenced by the architecture of Polyproc, the host software tools to be described are independent of the type of target hardware selected and, it is felt, are typical of the tools necessary for the development and test of application software for such systems.

A schematic representation of Polyproc is shown in **Figure 18-1**. As can be seen, it is made up of the target hardware under development, front-ended by a separate host machine. The system has been designed to provide a general purpose development environment, to aid in the design and test of application software for a range of real-time embedded computer systems comprising multiple processing elements. The target system may include anything from a single station containing one processor, up to many linked stations each of which contains multiple processing elements. Also, in order to make the system as general as possible, the target utilizes all Multibus [6] compatible hardware.

The front-end host machine provides users of the Polyproc system with a high-level interface to the various tools supported, and hence to the target system itself. The tool set supported includes a target-control package, program development utilities and also a range of performance monitoring and evaluation facilities as shown in **Figure 18-2**. The development aids include:

- an editor to allow application programs to be entered and, if necessary, modified

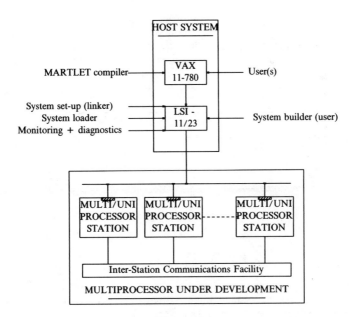

Figure 18-1

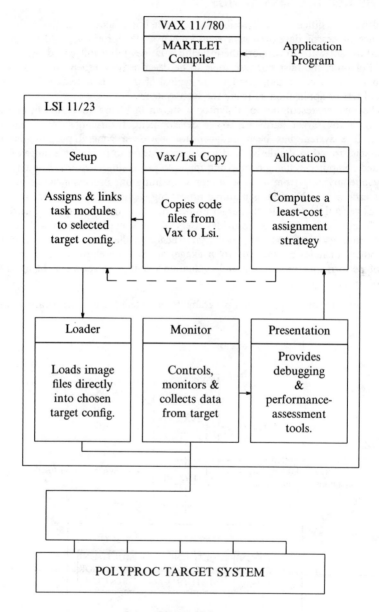

Figure 18-2

- a concurrent programming language; this is known as Martlet [7] and allows application software for the system to be written in a structured form as a suite of interacting, ADA-like [8] task modules

- system generation utility; this is an interactive program which, under control of the user, allows the suite of task modules comprising the application program to be assigned to individual processing elements of the target system

- a high-speed loading utility; this permits the individual processing and memory elements to be loaded with their appropriate code-images

- a range of general purpose run-time support facilities

To make use of the system, the user first writes the application program in the form of a suite of task modules. As with Ada, task modules can execute concurrently and communicate with each other to exchange information in a disciplined manner. The complete program is then compiled and, after any syntactic errors have been eliminated, the user runs the system generation program. This, in turn, takes the output from the language compiler and, interactively, allows the user to assign the individual tasks of the application program to specified processing elements in the target system. A memory image for each processing element is then created, containing the code for each task module assigned to that processor, together with an image containing a set of associated task-activation records for the shared-memory resident within each of the target stations. The latter are used by the run-time support software to implement inter-task communication and task scheduling. The user then runs the loader utility which down-loads each memory image, via the serial monitoring highway, into the appropriate processor or shared-memory (**Figure 18-1**). The monitor highway is based upon Ethernet [9] and each station contains an intelligent communications-control board implementing the monitor-station protocol. This board plugs directly into the station's Multibus giving direct access to all station memory -both local and shared. Finally, the user is provided with a range of run-time support facilities, which allow the complete program to be run, controlled, debugged and monitored via the control console of the host machine. These tools are now described.

18.3 RUN-TIME SUPPORT FACILITIES

A characteristic of many multiprocessor computer systems - particularly for embedded applications - is that there is normally, no overall software layer encompassing the complete system; rather, each node contains a local software shell controlling the operations within that station. This is the configuration adopted in Polyproc where each station contains a separate processor dedicated to running a "kernel" control program responsible for all run-time scheduling and task-management duties. Thus, it is only through the monitor machine that a user can gain a "global" picture of system operation. To provide access to specific facilities, the host software is organized as a number of functionally organized levels presented to the user as individual menus. The overall impression is of a tree-like structure down which users may traverse until they have completed the particular command or operation required (**Figure 18-3**). This framework has been adopted in order to impose a disciplined approach upon system-users, in an attempt to help prevent ill-considered commands being issued to the target system [10].

As can be seen, each level is presented to the user as a menu of possible options logically grouped together and selected by entering a single key-letter. The configuration illustrated reflects a conceptual view of the target system rather than any list dictated by solely architectural constraints of the target system. For any particular level, actions may either be selected or the user may climb to the preceding (upper) level. Selection of an option in a level will either cause that action to be performed or it will result in a descent to a lower, more specific level if further refinement of the request is necessary. In

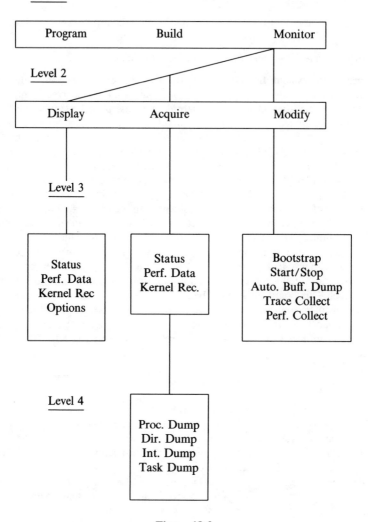

Figure 18-3

the event of any mistakes being made in selection, error control returns the user to the level from which the last command was issued.

In addition to the normal run-time management functions, the control kernel within each station can be instructed, by means of commands entered at the host console, to start recording the occurrence of specific, predefined events encountered during the running of a program. Each control kernel maintains a set of event buffers, organized as dual cyclic queues. Thus, at its occurrence, event related data - including time - are stored as an "event record" in the kernel buffer. Subsequently, depending upon the options chosen by the user for that particular kernel, when each buffer becomes full the contents will either be sent to the host machine automatically (Auto Collect) or may be sent in response to a specific request from the user (Acquire). The data collected from the target system may then be displayed and analysed by the host machine.

18.3.1 Program Debugging Aids

In both uniprocessor and multiprocessor systems, run-time errors may be caused either by an abnormal condition arising during the execution of a program - for example, divide-by-zero, stack overflow etc. - or by a logical flaw being present in the design of the program. However, in the case of multiprocessor distributed systems, a more subtle and essentially higher-level form of failure can also occur - tasks may be scheduled in such a way as to block certain system operations, system time constraints might not be met, tasks may try to call other tasks that have already completed execution etc. Initially, distributed multiprocessor software tends to behave as a number of distinct, separate programs exhibiting the typical uniprocessor errors previously described. As the debugging process continues, however, the "level" of the errors rises, and it is important to be able to perceive a global picture of system events to help locate, isolate and correct this higher-level class of error.

The primary means provided to carry out this function is the "Trace Collect" option. As with Ada, the minimum entity capable of concurrent operation in Martlet is the task module; tasks communicate by exchanging parameters during task-rendezvous and this level of system operation provides a convenient event with which to trace software behaviour. Thus, when in the Trace mode, the kernel logs each rendezvous occurring within its own station. Each event-log consists of the identities of the calling and called tasks and the global-time at which the event occurs. Two events are required to define each rendezvous: one event marks the entry call and one event marks the completion of the end-accept block. In this way, collections of such records constitute a history of all inter-task communications in those stations in which the Trace option has been selected.

Central to this approach is the concept of a global-clock against which all events, no matter where they occur, may be accurately registered. In this environment, the global-clock comprises a set of independent, local clocks capable of being started or stopped synchronously. This synchronism is achieved by means of the monitor-access link and so long as the global-clock period is kept long, relative to message transit times for the link, then each of the local clocks will appear synchronized. Further, to ensure the consistency of the global-clock, the individual clocks are constructed from identical hardware throughout the system and controlled by high accuracy crystals.

Clearly, the dynamic data collected by the host machine during such tracing will consist of a large number of similar, partially-ordered data records. Hence, it is important when displaying the results of a trace, for the user to be able to select specific and localized views of the overall software at a level related to that at which it is currently being investigated. In addition, since in a distributed multi-station implementation the physical separation of the two communicating tasks may well be causing the error, it is important that users can readily discriminate between tasks rendezvousing in the same station (local) and between tasks rendezvousing in different stations (remote). Furthermore, provision must be made to display the occurrence of interrupts (mapped, as with Ada, to entry calls) and error conditons. To achieve these aims, the following representations are used:

used:

$$A <-- - \to \quad \text{B Local entry call, A to B.}$$
$$A- \cdot >B \qquad \text{Remote entry call, A to B.}$$
$$A< \ - \ >B \quad \text{Local End-accept, B to A.}$$
$$A\leftarrow - \to B \ \text{Remote End-accept, B to A.}$$
$$A\leftarrow - \to C \qquad \text{Interrupt Service, A handles C.}$$
$$A<\text{****}>E \qquad \text{Error State, A finds error E.}$$

In addition, to help make the display output mirror the original program structure, nested entry calls are progressively indented. For example, consider a four-level, nested program segment of the form:

> TASK A calls TASK B then
> TASK B calls TASK C then
> TASK C calls TASK D.
> TASK D releases TASK C then
> TASK C releases TASK B and then
> TASK C calls TASK E.
> TASK B releases TASK A whilst
> TASK E releases TASK C.

If it is assumed that tasks A and B are resident in one station and tasks C, D and E in another, the output to display the above sequence would be as follows:

```
A --------- B
B - - - - C
C ------- D
C ------- D
B - - - - C
C ------- E
A ------- B
C ------ E
```

Clearly, while such a display indicates the rendezvous' encountered during program execution, it gives no indication of the time intervals between the various events. Consequently, all trace displays have an optional "switch" that allows timestamps associated with each event to be printed alongside each specific action. Collectively, these provide the basic tools for indicating task-level interactions between program segments and the following sections outline the options available to the user to scan through program execution histories following particular logical threads or noting specific actions.

Static Trace

The effect of this option is to cause the trace software, within the host computer, to search the file of event records looking for any actions involving the named task. Hence, using the same example given earlier, a static trace targeted upon Task C would produce the following:

```
B - - - C
C ------ D
C ------ D
B - - - C
C ------ E
C ------ E
```

Again, timestamps may be included and hence this form of trace can be particularly useful in checking the sequence of all entry calls and end-accepts encountered by a task, especially where such occurrences are determined by timeouts or some other non- deterministic event.

Running Trace

The purpose of this option is to allow users to follow the thread of execution of a set of rendezvous sequences. For example, using the same program segment as before, and further, assume that Tasks A, B, C and D all perform some collective processing function whilst the rendezvous between Tasks C and E is logically irrelevant to this function, a running trace would accurately portray the main sequence when targeted upon Task A:

```
A ------ B
B - - - C
C ----- D
C ----- D
B - - - C
A ------ B
```

The above facility is implemented by the trace software redefining the target task dynamically, each time the current target encounters an entry call or end-accept to another task. Thus, in the above example, Task A is the first target, followed by Task B and so on. Hence, once the end-accept from Task C to Task B has been executed, any further actions by Task C will be ignored, until that task is once again referenced by the current target.

Interactive Trace

While repeated use of the static and running traces with different initial targets can display accurately the task-level interactions within the program, the amount of output produced can, in practice, become excessive and, in some cases, repetitive. To help overcome this, and to allow particular regions of a program to be accessed more quickly, the static and running traces may be combined interactively. This allows the user to switch at will between the two options at any time during the trace process. Again, using the previous example, a typical user dialogue might produce the following:

```
A ------ B running
B - - - C running
C ----- D static
C ----- D static
B - - - C static
C ----- E static
C ----- E static
etc.
```

Since interrupts are mapped as external entry calls, some applications can produce a large number of interrupt-service requests over a comparatively short interval of time. In some instances, the effects of these requests might require investigation, but in many cases such repetitive events can be ignored. To facilitate this, the display of entry calls originating from interrupts has been made optional. Further, to aid in accessing required sections of trace information quickly, not only is a taskname required to act as a target variable but also an "occurrence value". This is a variable that can take a value from 1..n corresponding to an instance of that target within n such occurrences located by the value may be from 0 to 47 and this corresponds to the maximum number of entry-points in a Martlet task of 48; entries within a task are numbered sequentially starting from zero.

The overall effect is to provide the user with a powerful and flexible set of tools, which give complete control to follow the flow of execution of either small or large sections of complex, distributed software quickly and easily.

18.3.2 Performance Evaluation Aids

The purpose of the performance evaluation aids is to provide the user with both quantitative and qualitative insight into the operational characteristics of a program. The information presented, therefore, must illustrate such things as the degree of parallelism obtained within an implementation and the effects of system configuration changes as well as numerical performance data.

The data base which all performance displays use includes a file of event records collected by the monitor station in the manner previously described. Each record contains information about the flow of jobs executed by each processing element contained within the set of monitored stations. Linked with each event are a number of time-stamps, which mark important points associated with each event. In addition, each record can be allied with the particular processor being switched, and the station in which it resides.

The actual presentation of performance data to the user is an important design criterion. In many systems, performance data, especially at the system level, can be available but presented merely as a string of percentages or worse. Such lists may well contain the required information, but it is up to the user to extract relevant sections. Even then, the final form of presentation for the chosen data will probably be graphical - something the machine is perfectly capable of doing itself. The optimal solution is to provide the user with some broad view of system performance, and to give a number of options whereby the required areas can be located, isolated and displayed graphically. Indeed, the use of graphics allows not only quantitative performance displays to be easily generated, but also comparative, qualitative displays; permitting, for example, the effects of system changes to be easily recognized. In the laboratory system, two main graphical display-formats are available - time slice graphs for quantitative assessments, and a modified Kiviat display for qualitative evaluations.

Time Slice Graphs

A time slice graph is essentially a collection of one or more activity profiles, one for each named object. The running of each object is denoted by a horizontal line scaled to represent the duration of that object's run. The basic format of such graphs is particularly suited to displaying the performance of distributed, parallel software. For serial machines, the activation lines for each object would be mutually exclusive - moving up or down from any trace, no other would be encountered. For concurrent programs, more than one object can be running in the system as a whole at any one time. Thus, time slice graphs can give a very clear indication of the relative states of many concurrent software elements, as well as the actual time each element spends active. In this particular environment, the possible object-display space consists of all tasks contained within the set of stations monitored to acquire that data file. Such a space will contain not only user-written application tasks but also system level tasks and handlers. For example, a time slice graph could show up resource contention problems, possible uneven load balances and priority lockout (where certain tasks can be excluded from running by a constant stream of higher-priority ready tasks). Indeed, by forcing the Kernel of each station to record its own operations, control-program lockout [11] can be detected. This is analogous to the previous condition, except that it occurs when the demands made upon the controller's resources (schedulers, queue up-daters etc.) mean that overall performance is limited by the control program and not the capacity of the local processors. Displaying the execution profiles for system tasks (such as the communications tasks in Polyproc) can give a good insight into the operation not only of the system functions but of the interactions between system functions and user applications tasks.

As an example, **Figure 18-4** illustrates a time-slice graph for the program segment used in the previous section.

Modified Kiviat Figures

The idea of using circular graphs to display system performance data was first presented in 1973 [12] and these have become known as "Kiviat Graphs" after one of the authors. The idea was that by carefully selecting the various axes, the plotting of such graphs would produce easily recognisable figures or patterns which could highlight certain aspects of qualitative computer performance. The basic form of these graphs is shown in **Figure 18-5**. Each figure comprises an even number of axes equally spaced around a central point. A circle, drawn from this centre point defines a maximum (generally 100%) level for each system attribute represented by the axes. The axes are used to alternately represent good and bad functions of system behaviour - for example, cpu utilization, i/o channel usage etc. If a convention is adopted whereby the uppermost vertical axis is used for a "good" attribute then a resulting star pattern would show a system that was operating extremely well. Similarly, other patterns such as wedges, keelboats etc. would indicate

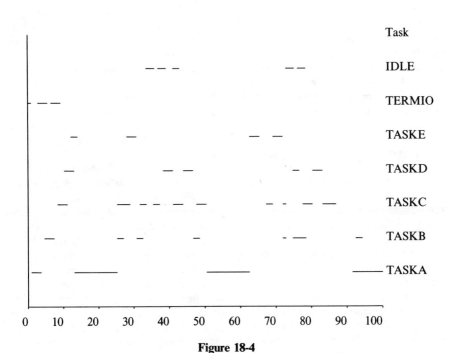

Figure 18-4

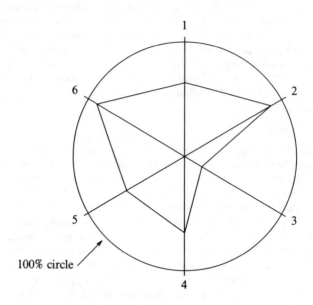

Figure 18-5

unbalanced system operation and help to highlight the disturbing factor or factors [13]. This method works well enough but has two main restrictions. To plot a Kiviat figure, users must supply an even number of system attributes - half good and half bad. In some cases, this could lead to unnecessary inclusions or important exclusions of some system characteristics and indeed, most profiles to date have used the cpu and i/o axes definitions employed in the original paper. Secondly, these figures have not been employed above the lowest system level and hence have not been available to help users cope with determining application-level software performance. The aim then, is to improve these existing methods, and to develop a user driven tool which will allow software profiles for application tasks running across a multiprocessor architecture to be easily derived. To do this, users are presented with a list of tasks from which they may choose significant tasks for display as a "Modified Kiviat figure" (MKF). For each chosen application or system task, the user is asked to specify whether the running of that task, on the assigned processor, constitutes a good or bad system attribute. Thus, a transaction-based system might, for example, have the tasks responsible for handling each transaction labelled as good while the tasks responsible for error logging might reasonably be labelled bad. To further improve the usability of such a tool, the converse state for each chosen element is calculated and plotted as a corresponding, neighbouring axis. This eliminates the need for users to specify an equal number of good and bad system attributes. Considering the above example, if the error logger has been defined as a bad attribute, and runs for twenty percent of the machine's time, then the profile will also contain an axis defining the "not-running" time of the error logging task as eighty percent and treating it as a good attribute. This not only helps in generating the figure, but it also helps to magnify the effect of any performance changes between profiles with the same elements but measured under different conditions. However, care must be taken in interpreting the MKF since, just because the running of a task is good, it does not necessarily follow that a system in which that task does not run is always bad.

As with the time slice graphs described above, the tasks chosen for display may be located anywhere within the distributed computer system. Thus, it is possible to construct MKFs that represent the performance of certain application functions even when in practice, these are fully distributed. Similarly, system-wide profiles can be generated - for example, generating a MKF from the idle tasks resident on each local processor could show overall computing-resource utilization. Continuous monitoring of such a system would mean that an animated "film" of the system's operation could be generated and displayed dynamically. Furthermore, MKFs can show the effect upon system operation of demands for localized or shared resources such as the communications channel. User and system tasks may be mixed at will, and the time-period over which the run-times are calculated varied. Associated with each MKF, a list is produced of the chosen tasks, whether they have been labelled good or bad, and the percentage run-times for each - no indication is given as to the physical location of the tasks.

It may be concluded from the above that the actual method and format of presentation of results using this approach are strongly influenced by the interpretation of the application by the user. As an example, **Figure 18-6** shows two MKFs derived from the example in the previous section. The first is for the single station configuration in which tasks A through E are defined as "good" system attributes whilst the running of the idle task is designated as "bad". As can be seen, the "good" axes (1, 3, 5 etc.) are generally fairly short reflecting the small amount of time required by each process. The obvious exception is the idle task which also runs for only short time but, by inference, this is now a "good" system attribute. The second MKF in **Figure 18-6** is intended to give a more qualitative analysis of the same application. For this, the idle times and the "output" times of the two processors used in a two station configuration are compared. The output actions of station 1 are concerned solely with the transmit task handling the entry calls made by task B to task C. Similarly, the input-output demands made in station 2 originate from the associated receiver task. As can be seen from the figure, when the axes are grouped into stations, the resulting figure is highly symmetrical indicating that the operation of the two stations, with respect to these criteria, is well balanced.

18.3.3 Implementation Overheads

With any instrumentation system there will always be overheads imposed by the measurement scheme. With the options available in this system, the tracing and performance measurement overheads are associated only with the switching of tasks - not with their internal workings. The degree of interference caused by the selection of either option will, in the case of the performance option, be constant, and in the case of the trace option, will, to some degree, vary. The overheads imposed by the performance option will remain constant irrespective of the type of software. Each task switch is logged, whatever the reason for that task being switched. Thus, by running an application that contains a known number of task switches for a long period of time, and measuring the difference between having the option enabled and disabled, a figure for the overhead imposed upon each processor switch can be obtained. Averaging the results for several runs returns:

Performance-Measurement Overheads
(per processor switch) = 13%

By employing a similar method, the overheads of the trace option can also be assessed. However, these overheads will not be constant. The Kernel inspects the reason for each switch and only if it is due to a flow control statement or to an error will the event be recorded. Thus, to measure the overheads imposed by this option, it is necessary not only

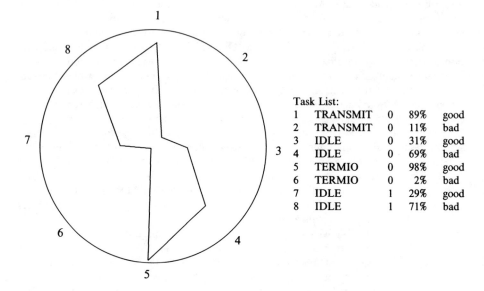

Task List:
1	TRANSMIT	0	89%	good
2	TRANSMIT	0	11%	bad
3	IDLE	0	31%	good
4	IDLE	0	69%	bad
5	TERMIO	0	98%	good
6	TERMIO	0	2%	bad
7	IDLE	1	29%	good
8	IDLE	1	71%	bad

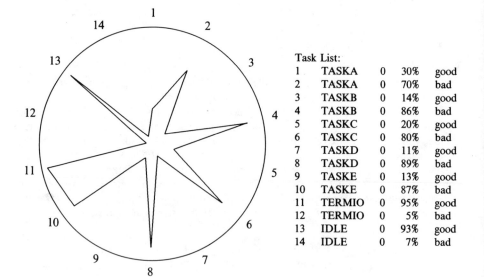

Task List:
1	TASKA	0	30%	good
2	TASKA	0	70%	bad
3	TASKB	0	14%	good
4	TASKB	0	86%	bad
5	TASKC	0	20%	good
6	TASKC	0	80%	bad
7	TASKD	0	11%	good
8	TASKD	0	89%	bad
9	TASKE	0	13%	good
10	TASKE	0	87%	bad
11	TERMIO	0	95%	good
12	TERMIO	0	5%	bad
13	IDLE	0	93%	good
14	IDLE	0	7%	bad

Figure 18-6

to know how many processor switches occurred, but also how many were recorded. Using a method similar to that above:

Trace-Measurement Overheads
(70% record rate and per switch) = 18%.

Thus, it is clear that even coding the measurement routines in a high-level language, with careful design the overheads imposed can be kept relatively low. One further point of interest is that, so long as the local buffers did not overflow (i.e. one half was transmitted while the other half was filling up) then there were no extra detectable overheads imposed by enabling or disabling the "auto-buffer send" option.

18.4 DISCUSSION AND CONCLUSIONS

The overall approach of using a functionally separate machine to monitor the target computer has proved both feasible and desirable. The system discussed has now been used by a number of people with varying degrees of experience, and the man-machine interface adopted has resulted in users being able to interact with the target system easily and safely. The direct presentation to the user of collected run-time error reports and event records has become one of the major debugging tools employed by users during the development of application software. These reports, in conjunction with gathered status information relating to any affected tasks, have proved a very quick means of locating run-time errors encountered during the early stages of debugging. In addition, the interactive trace facility which allows users to follow the flow of execution of a program, has proved particularly helpful in locating higher-level errors of the kind not normally encountered in serially-programmed computer systems. The trace facility has also enabled users to check their own conceptions of the expected behaviour of a program against what actually occurred in the target system at run-time. This is especially important in a parallel processing environment, in which many concurrent activities may be taking place simultaneously. This, coupled with the facility - the time-slice graph - to display the actual level of concurrency achieved within the target system at any given time, means that users can conduct meaningful experiments into the optimum design and configuration for any given system. In addition, the Kiviat figures have provided a powerful, user-driven means of demonstrating the effects of even minor system changes upon the performance of application software.

In the implemented system, there is scope for some investigations into alternative display formats used to show the calls made between tasks within a complete program. The current approach of using standard keyboard symbols is usable, but it effectively illustrates task interactions in a serial rather than a parallel form. One approach being considered is to generate a more formal picture of system behaviour using, for example, a Petri-net or finite-state machine kind of symbolic presentation. Alternatively, the display could be scaled vertically, to indicate the relative time spent between events, and horizontally, to show the parallelism apparent in each application. Clearly, a number of variants are possible.

A characteristic of most of the applications which have been investigated on the laboratory system to date, has been that all input and output data are generated and used by actual devices; for example, visual display units, disc controllers etc. Clearly, however, for some applications - certainly in the earlier stages of the development process - this may not be practicable, and so it is proposed that a separate "stimulus generator" will be implemented. This machine will be attached to the target system in the same fashion as the monitor is currently - via the monitoring link - and its function will be to generate input stimuli for, and absorb output data from, the target system. Further, it is proposed to enhance the data analysis facilities by providing the ability to create system "profiles". These are, essentially, a known set of system outputs (responses) for a predefined set of system inputs (stimuli), and it is envisaged that this feature will provide valuable information for the subsequent development and in-service maintenance of any given application system. In practice, to implement such a scheme it will be necessary to define not only the range of information used to compile the profile, but also over what period, and to what degree, any such profile is typical of actual system performance.

18.5 REFERENCES

1. W. Franta, H. Berg, and W. Wood, "Issues and Approaches to Distributed Testbed Instrumentation'," *IEEE Computer* (October 1982).

2. W. McDonald and R. Wayne-Smith, "A Flexible Distributed Testbed for Real-Time Applications," *IEEE Computer* (October 1982).

3. E. Gehringer, A. Jones, and Z. Segall, "The Cm* Testbed," *IEEE Computer* (October 1982).

4. R. L. Grimsdale, F. Halsall, F. Martin-Polo, and G. C. Shoja, "POLYPROC II - The University of Sussex Multiple Microprocessor," *Proc. IEEE 2nd. Int. Conf. on Distributed Computing Systems*, pp.95-104 (1981).

5. F. Halsall, R. L. Grimsdale, G. C. Shoja, and J. E. Lambert, "Development Environment for the Design and Test of Applications Software for a Distributed Multiprocessor Computer System," *IEE Proc. Computers and Digital Techniques*, pp.25-31 (January 1983).

6. *Intel Multibus Specification No. 9800683,* Intel Corporation, California, USA (1978).

7. R. L. Grimsdale, F. Halsall, F. Martin-Polo, and G. C. Shoja, "MARTLET: A Programming Language for a Distributed Multiple Microprocessor System," *Proc.ICS., 6th Euro.Reg.Conf. on Systems Architecture*, pp.403-414 (1981).

8. , "Ada Programming Language: Reference Manual," U.S. Department of Defense (July 1980).

9. R. Metcalf and D. Boggs, "Ethernet: Distributed Packet Switching for Local Area Networks," *CACM* **19** (July 1976).

10. D. A. Norman, "Design Rules Based Upon Analyses of Human Error," *CACM* **26**(4) (April 1983).

11. R. F. Vaughan and M. S. Anastas, "An Analysis of Multiprocessor Throughput in the Limit," *Journal of Digital Systems* **4**(2) (1980).

12. K. W. Kolence and P. J. Kiviat, "Software Unit Profiles and Kiviat Figures," *ACM/Sigmetrics Perf. Eval. Review* (June 1973).

13. M. F. Morris, "Kiviat Graphs - Conventions and Figures of Merit'," *ACM/Sigmetrics Perf. Eval. Review* (October 1974).

19 Cyba-M

D Aspinall

19.1 INTRODUCTION

When the microprocessor first appeared to the electronic engineer in the data sheets of the semiconductor industry, it was considered as something more significant than just the next level of integration which began when the separate transistor and diode components evolved into the logic gate. Just as the gate had brought the electronic engineer from the level of static and dynamic circuit analysis in the frequency domain through the study of transient response in the time domain and on to combinatorial and sequential logic circuit design, to use the microprocessor as a component would require an education in a new subject. The electronic engineers would need to add to their knowledge of the hardware technology by acquiring the knowledge, skills and techniques of Software Technology.

As part of this pedagogic exercise the Departments of Computer Science and Electrical and Electronics Engineering in the University College of Swansea collaborated to investigate the role of the microprocessor as a component in an information processing system. It was clear at the outset that the projected low cost of the integrated circuit components would lead to systems of many complex components including microprocessors and their associated memories. It was decided therefore to focus the collaborative project on the specification, design, implementation and use of a multi-microprocessor development environment.

The first phase of the project consisted of a dialogue between the hardware and software scholars from both disciplines to establish a common understanding of the problems, and to evolve a notation through which they could communicate. The specification of a multimicroprocessor development environment emerged from these discussions.

By this time it was clear that there was no accepted language for the programming of systems of concurrent cooperating processing elements. It was decided to experiment with a notation based upon the use of Petri Net Techniques which would enable the development of the applications programs. After agreeing the specification the two teams went their separate ways; the hardware team to analyse the specification, then to design and build the working system; the software team to develop the tools for program development on a separate mini-computer, which would eventually form part of the multiprocessor complex and act as development console. Eventually, the two came together as the hardware was commissioned, evaluated and then handed over as a working system to be used by the software group as a development environment.

By this time many students and research assistants has been involved in the project and moved on. Indeed, the main investigators moved from Wales to the University of East Anglia in Norwich and to U.M.I.S.T. in Manchester. At U.M.I.S.T., a joint project was established between the Departments of Computation and of Electrical Engineering and Electronics to maintain and use the CYBA-M multiprocessor. After long discussions with Welsh speaking colleagues in Swansea, it was decided to name the system by forming an acronym from the initial letters of Coleg Y Brifysgol Abertawe - University College of Swansea. M stands for Mynth. Data links to Norwich, Swansea and later to other research establishments enabled many workers to use the development facility. During this time, the system has been used in a variety of investigations:- evaluation of languages for real time concurrent systems, study of telephone exchange design, network architecture, reduction machines, applications in control, image processing and simulations.

Much experience has been gained in the maintenance of the hardware and software of a multiprocessor system.

It is not possible in this short paper to cover all the important features of this long complex project. In view of the other papers presented as part of this tutorial, we shall concentrate upon the hardware aspects of the project and attempt to highlight the lessons learnt by the electronic engineers to further their understanding of the role of the microprocessor as a component.

19.2 SPECIFICATION AND INITIAL DESIGN DECISIONS

The prime requirement was for a rigid physical interconnection structure to allow the close coupling of a small number, up to sixteen, of processing elements, each element to comprise a processor-memory pair or microcomputer. All processing elements would also share a common memory and a common set of input/output devices. The system had to enable the programming of a wide variety of interconnections between processes in the elements and in the shared input/output devices. Much emphasis was placed on the need to trace the different processing element state vectors during the development of low level programs.

It was decided to employ a direct shared memory interconnection scheme, which provided a structure for the programmable interconnection of processing elements as well as the shared memory concept. A separate shared image memory structure was used to provide the input-output ports. The 8080 microprocessor was selected from the small number available at the start of the project. This has an address space of 64 K-bytes which is divided as follows:

Local Memory	32 K-bytes (per processor)
Shared Memory	16 K-bytes
Shared Image Memory	16 K-bytes
Total Memory	= 512 K-bytes

The arrangement is shown in **Figure 19-1**.

Program development requires facilities for loading, running and monitoring the program. In this environment the problem is not only to load, run and monitor up to 16 separate programs but also to monitor their interworking. The basic programmer interface to the system is provided through a VDU keyboard attached by a privileged route to one of the processing elements (PE15) as shown in **Figure 19-2**. Other facilities such as a floppy disc system, line printer and modems for remote operation are also allowed a

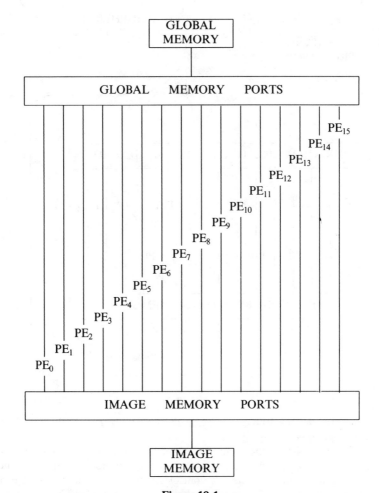

Figure 19-1

privileged route into PE15.   This processing element supports a job control language to enable development activities.   The loading of each program into the local memory of its assigned processing element, from the file held on a floppy disc, is achieved by providing separate routes between each processing element and PE15, as illustrated in **Figure 19-2**. The connections to the global and image memory ports are indicated to correspond to **Figure 19-1**. The additional routes between each element and the direct local memory access unit are shown. Also shown are the routes from each processing element to the image memory. These routes are provided to enable a copy of each of the significant registers within the microprocessor and its associated control logic, to be made accessible in the image memory. Thus the processing element PE15 may read the image memory to establish the state of each processing element.

To summarize, the extra connections shown in **Figure 19-2** enable the loading of programs and the issue of commands to run and halt them. Furthermore, every active register in each processing element may be read by PE15, as may all the global memory and all the image memory. These data may be dumped onto floppy disc, copied to the line

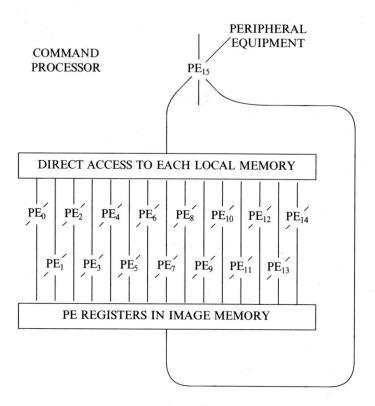

Figure 19-2

printer or displayed on the VDU, to provide the programmer with all the information necessary for program development.

Preliminary discussions on the establishment of a basic design methodology led to a detailed specification of certain direct hardware commands, to facilitate the control of the individual elements through the job control language. In addition to the normal commands of a JCL for a single processor, there are commands which cause a printout of the processing elements within the system; which cause the system to halt on certain breakpoint, or stack limit, traps; and which enable a printout of the state of the processing elements on a halt. These extra facilities add to the complexity of each processing element, some of them requiring 20 or so sequential operations. These operations are controlled by a separate sequential state machine within each processing element. This separate machine is known as the *control slave processor*.

19.2.1 Control Slave Specification

The specification of the control slave is important for two reasons: first, it is a complex piece of hardware, which could grow in a heuristic manner and exceed the space limitations quite easily. Second, it forms only a small portion of the command console system, the rest being program, and the designer of the software must have an unambiguous statement of the operation of the slave - particularly since the hardware and software must be delivered together, and neither can be fully tested without the other. The functions of the control slave cannot be categorized easily, but all are provided to aid program testing.

The control slave performs the following functions:

- Store last instruction (considered essential for easy fault finding)
- Breakpoint control (used for single step)
- Time out for faulty or non-existent memory
- Detect halt instruction
- Set trap error (changing breakpoint register while enabled)

Control slave forces its processor to:

Reset (initialize at start-up and after fault)
Start executing user program
Stop executing user program
Dump processor state
Stopall the processors (a special hardware command)

Control slave obeys the following commands:

Enable or disable   - Breakpoint operation
                                - Stopall on halt
                                - Stopall on breakpoint hit
Clear trap error

The response of the control slave to all expected events is described by a transition diagram. Transitions can be caused by hardware events, or by the main commands, which are generated by the command processor when a conventional processor instruction is obeyed, i.e. by software.

The transition diagram is the interface specification between the hardware and software of the command console, and this approach has been found to be extremely valuable in providing a clear definition of the control slave action. Every command issued by the processor produces an acknowledgement by the control slave. This transition diagram describes only one of the many state machines required to implement control slave.

Stopall: A facility considered to be one of the most important features of the control slave. As soon as a fault condition is recognised, stopall is generated by the slave detecting the fault, and all processors are automatically stopped. The main fault conditions are caused by:

Ilegal access, which causes a time-out because the memory location addressed does not respond; also when S (local memory bus) attempts an access if S local memory is not set.

Issuing an invalid command which causes the slave to enter the fault state. The slave is designed to be ignorant where command execution is concerned, and it expects the command processor to issue correct commands. The transition diagram defines the valid and invalid commands.

Stopall can be enabled or disabled when a breakpoint hit occurs, or if a halt instruction is obeyed. Stopall can only be removed by issuing a valid command to the control slave.

19.2.2 Process Flags

Binary *semaphores* are provided in a special memory, located for convenience in the shared image memory. Each word is automatically cleared during a read cycle so that a '1' set in a location can only be read once. The locations may also be accessed in the normal way, so the command console may examine them non-destructively.

Available word: The process flags are provided to control the sharing of software resources. The *available* word is identical in operation, but is associated with hardware resources. All devices on the shared image memory have an *available* word which must be examined before the resource is accessed. Each control slave and command control word contain such a register.

19.3 HARDWARE DESIGN CONSIDERATIONS

The most important design criterion was the need to make the total CYBA-M a completely synchronous machine. The physical size is restricted to ensure low clock skew over the whole system, and established design methods ensured that problems of synchronization at the multiport memories did not exist [1].

The processor, the 8080, was selected when it was considered to be the only one suitable for the task. Only four of its instructions have not been supported and these are of no direct value. Some of the other significant facts concerning the hardware design are presented below.

19.3.1 Global Memory

A 16-port memory, with 10 M byte/sec data rate, is constructed from a five- stage pipeline which operates with a beat period of 100 ns. The operations, in order starting from requests generated by the node switch, are:

(1)   Generate the next serve address

(2)   Arbitrate

(3)   Transfer address and data from port to store

(4)   Perform memory cycle

(5)   Transfer data from store to port

The pipeline arrangement works most efficiently when the traffic is high, a condition which arises when contention is most likely to be a problem. However, when the traffic is low, there is a 400 ns delay between request and serve, which incurs one delay beat in the 8080.

Arbitration Circuit : A snapshot with pre-emptive priority is used to determine the next serve address; an algorithm which ensures that all processors will get served. A field programmable logic array (FPLA) is used to implement the priority logic, the serve address logic, and the logic to enable the snapshot. Simply by changing the PLA pattern, other serve algorithms can be implemented.

19.3.2 Image Memory

The shared image memory is a distributed structure designed on a bus of 2 metres, which passes along the backplane of the image memory card frame and the processor card frame. Each bus cycle takes 400 ns, and may be extended by the destination logic for up to three cycles for slower memory components. The priority logic is functionally identical to the global memory circuit, including the FPLA; otherwise, the system is conventional. To stop the time out on the control slave, the destination logic must generate an acknowledge signal, the lack of which indicates a vacant address location. In this event, the bus controller automatically proceeds to serve the next request on the next bus cycle.

19.3.3 Slave Processor

The control slave is the most complex single system in the multiprocessor. It consists of 15 state machines, the largest of which occupies 44 product terms in a 14-input 8-output FPLA. Another FPLA implements two more state machines. Cost was less important than the space saved by the use of FPLA's. One major difficulty was the testing of the logic with FPLA's present. Returning faulty FPLA's for reprogramming by the supplier was unacceptable, and a real time FPLA emulator system was essential.

19.4 SOME PERFORMANCE MEASUREMENTS

One of the objectives of measuring the performance of CYBA-M is to assess how the overall machine performance degrades as the number of processing elements concurrently accessing either the global or image memories increases. The measurements indicate when the shared memory areas become a "bottleneck" in either interprocessor communications, access to shared code, or peripheral data transfers. The results may be used to calibrate the machine, to assist in the derivation of optimum solutions to particular application problems.

19.4.1 Performance Tests

The test consists of moving a block of data from the global memory into a number of processing elements. The data are moved from the global memory, one byte at a time, into an internal processor register. Each data byte transferred overwrites the previous contents of the register. Although this may appear to be a meaningless test, it does permit the maximum amount of memory activity to be generated. Two such tests are performed:

Test 1 (Global) :- The program to transfer the data block is located in global memory, and is accessed concurrently by all the processing elements involved in the block transfer.

Test 2 (Image):- The program to transfer the data block is located in a read-write storage area in image memory, and is accessed concurrently by all the processing elements involved in the block transfer.

The performance of a shared memory is determined by the number of processing elements which are attempting to access the memory simultaneously. The processing elements interfere with each other, and therefore cause delays in accessing the memory. The performance of the memory may be predicted by assuming that all the processing elements access the shared memory with the same request distribution. In this case, Weitzman [2] defines an "effective memory utilization factor" (r), which represents the fraction of a processing element cycle time that is spent in a contended memory cycle. For a CYBA-M processing element, $r = t_N/t_A$, where t_N = memory cycle time and t_A = average time between memory requests. It is then possible to predict the probability that the memory is locked due to concurrent memory requests from N processing elements, and hence derive the normalized memory throughput ratio, T, (or rate of memory cycles), relative to one processing element having uncontended access to the shared memory. The resulting performance equation is:

$$T - \frac{t_A}{t_N}\left[1 - \left(\frac{T}{N\left[1 - \frac{t_N}{t_A}\right]}\right)^N\right] = 0$$

For the global memory, $t_N = 100$ns and for the image memory, $t_N = 800$ ns; access to the image memory area requires two image memory bus cycles. In the test programs, when the data transfer program is in global memory, t_A to global memory $= 2.04$ microseconds, and when the data transfer program is in the image memory, t_A to image memory $= 2.75$ microseconds. These figures are derived from the test program and are calculated by dividing the time the microprocessor takes to execute one cycle of the test program by the number of memory cycles in the program loop. The timing calculations are simplified as the microprocessor only accesses the data block in a tight program loop of six instructions. The loop time for the global memory loop is 18.4 microseconds, while that for the image memory based loop is 24.8 microseconds; that is, 800 ns extra for each of the instruction/operand fetch memory cycles, of which there are 8.

The performance measurements on transferring a 5000 byte data block for test 1 and test 2 were carried out. The theoretical performance equation gives T as approximately proportional to N, for $N < t_A / t_N$. The actual performance results were in agreement with the theory.

It is worthy of note that in test 1 the initial performance results indicated a performance degradation of approximately 0.5% per processing element when N processing elements are accessing the global memory concurrently. For a 16 processor application, this represents 92% processor utilization under circumstances where all the memory accesses are made to the global memory. With real applications programs, where the code and workspace are located in the local memory of a processing element, only a few references are made to the shared memory, which reduces contention to negligible levels, and the processor utilization approaches 100%.

On the image memory, however, the contention is more dominant, it being eight times slower than the global memory. **Figure 19-3** shows the mid-point and deviation for the experimental results up to 14 processors. The spread of the results is due to interference caused by contention, and the situation is aggravated by the processors becoming locked into a synchronization pattern. This appears to produce an average throughput that is greater than that predicted by theory, and may explain why the experimental results outperform the theory. The effects of synchronization of this type have been noticed on many of the applications studied, particularly when deterministic load patterns have been applied.

19.5 CONCLUSIONS

The success of any microprocessor implementation depends upon the care and discipline exercised at an early stage of the project to produce a clear specification of the system, providing a precise statement of the software designers requirements to be satisfied by the hardware designer. Hardware and software actions causing state transitions by an appropriate hybrid state machine must be clearly separated. Once this has been achieved the hardware design can proceed to deal with the usual problems of cost- effective performance tradeoffs. During this project the FPLA emerged as a significant implementation component. The development of the system for programming these arrays formed a

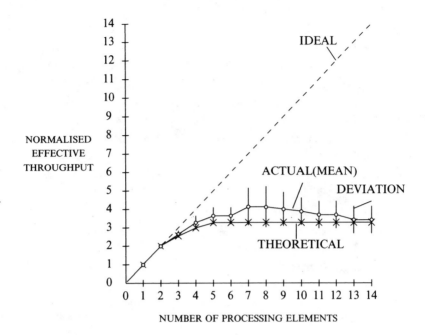

Figure 19-3

significant part of the project in its early days, as did the development of hardware analysis techniques based upon the logic state analyser instruments as they became available.

The complete hardware and software of the CYBA-M development environment has been operating reliably for many years and has provided many research students and staff with their first experience of a multimicroprocessor project. Many of problems solved during the project have given insights on how to make the best use of the newer microprocessor components which have been introduced since we first met an advanced 8 bit microprocessor, the 8080.

19.6 REFERENCES

1. M. Pechovcek, "Anomalous Response Times of Input Synchronisers," *IEEE Transactions on Computers* **C-25**, pp.133-139 (1976).

2. C. Weitzman, *Distributed Micro/Minicomputer Systems,* Prentice-Hall (1980).

3. D. Aspinall, "Multi-microsystems'," *Proceedings of INFOTECH State of the Art Conference*, pp.47-62, Future Systems, London (1977).

4. D. Aspinall and E. Dagless, "Overview of a Development Environment," *Microprocessors and Microsystems* **3**(7), pp.301-305 (September 1979).

5.   D. Aspinall, "The Microprocessor as Component and Tool," *Electronics and Power*, pp.791-795 (November/December 1979).

6.   E. L. Dagless, "A multi-processor - CYBA-M," pp. 843-848 in *Information Processing 77*, ed. B. Gilchrist, North Holland (1977).

7.   E. L. Dagless, M. D. Edwards, and J. T. Proudfoot, "The Shared Memories In The CYBA-M Multimicroprocessor," *IEE Proceedings Part E* **301** (July 1983).

8.   J. T. Proudfoot, "The Use of Programmable Logic Arrays," *Electronics and Power* **26**(11), pp.883-887 (1980).

9.   E. L. Dagless and D. Aspinall, "A Feasibility Study of the Use of FPLA's," Report of ACTP No. 3008 (July 1978).

10. R. Dowsing, "Software for CYBA-M," *Microprocessors and Microsystems* **3**(7), pp.306-310 (September 1979).

11. R. Artym, *Software Practice and Experience*, 1982.

12. S. J. Young, "Inter-Process Communication Primitives for DSM Multiprocessors," pp. 327-331 in *Implementing Functions*, ed. G. Noguez, North Holland (1981).

13. P. C. Burkimsher, "EMU : A Multiprocessor Software Debugging Tool," *Software and Microsystems* **1**(2), pp.41-47 (February 1982).

14. D. Aspinall, E. L. Dagless, and R. D. Dowsing, "Design Methods for Digital Systems including Parallelism," *Electronic Circuits and Systems* **1**(2), pp.49-56 (January 1977).

15. R. D. Dowsing and E. L. Dagless, "Design Methods for Digital Systems: I - Concurrency Constructs," *Computers and Digital Techniques* **2**(3), pp.93-99 (August 1979).

20 POLYPROC

F Halsall

20.1 BACKGROUND AND AIMS

Computer systems which utilize multiple processors offer a number of advantages over uniprocessor systems in a number of real-time application environments. Typically, these include increased throughput, improved levels of system availability, ease of incremental growth, and so on.

Although at the time of inception of this project it was possible to assemble a multiprocessor computer system from currently available commercial products - single board computers, intelligent peripheral boards, etc. - there were not suitable software tools - language compilers, run-time diagnostic aids, etc. - to allow application software for such systems to be written and tested in a systematic way. The main aim of this project, therefore, was to develop a methodology, and create a development environment, for the design and production of high quality applications software in distributed multiprocessor computer systems, intended for use in a range of real-time embedded applications.

20.2 A MULTIPROCESSOR DEVELOPMENT ENVIRONMENT

When developing the software and hardware for a dedicated microprocessor-based system, it is normal practice to use the various software and hardware tools - editors, debuggers, in-circuit emulators, etc. - provided with a microprocessor development system (MDS), to enable the software under development to be conveniently entered and edited, and subsequently tested on the actual target hardware configuraiton. Although this is a suitable approach for developing such systems, the limited facilities available with an MDS means that they are not suitable for developing more sophisticated multiprocessor-based systems.

The approach adopted in this project, therefore, was to utilize a separate host computer, to provide a flexible user interface with the target multiprocessor system under development.

All application software is entered, compiled, linked and edited on the front-end host machine, and the resulting memory images are then down-loaded and tested on the selected target hardware configuration. In addition, the front-end machine contains a range of performance monitoring and diagnostic aids, to provide the user of the system with a convenient set of facilities for debugging the particular target multiprocessor system under development.

20.2.1 Target Hardware Configurations

The distributed multiprocessor system to be described has been implemented to investigate a variety of real-time embedded computing applications, such as flight simulators, robotics, process control etc. In applications of this type, the overall processing function is often distributed naturally over a localized area. In a flight simulator, for example, the processing is distributed among the many items of equipment - visual system, motion control etc. - around the simulator, whereas, in a robotics application, the processing is distributed through equipment distributed around the plant or site.

A logical evolution of this physical distribution of processing functions is to implement each function by means of a separate computing unit or station. The stations which make up the system are then linked together to perform the overall system-processing function. The level of processing power required within a station will, of course, vary, and will depend on the amount of local processing required at that site. At one extreme, a station may require only a single processing element; whereas, at the other, a station may require a large number of elements. Similarly, different applications will require varying numbers of stations.

In order to cater for a wide range of different application requirements, the system development facilities have been designed to support a number of alternative target hardware configurations. Thus a system may include just a single autonomous multiprocessor station. Alternatively, a system may be made up of a number of similar stations, linked together, and collectively executing a single application program. Some of the alternative target hardware and associated software configurations are illustrated in **Figure 20-1**.

Station Design

In each of the target systems a station can consist of a selected number of processing elements, each with an amount of local or private memory. In addition, in a multiprocessor station, each element has access to a common shared memory which is used primarily as a means for fast communication between processing elements within the same station. Also, in order to maximize the level of concurrency within a multiprocessor station, a separate processing element is designated as a master or control processor, dedicated to the task of controlling and scheduling the other processors within that station.

The processor adopted for the system is the Intel 8086, and a station consists of a number of SBC 86/12A single-board computers which plug directly into the main station bus. This is based on the Intel Multibus, and additional shared memory and peripheral interface boards also plug directly into the same bus. Each processor board contains an 8086 CPU, an amount of local memory (PROM and RAM), various peripheral interfaces and timers and, if required, additional special purpose co-processors to enhance the processing capabilities of the host local processor. A schematic of a station is shown in **Figure 20-2**.

Interstation Communications

The stations which make up the system are linked together by means of a communications network. Since, in the application areas considered, stations may be distributed over a local area, the communications subsystem selected for use with the laboratory development facility is based on a serial coaxial bus network. The overall software structure, however, is independent of the type of interstation communications network. A standard interface is utilized between the main station software and the communications processor, and it is the latter which implements the appropriate network-dependent

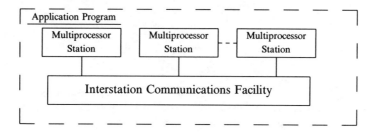

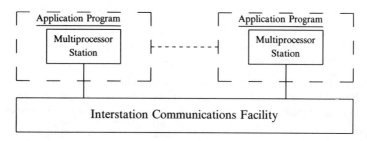

Figure 20-1

protocol. Thus alternative communications protocols and topologies may be used, simply by changing the communications-processor board within each station.

20.2.2 Software Development Tools

A feature of many real-time embedded systems of the type considered is that the application software, once designed and tested, is usually static; that is, the suite of task modules which make up the application program are normally statically assigned to the individual processing elements in the selected target system.

Also, there is normally a need to communicate data between tasks, so that the status of inter-related devices can rapidly be communicated between the tasks that control the devices.

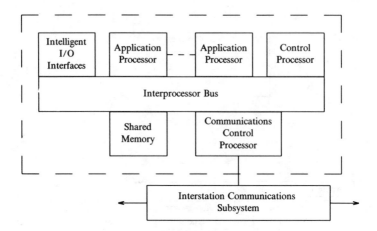

Figure 20-2

The aim of the system designer is thus to partition the application requirements into suitable subfunctions or tasks that can execute concurrently and communicate with each other, and then to distribute and statically assign the resulting program code to selected processing elements in the hardware configuration to be used. The methodology adopted for the design and test of application software for the laboratory multiprocessor is:

- Define and analyse the application requirements and partition the application into a number of subfunctions or task modules that can execute concurrently

- Define the function of each task module and the specification of the interface to be used for inter-task communication

- Code each component task module using a suitable concurrent programming language and compile the complete program

- Assign the compiled code of each task to a specific processor in the selected target hardware configuration and create the memory image for each processor together with the associated data structures for use by the run-time support software

- Run and monitor the performance of the application on a suitable development system and identify and correct any programming errors

- Try alternative partitioning and assignment strategies to obtain an optimum run-time system

The first step in the design is to define clearly the application requirements, and to partition the application into a number of reasonably sized operations or tasks which can, if necessary, be carried out concurrently. Clearly, some tasks, such as those concerned with the control of a specific device or piece of equipment, can be identified readily; others may be less obvious, but necessary in order to exploit the potential advantages offered in terms of, for example, enhanced throughput or system reliability. After the partitioning operation has been performed, a detailed specification of the function of each task is produced, together with a specification of the necessary intertask communication parameters to be used. Parallelism within the system exists, therefore, at the task level, where a task, when implemented in actual code, is a reasonably sized program module. Although there are no inherent built-in limitations to the size of tasks, the system designer typically partitions the application in order, first, to exploit the potential advantages offered by the multiprocessor and, second, to minimize the number of requests for intertask communication.

The second step is to select a suitable concurrent programming language to code each task module. Clearly, the language selected must contain the necessary concurrency features to provide for intertask communication in a well defined manner; and the language compiler should contain suitable compile-time checks to ensure their correct usage.

Since, up to this point, the application software is not tied to a specific hardware configuration, the next step is to take the output from the language compiler, and to distribute and assign the object code of each task module to a specific processor within the target system. This is known as the system configuration phase; and is in turn performed by a system configuration program [1]. This is an interactive program which takes as input the output from the language compiler and in turn produces a memory image for each processor within the system, together with associated data structures for use by the run-time support software to effect intertask communication.

In order to identify and locate possible errors in both the partitioning of the applications software and the specified assignment, the memory images for each processor generated by the system configuration program are first downloaded and run on a laboratory development facility. This consists of the actual target multiprocessor hardware front-ended by a single processor host machine. The latter runs both the compiler for the applications programming language and the system configuration program. The run-time support software in the multiprocessor under development, in addition to performing the normal run-time support functions concerning the scheduling of tasks and processors, and the synchronizing and managing of intertask communications, contains additional run-time diagnostic and performance monitoring aids. Thus any run-time errors are detected, and appropriate trace and diagnostic messages output to the host machine. Also, the performance of the specified task distribution is monitored, and alternative partitioning and assignment strategies can be tried and their effects monitored.

Finally, after all errors in the applications program have been corrected and the optimum distribution of task modules determined, the memory images for the actual applications hardware are produced.

The various software tools which have been designed and implemented for use with this methodology are:

(1) A concurrent programming language: this is known as Martlet and has been developed to enable a programmer to write applications software as a suite of task modules which execute concurrently and communicate with each other in a synchronized way.

(2) A system configuration program: this is known as Setup; it is written in Pascal and runs interactively on the front- end machine. It allows users of the system to perform the assignment of task modules to the individual processing elements which make up the selected target system and generates the necessary intertask and interprocessor data structures for use by the run-time support software.

(3) The run-time support software: this forms the interface between the distributed suite of task modules and the selected hardware configuration. Essentially, it implements all intertask communication requests, and the scheduling of tasks and processing elements.

(4)   Loading and performance monitoring and diagnostic software: this is primarily resident in the host machine, but a part is also in firmware, on a special card in each station, to allow application software to be down-loaded from the host machine prior to testing; and performance monitoring and diagnostic data to be gathered whilst the system is running.

Applications Programming Language

Although a number of programming languages which support concurrent processing are available [2, 3, 4, 5], the majority are based on the monitor concept [6] and are intended primarily, therefore, either for a uniprocessor system or possibly for a multiprocessor system which employs a single shared-memory architecture [7]. Consequently, since it was intended to investigate architectures which contained distributed properties, it was felt that a language providing a message-based intertask communication and synchronization mechanism offered a more flexible solution. Moreover, it is essential that these mechanisms must be an integral part of the language in order to obtain the full advantages of compile-time checks.

Although no such languages are as yet commercially available for a multiprocessor system, the specification for the US Department of Defence language Ada [8] contains many of the features just outlined, especially the tasking features proposed for multiprocessor implementations. In order to exploit these, therefore, it was decided to take an existing sequential language - Pascal [9] - and to modify and extend this to include some of the features proposed for Ada. The resulting language is known as Martlet [10] and this is currently being used to produce application software for the system.

In brief, a Martlet program consists of a suite of task modules which communicate by exchanging typed parameters, and synchronization is achieved using the concept of a rendezvous [8]. Other facilities in Martlet are a 'delay' statement, the handling of interrupts as external entry calls, a 'port' statement, multiple-task instances and exception handling facilities. These are all discussed in detail in [10].

System Configuration Program

After the applications program has been compiled, the compiler output is used as input to the system configuration program. This is written in Pascal, and interacts with the system designer to create a memory image for each processor element in the multiprocessor structure.

The program first requests the system hardware configuration to be used, and then the names of the files output by the compiler containing the object code and the corresponding control information. It then systematically reads the code and control information for each task, and requests the identity of the processor to which each task is to be assigned, and the priority to be assigned to the task. Also, if the task has parameters associated with it, the values to be assigned to them are requested. The program then creates the data structures required by the run-time support software, both to schedule the running of the tasks and to manage any intertask communication requests. This includes , for each task that requires to communicate with a task in a different station, the creation of a pair of pseudo-communication tasks: one in the calling task station (transmit) and the other in the called task station (receive). This is shown diagrammatically in **Figure 20-3**. Thus, whenever a task wishes to communicate with a remote task, on receipt of the intertask communication request, the control processor schedules the associated pseudo-called task in the normal way. The latter then communicates with the requested remote pseudo-calling task, using the communications subsystem, which makes the intertask communication request on its behalf. In this way, all intertask

STATION 1   STATION 2

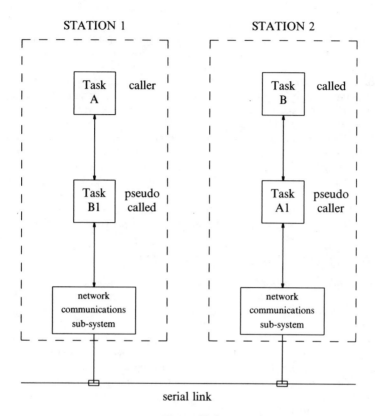

serial link

Figure 20-3

communication within a station is handled in a standardized way by the control processor, and is independent of both the physical location of the communicating tasks and the specific network protocol adopted.

Each task within the system has a unique identifier assigned to it which includes both the station address and the task address. Thus, whenever two pseudo-tasks wish to communicate, a simple handshake protocol is followed using the communications network. The requesting pseudo-task first sends a request-for-entry message via the network to the addressed pseudo-task, which in turn responds with a ready-to-accept message when it is scheduled. Parameter values associated with the entry call are then sent, and the remote pseudo-task makes a normal entry call on behalf of the calling task. Finally, after the call has been accepted and processed, any result parameters are returned to the calling task via the two pseudo-tasks in a similar way. The system configuration program then generates the memory image for each processor and shared memory resulting from the specified assignments, and the system designer may, if he requires, display these on the VDU screen.

Run-time Support Software

The control processor within a station contains an executive program known as the station or control kernel [11]. In addition, since, with the selected hardware, a control processor cannot physically access the working registers of another processor, each local processor contains a small kernel which simply runs the task the control kernel has selected.

A schematic diagram of the run-time support software within a station is shown in **Figure 20-4** and a detailed description can be found in [11].

In summary, the control kernel is implemented in two parts: the kernel data structures, which are created by the system configuration program, and the kernel routines.

The kernel data structures are situated in the station shared memory, since they are used by both the control kernel and the local kernels to effect the scheduling of tasks and to control interprocessor communication. They are shown in **Figure 20-5** and contain a linked list of task activation records, a list of processor status records, a task directory and an interrupt map table [11].

The control kernel routines are shown in outline in **Figure 20-6**. The scheduler routine is called whenever one of the ready queues associated with a local processor is updated. The task switching routine is called either as a result of scheduling, or when a local processor requests the current task it is running to be suspended. The local processor can request one of four actions: accept, entry call, end-accept or request interrupt service, which are handled by separate routines. The main kernel routine has two segments: the initialization segment, and the segment which performs the polling of flags.

20.3 LABORATORY DEVELOPMENT FACILITY

Once the memory images for each local processor and shared memory above been created, they are then down-loaded and run on a laboratory development facility in order to locate any possible errors in the applications program, and to monitor its performance during the test and run-time phases.

The development facility includes the actual target multiprocessor hardware, front ended by a uniprocessor host machine, as shown in **Figure 20-7**. During development, the latter contains the Martlet compiler and the system configuration program, and also status monitoring and performance measurement software. In addition, the host is used

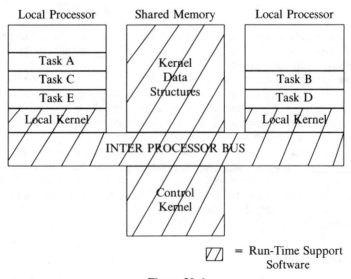

Figure 20-4

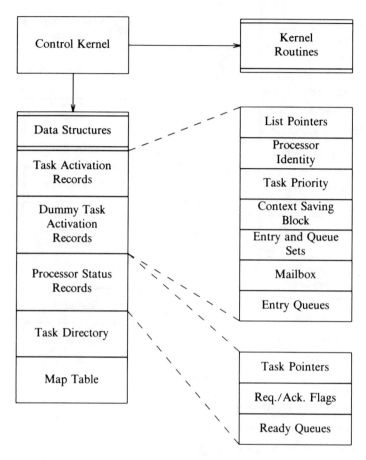

Figure 20-5

in the run-time system for monitoring and diagnostic purposes.

Communication between the host and the one or more stations in the target system is by means of a high bit-rate serial communications link which handles all communications with the host system. The system designer and/or service engineer can thus enter commands at the host terminal (which result in specific control messages being sent to selected stations in the system), and the station development board, in co-operation with the station control kernel, initiates the specified actions. These include commands to down-load the memory images for each processor, initiate the running of the application tasks, and also commands to collect and display on the host terminal, station status information and performance monitoring data. In addition, any run-time errors detected by the control kernel are immediately reported to the host station, which then displays the appropriate error message on the host console.

The station status information is of particular interest, either when an error message is reported or when the current system state is required. It is provided only when specifically asked for by the host. The control kernel responds to the request by formulating a suitable response message containing the requested status information, and this is then sent by the CCP to the host. It may include:

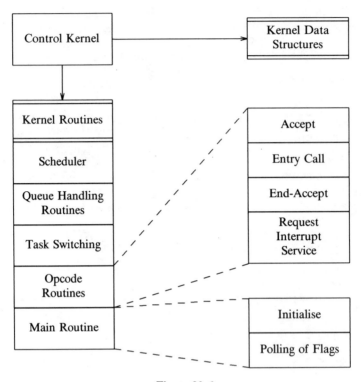

Figure 20-6

- the status of each processor in the station

- the directory list of tasks in the station

- the current state of all interrupt flags

- the state of each task in the station (running or suspended)

- the entry call on which a task is suspended or is waiting to receive

- the task currently being run by each processor in the station.

Performance monitoring data is recorded continuously by the control kernel within each station, in a circular buffer, and the current contents of the buffer may be requested at any time by the host. The performance data includes a record of all the main events that have occurred, together with associated time stamps. The events include control kernel calls for intertask communication and also the scheduling of local processors.

In order to monitor the specified assignment during the development phase, such information as the time a processor is idle, the frequency with which a task is called by other tasks, the length of the ready queue of each processor, the frequency of interstation communication between tasks etc. is also recorded. The system designer can thus try different partitioning and assignment strategies and monitor their effects.

Once the application software has been fully tested, and the optimum partition and assignment determined, the memory image for each processor is produced, and the host processor is then used, if required, in a maintenance/diagnostic role.

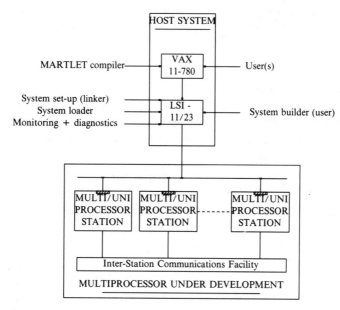

Figure 20-7

20.4 DISCUSSION

The development environment which has been described enables applications software for a distributed multiprocessor computer system to be designed and implemented in a systematic way. The function and design of the various software components which are used in the methodology have been described, and the structure and facilities provided in a laboratory development facility presented.

The provision for target systems, made up of of multiple linked multiprocessor stations with disjoint address spaces offers considerable flexibility, and makes the described system applicable to a wide range of application environments. Also, the use of a separate processing element for the control of all interstation communications means that the interstation communications facility can be readily varied, with minimal effect on the applications software.

Although the rendezvous concept provides a safe and easy-to-use mechanism for communication and synchronization between tasks, it creates a heavy demand on the run-time kernel software for its implementation. Hence the use of a separate dedicated processor to run the main station kernel significantly improves the concurrency of the system, especially when the station contains multiple local processors. If a particular station requires the use of only a single local processor, however, an additional processor for the control kernel is clearly less justified. Indeed, to meet this possible requirement, the laboratory development facility also offers the possibility of using a station which contains a single combined local and control processor.

The use of a separate control kernel to manage all the other processors in a station neatly overcomes many of the potential synchronization and deadlock problems associated with multiple processors accessing shared-data structures. With this arrangement, however, the overheads involved in mapping interrupts into entry calls to high-level service tasks is relatively high, and, consequently, in order to meet the real-time response constraints of certain devices, it is necessary in the development system to handle a significant amount of the processing of interrupts using low-level service routines. This clearly erodes the advantages of processing interrupts using high-level service tasks, and hence, for those devices which have a very fast time-critical response requirement, a special dedicated processor must normally be used for their control.

20.5 REFERENCES

1. M. Dowson, B. Collins, and B. McBride, "Software strategy for multiprocessors," *Microprocessors and Microsystems* **3**, pp.263-266 (1979).

2. P. Brinch Hansen, "The programming language concurrent Pascal," *IEEE Trans.* **SE-1**, pp.199-207 (1975).

3. N. Wirth, "MODULA: A language for modular programming," Report 18, Institut fur Informatik ETH (1976.).

4. D. W. Bustard, "PASCAL PLUS: A description," Interim Report, Department of Computer Science, The Queen's University of Belfast (October 1977).

5. R. A. Fraley, "SYSPAL - A Pascal based language for operating system implementation," *Proceedings of AFIPS Spring Computer Conference*, pp.32-35 (1978).

6. C. A. R. Hoare, "Monitors: An Operating System Structuring Concept," *Comm ACM* **17**(10), pp.549-557 (1974).

7. P. Brinch Hansen, "A keynote address on concurrent programming," *IEEE Computer*, pp.50-56 (May 1979).

8. J. D. Ichbiah, J. G. P. Barnes, J. C. Heliard, B. Kreig-Brueckner, O. Roubine, and B. A. Wichmann, "Rationale and preliminary ADA reference manual," *SIGPLAN Notices* **14**, Parts A and B (1979).

9. K. Jensen and N. Wirth, "PASCAL: User manual and report," in *Lecture notes on Computer Science, Vol. 18*, Springer Verlag Berlin Heidelburg, New York (1974).

10. R. L. Grimsdale, F. Halsall, F. Martin-Polo, and S. Wong, "Structure and Tasking Features of the Programming Language Martlet," *Computers and Digital Techniques, Proc.IEE* **129**(2), pp.63-69, Pt.E (1982).

11. G. C. Shoja, F. Halsall, and R. L. Grimsdale, "A control kernel to support Ada intertask communication on a distributed multiprocessor computer system," *Software and Microsystems* **1**(5), pp.128-134 (1982).

Part V

Modelling and Verification

S. Abramsky
A. J. R. G. Milner

21 Using Algebra for Concurrency

A. J. R. G. Milner

21.1 INTRODUCTION

A prominent feature of any algebra is that its expressions, by their form, either exhibit the structure of the objects which they represent, or exhibit the way in which those objects were built, or could be built, or may be viewed. Often indeed an object does not *possess* structure, but we *impose* structure upon it by our view of it - and thereby understand it better. A rectangular array of numbers, for example, is not of itself a row of columns, nor is it a column of rows; these are views which we impose upon it, and any linear expressions of such an array will impose some such biased view.

So it is no accident that algebra is useful in understanding complex distributed systems; for such systems must have many parts (else they would not be complex), and a structured view is essential in understanding something with many parts.

In designing an algebra for distributed systems, we are faced first with an inherent difficulty; the connectivity of the components is not in general tree-like, whereas the structure of an algebraic expression is always tree-like. It follows that the connectivity of a system is not expressible merely by the form of an expression. However, the analysis of an expression into subexpressions will express the analysis of the system into subsystems - and the expressions will often be chosen in such a way that the subsystems which are thus identified are physically meaningful, and possess properties from which properties of the complete system follow naturally.

A more detailed problem in algebra is: what is the nature of the connecting links between the subsystems of a distributed system? In a system such as the following (**Figure 21-1**) do the arcs represent directed channels carrying data from one node to another, in which case do they have memory capacity? Or do they represent simply the contiguity of the objects represented by the connected nodes - an interface across which they exchange an immediate interaction? And in either case does the forked arc from B to A and C carry a communication between B and *both* A and C, or does it signify that a single communication occurs between *either* B and A *or* B and C but not both?

One modest purpose of this chapter is to show that the precise answers to these questions can indeed be given by choosing one algebra or another, and that the different choices differ markedly. In section 21.2 we look at an algebra in which the arcs represent unbounded queues of data elements. In sections 21.3 - 21.6 we look at more primitive (but more general) models in which arcs are immediate interfaces; in this case

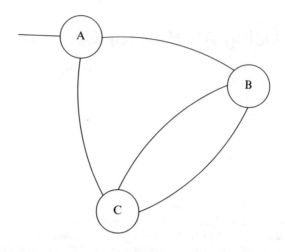

Figure 21-1

the queues of section 21.2 would themselves be represented by nodes of a particular nature. Another - not so modest - purpose is to illustrate in each case that algebraic proofs of system properties can indeed be carried out. We have no space either to treat complex examples or to show the full richness of the algebraic theories concerned. Instead we hope that readers will find interest in the significance and importance of the fundamental choices in building an algebraic model - namely, fixing the nature of the *objects,* and fixing the basic *operators* by which a rich enough class of objects can be built.

In the final section 21.7, we comment very briefly upon the relation between algebra and other theoretical tools for analysing concurrent systems.

21.2 PIPELINING : KAHN NETWORKS

A particularly simple and attractive form of concurrency is proved by the dataflow idea which arose first from the work of Jack Dennis at MIT and his group, but was put on an algebraic footing by Gilles Kahn - first at Stanford and then at IRIA (now INRIA) near Paris.

Simple networks are considered in which each node receives a (possibly infinite) sequence of values along each of zero or more output lines. If an output line serves more than one succeeding node, then its values go to all of them. There may be loops in the network, and typically some lines are designated as inputs and outputs of the entire network. An example is shown below, in which the nodes are uninterpreted (**Figure 21-2**). In this network, the node F_2 may be interpreted as as a function of two input sequences, yielding one output sequence; the other nodes similarly.

The question is: given the functions F_1, F_2 and F_3, how may we express the function represented by the entire network, which takes input sequences x and y and yields output sequence z? The answer is gained simply by introducing an unknown w standing for the

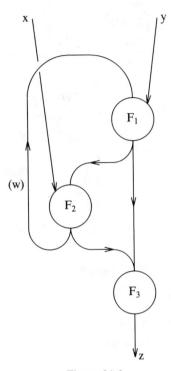

Figure 21-2

sequence of values which travel along the single arc which loops back from F_2 to F_1. For then the output F_1 is $F_1 (w,y)$ - a sequence - and this is fed into F_2 , so that w satisfies the equation

$$w = F_2(x,F_1(w,y))$$

and it can be shown that under simple conditions there is a unique solution to this equation - though depending on F_1 and F_2 it may be an infinite, finite or even empty sequence. Finally, since F_3 receives as inputs w and F_1 (w,y), the output z is given by

$$z = F_3(w,F_1(w,y))$$

As a more concrete example, consider the following net S_1 (with no input and one output line). We can calculate that it generates the sequence $S_1 = 1.2.3. \cdots$ of all positive integers. (**Figure 21-3**) To do this, we must first interpret the four nodes:

ZERO = 0. ϵ (a zero, followed by the empty sequence ϵ)
ONES = 1.ONES   (the infinite sequence of ones)
THEN(x,y) = first(x).y   (the sequence y preceded by the first
                                    member of the sequence x)
PLUS(x,y) = (first(x) + first(y)) .PLUS(rest(x),rest(y))
                                    (adds the pairs of inputs, one by one)

Note that any sequence x can be split into its leading member first(x) and its remaining sequence rest(x). The sequence S_1 generated by the whole net clearly satisfies

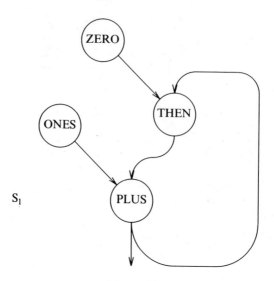

Figure 21-3

$$S_1 = PLUS(ONES, THEN(ZERO,S_1)) \tag{1}$$

We can begin computing S_1 as follows:

$$S_1 = PLUS(ONES, THEN(0.\epsilon,S_1))$$
$$= PLUS(1.ONES, 0.S_1)$$
$$= 1. PLUS(ONES, S_1) \tag{2}$$

To go further, let us define inductively

$$S_{k+1} = PLUS(ONES, S_k) \quad (k = 1,2, \cdots) \tag{3}$$

If we can show that for all $k \geq 1$

$$S_k = k.S_{k+1} \tag{4}$$

then we have what we want, for it will follow that

$$S_1 = 1.S_2 = 1.2.S_3 = 1.2.3.S_4 = \cdots$$
$$= 1.2.3. \cdots$$

So let us prove (4) by induction on k. It certainly holds for $k = 1$, since $S_1 = 1.S_2$ follows from (2) and (3); so now assume that (4) holds at k, and prove it at $k + 1$:

$$
\begin{array}{ll}
S_{k+1} = PLUS(ONES, S_k) & \text{by definition of } S_{k+1} \\
= PLUS(1.ONES, k.S_{k+1}) & \text{by assumption} \\
= (k+1).PLUS(ONES, S_{k+1}) & \text{by PLUS} \\
= (k+1).S_{k+2} & \text{by definition of } Sk+2
\end{array}
$$

which is what we wanted.

Nets of this kind can, in a very succinct manner, compute interesting and nontrivial functions. Wadge (in his work on LUCID) and others have given many examples, and the proofs can always be carried out in the above algebraic style - which is definitely a mathematical style rather than a specialised program-proof methodology.

Certainly the nets exhibit a form of concurrency and communication, namely "pipelining"; what are their limitations? First, the model and the proof method become considerably more complex as soon as the nodes are not assumed to be determinate - or at least not fully described as functions; an example of a non-determinate node is the MERGE (**Figure 21-4**) in which it is known that z contains all members of x and of y in the right order, but interleaved in an unspecified manner (eg. according to order of arrival, which is not specified in the model). Such non-determinism can be very useful. Second, the model attains its simplicity partly by omitting one feature of behaviour which we may sometimes wish to take into account, namely the relative order in which the input elements are received and the output elements delivered in a network. For - considering our first illustrated net with nodes F_1, F_2 and F_3 - the solution which determines z as a function of x and y does not indicate how many elements from x and y are absorbed before the first, second, $\cdots$ element of z is generated

A third limitation is that any realization of the model will require unbounded memory capacity to represent the queues of values which build up on internal arcs of a network. It is important to be able to ignore this detail at a high level of modelling, but if memory capacity is to be modelled then the Kahn networks are not the appropriate tool.

To achieve a general model of communicating agents which removes these limitations involves, apparently, a totally different approach. We illustrate one such approach - but emphasize that the purity of the Kahn model should tempt us to use the latter whenever we can accept its limitations.

21.3 INTERACTING AGENTS

We now look at a algebraic way of presenting agents which interact with other agents linked to them. A convenient simplification, to begin with, is to treat interaction as neither input nor output of values, but as a symmetric handshake between two (or perhaps more) agents; its occurrence carries no value from one agent to another, but merely means that *something* (eg. a high voltage pulse), rather than *nothing*, has occurred. Each agent - which may be realised by one or many processors - carries sites or ports on its periphery at which such events may occur; a Greek letter may be conveniently used both to name the port and to stand for an event occurring at that port. Here is an agent with two ports (**Figure 21-5**). If we wish P to be an agent which alternates between α and β events, then it may be specified by the equation

$$P = \alpha.\beta.P$$

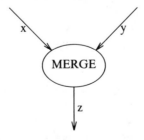

Figure 21-4

Figure 21-5

Of course, by expanding this, we can obtain

$$P = \alpha.\beta.\alpha.\beta.\alpha. \cdots$$

showing that the order of events (here, a strict alternation) at different ports is indeed recorded. A slightly more complex agent (**Figure 21-6**) which alternately performs *either* α_1 *or* α_2, then β, may be defined by the equation

$$Q = \alpha_1.\beta.Q + \alpha_2.\beta.Q$$

(which may be abbreviated by $Q = (\alpha_1 + \alpha_2).\beta.Q$); here the binary operator "+" between agent expressions indicates that either arm may be entered, but not both, during a computation. Thus we already have two operations on agent expressions; summation - meaning disjunction - and the prefixing ($\alpha.$) of an atomic action at a particular port.

Typically, an agent P will have the form

$$P = \Sigma(\alpha_i.P_i)$$

where i ranges over some set, indicating the possible next actions of P.

We will not yet deal with how to stick agents together to form bigger agents; even with the slender resources introduced so far we can represent the handling of data values. For suppose we wish an agent (**Figure 21-7**) to represent a buffer with capacity one, alternately receiving values in N (non-negative integers) at port α and delivering them at β . We may do this by taking α to stand for a single port, but for a family $\{\alpha_i \mid i\epsilon N\}$ of ports, one for each value; likewise β . Then our buffer can be defined

$$B = \sum_{i\epsilon N} (\alpha_i.\beta_i.B)$$

A convenient notation for this (avoiding writing Σ too often) is gained by introducing variables x,y, $\cdots$ over N - or whatever data domain is appropriate - and taking the first occurence of such a variable to imply summation over N :

$$B = \alpha x.\beta x.B$$

A rather different - but equally simple - agent with two ports is a storage register which can be assigned a value at α and can deliver its current value at β. (**Figure 21-8**) The parameter v in R(v) indicated the current value stored in the register, and - using a variable as indicated above - we can define R(v) thus:

$$R(v) = \alpha x.R(x) + \beta v.R(v)$$

The importance of this example is that the formalism can treat both passive agents - e.g. memory - and active agents on exactly the same footing. This is valuable in many applications; if we consider the systolic arrays discussed by Mead and Conway, for example, then we find agents where memory capacity and processing power are united in the same element, and it would be irksome to have these roles treated by different notations.

It is often helpful to represent the possible "courses of action" of an agent graphically. For this purpose we can use a *derivation tree*. If we expand the agent Q, given above, a

Figure 21-6

Figure 21-7

Figure 21-8

little way, then we get

$$Q = \alpha_1.\beta.(\alpha_1.\beta.Q + \alpha_2.\beta.Q) + \alpha_2.\beta.(\alpha_1.\beta.Q + \alpha_2.\beta.Q)$$

and we can conceive the indefinite expansion by a tree (**Figure 21-9**). Such a tree represents both the action sequences which are possible (these are the paths of the tree) and the possible alternatives at each point in an execution (these are the branches from a node).

One final point before considering the composition of agents: the treatment is so far ambiguous in the sense that it has not been determined whether our agents are synchronous (forced to do something at every tick of a universal clock) or asynchronous (able to wait indefinately until an interaction is expected or demanded by the environment). Operators which *compose* agents cannot remain uncommitted in this sense; from now on we shall adopt the second (asynchronous) alternative, but here remark that a synchronous calculus is equally possible.

21.4 PRODUCT OF AGENTS

The focal point of an algebra of concurrent communicating agents, such as we are discussing, is undoubtedly the choice of an operator (a kind of product) which puts together two agents to make a single agent, whose behaviour reflects both the independent actions of each component and also their mutual interaction.

Let us consider two agents P and Q, which are buffer-like (as our very first example): (**Figure 21-10**) We revert to the simple form in which values are not carried by handshakes, but the addition of values poses no real difficulties. Notice that we have arranged P and Q to share a port name β; this arrangement can be made by using "renaming" operators which we do not consider in this paper.

Now following the method of Hoare and his group, and also of George Milne, we wish to "muiltiply" P and Q together to form an agent which may be pictured as in **Figure 21-11** in which the actions of α and γ may occur independently, but the action β may occur (as "interaction") when both P and Q are capable of it. Let us denote this product operator by $\&_\beta$ - we may call it β-*synchronization*. There will be such an

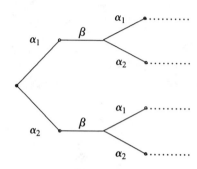

Figure 21-9

$$P = \alpha . \beta . P \qquad\qquad Q = \beta . \gamma . Q$$

Figure 21-10

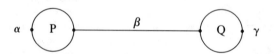

Figure 21-11

operator $\&_\alpha$ for any action α, and in general we may wish to use $\&_A$, *A-synchronization*, for any set A of actions. Sticking to $\&_\beta$, and recalling that we wish to consider agents expressed in the form $\Sigma\alpha_i.P_i$, what equation should be satisfied by

$$(\Sigma\alpha_i.P_i)\&_\beta(\Sigma\gamma_j.Q_J) \qquad ?$$

The product agent should be available to do any α_i which is $\neq\beta$, *or* any γ_j which is $\neq\beta$, *or* β itself provided $\alpha_i = \beta = \gamma_j$ for some i and some j. So we propose:

If $P \equiv \sum(\alpha_i.P_i)$ and $Q \equiv \sum(\gamma_j.Q_j)$,

then

$$P \&_\beta Q = \sum_{\alpha_i \neq \beta} \alpha_i.(P_i \&_\beta Q) + \sum_{\gamma_j \neq \beta} \gamma_j.(P \&_\beta Q_j)$$
$$+ \sum_{\alpha_i = \gamma_j = \beta} \beta.(P_i \&_\beta Q_j)$$

The first and second sums represent the independent actions of P and Q respectively, while the third represents their interactions for all pairs i,j such that $\alpha_i = \beta = \gamma_j$. Such a general equation may be less easy to understand than a particular case, so let us calculate $P \&_\beta Q$ for our particular case in which $P = \alpha.\beta.P$ and $Q = \beta.\gamma.Q$. We proceed as follows:

$$P \mathbin{\&_\beta} Q = \alpha.(\beta.P) \mathbin{\&_\beta} \beta.(\gamma.Q) \tag{1}$$

$$= \alpha.(\beta.P \mathbin{\&_\beta} \beta.(\gamma.Q))$$

Here we have used the product rule once, noting that the only possible first action is α performed by P, since P cannot yet allow Q to perform β. Now we shall be able to find some equations which determine the behaviour $P \mathbin{\&_\beta} Q$, for we have

$$\beta.P \mathbin{\&_\beta} \beta.(\gamma.Q) = \beta.(P \mathbin{\&_\beta} \gamma.Q) \tag{2}$$

$$= \beta.(\alpha.\beta.P \mathbin{\&_\beta} \gamma.Q)$$

$$= \beta.(\alpha.(\beta.P \mathbin{\&_\beta} \gamma.Q) + \gamma.(\alpha.\beta.P \mathbin{\&_\beta} Q))$$

(this step reflects independent action by either component).

Also,

$$\beta.P \mathbin{\&_\beta} \gamma.Q = \gamma.(\beta.P \mathbin{\&_\beta} Q) \tag{3}$$

$$= \gamma.(\beta.P \mathbin{\&_\beta} \beta.\gamma.Q)$$

while $\alpha.\beta.P \mathbin{\&_\beta} Q$ is just the original $P \mathbin{\&_\beta} Q$.

If we put (1), (2) and (3) together, and write R for $(P \mathbin{\&_\beta} Q)$ and S for $(\beta.P \mathbin{\&_\beta} \beta.\gamma.Q)$, we get the simple equations

$$R = \alpha.S \tag{4}$$

$$S = \beta.(\alpha.\gamma.S + \gamma.\alpha.S)$$

Apparently, then, our composite agent R first performs α , then repeatedly performs β followed by α and γ in either order. In this simple case at least, we have been able to deduce a product-free description of the product of two agents; the equations (4) might have been written down to describe the behaviour of a single agent R with three ports (**Figure 21-12**). Such transformations of description are the essence of the algebraic approach. It may be compared with the algebra of regular expressions, which describe the behaviour of finite automata in classical automata theory. But automata theory failed to provide a notion of produce which was adequate to express how two concurrent automata can interact.

At this point, we should ask whether our product $P \mathbin{\&_\beta} Q$ has given us what we want. *On the one hand,* we noted that it could again be "β-synchronized" with yet another agent, T say, which is also capable of performing β from time to time. The resulting agent $P \mathbin{\&_\beta} Q \mathbin{\&_\beta} T$ could be pictured as in **Figure 21-13** which reflects that the action β will only be performed when *all three* agents are capable of it; thus β-synchronization permits us to model multi-way (not just two-way) handshakes. In passing, we note that it is easy to show that $\&_\beta$ is both communicative and associative, that is:

Figure 21-12

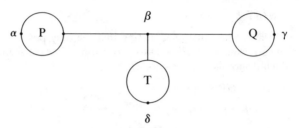

Figure 21-13

$$P \,\&_\beta\, (Q \,\&_\beta\, T) = (P \,\&_\beta\, Q)\&_\beta\, T$$

$$P \,\&_\beta\, Q = Q \,\&_\beta\, P$$

and such algebraic laws are essential in a smooth calculus.

On the other hand, we may have wished somthing different for the product of P and Q. For we may argue that the intermediate port β should serve only for interaction *between* P and Q, and that it should not be visible or accessible outside the product. In other words, we look for a form of the product in which the only remaining visible actions are α and γ .

Following Hoare and Milne, we choose to achieve this not by modifying the product, but by introducing an operation called *hiding* which may be applied to any agent to conceal some of its actions. Specifically, if R is some agent possibly capable of performing β from time to time, then

$$R \,/\, \beta$$

will represent R's behaviour with all β actions omitted. (Of course we have operators " $/\,\alpha$ " for all actions α , and operators "$/A$" for all sets A of actions.) Thus instead of forming the product $R = P \,\&\, Q$ of our two agents, we shall often prefer to form the *hidden* product $R' = (P \,\&_\beta\, Q) \,/\, \beta$; looking back at equation (4) above, we shall expect R' to satisfy instead the equations.

$$R' = \alpha.S' \tag{4'}$$

$$S' = \alpha.\gamma.S' + \gamma.\alpha.S'$$

i.e. the hidden product first performs α , and therafter repeatedly performs α and γ in either order. We shall not give the exact definition of the hiding operators here; it requires refinements which would take up too much space.

There are variants of the product operators $\&_\alpha$ and $\&_A$. Instead of pursuing them further, we shall now look briefly at an alternative originally introduced by the author; it has an advantage over the above in that just one product operator is required, in place of a family of operators indexed by actions α or by sets A of actions, but a disadvantage (in the form given here) that it models only two-way (not multi-way) handshakes. Part of the purpose of describing two approaches in this paper is to dispel the tempting impression that there is one clearly best algebra of concurrent processes.

21.5 AN ALTERNATIVE AGENT PRODUCT

To define an alternative product, we make a new assumption, namely that for every action α there exists an *inverse* action $\bar{\alpha}$, and that an interaction may occur between two agents whenever they may perform inverse actions. Moreover, this interaction constitutes for the product agent a distinguished action - denoted by the symbol τ - which we may call the *silent* action. By this means we can get away with just a single operator, called *composition* and denoted by "$|$", in place of the family $\&_\beta$ of operators - though (as here presented) we thereby sacrifice multi-way handshakes and retain only two-way handshakes.

Let us treat the same example as before (**Figure 21-14**) (Note that we have named one of Q's ports inversely to one of P's ports, to make the product work). Rather than writing down a general equation for the product $(\Sigma\alpha_i.P_i) \mid (\Sigma\gamma_j.Q_j)$, we shall state the rule informally: the next action of $P\mid Q$ can be *either* an action which is possible for P or Q independently, *or* a τ action if P and Q can perform inverse actions.

We now begin to compute $P\mid Q$: (**Figure 21-15**)

$$P\mid Q = \alpha.\beta.P \mid \bar{\beta}.\gamma.Q$$
$$= \alpha.(\beta.P\mid\bar{\beta}.\gamma.Q) + \bar{\beta}.(\alpha.\beta.P \mid \gamma.Q)$$

No inverse actions were possible (hence no τ action results) on this first step. But the second term, which was absent when we worked out $P \&_\beta Q$, represents the possibility that Q's $\bar{\beta}$ action may be complemented by a β-action performed not by P but by some further agent P' to be added later. In other words, systems like **Figure 21-16** can be formed by this product operation, representing how Q may interact with *either* P *or* P' (but not both) through the same port. There is a disjunctive quality in "$|$" which contrasts with the conjunctive quality of " $\&_\beta$ ".

If we were to proceed further in computing $P\mid Q$ we would get a rapid expansion; for example, for one of the terms we would get

$$\beta.P\mid\bar{\beta}.\gamma.Q = \beta.(P \mid \bar{\beta}.\gamma.Q) + \tau.(P\mid\gamma.Q) + \bar{\beta}.(\beta.P\mid\gamma.Q)$$

since the three possibilities of *independent* action, by either component and *inter*action, are all present.

But we can avoid so much expansion by using an analogue to the hiding operator. This time, we require something a little different; we use an operator $\setminus \beta$ called *restriction*. The effect of $R \setminus \beta$ is to discard from R all alternatives (appearing as summands of R) which begin with either β or $\bar{\beta}$. This means that the only use of these actions within R is to permit interaction between different components of R (yielding τ actions for R itself).

$$P = \alpha . \beta . P \qquad\qquad Q = \bar{\beta} . \gamma . Q$$

Figure 21-14

Figure 21-15

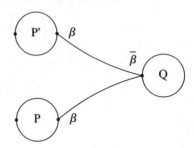

Figure 21-16

Let us now compute, not P|Q, but $R'' = (P \mid Q) \backslash \beta$:

$$R'' = (\alpha.\beta.P \mid \overline{\beta}.\gamma.Q) \backslash \beta$$
$$= \alpha.(\beta.P \mid \overline{\beta}.\gamma.Q) \backslash \beta$$
$$= \alpha.\tau.(P \mid \gamma.Q) \backslash \beta$$

At each step, alternatives involving uncomplemented actions β or $\overline{\beta}$ have been discarded. We now compute $S'' = (P \mid \gamma.Q) \backslash \beta$:

$$S'' = (\alpha.\beta.P \mid \gamma.Q) \backslash \beta$$
$$= \alpha(\beta.P \mid \gamma.Q) \backslash \beta + \gamma.R''$$
$$= \alpha.\gamma.(\beta.P\ Q) \backslash \beta + \gamma.R''$$
$$= \alpha.\gamma.\tau.S'' + \gamma.\alpha.\tau.S''$$

Putting these together, we have obtained the following product-free description of our composite agent R'' :

$$R'' = \alpha.\tau.S''$$
$$S'' = \alpha.\gamma.\tau.S'' + \gamma.\alpha.\tau.S'' \qquad (4'')$$

If we compare this with the equation (4′) in the previous section, we see that the only difference is in the presence of some τ actions, which are so to speak traces of internal communications. In fact there is mathematical justification for the algebraic law

$$\alpha.\tau.P = \alpha.P$$

(for arbitary α and P), and this law removes all difference between (4′) and (4″) !

There is a pleasant duality between the pair of operators ($\&_\beta$, $/\beta$) on the one hand, and the pair ($\mid$, $\backslash \beta$) on the other:

$\&_\beta$ (β synchronization) *demands* certain interactions;

$/\beta$ (β hiding) *releases* β from further synchronisation demands; while

$|$ (composition) *permits* both independent action and interaction;

$\setminus\beta$ (β restriction) *inhibits* certain uncomplemented actions.

In both cases, the lesson learned is that a pleasant algebraic treatment is obtained by separating the synthesis of concurrent agents into two phases: a product operation which takes account of their interaction, and an encapsulation operation which prevents external access to internal interfaces. The importance of the separation is that a binary product operation can be applied repeatedly - to link an arbitary number of agents together - before applying an encapsulation operation to "enclose" the composed system.

21.6 A BIGGER EXAMPLE

Consider the following system: (**Figure 21-17**) It consists of a ring of n identical agents, each waiting for a communication from its predecessor in the circular order (as indicated by the little arrows) except for $C_{1'}$ which is waiting for a communication on its a_1 port. It is intended to act as a distributed schedular for n independent agents $P_1 \cdots, P_n$ (not shown). P_i will be connected to C_i at both ports α_i and β_i ; P_i requests (at α_i) to initiate a certain activity, and indicates (at β_i) when it has completed the activity. The scheduling discipline is as follows:

(1) Requests are treated in cyclic order, starting with P_1 ;

(2) Each P_i must alternate between α_i and β_i - i.e. it cannot be running more than one instance of the activity at any time.

It is quite easy to define the agents C_i , and then put them all together, using either product operator; moreover, the algebraic proof that the resulting system has the two desired properties is not hard. If we are going to use the second form of agent product,

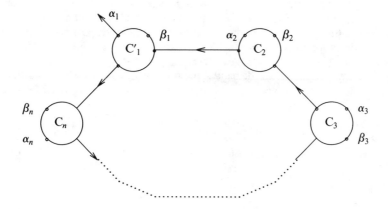

Figure 21-17

then we will define C_i as follows: (**Figure 21-18**)

$$C_i = \overline{\gamma}_i.C_i'$$

$$C_i' = \alpha_i \, (\gamma_{i+1}.\beta_i.C_i + \beta_i.\gamma_{i+1}.C_i)$$

(where subscript addition is modulo n)

Intuitively, C_i first learns (at $\overline{\gamma}_i$) from his predecessor that he may now grant a request (at α_i); after that request he then transmits request permission (at γ_{i+1}) and receives termination signal (at β_i) in either order; he then repeats.

It is not hard to see that this system works. In fact, the scheduler is expressed as

$$S = (C_1'|C_2| \;\; \cdots \;\; | C_n)\backslash \gamma_1 \backslash \gamma_2 \; \cdots \; \backslash \gamma_n$$

and the formulation and proof that S satisfies properties like (1) and (2) above is not difficult. It has been given as an example in the author's book "A Calculus of Communicating Systems", and can equally well be treated using the operators $(\&_\beta, /\beta)$ instead of $(|, \backslash \beta)$.

21.7 CONCLUSION

This short introduction to an algebraic approach to concurrency has necessarily omitted some intricate details, as well as paying no attention to other algebraic approaches (for example, Vaughan Pratt has suggested an approach which generalises the Kahn networks in a different manner). What we hope to have shown is that four kinds of operator - namely atomic action (α.), summation ($+$), product ($\&_\beta$ or $|$) and encapsulation ($/\beta$ or $\backslash \beta$) - together give great expressive power, amd moreover satisfy interesting algebraic identities.

In a methodology for proof about particular systems, we almost certainly need more than "just" algebra. With algebra, we can typically prove equations between agent expressions; we often wish also to prove that an agent possesses some property which is not expressible by an equation. It is therefore important to look at the relation between such algebras and logics - Temporal or Modal logics - designed to express interesting properties of processes.

Another important relationship to study is between the algebraic approach and Net Theory. The emphases of these models are different; communication is the cornerstone of the algebra (in the present approach), while Net Theory emphasizes casual independence, provides a totally different graphical aid to intuition, and provides different tools for abstraction.

Finally, synchronous systems demand some form of treatment. The author has found one way of integrating the above asynchronous algebra with an algebra of synchronous

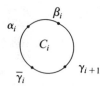

Figure 21-18

(clocked) systems; this method has some mathematical simplicity - for example, the algebra becomes more conventional, being at least a semi-ring (with agent sum and product as the semi-ring operations) - but by no means obviously the best integration possible.

21.8 REFERENCES

1. R. Milner, "Process; a Mathematical Model of Computing Agents," pp. 157-174 in *Logic Colloquium 72*, ed. H. E. Rose and J. C. Shepherdson, North Holland (1973).

2. G. Milne and R. Milner, "Concurrent Processes and their Syntax," *J.ACM* **26**(2), pp.302-321 (1979).

3. R. Milner, "A Calculus of Communicating Systems," in *Lecture Notes in Computer Science Volume 92*, Springer-Verlag (1980).

4. R. Milner, "Calculi for Synchrony and Asynchrony," *J. Theoretical Computer Science*(25), pp.267-310 (1983).

5. R. Milner, "Flowgraphs and Flow Algebras," *J. ACM* **26**(4), pp.794-818 (1979).

6. M. Hennessy and R. Milner, "Algebraic Laws for Nondeterminism and Concurrency," CSR-133-83 Computer Science Dept, Edinburgh University (1983).

7. R. Milner, "A Complete Inference System for a Class of Regular Behaviours," *to appear in J. Computer and Systems Sciences* (1982).

8. R. Milner, "A Modal Characterisation of Observable Machine Behaviour," in *Lecture Notes in Computer Science Volume 112*, Springer-Verlag (1981).

9. M. Hennessey and C Stirling, "The Power of the Future Perfect in Program Logics," Report CSR-133-83, Computer Science Dept, Edinburgh University (1983).

10. M. Hennessy and G. Plotkin, "A Term Model for CCS," *Proc 9th MFCS, Poland*, Springer-Verlag (1982).

11. M. Hennessy, "A Term Model for Synchronous Processes," Report CSR-77-81, Computer Science Dept, Edinburgh University (1981).

12. G. Kahn and D. MacQueen, "Coroutines and Networks of Parallel Processes," *Proc IFIP 77 Congress*, North Holland (1977).

13. D. MacQueen, "Models for Distributed Computing," Report No. 351, INRIA-Laboria, Paris (1979).

14. C. A. R. Hoare, S. D. Brookes, and A. D. Roscoe, "A Theory of Communicating Sequential Processes," Technical Monograph PRG-16, Computing Laboratory, Oxford University (1981).

15. G. Milne, "CIRCAL: A Calculus for Circuit Description," Report CSR-122-82, Computer Science Dept, Edinburgh Universty (1982).

15. R. De Nicola and M. Hennessy, "Testing-equivalences for Processes," Report CSR-123-82, Computer Science Dept, Edinburgh University (1982).

15. M. Hennessy, "Synchronous and Asynchronous Experiments on Processes," Report CSR-125-82, Computer Science Dept, Edinburgh University (1982).

22 Reasoning About Concurrent Systems

S. Abramsky

An attractive model for a concurrent system of any kind is a *graph,* with *nodes* which represent subsystems, and *arcs* which represent connections or interfaces between subsystems. In the case of distributed systems a tempting interpretation of such graphs immediately suggests itself: nodes correspond to *processes,* and the arcs to *communication channels* between processes. Of course to proceed further, we must say what processes are, and how they communicate with each other. Many of the current approaches to distributed computing comprise variations on this theme. Our aim here is to explore one such variation, which is closely linked to a programming style, of *functional* or *applicative* programming, seen as being of major importance in the new generation of computing technology. We shall place particular emphasis on the amenability of the functional style to mathematical reasoning about program behaviour.

That conventional, sequential programs can be viewed as functions is not too surprising. The way we use such programs is to supply them with input data, execute them, and gather the output. The natural abstraction of such a program is the input data/output data correspondence it implements, i.e. the mathematical function it computes. One can then turn around this interpretation of *programs* as *functions,* and develop a notation for describing functions directly, in a mathematical style. As long as we are careful in the design of our notation, e.g. so that the functions we can define are computable, our mathematical definitions of *functions* can be viewed as *programs.* This is the basic idea of functional programming

22.1 INTERACTIVE PROGRAMS

22.1.1 Sequences

Our first problem in extending this approach to distributed or concurrent programs is that such programs exhibit a much richer variety of behaviour in the way they interact with their environment than do conventional programs. We can illustrate this by reference to a simple interactive program, without bringing in concurrency explicitly (although of course interaction between a program and its user can be viewed as a system of two communicating processes). In contrast to our sequential program model (**Figure 22-1**) where all the input is represented initially, the program computes, and output is returned, an interactive program starts to execute, is provided with initial input, produces some initial output, waits for more input, and so on. Clearly the ability to

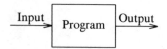

Figure 22-1

interpret program behaviour of this kind as functional in character is essential if there is to be any hope of extending the functional style to distributed and concurrent computing. How can this be done? The essential idea is to convert *actions* or *events* (the basic ingredients of the imperative or procedural view of computation) into *data* (the basic ingredient of the declarative, in our case the functional, view). The events in our system, comprising a single interactive program, are: *arrival* of successive items of input data, and *departure* of successive items of output. What matters logically about the input items is not *when* they arrive, but their values, and the order in which they arrive. Thus the natural abstraction for the input is as a *sequence* of basic data items; similarly for the output. The entire program behaviour can then be viewed as a function *from* sequences (of inputs) *to* sequences (of outputs).

As a first example, consider an interactive program whose task is to read a sequence of integers from the input, and output the corresponding sequence of their successors. What marks this an *interactive* program is that the program must output the successor of each input item *without* waiting for any more input. Thus if I supply a 1 as first input item, I should get back a 2 as output whether I provide any more input or not. The important point is that *all this can be expressed purely functionally*. For example, the equation

$$hd(f(1:x)) = 2$$

says that the required function f must map any input sequence beginning with a 1 to an output sequence beginning with a 2, no matter what the rest of the input sequence may be - it may be empty. (NB: in the above equation, the symbol ":" denotes a prefixing operator, used e.g. in " a:x " to construct a sequence from a basic data item a and a sequence x. The hd" operator returns the first item of a sequence; and if undefined if the sequence is empty. Thus hd(a:x)=a.)

The required function f can be defined thus:

$$f(a:x) = (a+1) : f(x)$$

We can then use this equation to calculate:

$$f(1:2:3:y) = 2:f(2:3:y) = 2:3:f(3:y)$$
$$= 2:3:4:f(y)$$

by successively substituting 2:3:y , 3:y , y for x .

22.1.2 History and State Information

One property of the function f which we have defined is that its i'th output value depends only on the i'th value, and not on any of the previous input values. We say that such a function is *history independent,* since at the stage when the i'th input value x_i is being inspected, we can regard the sequence of previous inputs, $x_0, \cdots, x_{i-1}$ as a "history" of our previous interactions with the program. There is of course nothing to stop us writing programs in a purely functional style which *do* take account of previous inputs. For example, consider a parity counter program which is to read a sequence of inputs, and for each n'th input is to output 0 if n is even, and 1 if n is odd. This must be the simplest history dependent program, since one bit of information about the history is required! A functional definition is:

$$parity(x) = p(x,0)$$

$$p(a{:}x,0) = 0{:}p(x,1)$$

$$p(a{:}x,1) = 1{:}p(x,0)$$

Note how the auxiliary function p uses an additional parameter to hold the required information bout the history. This parameter can be thought of as providing *state information.* (In automata theory, the state of a machine may be thought of as an equivalence class of histories, i.e.input-tape sequences.) Using this idea, interactive programs which respond to inputs by modifying a state and/or producing outputs can be written rather elegantly in a purely functional style. Examples of such programs include interactive editors, databases and interpreters. For example, in an editor the state parameter would correspond to the file being edited, the input sequence to the edit command stream, and the output sequence to the editor prompts and file display information. A number of programs of this kind are developed in [1]. Thus the scope of this method is much wider than might at first be apparent.

22.2 CONCURRENT PROGRAMS

22.2.1 Function Families

We now turn from the simple interactive programs, which can be thought of as single-process systems, to multi-process concurrent systems. We will represent multiple-process systems pictorially by directed graphs. The nodes will correspond to processes, each of which will be an "interactive program" of the kind already discussed, but generalized to allow more than one input sequence (more than one output sequence is also possible but we shall not need this for the moment). The arcs will correspond to the sequences, which are now to be thought of as histories of communications between processes. Each directed arc will represent a communication channel from the process at its source node - the producer - to the process at its target node - the consumer. the nature of the communication is *buffered;* the producer need not handshake with the consumer before emitting a value on the channel. It will be convenient to allow arcs to be "split" so as to be connected to several target nodes. This is to be understood as a non-contentious form of sharing, equivalent to duplication of the arcs: the *same* values go to every target.

In terms of our functional notation, the transition from single-process to multiple-process systems corresponds to the generalization from defining a single function over sequences to defining a family of functions. Corresponding to *cycles* in our graph of processes and communication channels there will be *recursion* in our definitions. Thus once again a property of *behaviour* - in this case feedback - is mirrored by a construction on *data* - in this case recursive function definition. (In functional programming, functions themselves are just another type of data - in fact in a very austere functional languages, such as pure lambda-calculus, they are the *only* data type.)

As a first example, consider the process network **Figure 22-2** where the processes F and G have the following behaviour: F first emits a 1 on its output (without requiring any input) and then copies its input, item by item, to its output. G repeatedly takes a pair of items from its two input sequences and outputs their sum. Functionally, we can write:

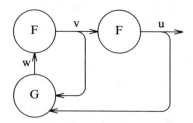

Figure 22-2

$$F(x) = 1{:}x$$

$$G(a{:}x,\ b{:}y) = (a+b){:}\ G(x,y)$$

The whole system can be described by giving names to each of the arcs appearing in the graph, as we have done in the figure, and writing a functional equation for the "behaviour" of each arc, i.e. its value as a sequence:

$$u = F(v)$$

$$v = F(w)$$

$$w = G(u,v)$$

Note that the "splitting" of the arcs u and v in the figure is reflected in the equations, since e.g. v appears as a parameter in both the first and the third equation. Also, the cyclic nature of the graph is reflected in the mutual recursion between the definitions of u, v and w - thus u is defined in the terms of u, v in the terms of w , and w in terms of u and v. Because of this mutual recursion, it might seem that the system must deadlock, with no useful information being produced. As we shall see, this is not the case.

First we will rewrite the above equations, using our definitions of F and G :

$$u = 1{:}v$$

$$v = 1{:}w$$

$$w = G(u,v)$$

where

$$G(a{:}x,\ b{:}y) = (a+b)\ {:}G(x,y)$$

Regarding u as the output of the whole system, we want to show that it generates the sequence of *Fibonacci numbers,* i.e. the sequence given by

$$F_0 = 1 \quad F_1 = 1 \quad F_{n+2} = F_n + F_{n+1}$$

This will be our first example of how the functional style lends itself to simple and elegant methods of proof. Our argument will exhibit the mathematical character of our equations; but keep in mind that the conclusion of the argument will provide information about the behaviour of a concurrent, multi-process system. It is the duality of point-of-view, between the *mathematical* properties of a notation and its *computational* interpretation, which provides much of the motivation for what we are doing.

Turning to the proof, we first (re-) describe the sequences u,v,w in index notation:

(I) $u_0 = 1$ $\qquad u_{k+1} = v_k$
(II) $v_0 = 1$ $\qquad v_{k+1} = w_k$
(III) $w_k = u_k + v_k$

These descriptions can be read off directly from the defining equations for u, v and w. (Of course in a more formal proof, we would have to give a detailed justification.) Now what we want to show is:

$\forall k \; u_k = F_k$

We argue by induction on k.

First $F_0 = 1 = u_0$

$\qquad F_1 = 1 = v_0 = u_1$

directly from the equations for F and (I) and (II) . We now show that $F_{k+2} = u_{k+2}$, assuming $F_k = u_k$ and $F_{k+1} = u_{k+1}$.

$$
\begin{aligned}
u_{k+2} &= v_{k+1} & &\text{(I)} \\
&= w_k & &\text{(II)} \\
&= u_k + v_k & &\text{(III)} \\
&= u_k + u_{k+1} & &\text{(I)} \\
&= F_k + F_{k+1} & &\text{inductive hypothesis} \\
&= F_{k+2} & &\text{definition of F}
\end{aligned}
$$

Arguments of this kind, where we reason about streams in an elementwise fashion, are formalized particularly neatly in the LUCID system of Ashcroft and Wadge [2, 3]. The programming notation of LUCID can be regarded as a (deliberate) restriction of the general functional style we are using.

22.2.2 Hamming's Problem

As a further example of reasoning of this kind, we consider the functional solution of "Hamming's Problem", which is: to generate a sequence of integers in ascending order satisfying the following properties:

(P1) 1 is in the sequence

(P2) If n is in the sequence, so are 2n, 3n and 5n

(P3) Nothing is in the sequence except as required by (P1) and (P2)

We need an auxiliary function to merge two sequences of integers in ascending order, omitting duplicates:

$$
\begin{aligned}
M(a{:}x, b{:}y) &= a{:}M(x,y) & &\text{if } a{=}b \\
&= a{:}M(x, b{:}y) & &\text{if } a{<}b \\
&= b{:}M(a{:}x, y) & &\text{if } a{>}b
\end{aligned}
$$

We can now define a solution to Hamming's Problem as a process network (**Figure 22-3**). Here F is the same function as we used in the previous example (**Figure 22-2**). The xn functions, n = 2,3,4,5, are defined thus:

$$\text{xn } (a{:}x) = (a{\times}n){:} \, \text{xn}(x)$$

The equations defining our network are then:

$$u = F(v) = 1{:}v$$

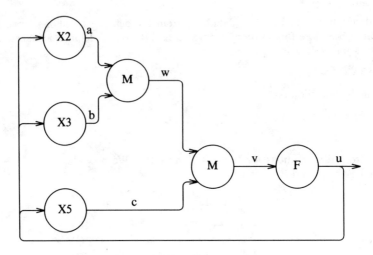

Figure 22-3

$$v = M(w,c)$$
$$w = M(a,b)$$
$$a = x2(u)$$
$$b = x3(u)$$
$$c = x5(u)$$

22.2.3 Deadlock and Convergence

Taking u as the output of the whole system, we shall prove that the system *never deadlocks,* i.e. that at any stage, more output will always be produced, or equivalently, u is infinite. This amounts to saying that for any k, the k'th term of u is a well defined integer, which we shall write

$$u_k \!\downarrow$$

(to be read: u_k *converges*).

We again write properties of the sequences in index form:

(I) $u_0 = 1$ $u_{k+1} = v_k$

(II) $a_k\!\downarrow$ & $b_k\!\downarrow$ & $c_k\!\downarrow$ if and only if $u_k\!\downarrow$

(III) if $x_k\!\downarrow$ and $y_k\!\downarrow$ then $M(x,y)_k\!\downarrow$

Properties (I) and (II) are immediate from the definitions; note that x2 etc. are history-independent functions. Property (III) needs a little thought. We note that at each stage the merge process defined by M inspects one item from each input sequence, consumes *at most* one item from each input sequence, and produces exactly one item on its output. Thus to produce k items, it must inspect at most k items from each input. The existence of k items on each input is therefore sufficient to ensure the existence of k output items. (It is *not* necessary - e.g. the merge process may inspect no more than one item from the first input in producing the k output items. Question - in which case does this arise?)

We now prove that $\forall k\ u_k\downarrow$ by induction on k.

For $k=0$, $u_0=1$ by (I).

Now assume $u_k\downarrow$.

$u_{k+1} = v_k$ by (I)

$v_k = M(w,c)_k$, so $v_k\downarrow$ if $w_k\downarrow$ and $c_k\downarrow$ by (III)

$w_k = M(a,b)_k$, so $w_k\downarrow$ if $a_k\downarrow$ and $b_k\downarrow$ by (III)

so $u_{k+1}\downarrow$ if $a_k\downarrow$ & $b_k\downarrow$ & $c_k\downarrow$ if and only if $u_k\downarrow$ by (II)

but $u_k\downarrow$ by induction hypothesis. So $u_{k+1}\downarrow$.

Certain cases of this kind of analysis for deadlock freedom are simple enough to be automated. See [4].

22.3 DYNAMIC NETWORKS

We now turn to a final example of a concurrent program, which will serve two purposes. Firstly, the process networks we have considered so far have been *static* in character: there are a fixed number of processes, which remain unchanged throughout the computation. The functional style also allows us to describe a certain class of networks which grow dynamically. The form of growth which can be described is where a single node of the network is replaced by a sub-network, with the connections to the rest of the network left unchanged. Our example will illustrate how such dynamic networks can be used. It will also provide an opportunity to illustrate an alternative approach to proving facts about concurrent systems behaviour described in a functional style.

Our example is a system whose output sequence will be the prime numbers in ascending order. The method used will be a parallel form of the sieve of Eratosthenes. The dynamic network growth will be used to generate the array of parallel processes comprising the sieve. The reader is challenged to give a proof of the correctness of this program based on an operational understanding of its behaviour. By contrast, use of appropriate forms of mathematical induction will allow an elegant correctness proof. We shall use the notation "n!m" to mean "n divides m" (n, m integers), and "n¡m" to mean "n does not divide m". Our equations are as follows:

$P = \text{Sift}(I(2))$

$I(n) = n{:}I(n+1)$

$\text{Sift}(a{:}x) = a{:}\text{Filter}(a, \text{Sift}(x))$

$\text{Filter}(p,a{:}x) = \text{Filter}(p,x) \quad \text{if } p!a$

$\qquad\qquad\quad = a{:}\text{Filter}(p,x) \quad \text{if } p¡a$

Then we claim that P is the required sequence. Intuitively, it is clear that I(2) (or I2) is the sequence 2,3,4, $\cdots$ of integers from 2. Filter(p,x) generates the subsequence of x obtained by removing elements divisible by p. The sieve process (Sift) works by creating one copy of the filter process for each prime generated thus far. Thus after $k+1$ primes have been generated, we can picture the appearance of the network as in **Figure 22-4**.

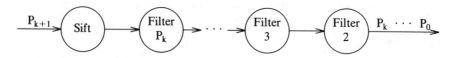

Figure 22-4

Of course, the activity of generating new integers to test and passing them through the sieve can proceed in a highly parallel pipelined fashion, so there are many possible "pictures". This should suggest why reasoning based on the mathematical properties of the equations is to be preferred. A solution for this problem in Hoare's CSP language, with a very similar process structure, but a quite different behaviour with respect to inter-process synchronization, is given in [5].

22.3.1 Structural Induction

We now turn to the question of how we can prove the correctness of this last example. The method we shall use is a form of structural induction on sequences (in this case, sequences of integers). That is, to prove a property ϕ of sequences, we prove:

(1) ϕ holds for the empty sequence, which we write Ω.

(2)   If ϕ holds for a sequence x, then for any integer a, ϕ holds for a:x.

and conclude that ϕ holds for *all* sequences. The basis for this method of proof is that all sequences are built up from the empty sequence by prefixing. However, there is a subtlety. As we have seen in previous examples, and indeed as we expect in the present case, the output of our system may well form an *infinite* sequence, while proving (1) and (2) only guarantees that ϕ holds for any *finite* sequence. To ensure the validity of our proof method, we must also prove

(3) ϕ is such that, if it holds for all finite initial segments of an infinite sequence, it holds for the infinite sequence as well.

we say that ϕ *admits induction* or is *admissible* if it satisfies (3). A full explanation of the issues raised here would take us too far afield, but they are important and fascinating. For further discussion of admissibility see [6]. For theoretical foundations, see [7] and [8]. In what follows, we shall omit proofs of admissibility for the properties we shall consider. (There are in fact syntactical checks for admissibility when properties are formalized in the predicate calculus.)

The proof of correctness we shall give follows closely the outline in [9]. It proceeds in structured fashion, by way of five lemmas.

Lemma 1

I2 is the sequence of integers in ascending order from 2. We leave the proof of Lemma 1 as an exercise.

Lemma 2

∀ p,L Filter(p,L) is a subsequence of L containing exactly those elements of L not divisible by p.

Proof

By structural induction on L.

(1) $L = \Omega$. Filter(p,Ω) = Ω, so this case is trivial.

(2)   L = a:x. By induction hypothesis, Filter(p,x) is a subsequence of x, therefore Filter(p,x) and a:Filter(p,x) are both subsequences of a:x. Again by induction hypothesis, Filter(p,x) contains exactly those elements of x not divisible by p; therefore the subsequence of elements of a:x not divisible by p is given by a:Filter(p,x) if p¡a, and by Filter(p,x) if p!a, i.e. by Filter(p,a:x).

Lemma 3

∀ L Sift(L) is a subsequence of L.

Proof

By induction on L.

(1) $L = \Omega$. Sift(Ω) = Ω, so this case is trivial.

(2)   L = a:x. By induction hypothesis, Sift(x) is a subsequence of x, and by Lemma 2, Filter(a,Sift(x)) is a subsequence of Sift(x); therefore Sift(a:x) = a:Filter(a,Sift(x)) is a subsequence of a:x.

Lemma 4

∀ L if L is an increasing sequence of integers and p occurs in Sift(L), no other multiples of p (than p itself) occur in Sift(L).

Proof

By induction on L.

(1) $L = \Omega$. Trivial by Lemma 3.

(2)   L = a;x. Suppose p occurs in Sift(a:x).
Subcase (i): a=p. By Lemma 2, no multiple of a will occur in Filter(a,Sift(x)).

Subcase (ii): a≠p. Since L is increasing and p occurs in L, since it occurs in Sift(L), and by Lemma 3 Sift(L) is a subsequence of L, we must have a<p, so a is not a multiple of p. By induction hypothesis, no multiple of p other than itself occurs in Sift(x).

Lemma 5

∀L, if every element of L is >1, and p is a prime occurring in L, p occurs in Sift(L).

Proof

(1) $L = \Omega$. Trivial.

(2)   L = a:x.

Subcase (i): p=a Sift(a:x) = a:Filter(a,Sift(x)), so p occurs in Sift(L).

Subcase (ii): p≠a. Then p must occur in x, therefore in Sift(x) by induction hypothesis. By Lemma 2, p occurs in Filter(a,Sift(x)) if and only if p is not divisible by a. Since p is prime, it is divisible only by itself and 1. Since a$\neq$1 by the assumption on L, and a$\neq$p, p occurs in Sift(L).

Correctness of Primes Program

The sequence of integers P is exactly the sequence of prime numbers in ascending order.

Proof

Since all primes are integers >1 by Lemma 1 all primes are members of I2, hence by Lemma 5 of P = Sift(I2). Since any non-prime is a multiple of primes, by Lemma 4 no non-prime number can occur in P. Finally, by Lemma 3 P is a subsequence of I2, hence the primes appear in ascending order.

It is interesting to note that our correctness proof does not contain any argument for the deadlock-freedom of the program, i.e. that p is infinite. The fact that the program is deadlock-free reduces to the purely mathematical fact about the integers that there are definitely many primes! This reduction of a significant fact about program behaviour to a mathematical fact about a data type is typical of program verification in general, but of functional programming in particular.

The examples we have been considering have necessarily been rather small, and their subject-matter not perhaps of great practical importance. The reader should not be misled. The ideas and methods we have been discussing have a wide range of potential applications. The challenge to realize this potential is open.

22.4 TIME DEPENDENCY

We now turn to an important - possibly the most important - aspect of concurrency and distributed computing, namely synchronization, and time-dependent system behaviour. It should be emphasised that the approach we have been using thus far does *not* extend to the description of time-dependent behaviour. It does allow the description of a limited form of synchronization, namely producer-consumer synchronization of the kind implicit in the use of buffered communication channels. However, it seems clear that operating systems, process control systems, and any kind of hardware system considered at a sufficiently fine grain of detail, all exhibit time-dependent behaviour of one sort or another. We are faced with a dilemma: do we accept the fact that the functional style is inadequate to deal with these important aspects of distributed computing, or do we try to extend it to handle time-dependency, at the risk of destroying the very properties which originally made the style attractive? Some interesting work has been done on these matters, but the outcome is at present inconclusive. We shall do no more here than indicate one of the main directions, and hope that the reader may be tempted into further study.

A standard example of time-dependent behaviour is provided by the *airline reservation system*. Here we have a shared database containing flight reservation information, which is accessed by a number of geographically distributed terminals. Requests for reservations should be processed at the database in their order of arrival, and replies routed back to the requesting terminal. If we separate the input and output functions of the terminals, we have the situation in **Figure 22-5**.

The problem is how the two input sequences are to be processed by the Database process? Within each sequence, the order of inputs is well defined, but the requirement that items from two independent sources should be processed in their order of arrival appeals to information about the ordering of items on Input 1 relative to items on Input 2 which is *not available* in the system as it stands. To expose the problem more clearly, we factor

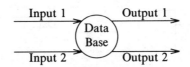

Figure 22-5

it as in **Figure 22-6**.

Now the problem is located in the task of serializing two independent sequences in the order of availability of their items. The process which does this is usually called *merge*.

If we had a primitive "function" merge, the behaviour of the whole system could be described as follows:

Output1, Output2 = Db(u)

u = Merge (Input1, Input2)

Here Db is the function to implement the database, which is essentially just a simple interactive program of the kind we began by considering. Have we then solved our problem, of describing time-dependent systems in the functional style? The notation suggests we have, but here the notation is misleading. It suggests that merge is a function from a pair of input sequences to an output sequence. But if merge is to perform its task of interleaving the two input sequences in time order, it cannot be anything of the sort. The point is that part of the information on which it is basing its decisions as to how to perform the interleaving is being suppressed. We could write

Merge (x,y,tx,ty)

as a function where tx is a sequence of integers such that $(tx)_k$ is the time at which x_k becomes available, and similarly ty. But then, how are we to supply values for tx and ty in calls of merge? Moreover, reasoning explicitly about absolute times in order to understand systems behaviour seems something to be avoided.

How, then, are we to understand merge? One main approach is to view it as a *nondeterministic operator,* which can on different occasions of use yield different results for the same inputs. Thus the first item of the sequence

Merge (a:x,b:y)

may be *either* a *or* b; we cannot predict which. In order to recover a functional meaning for merge, we can then say it maps a pair of input sequences to a *set* of output sequences, representing the different possible results, i.e. the various ways in which the interleaving might be performed. But then we must revise our account of the meaning of *all* functions to work on sets. For example, the function Db for **Figure 22-6** must now be defined over *sets* of possible input sequences. The meanings of functional programs become considerably more complex, and so unavoidably does reasoning about them. Moreover, there are additional problems connected with the issues of *fairness* in the interpretation of merge. A considerable amount of work has been done on the semantics of merge; e.g. [10, 11, 12, 13]. It seems fair to say that no satisfactory formalism for reasoning about functional programs with merge has yet been proposed.

Thus functional programming with merge is not yet understood adequately from the *theoretical* point-of-view. However, it can be - and has been - implemented and experimented with. The author and Richard Sykes have shown that with the addition of time-ordered merge, the functional style is adequate to describe complete operating systems,

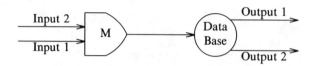

Figure 22-6

interactive applications, robot-manipulation etc. Programs of this kind, displaying the required time-dependent behaviour, have been demonstrated. Work on similar lines has also been carried out by Henderson and Jones [1, 14].

We thus have a gap between theory and practice. It remains to be seen whether an adequate theoretical foundation for the experimental work can be developed.

22.5 REFERENCES

1. P. Henderson, "Purely Functional Operating Systems," in *Functional Programming*, ed. Darlington, Henderson and Turner, Cambridge University Press (1982).

2. E. Ashcroft, "LUCID - A Formal System for Writing and Proving Programs," *SIAM Journal on Computing* (1976).

3. E. Ashcroft and W. Wadge, "LUCID, a non-procedural language with iteration," *CACM* (1976).

4. W. Wadge, "An Extensional Treatment of Dataflow Deadlock," *Springer Lecture Notes in Computer Science* **70** (1979).

5. C. A. R. Hoare, "Communicating Sequential Processes," *CACM* (1978).

6. M. Gordon, R. Milner, and C. Wadsworth, "Edinburgh LCF," *Springer Lecture Notes in Computer Science* **78** (1980).

7. G. Kahn, "A Simple Theory of Parallel Programs," *IFIP Congress Proceedings* (1974).

8. D. Scott, "Lectures on a Mathematical Theory of Computation," Programming Research Group Monograph, Oxford (1981).

9. G. Kahn and D. MacQueen, "Coroutines and Networks of Parallel Processes," *IFIP Congress Proceedings* (1977).

10. S. Abramsky, "On Semantic Foundations for Applicative Multiprogramming," *Springer Lecture Notes in Computer Science* **154** (1983).

11. M. Broy, "Finite and Infinite Networks of Processes," Technical University of Munich (1983).

12. F. Boussinot, "Proposition de Semantique Nouvelle," *Theoretical Computer Science* (1982).

13. D. Park, *The 'Fairness' Problem and Non-Deterministic Computing Networks,* Warwick University (1982).

14. S. Jones, *Abstract Machine Support for Purely Functional Operating Systems,* Oxford (1983).

Index

The following acronyms are used in this book.

AMPS	Applicative Multiprocessing System
APM	Abstract Prolog Machine
CDB	Completed Database
CSP	Cooperating Sequential Processes
CTL	Compiler Target Language
CWA	Closed World Assumption
DAP	Distributed Array Processor (ICL)
DDP	Distributed Data Processor (Texas Instruments)
DFS	Distributed File System
DP	Distributed Processes
FEL	Function Equation Language
GCF	Generalized Control Flow
ICST	Imperial College of Science and Technology (London)
IPC	Inter-process communications
JNT	Joint Network Team U.K.
KRC	Kent Recursive Calculator
KUDOS	Keele University Distributed Operating System
LAN	Local Area Network
MIMD	Multiple Instruction Multiple Data
MISD	Multiple Instruction Single Data
MKF	Modified Kiviat Figures
OSI	Open Systems Interconnection
NSA	Novel Sequential Architectures
PCRA	Packet Circulation Ring Architecture
PTA	Physical Tree Architecture
PRA	Pipelined Ring Architecture
RPC	Remote Procedure Call
SIMD	Single Instruction Multiple Data
SISD	Single Instruction Single Data
TASS	Template Assembler
UID	Unique Identifier
VTA	Virtual Tree Architecture

A.P.I.C. Studies in Data Processing
General Editors: Fraser Duncan *and* M. J. R. Shave

In Preparation

053672Bj
26 -6 -85